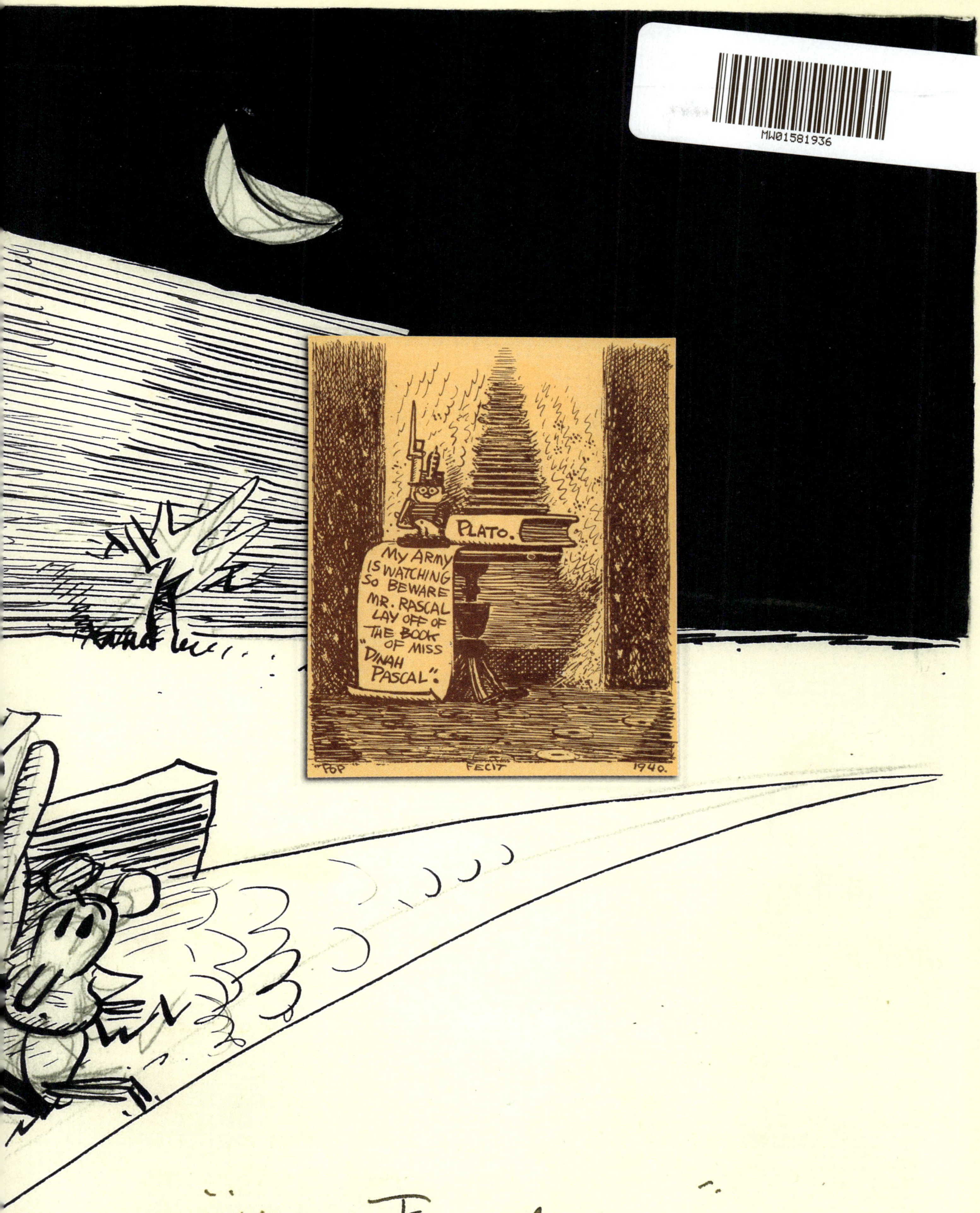
PLATO.
MY ARMY IS WATCHING SO BEWARE MR. RASCAL LAY OFF OF THE BOOK OF MISS "DINAH PASCAL".
"POP" FECIT 1940.

To Harry Frandsen
MIT LUFF UND DEWOTION — from
GEO HERRIMAN

KRAZY KAT

& THE ART OF

GEORGE HERRIMAN

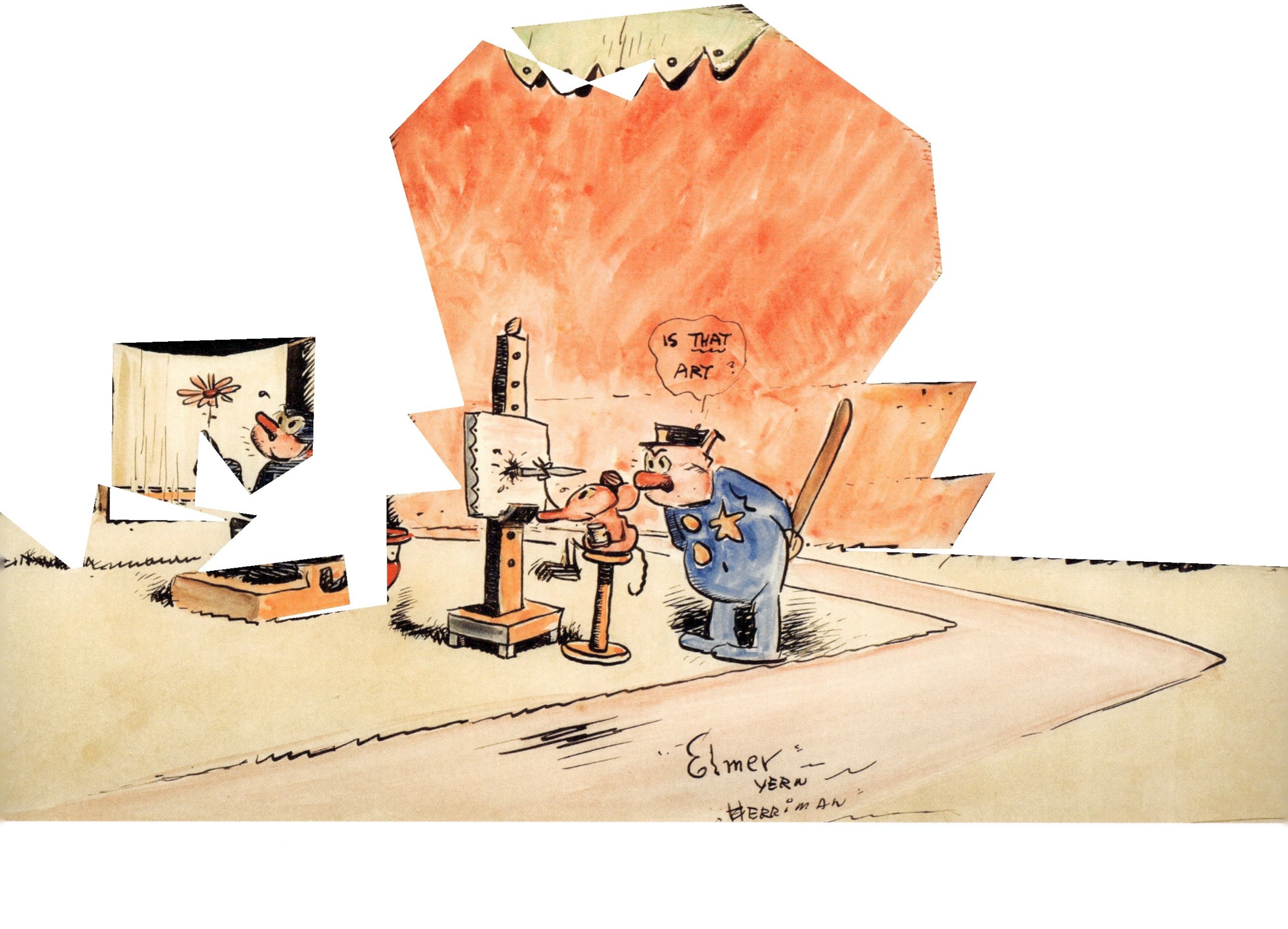
IS THAT ART ?
Elmer
YERN
HERRIMAN

KRAZY KAT

& THE ART OF GEORGE HERRIMAN

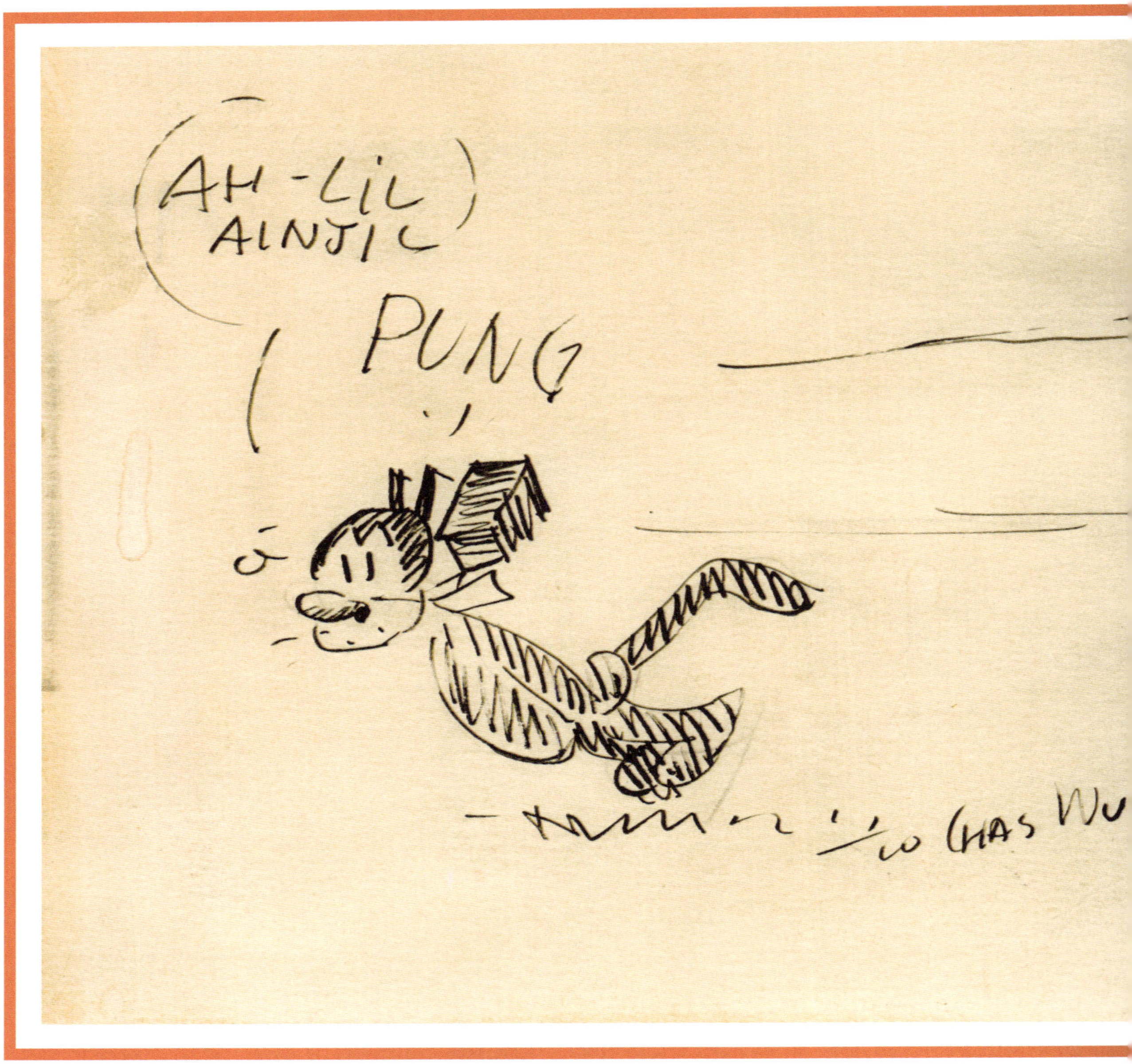
AH-LIL AINJIL
PUNG

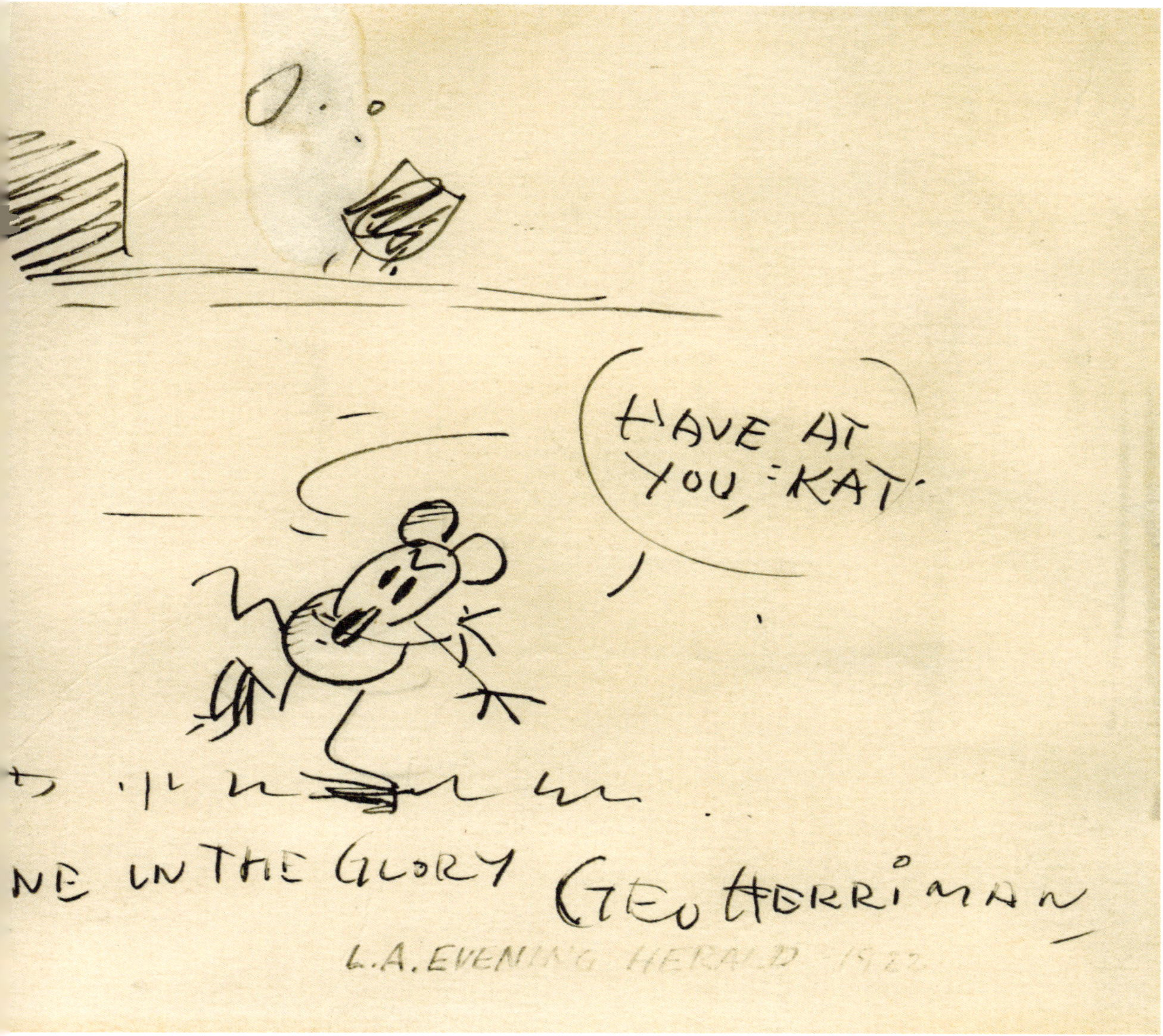
HAVE AT YOU, KAT
NE IN THE GLORY
GEO HERRIMAN
L.A. EVENING HERALD

A CELEBRATION

Edited & designed by
CRAIG YOE

ABRAMS COMICARTS, NEW YORK

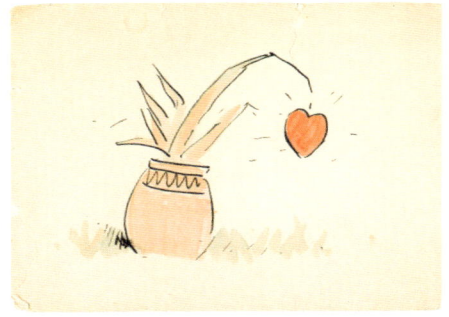

"Klizia,"
The humor, creativity, and love *Krazy Kat* readers
experienced daily I have with you.
—"Kraig"

Visit GeorgeHerriman.com

If you like this book, please blog, Facebook, and tweet about it! To contact the author, please e-mail craig@yoe.com. Visit the International Team of Comics Historians blog at www.TheITCHblog.com. Friend Craig Yoe on Facebook!

If you have any artwork or ephemera you want to lend or sell for future editions of this book, please contact Craig Yoe.

A loving brick zipped to all the generous individuals and institutions who made this book possible:

Yoe Studio: Craig Yoe & Clizia Gussoni (Chief Executive Officers and Creative Directors); Sandy Schechter (VP of Research); Carl Linich (Editorial Associate); Nancy Bond, Luke McDonnell, Mark Lerer, Elizabeth Savanella, Victoria Savanella, and Maggie Uschakow (Design Associates); Steve Bennett, David Burd, Beth Davies-Stofka, David Donihue, Steven Thompson, Doug Wheeler (Media Associates).

These people deserve special mention: Dee Cox, George Herriman's granddaughter, for her generosity and the pleasure of working with her; Bill Blackbeard, for rescuing so many comic strips from oblivion, especially his favorite, *Krazy Kat*; Patrick McDonnell, Karen O'Connell, and Georgia Riley de Havenon for writing their groundbreaking Abrams book, *Krazy Kat: The Comic Art of George Herriman*, which established Herriman as a true Artist; and Rick Marschall, for his invaluable knowledge, books, and friendship. Michael Tisserand, who is writing a much anticipated biography of Herriman, was an invaluable resource and generously helped.

A deep thank-you to Charles Kochman and his associates at Abrams (Neil Egan, Sofia Gutiérrez, and Scott Auerbach) for their friendship and guidance.

A special thank-you to the essay writers: Jay Cantor, Dee Cox, Harry L. Katz, Craig McCracken, Richard Thompson, and Douglas Wolk. A very special thank-you to Bill Watterson.

Craig Yoe's collection of Herriman art appears on the following pages: endpapers and pages 2–3, 6, 8, 31, 32, 33, 36, 42, 50, 68, 78, 150, and 151 (left).

Craig Yoe's collection of Herriman images and ephemera appears on the following pages: 16–17 (top), 19, 20, 21, 22, 23, 24, 25, 26, 30, 39, 79 (top left and middle), 83, 119, 121, 122, 123 (bottom), 124–125, 126, 143, 144, 145, 148, 149, 151 (right), 152, 155, 156, 157, 159–161, and 163.

Thank you to the individuals and institutions who generously lent art: Rob Andrews (pp. 46–47, 55, 56, 67, 71, 88); Bernhard Angerer (p. 69); Mel Brinkman (pp. 90–91); Russ Cochran (p. 70); Dee Cox (front endpapers; pp. 4, 130, 131, 132, 133, 141, 166, bottom); Steve Donnelly (pp. 43, top; 49, bottom; 74, 174); Chris Englund (p. 66); John Fawcett/Fawcett's Maine Antique Toy & Art Museum (pp. 89, 98, 106–107); Geppi's Entertainment Museum (pp. 43, bottom; 63); Jack Gilbert (p. 58); Glen Gold (pp. 105, 112); George Hagenauer (pp. 48–49, top); Richard Halegua (pp. 102–103); Heritage Auction Galleries (pp. 92–93, 135); Jud Hurd (p. 142, bottom); Illustration House (pp. 57, 60, 62, 65, 72, 97, 104); International Museum of Cartoon Art Collection, The Ohio State University Billy Ireland Cartoon Library & Museum (pp. 108–109); Carsten Laqua (p. 175); Harvey Leake (pp. 110–111); Library of Congress (pp. 44–45, top); Bernard Mahe (pp. 59, 94–95); Rick Marschall (p. 140); Craig McCracken (pp. 34, top; 73, 100–101); Patrick McDonnell, with the help of John Carlin (pp. 61, 64, 66); Ulrich Merkl (pp. 44–45, bottom); Peter Merolo (pp. 34, bottom; 142, top; 172–173); Marion Pickens (p. 99); The Raguse Family (p. 1); Jerry Robinson (pp. 146–147); Chris Wrenn (pp. 43, middle; 48, bottom; 96).

Thank you to the individuals and institutions who generously lent images and ephemera: Bob Beerbohm (pp. 120, 158); Warren Bernard (p. 136); Bill Blackbeard, with the help of Mark Van Landuyt (pp. 14–15); Mel Brinkman (pp. 79, bottom; 80–81, 82); Dee Cox (pp. 5; 166, top; 167, 168); Chris Ecker (p. 123, top); Geppi's Entertainment Museum (p. 171); David Gerstein (p. 79, top right); International Museum of Cartoon Art Collection, The Ohio State University Billy Ireland Cartoon Library & Museum (p. 162); Alan Kaplan (pp. 16–17, bottom; 35); Charles Kochman (p. 118); Rick Marschall (pp. 164–165); Craig McCracken (pp. 18, 153, 154–155); Bonnie Robinson (p. 147); Rob Stolzer (pp. 134, 170).

Photography: Mariama Anderson and James Knight (p. 99); Tim Fuller (front endpapers; pp. 4, 5, 130, 131, 132, 133, 141, 166, 167, 168); Ron Garofalo (pp. 90–91); Hal Hagy (p. 89); Jeff Park (p. 1); and William Thuss (pp. 98, 106–107).

Thank you to the following consultants: Giovanna Anzaldi, Jon Barli, Jerry Beck, James Carlsson, Lucy Caswell, Robert Chris, Faye Desmond, Dan Donnelly, Rich Donnelly, Sara Willett Duke, Jeff English, Chris Gaslin, David Gerstein, Greg Goldstein, Andy Hershberger, Eddie Ibrahim, Robert Kass, Denis Kitchen, Joan Allyn Kodish, Peter Maresca, Angela Meyer, Glenn Mott at King Features, Rob Pistella, Craig Raguse, Mike Richardson, Jenny Robb, Lee Salem, Gary Sassaman, David Scroggy, Francesco Spreafico, Tommy José Stathes, and Susan Allen Yonas.

Herriman often didn't date his paintings and drawings. Dates are specified when known. A best effort has been made to organize the images into specific sections but, like the landscapes of Coconino County, the definition between painting, greetings, and specialty drawings can shift. Speaking of Coconino County, Herriman spelled it sometimes with "K"s and sometimes with "C"s. We have preserved Herriman's and the essay writers' preferred spelling in their specific contexts. In the "Four-Color Feline" section, the strips are in chronological order. In the "A Month of Sundays. Years, Even!" section, the strips are grouped aesthetically.

Every effort has been made to properly credit the owners of Herriman art and ephemera, and the legal rights holder of any text. Every effort has been made to properly cite if a piece has been unpublished. We apologize for any oversight and we'll gladly make corrections in reprints.

Editor: Charles Kochman
Assistant Editor: Sofia Gutiérrez
Designer: Craig Yoe/YOE! Studio
Design Manager: Neil Egan
Production Manager: Ankur Ghosh

Library of Congress Cataloging-in-Publication Data:

Krazy Kat and the art of George Herriman: A Celebration / [edited by] Craig Yoe.
 p. cm.
Includes bibliographical references and index.
ISBN 978-0-8109-9594-9 (alk. paper)
1. Herriman, George, 1880–1944. Krazy Kat. 2. Herriman, George, 1880–1944.
I. Yoe, Craig.
PN6728.K7K73 2010
741.5'6973—dc22
      2010001212

Compilation, preface, and "A Life in Panels" copyright © 2011 Craig Yoe. All other visuals and text are copyright the creators or rights holders where applicable. Essays by Jay Cantor, Dee Cox, Harry L. Katz, Craig McCracken, Richard Thompson, and Douglas Wolk copyright © 2011 the authors.

Krazy Kat™ Hearst Holdings, Inc.

Bill Watterson's appreciation reprinted by his permission from *The Komplete Kolor Krazy Kat* (Remco World Service Books, 1980), edited by Rick Marschall.

Gilbert Seldes' essay: Reprinted with the permission of Russell & Volkening as agents for the author. Copyright © 1924 by Gilbert Seldes, renewed in 1952 by Gilbert Seldes.

Published in 2011 by Abrams ComicArts, an imprint of ABRAMS. All rights reserved. No portion of this book may be reproduced, stored in a retrieval system, or transmitted in any form or by any means, mechanical, electronic, photocopying, recording, or otherwise, without written permission from the publisher.

Abrams ComicArts is a registered trademark of Harry N. Abrams, Inc., registered in the U.S. Patent and Trademark Office.

Printed and bound in China

10 9 8 7 6 5 4 3 2 1

Abrams ComicArts books are available at special discounts when purchased in quantity for premiums and promotions as well as fundraising or educational use. Special editions can also be created to specification. For details, contact specialmarkets@abramsbooks.com or the address below.

115 West 18th Street
New York, NY 10011
www.abramsbooks.com

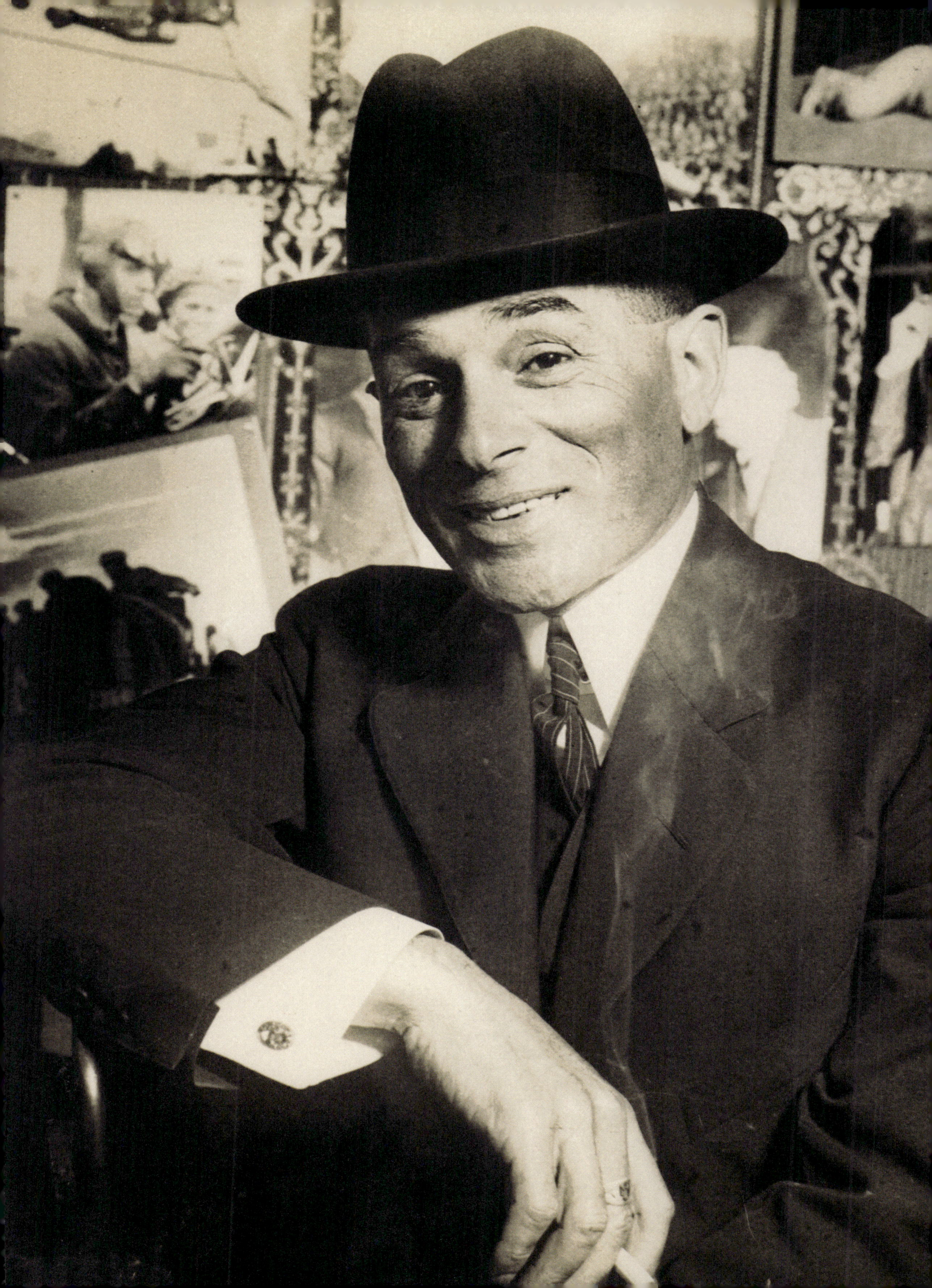

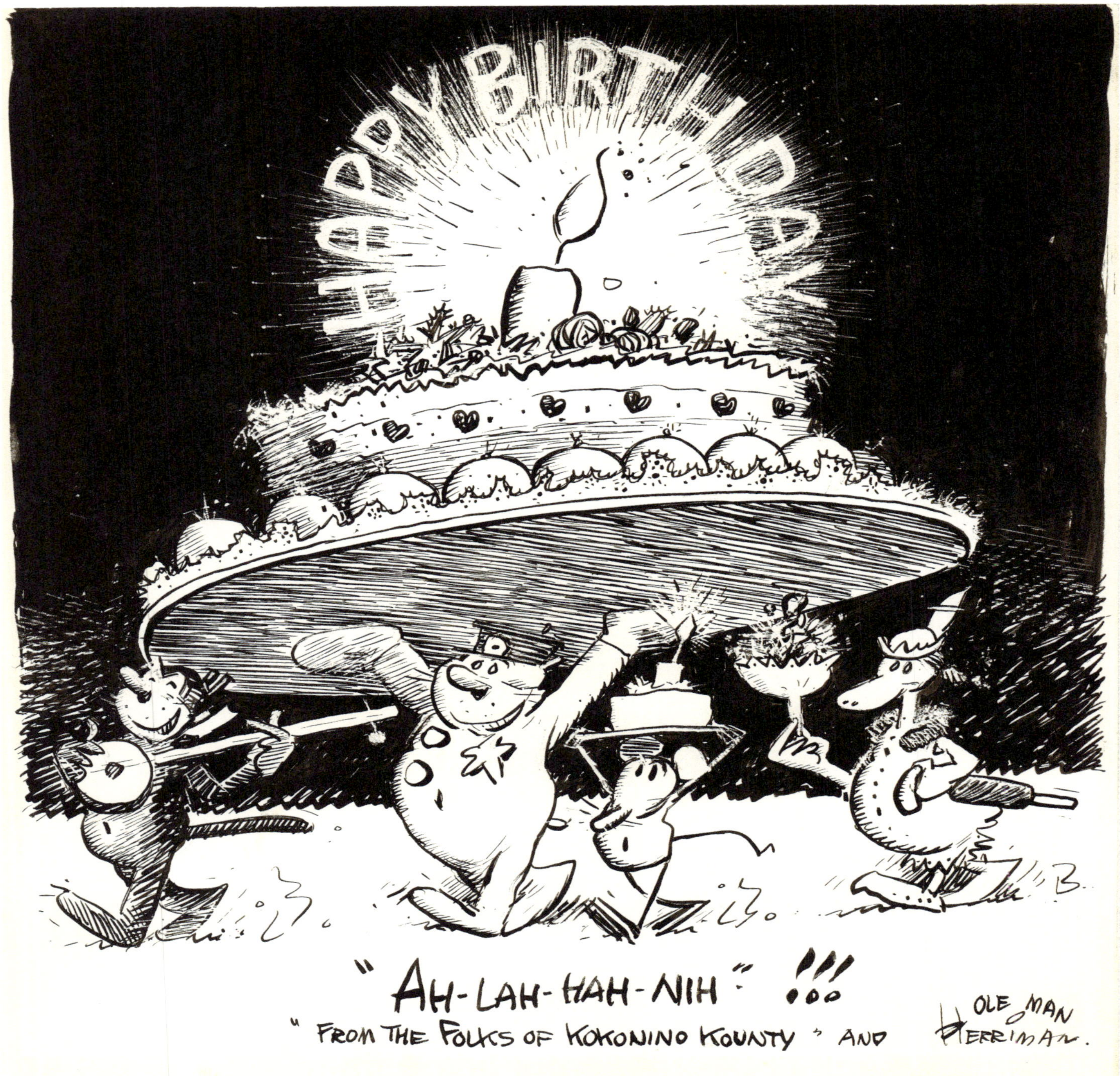
HAPPY BIRTHDAY
"AH-LAH-HAH-NIH"!!!
"FROM THE FOLKS OF KOKONINO KOUNTY" AND OLE MAN HERRIMAN.

ABOVE A specialty drawing for the fiftieth anniversary of the *Los Angeles Times,* 1931.

ENDPAPERS Previously unpublished drawing by George Herriman done as a gift to Harry Frandsen, with the dedication "mit luff und dewotion." Herriman drew the bookplate for his granddaughter Dinah Pascal (Dee Cox) when she was five years old. Dee says, "The Plato reference is because Pop hoped I would learn to love literature."

HALF-TITLE PAGE "Is *that* art?" Offissa Pupp asks. The inscription reads, "'Elmer'—Yern—Herriman." Elmer "Al" Raguse Sr. was the director of sound at Hal Roach Studios. Late 1930s. Previously unpublished.

TITLE PAGE Curiously, the only known specialty drawing depicting the classic scene of Ignatz throwing a brick at Krazy. The inscription on this beauty reads, "To Chas Wunder, Thine in the Glory, Geo Herriman." 1922. Previously unpublished.

COPYRIGHT PAGE An unpublished hand-drawn greeting from George Herriman to a family member.

PREVIOUS PAGE An unpublished photo of a young and jubilant George Herriman.

Contents

An Appreciation: A Few Thoughts on Krazy Kat Bill Watterson — 9

Preface: A Strip Load of Bricks Craig Yoe — 11

A Life in Panels Craig Yoe — 13

Four-Color Felines — 18

Warped with Fancy, Woofed with Dreams Harry L. Katz — 27

Oh, What a Gift! — 30

The Krazy Kat That Walks by Himself Gilbert Seldes — 37

Original Thoughts Daily — 42

Krazy Kat E. E. Cummings — 51

A Month of Sundays. Years, Even! — 54

It's Krazy, I Tell You. KRAZY! Craig McCracken — 75

Kat-Toons — 78

KKKKRRRAaaaAZZZEEEEEE! Richard Thompson — 85

The Fine Art of Cartooning — 88

A Genius of the Comic Page Summerfield Baldwin — 113

Kat Books — 118

Reply to an Inquiry by Ignatz Mouse Jay Cantor — 127

Greetings from Coconino County — 130

The Gift Douglas Wolk — 137

Special Specialty Drawings — 140

This Is About Garge Herriman Tad Dorgan — 149

Toyland, Toyland. Krazy Kat and Ignatz-land — 152

Toots Herriman Tells the World About Krazy Kat William Paul Langreich — 159

Picture Perfect — 162

Remembering My Grandfather, George Herriman Dee Cox — 169

Bibliography — 174

Index — 175

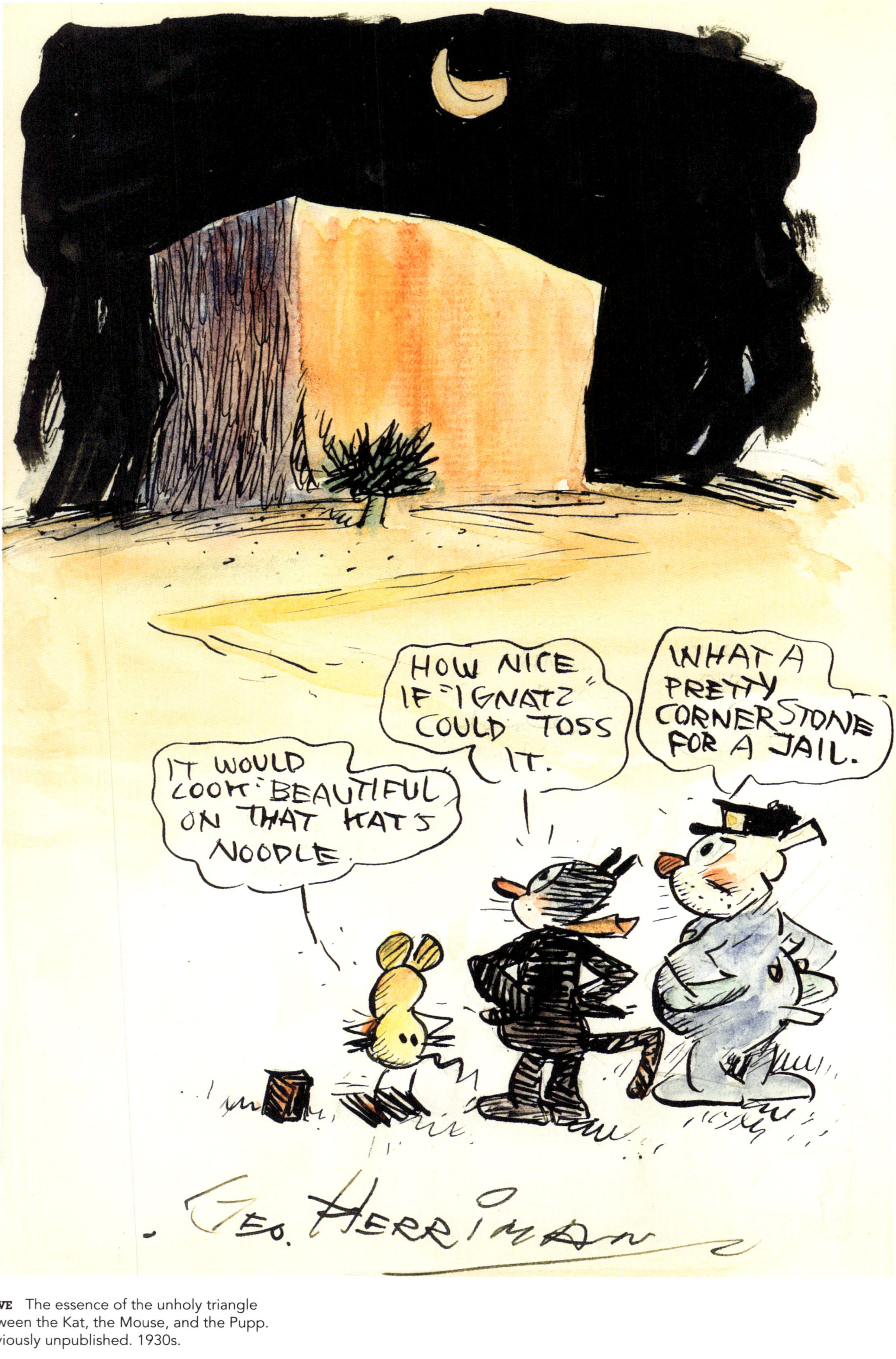
WHAT A PRETTY CORNERSTONE FOR A JAIL.
HOW NICE IF "IGNATZ" COULD TOSS IT.
IT WOULD LOOK BEAUTIFUL ON THAT KAT'S NOODLE.
GEO. HERRIMAN

ABOVE The essence of the unholy triangle between the Kat, the Mouse, and the Pupp. Previously unpublished. 1930s.

An Appreciation
A Few Thoughts on Krazy Kat
by Bill Watterson
This essay first appeared in *The Komplete Kolor Krazy Kat* Volume 1: 1935–1936, edited by Rick Marschall (Remco Worldservice Books, 1990).

As a cartoonist, I read *Krazy Kat* with awe and wonder. *Krazy Kat* is such a pure and completely realized personal vision that the strip's inner mechanism is ultimately as unknowable as George Herriman. Nevertheless, I marvel at how this fanciful world could be so forcefully imagined and brought to paper with such immediacy. THIS is how good a comic strip can be.

Interestingly, *Krazy Kat* gains its momentum less from the personalities of its characters than from their obsessions. Ignatz Mouse demonstrates his contempt for Krazy by throwing bricks at her; Krazy reinterprets the bricks as signs of love; and Offissa Pupp is obliged by duty (and regard for Krazy) to thwart and punish Ignatz's "sin," thereby interfering with a process that's satisfying to everyone for all the wrong reasons. Some thirty years of strips were wrung out of that amalgam of cross-purposes. The action can be read as a metaphor for love or politics, or just enjoyed for its lunatic inner logic and physical comedy.

Despite the predictability of the characters' proclivities, the strip never sinks into formula or routine. Often the actual brick tossing is only anticipated. The simple plot is endlessly renewed through constant innovation, pace manipulations, unexpected results, and most of all, the quiet charm of each story's presentation. The magic of the strip is not so much in what it says, but in how it says it. It's a more subtle kind of cartooning than we have today.

To the bewilderment of many readers, there are few endings in *Krazy Kat* that qualify as "punchlines." Instead, it's the temperament of the writing and drawing throughout the strip that is the joke. If you don't think it's funny that a strip should have an intermission drawing, or that a character would refer to his tail as a "caudal appendage," you're reading the wrong strip, and it's your loss.

Quirky, individual, and uncompromised, *Krazy Kat* is one of the very few comic strips that takes full advantage of its medium. There are some things a comic strip can do that no other medium, not even animation, can touch, and *Krazy Kat* is a virtual essay on comic strip essence.

In their headlong rush for the "gag," most cartoonists run right past the countless treasures Herriman uncovered simply by taking his time to explore the freedom of his medium. The self-consciously baroque narrations and monologues ("From the kwaint konfines of the kalabozo del kondado de Kokonino—Offissa Pupp gives answer") show that words can be funny in themselves, just as drawings can. The sky turns from black to white to zigzags and plaids simply because, in a comic strip, it CAN. No other cartoonist ever approached his blank sheet of paper with so much affection for all its possibilities.

The scratchy drawings delight me no end. They have the honesty and directness of sketches. So many of today's strips are slick and polished, the inevitable result of assistants trying to develop a mechanical style that can be continued indefinitely. The drawings in *Krazy Kat* are whimsical, idiosyncratic, and filled with personality. The bold design of the Sunday strips neatly complements the flat expanses of color or black, and the wonderful hatching brings character to the otherwise posterish approach.

Nothing in *Krazy Kat* had a supporting role, least of all the Arizona desert setting. Mountains are striped. Mesas are spotted. Trees grow in pots. The horizon is a low wall that characters climb over. Panels are framed by theater curtains and stage spotlights. Monument Valley monoliths are drawn to look more like their names. The moon is a melon wedge, suspended upside down. And virtually every panel features a different landscape, even if the characters don't move. The land is more than a backdrop. It is a character in the story, and the strip is "about" that landscape as much as it is about the animals who populate it.

As the artwork is poetic, so is the writing. With the possible exception of *Pogo,* no other strip derives so much of its charm from its verbiage. *Krazy Kat's* unique "texture" comes in large part through the conglomeration of peculiar spellings and punctuations, dialects, interminglings of Spanish, phonetic renderings, and alliterations. *Krazy Kat's* Coconino County not only had a look; it had a sound as well. Slightly foreign, but uncontrived, it was an extraordinary and full world.

Darn few comic strips challenge their readers any more. The comics have become big business, and they play it safe. They shamelessly pander to the results of reader surveys, and are produced by virtual factories, ready-made for the inevitable T-shirts, dolls, greeting cards, and television specials. Licensing is where the money is, and we seem to have forgotten that a comic strip can be something more than a launchpad for a glut of derivative products. When the comic strip is not exploited, the medium can be a vehicle for beautiful artwork and serious, intelligent expression.

Krazy Kat was drawn well over half a century ago, and yet it's a much more sophisticated use of the comic strip medium than anything we cartoonists are doing today. Of course, a 1930s Sunday *Krazy* filled the entire newspaper page, whereas editors today usually cram at least four strips in the same amount of space. This reduction of size greatly limits what can be drawn and written and still remain legible, and it goes a long way toward explaining the comics' devolution.

Even so, the whiteness of paper is still vast, uncharted territory, ripe for exploration. There are plenty of exotic lands for a cartoonist to map, if he or she will leave the well-worn paths and strike off for the wilds of the imagination. *Krazy Kat* is like no other comic strip before or after it. We are richer for Herriman's integrity and vision.

Krazy Kat was not very successful as a commercial venture, but it was something better. It was art.

***Bill Watterson** is the creator of the comic strip* Calvin and Hobbes.

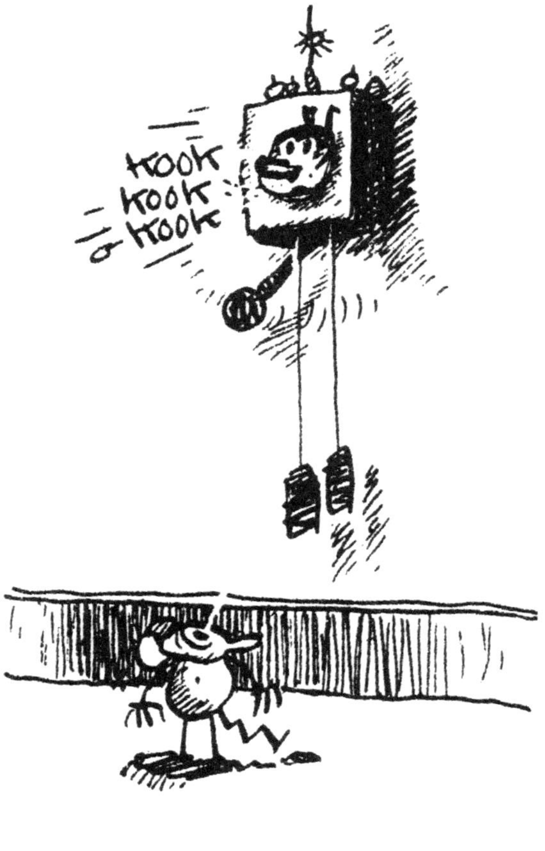

kook
kook
kook

Preface
A Strip Load of Bricks
by Craig Yoe

The bonking on the bean via a brick of the kat called Krazy is the defining moment of George Herriman's *phantasy*. Or defining *moments*—plural—if there is such a thing. The Act is repeated over and over again. *ZAP! POW!* Ohhh, geez, it's a grim, aggressive, violent, horrible act; criminal, even. The local *loco* lawman, the Pupp, has made it his mission to stop the violence. Jail the perp. Protect not the Kute Kat, the Kuddly Kat, the Kool Kat, but the *Krazy* Kat—from herself. (From *his* self? *Its?*) This Kitten gone Wrongo, this Kat, tolerates the abuse, *wants* the abuse. Sick Sick Sick. Unconscionable.

But right or wrong—and I unwaveringly think this Hit on the Head with a Heavy Object is wrong—sweet dreams are made of this. Who am I to be disagreeable? Some meeces want to abuse you. (I hate those meeces to pieces.) And some kats of the krazy variety want to be abused. Well, who among us hasn't enjoyed an aggressive kiss, a playful hair tug, a light spank? But brick bonks on beans? Doesn't this go beyond playful S&M and over to the dark side? A kat could get hurt! Is Krazy's responsive "Darling!" a Safe Word? Does he/she have lines not to be crossed, drawn in the sand or on the funnies page—we can only hope she/he/it does—or is this Kraziness Kertifiable?

This mouse-to-mouser violence isn't a product of the environment. The landscape around this masochistic madness is moving mesas that are calm, gentle, lulling—yes, even in a druggy, psychedelic, surreal way. They have even been called Poetic by more than a few wags, some of them in this very book. And in the County of Coconino, there certainly is law and order. Kop. Kop with Klub. A jailhouse that rocks. Paper. Scissors. Rock. Dog. Cat. Mouse. But the mouse has turned. He faces his natural aggressor, and his natural aggressor's natural aggressor. This mouse (married, BTW) refuses to be the victim. Instead he fights back. Mad as Herriman, hmmm? and not going to take it anymore? Eye for eye? Truth for truth? The so-called vermin mouse takes on the cat *and* the dog. And this mouse, this Rebel with a Kause, brings it on. Ignatz the roaring mouse becomes the aggressor. Political romantics will call him the proletariat rising up angry. BDSM practitioners would identify him as the Dom taking control. The Offissa Pupp in all of us might shake his finger, or more likely his klub, at this monarch of mischief, this mouse marauder—while secretly admiring his tenacity. Refusing to march to anything but a different drummer's beat, Ignatz only katapults his own brick maker's brick!

And who is Ignatz?! Don't we have just to look into ourselves to see? As far as we have evolved, don't we have to answer the question "Are you a Man or a Mouse?" too many times with a squeak? Wouldn't we, for once, want to take a hardened-clay parallelepiped and toss it at the Status Quo? We all have this proclivity toward violence. This violence takes deplorable forms on football fields and battlefields, with Nations flinging bricks to the point that we have nothing less than a krazy, precarious planet. A pox on this lack of pax.

But maybe just one well-aimed punk rock ignatzed onto humanity's head would make us feel like we've truly accomplished something Good and Right in life. Is *that* a crime? If so, then I'll do the time!

What inspires me to be a zapping zealot? Merely the scribblings and scratchings of this master Zen cartoonist on a three-ply cotton Bristol board. Did I call him a cartoonist? He's really a Fine Artist (as if that's somehow better—it's really not). No, scratch this whole thing. Herriman's not even a combo of the two, cartoonist and Fine Arteest. I'm trying to assign him mortal status here when he's clearly a god. I've viewed thousands of vintage photos of master cartoonists, everyone from Milt Gross to Jack Kirby, at their drawing boards. Hell, I've watched John Stanley and Carl Barks draw at their drawing boards. But I'm mesmerized by the photos of George Herriman at his drawing board. He seems to be so in control. His hat sits on his head like a crown. George Herriman, King of All He Surveys. I could never imagine King Herriman having artist's block when he blocked out his panels. His thoughts must have just flowed.

For more than thirty years, Herriman wrote it, staged it, drew it, inked it. Let's begin those "it"s with capital "I"s. Wrote It, staged It, drew It, inked It. "It" being the supreme artistic expression that man has achieved. *Krazy Kat* by the King Krazy Kat hisself, George Herriman. It's about violence. It's about sick love. It's about poetry. It's about how life shouldn't be and how life should be. Let's all go and live in the panels. No more safe distance, viewers. Let's leap in and feel the desert heat, experience the vertigo of the changing landscapes, hear the bricks zapping by our ears—those heat-seeking missiles without mercy helping us all get in touch with our felines. Dark felines like Krazy.

It's Krazy, I know.

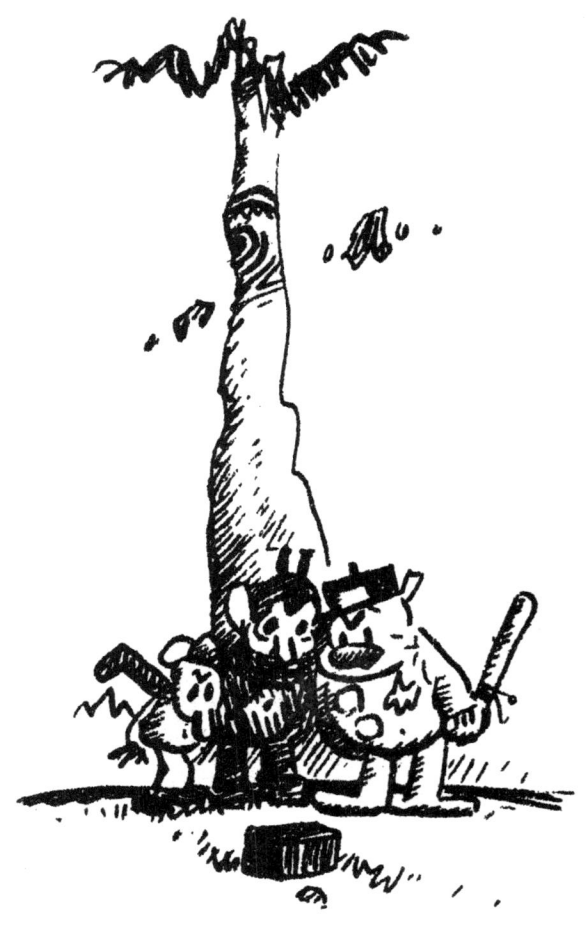

A Life in Panels

by Craig Yoe

The creator of the zenith of comic strip art, George Joseph Herriman, was born on August 22, 1880, in New Orleans. Herriman was about ten years old when his family moved to Los Angeles, as many African American Creole families did, to escape the restrictions of the Jim Crow laws.

Herriman never publicly acknowledged his ethnicity, probably fearful of its effects on his reputation. Some people believe that Herriman always wore a hat to hide his "kinky" hair, but it's also been suggested that the hat covered an unsightly bump. Herriman's death certificate lists him as *Caucasian*.

In a letter to William B. Ziff, of the Ziff Davis publishing company, for a feature in *Ziff's* (April 1926), Herriman gave this early biographical snippet: "Once, when a youth, I aspired to become a baker, a kneader of dough, to mold bread and fashion a doughnut or stencil a cookie. Full of the spirit of adolescence I buried a dead mouse in a loaf of bread once—it found its way into a tough family and not only did I get a sweet trimming but I got the air also. In another bakeshop, I thought it cute to salt the doughnuts instead of the accustomed sugaring. Wam!! 'Stars' and everything—out on the pavement again—a good baker at large. Another shop; and I slit a 200 pound sack of flour over a four foot five inch baker—we barely got him out alive, when we did, looking like a 'pose plastique,' he took away the last remnant of ambition out of me. Then I became a cartoonist—as a sort of revenge on the world.

"We're doing our stuff for Mr. W. R. Hearst, but don't let him know anything about it. Oy, if he should know! And if you want to know, we love the desert, the dry old desert, and that's where you will find us when the last drop of ink is out of our bottle and the pen snaps."

Herriman began his career as an engraver at the *Los Angeles Herald* in 1897, where he produced spot illustrations, political cartoons, and daily strips. In 1900 the artist moved to New York, where he sold cartoons to *Judge* magazine and painted signs for sideshows in Coney Island, where he was occasionally a carny barker.

Between 1901 and 1910, Herriman produced his first regular strip, *Musical Mose*, as well as other features, such as *Acrobatic Archie, Professor Otto and His Auto, Major Ozone's Fresh Air Crusade, Mary's Home from College,* and *Gooseberry Sprig*.

On June 20, 1910, the artist inaugurated *The Dingbat Family* for the *New York Evening Journal*, a Hearst paper. The strip featured the adventures of an ordinary family dealing with their annoying upstairs

FOOTBALL OF THE FUTURE, AN INSPIRATION BY HERRIMAN

TRACEAELE TO HARVARD'S EMPLOYMENT OF METAL PADDING IN LAST SATURDAY'S GAME WITH WEST POINT.

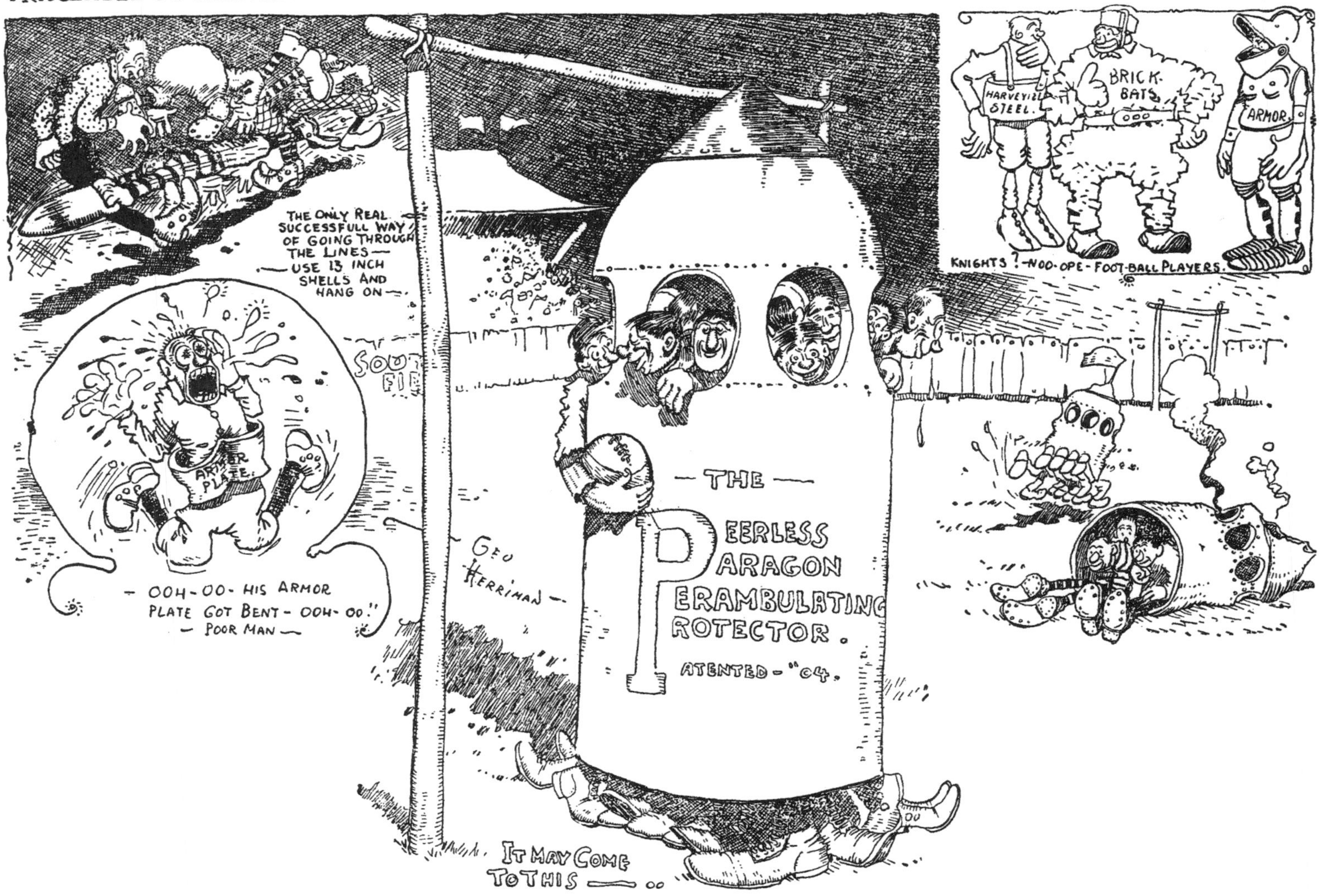

THE ONLY REAL SUCCESSFULL WAY OF GOING THROUGH THE LINES — USE 13 INCH SHELLS AND HANG ON —
HARVEYIZED STEEL.
BRICK-BATS
ARMOR
KNIGHTS? - NOO-OPE - FOOT-BALL PLAYERS.
ARMOR PLATE
— OOH - OO - HIS ARMOR PLATE GOT BENT - OOH - OO." — POOR MAN —
GEO HERRIMAN
— THE —
PEERLESS PARAGON PERAMBULATING PROTECTOR.
PATENTED - "04.
IT MAY COME TO THIS —

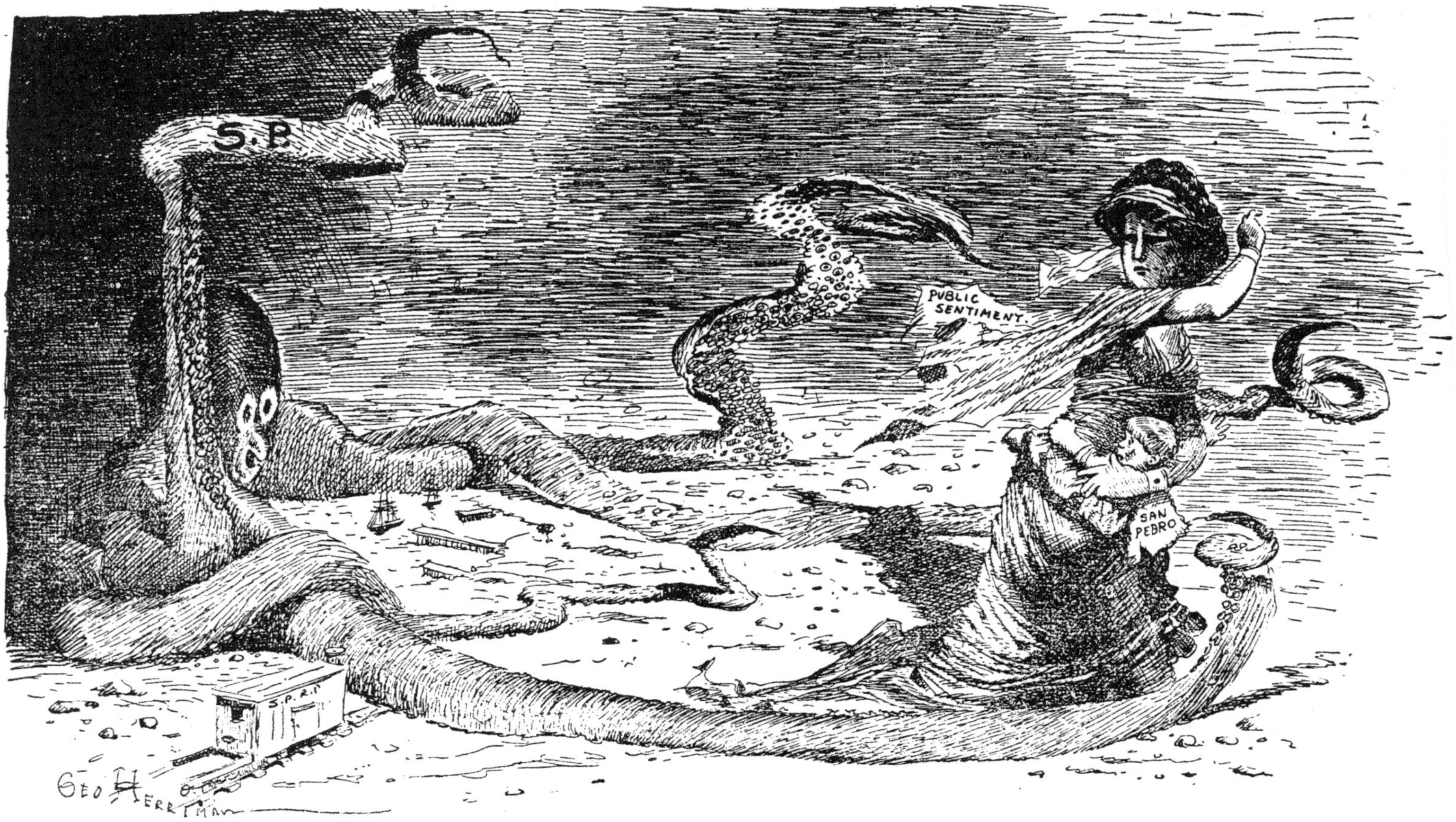

S.P.
PUBLIC SENTIMENT
SAN PEDRO
S.P.R.R.
GEO HERRIMAN

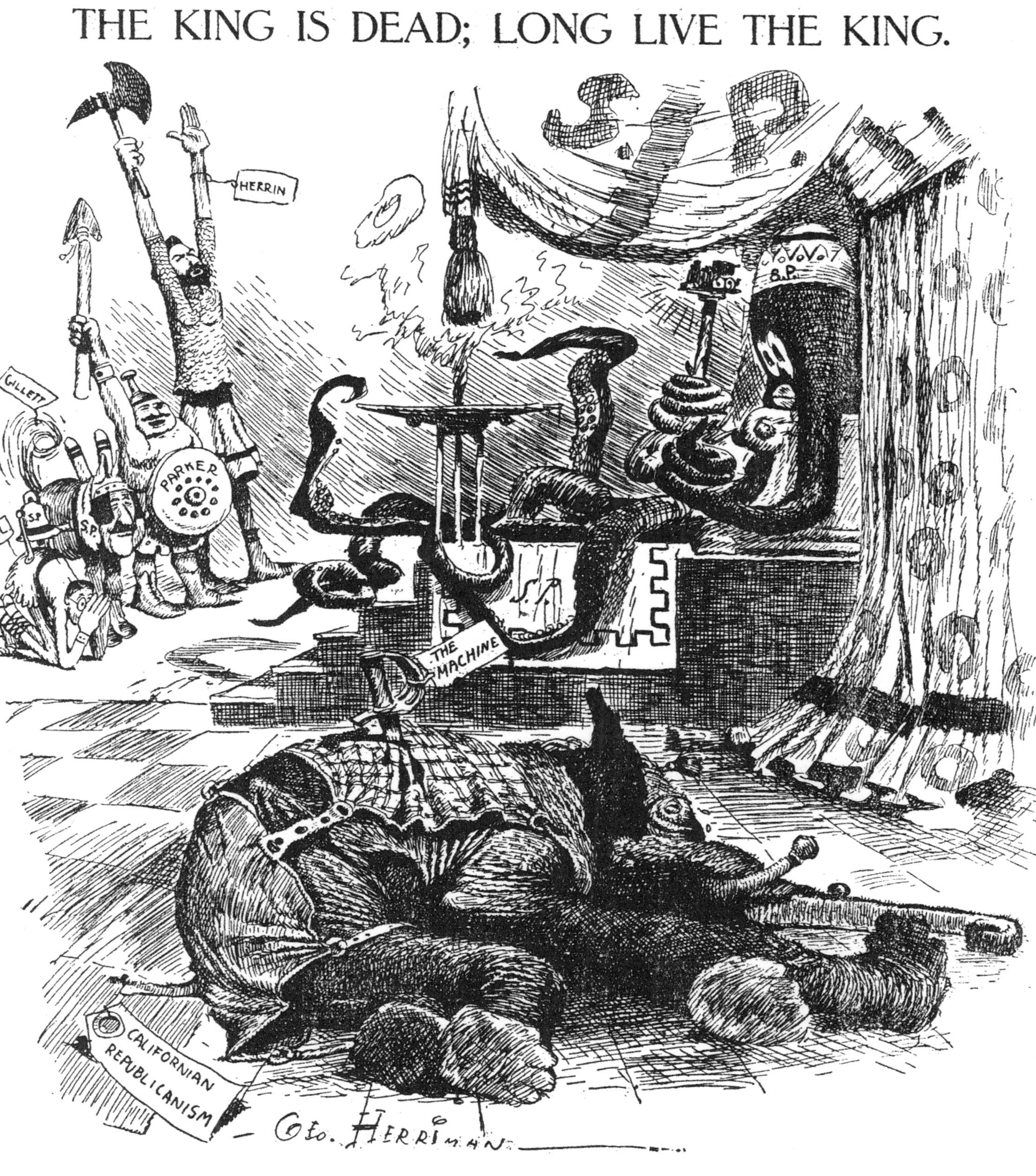
THE KING IS DEAD; LONG LIVE THE KING.
S.P.
HERRIN
GILLETT
PARKER
BELL
S.P.
THE MACHINE
CALIFORNIAN REPUBLICANISM
GEO. HERRIMAN

OPPOSITE AND ABOVE Very early in his career, George Herriman drew a plethora of sports and political cartoons before devoting himself full time to comic strips. Circa 1904.

RIGHT On July 26, 1910, Ignatz Mouse historically throws an object at Krazy Kat's head for the first time (fifth panel, bottom). The title of this daily comic strip is "Mr. Dingbat Demands His Rights" from *The Family Upstairs*.

BELOW Ignatz and Krazy started off as a little adventure that ran at the bottom of the main storyline featuring the Dingbats. On November 11, 1912, just for one special day, Herriman drew not only a strip reversal, but also a role reversal for all his characters. Ignatz and Krazy became the main feature, while E. Pluribus Dingbat and his wife, Minnie, dressed up like the mouse and the cat, took a subservient position.

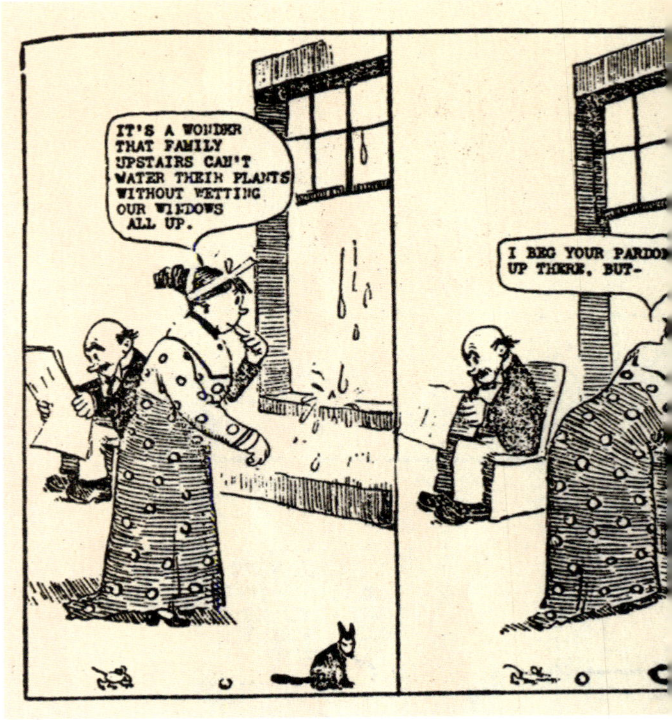
IT'S A WONDER THAT FAMILY UPSTAIRS CAN'T WATER THEIR PLANTS WITHOUT WETTING OUR WINDOWS ALL UP.
I BEG YOUR PARDO UP THERE, BUT-

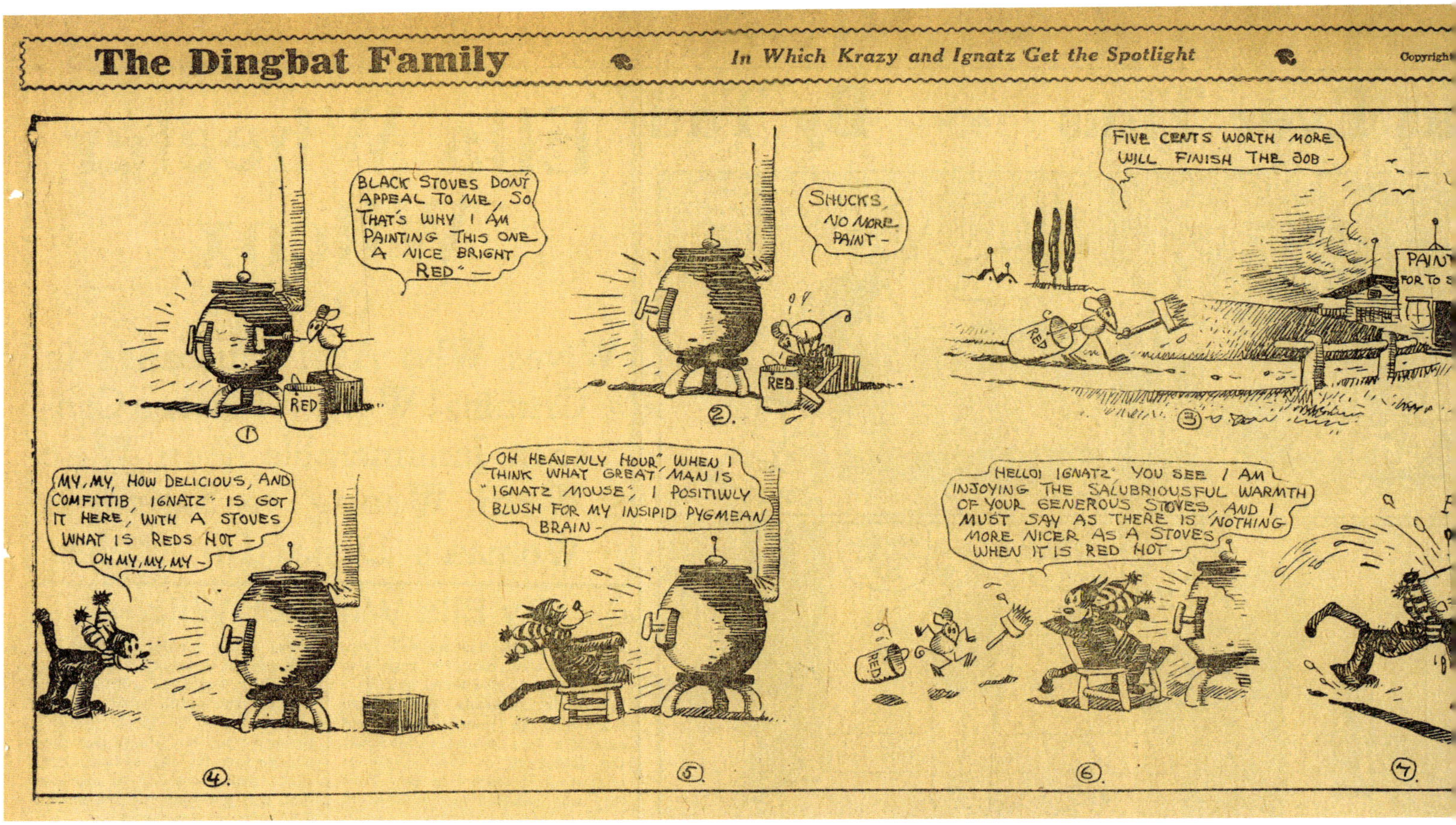
The Dingbat Family
In Which Krazy and Ignatz Get the Spotlight
BLACK STOVES DON'T APPEAL TO ME, SO THAT'S WHY I AM PAINTING THIS ONE A NICE BRIGHT RED—
RED
SHUCKS, NO MORE PAINT—
RED
FIVE CENTS WORTH MORE WILL FINISH THE JOB—
RED
MY, MY, HOW DELICIOUS, AND COMFITTIB, IGNATZ IS GOT IT HERE, WITH A STOVES WHAT IS REDS HOT— OH MY, MY, MY—
OH HEAVENLY HOUR, WHEN I THINK WHAT GREAT MAN IS "IGNATZ MOUSE", I POSITIWLY BLUSH FOR MY INSIPID PYGMEAN BRAIN—
HELLO! IGNATZ YOU SEE I AM INJOYING THE SALUBRIOUSFUL WARMTH OF YOUR GENEROUS STOVES, AND I MUST SAY AS THERE IS NOTHING MORE NICER AS A STOVES WHEN IT IS RED HOT—
RED

neighbors. In fact, for a short time, Herriman renamed his feature *The Family Upstairs,* even though he never pictured the residents above in his strip. Herriman was the first to use the word *dingbat* to indicate a silly, empty-headed person.

In *The Dingbat Family,* the artist used the bottom part of each panel to visually narrate the stories of the Dingbats' pet, Krazy Kat, and a mouse named Ignatz. These cat-and-mouse games were unrelated to those of the Dingbats. Herriman stated that he was using the "waste space." On July 26, 1910, Ignatz Mouse threw a hard object (a pebble, not yet a brick) at Krazy Kat's head for the first time. Eventually, bonking Krazy's brain with a brick, with all its attendant meanings, became the strip's main motif. In 1913, Krazy Kat and Ignatz finally had a strip on their own, while *The Dingbat Family* folded in 1916.

Herriman's creative use of language narrates the whimsical adventures of three characters—Krazy, Ignatz, and Pupp—locked in a love triangle. The unfortunate feline is in love with Ignatz, who does not reciprocate his (or her? Krazy's gender was never clearly established) feelings and likes to hurl bricks at the cat's head. This violent treatment only seems to throw Krazy

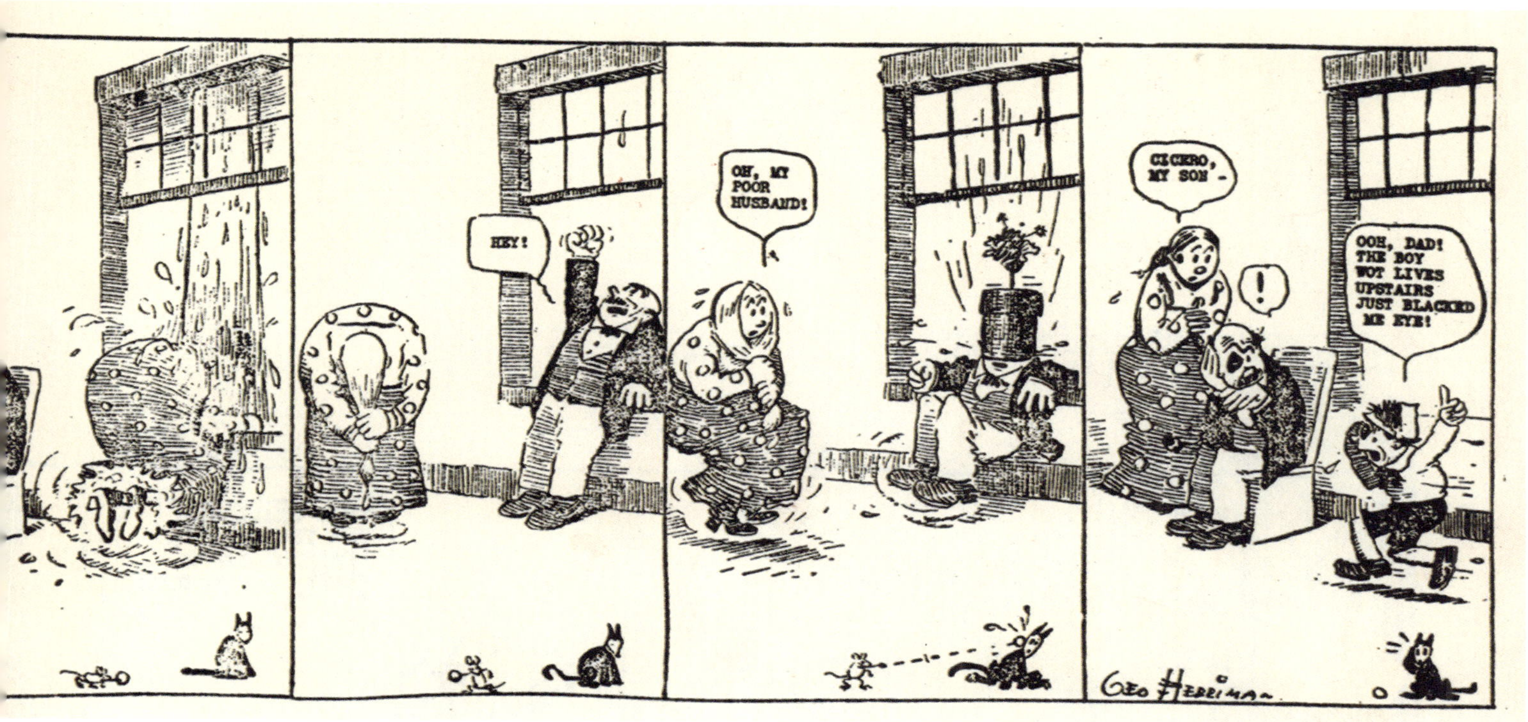
HEY!
OH, MY POOR HUSBAND!
CICERO, MY SON -
!
OOH, DAD! THE BOY WOT LIVES UPSTAIRS JUST BLACKED ME EYE!
GEO HERRIMAN

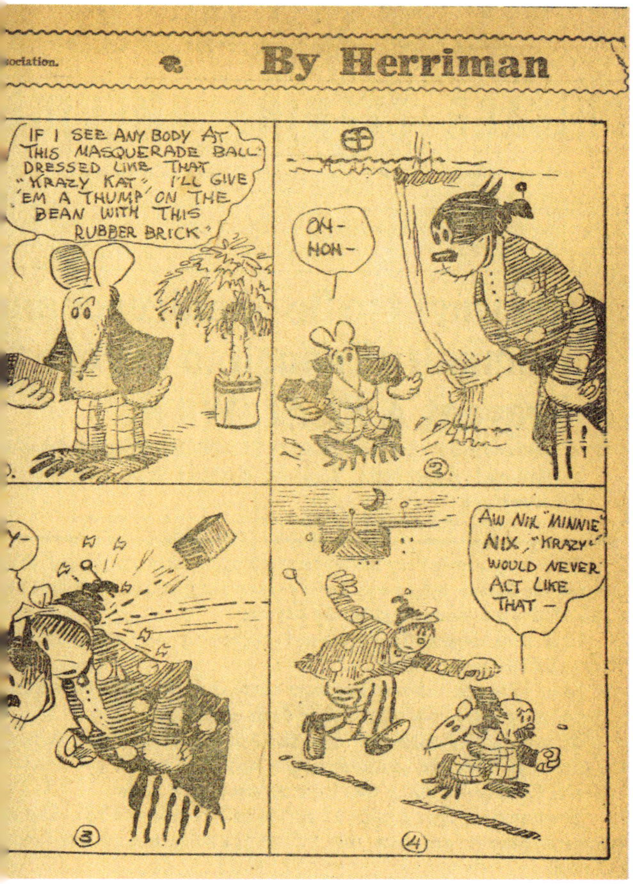
By Herriman
IF I SEE ANY BODY AT THIS MASQUERADE BALL DRESSED LIKE THAT "KRAZY KAT", I'LL GIVE 'EM A THUMP ON THE BEAN WITH THIS RUBBER BRICK"
OH-HON-
AW NIX "MINNIE" NIX, "KRAZY" WOULD NEVER ACT LIKE THAT -

more deeply in love. The third character, Offissa Pupp, besotted with Krazy and motivated by a strong sense of duty, tries to bring sanity back by locking up the repeat offender, Ignatz.

In regard to Krazy's undetermined gender, Herriman told movie director Frank Capra, who watched the artist drawing at the Hal Roach Studios, "I don't know. I fooled around with it once; began to think the Kat is a girl—even drew up some strips with her being pregnant. It wasn't the Kat any longer, too much concerned with her own problems—like a soap opera. Know what I mean? Then I realized Krazy was something like a sprite, an elf. They have no sex. So that Kat can't be a 'he' or a 'she.' The Kat's a sprite—a pixie—free to butt into anything. Don't you think so?"

The strip features many other characters, such as Mrs. Kwak Wakk, "Bum Bill" Bee, and Don Kiyote, and ever-changing landscapes in an imaginary version of the desert of Coconino County, Arizona.

The characters speak in a poetic soup of phonetically spelled words inspired by an ethnological mix of Creole, African American, and Brooklyn English, as well as Yiddish, Spanish, and American Indian languages.

The strip's subtleties and surrealism never made it very popular with the public en masse, but it had an enthusiastic following among artistic and intellectual circles. In 1924 writer Gilbert Seldes dubbed Herriman "the counterpart of Chaplin in the comic film" in his essay on *Krazy Kat* in *The Seven Lively Arts* (reprinted in this book starting on page 37). President Woodrow Wilson never missed reading it. E. E. Cummings called it "a meteoric burlesk melodrama." Legend has it Picasso was a fan. If he wasn't, he should have been. Disney to de Kooning were devotees. E. B. White sung his praises. But the artist's most ardent supporter was William Randolph Hearst. Hearst owned the King Features Syndicate and refused to drop Herriman's *Krazy Kat* even when it was carried by fewer than fifty papers. It was reputedly Hearst who ordered the strip to be cancelled in 1944, upon learning of Herriman's passing because no one could replace the artist. *Krazy Kat* is possibly the first important strip to die with its creator.

Two family tragedies marked Herriman's life. On September 29, 1931, his wife of twenty-nine years, Mabel, died in a car accident, and in 1939 his daughter Bobbie passed away at age thirty. He retired to a lonely existence, brightened only by his cats and dogs. Herriman died on April 25, 1944, of "non-alcoholic cirrhosis of the liver" and, at his request, his ashes were scattered over Monument Valley in Arizona.

Four-Color Felines

Krazy Kat had maybe not nine, but a number of lives in a variety of media. Her most wonderful life, however, was in the color Sunday newspapers.

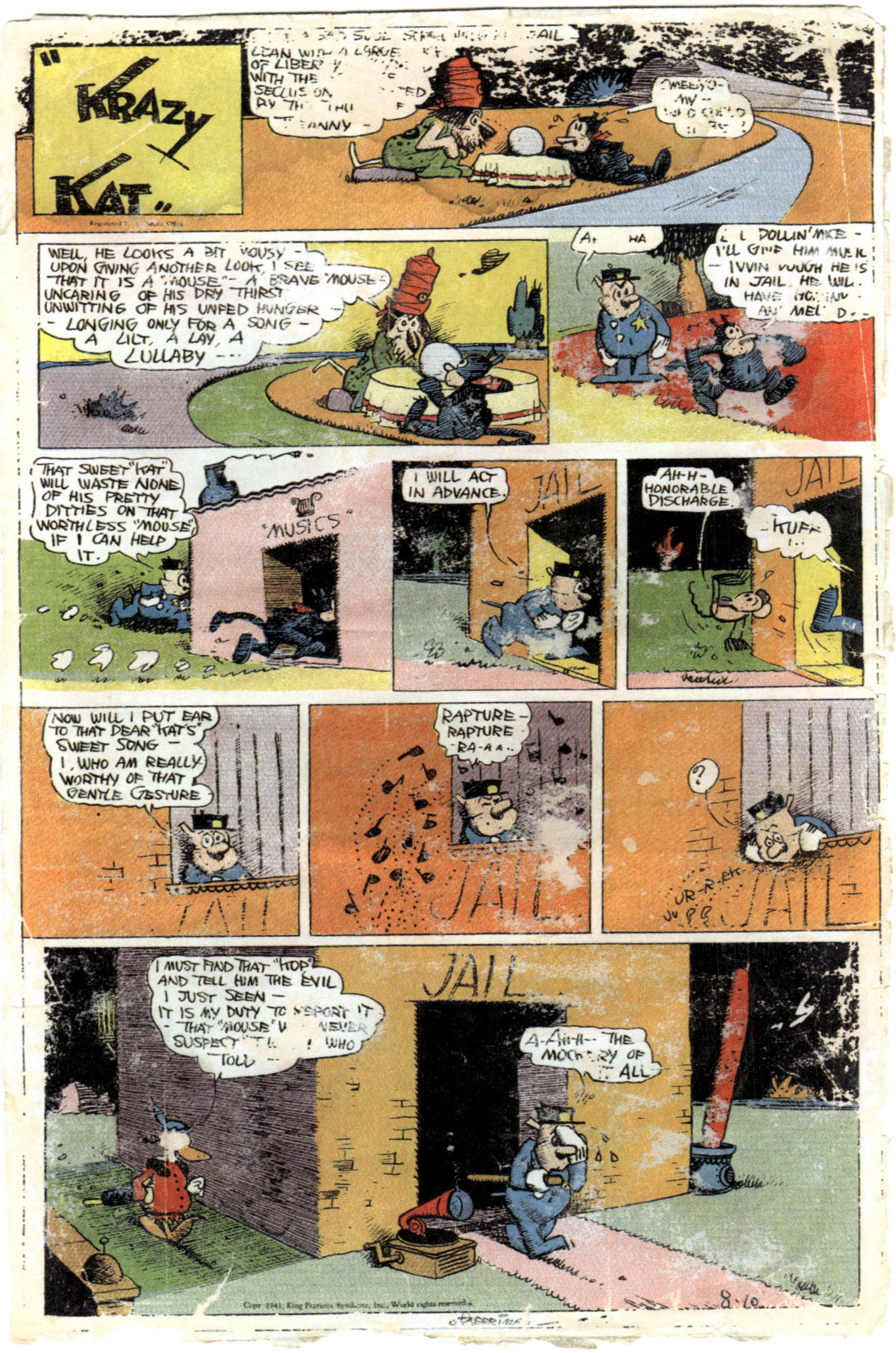

"KRAZY KAT"
WELL, HE LOOKS A BIT LOUSY - UPON GIVING ANOTHER LOOK, I SEE THAT IT IS A "MOUSE" - A BRAVE "MOUSE" - UNCARING OF HIS DRY THIRST UNWITTING OF HIS UNFED HUNGER - - LONGING ONLY FOR A SONG - A LILT, A LAY, A LULLABY - - -
THAT SWEET "KAT" WILL WASTE NONE OF HIS PRETTY DITTIES ON THAT WORTHLESS "MOUSE" IF I CAN HELP IT.
"MUSICS"
I WILL ACT IN ADVANCE.
JAIL
AH-H- HONORABLE DISCHARGE.
JAIL
-KUFF
NOW WILL I PUT EAR TO THAT DEAR "KAT'S" SWEET SONG - I, WHO AM REALLY WORTHY OF THAT GENTLE GESTURE
JAIL
RAPTURE - RAPTURE - RA-A-A..
JAIL
JAIL
I MUST FIND THAT "KOP" AND TELL HIM THE EVIL I JUST SEEN - IT IS MY DUTY TO
JAIL
Copr 1941, King Features Syndicate, Inc., World rights reserved.
8-10

RIGHT A rare color printer's proof sheet. August 10, 1941. Previously unpublished.

OPPOSITE February 14, 1937.

21437

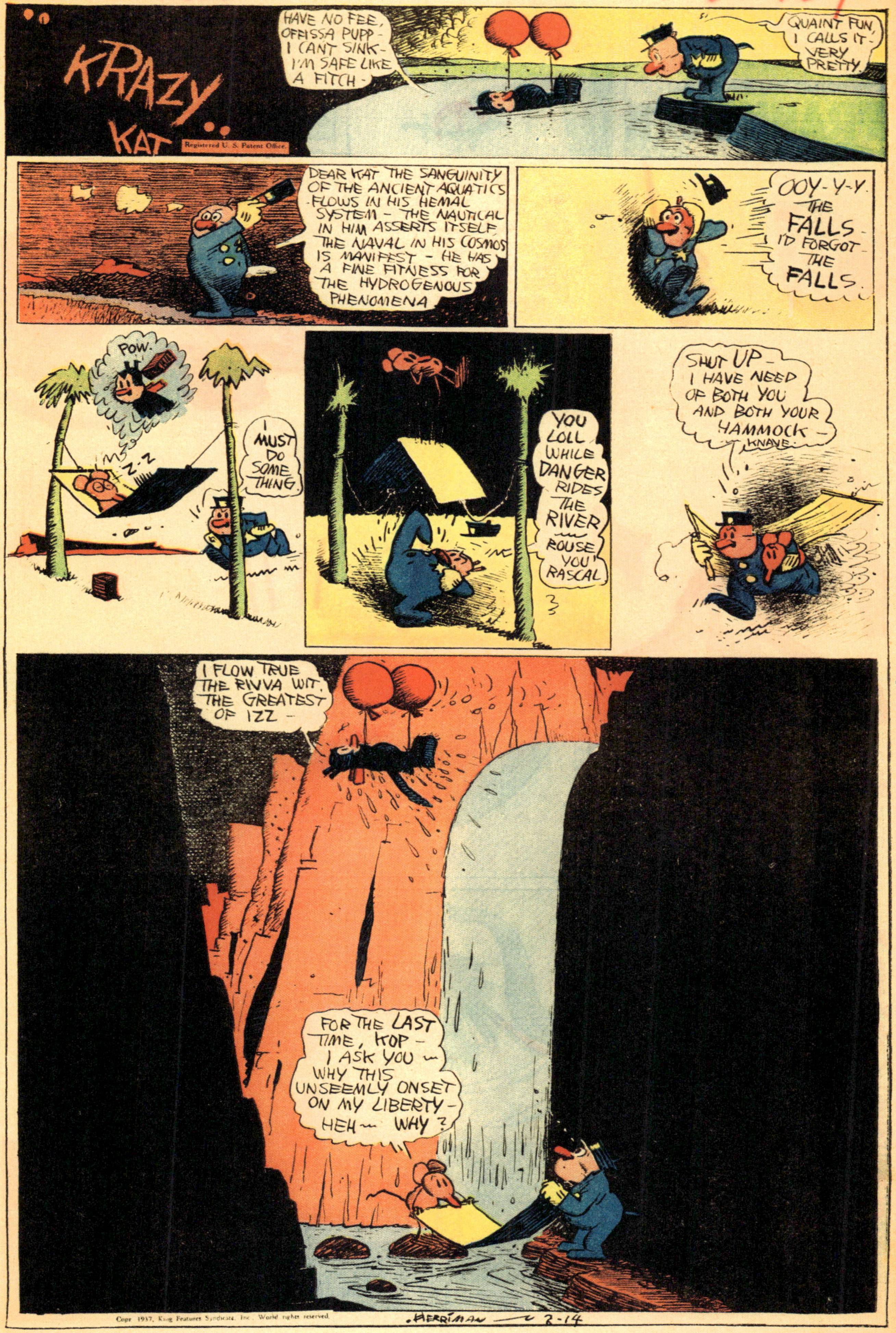
KRAZY KAT
Registered U. S. Patent Office.
HAVE NO FEE, OFFISSA PUPP - I CAN'T SINK - I'M SAFE LIKE A FITCH -
QUAINT FUN, I CALLS IT - VERY PRETTY.
DEAR KAT THE SANGUINITY OF THE ANCIENT AQUATICS FLOWS IN HIS HEMAL SYSTEM - THE NAUTICAL IN HIM ASSERTS ITSELF THE NAVAL IN HIS COSMOS IS MANIFEST - HE HAS A FINE FITNESS FOR THE HYDROGENOUS PHENOMENA
OOY-Y-Y THE FALLS I'D FORGOT THE FALLS.
POW.
Z-Z
I MUST DO SOME THING
YOU LOLL WHILE DANGER RIDES THE RIVER — ROUSE YOU RASCAL
SHUT UP - I HAVE NEED OF BOTH YOU AND BOTH YOUR HAMMOCK - KNAVE.
I FLOW TRUE THE RIVVA WIT THE GREATEST OF IZZ -
FOR THE LAST TIME, KOP - I ASK YOU - WHY THIS UNSEEMLY ONSET ON MY LIBERTY - HEH - WHY ?
Copr 1937, King Features Syndicate, Inc. World rights reserved.
HERRIMAN 2-14

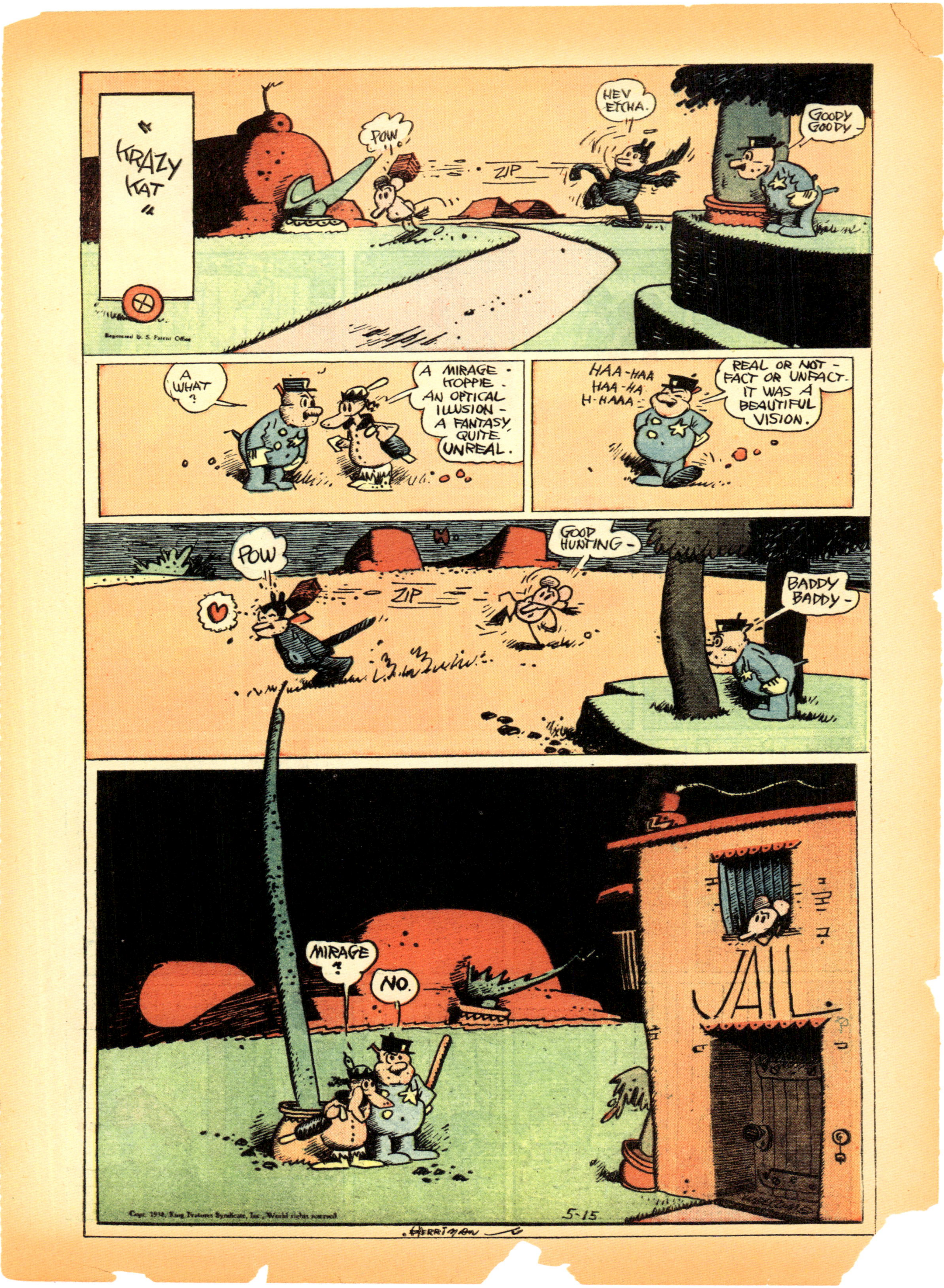
"KRAZY KAT"
Registered U. S. Patent Office
POW
ZIP
HEY ETCHA.
GOODY GOODY -
A WHAT ?
A MIRAGE - KOPPIE - AN OPTICAL ILLUSION - A FANTASY, QUITE UNREAL.
HAA-HAA HAA-HA H-HAAA
REAL OR NOT - FACT OR UNFACT. IT WAS A BEAUTIFUL VISION.
POW
ZIP
GOOD HUNTING -
BADDY BADDY -
MIRAGE ?
NO.
JAIL
Copr. 1938, King Features Syndicate, Inc., World rights reserved
5-15
HERRIMAN

ABOVE May 15, 1938.

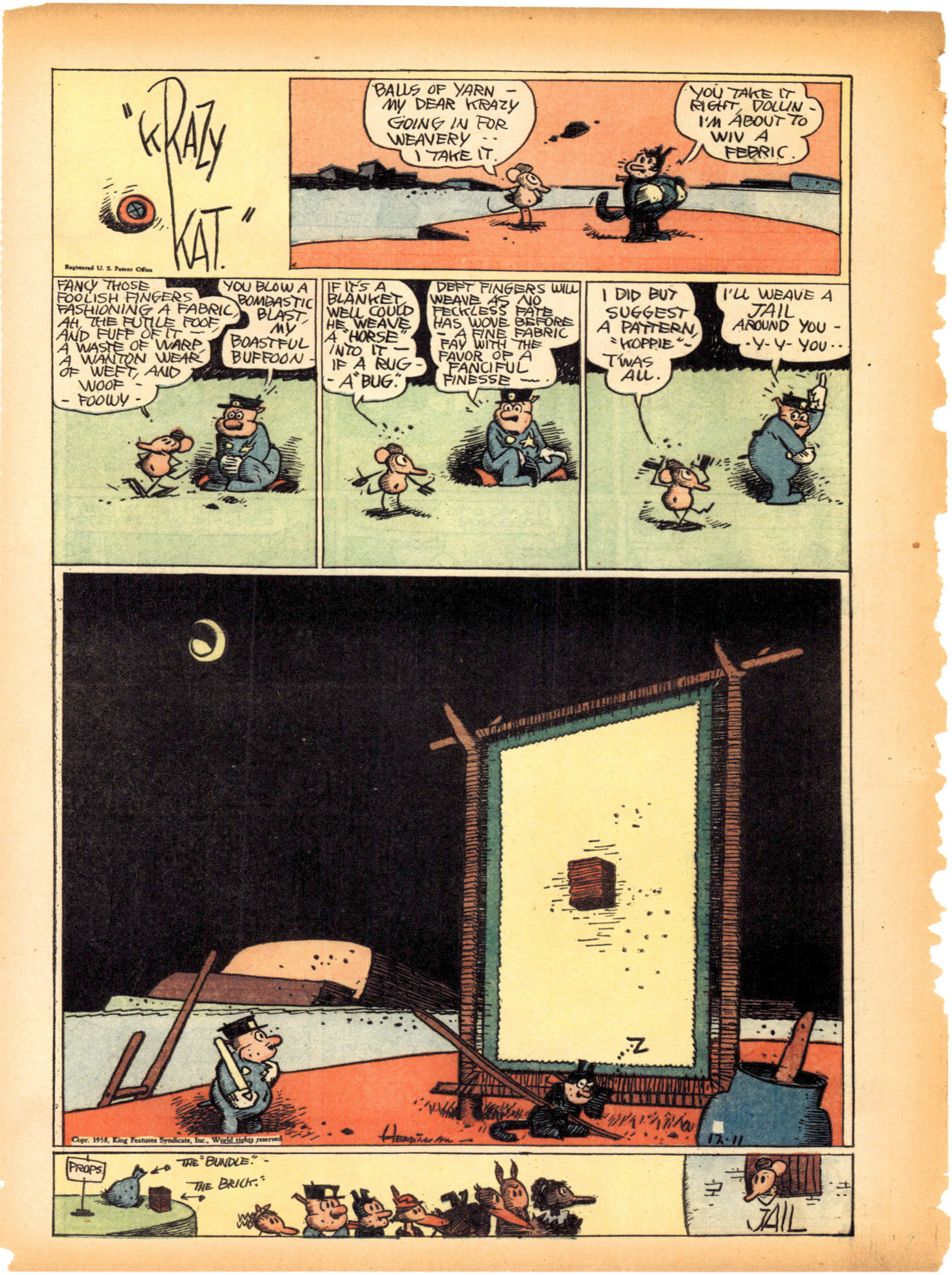
"KRAZY KAT."
Registered U. S. Patent Office
BALLS OF YARN — MY DEAR KRAZY GOING IN FOR WEAVERY - - I TAKE IT.
YOU TAKE IT RIGHT, DOLLIN — I'M ABOUT TO WIV A FEBRIC.
FANCY THOSE FOOLISH FINGERS FASHIONING A FABRIC, AH, THE FUTILE FOOF, AND FUFF OF IT — A WASTE OF WARP, A WANTON WEAR OF WEFT, AND WOOF - - FOOWY -
YOU BLOW A BOMBASTIC BLAST, MY BOASTFUL BUFFOON -
IF IT'S A BLANKET, WELL COULD HE WEAVE A "HORSE" INTO IT — IF A RUG - - A "BUG."
DEFT FINGERS WILL WEAVE AS NO FECKLESS FATE HAS WOVE BEFORE — A FINE FABRIC FAY WITH THE FAVOR OF A FANCIFUL FINESSE —.
I DID BUT SUGGEST A PATTERN, "KOPPIE" - T'WAS ALL.
I'LL WEAVE A JAIL AROUND YOU - -Y- Y- YOU - -
Z
Copr. 1938, King Features Syndicate, Inc., World rights reserved
HERRIMAN
12-11
PROPS.
THE "BUNDLE." -
THE BRICK."
JAIL

ABOVE December 11, 1938.

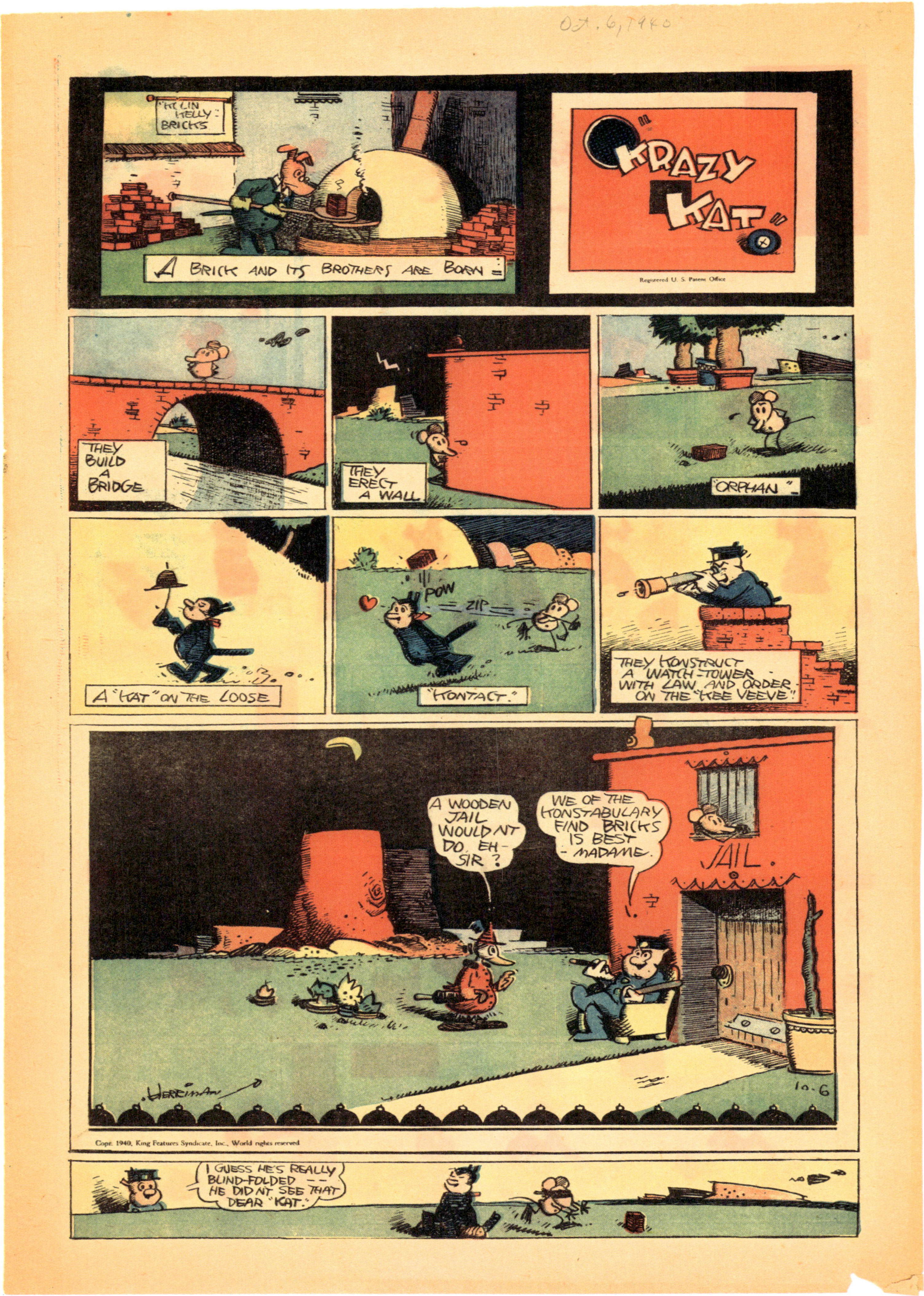

Oct. 6, 1940
"KOLIN KELLY" BRICKS
A BRICK AND ITS BROTHERS ARE BORN -
"KRAZY KAT"
Registered U. S. Patent Office
THEY BUILD A BRIDGE
THEY ERECT A WALL
"ORPHAN" -
A "KAT" ON THE LOOSE
POW
ZIP
"KONTACT."
THEY KONSTRUCT A WATCH-TOWER - WITH LAW AND ORDER ON THE "KEE VEEVE"
A WOODEN JAIL WOULD NT DO, EH SIR?
WE OF THE KONSTABULARY FIND BRICKS IS BEST - MADAME.
JAIL.
HERRIMAN
10-6
Copr. 1940, King Features Syndicate, Inc., World rights reserved
I GUESS HE'S REALLY BLIND-FOLDED -- HE DID NT SEE THAT DEAR "KAT."

ABOVE October 6, 1940.

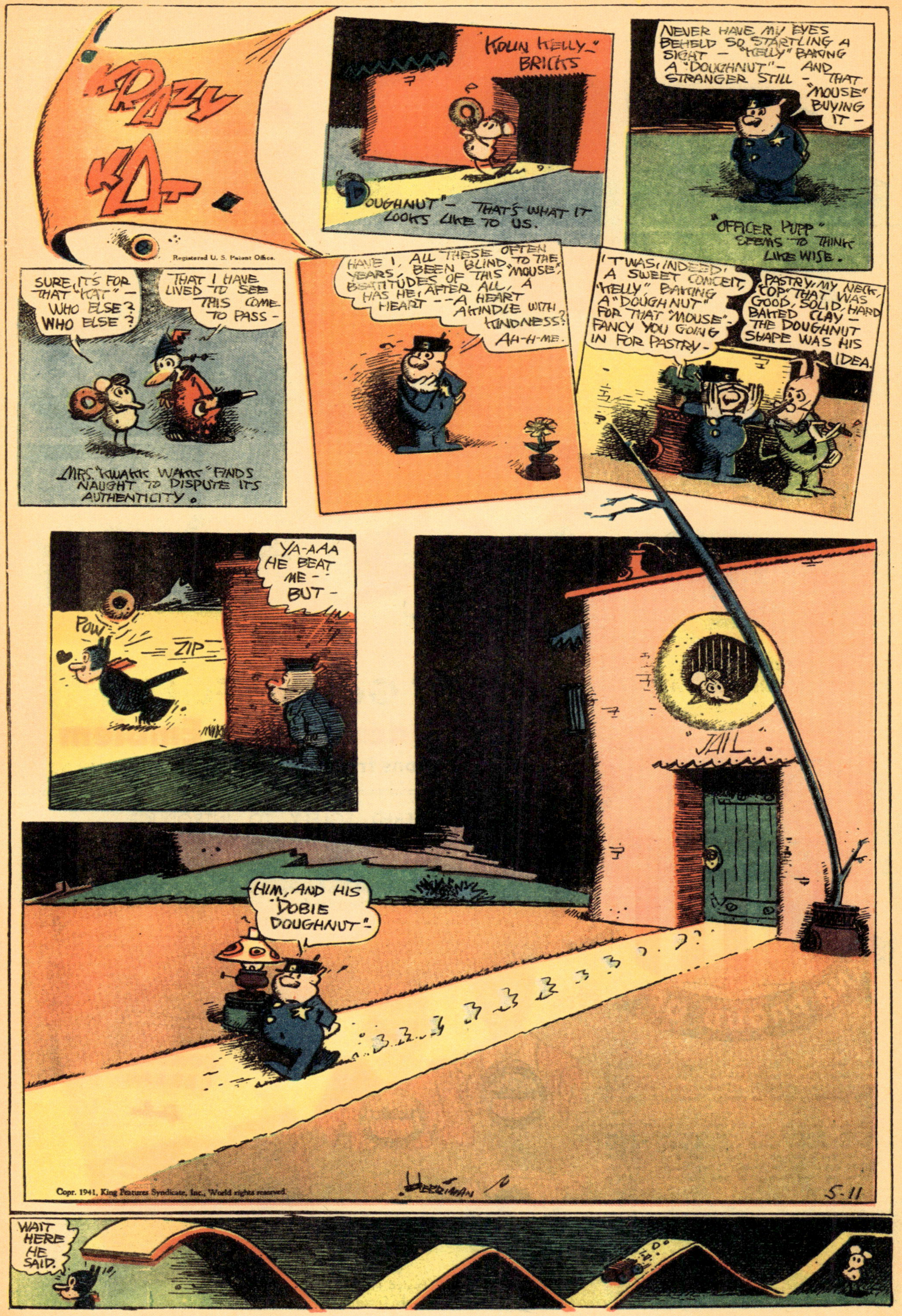
KRAZY KAT.
Registered U. S. Patent Office.
"KOLIN KELLY" BRICKS
"DOUGHNUT" — THAT'S WHAT IT LOOKS LIKE TO US.
NEVER HAVE MY EYES BEHELD SO STARTLING A SIGHT — "KELLY" BAKING A "DOUGHNUT" — AND STRANGER STILL — "THAT "MOUSE" BUYING IT —
"OFFICER PUPP" SEEMS TO THINK LIKEWISE.
SURE, IT'S FOR THAT "KAT" — WHO ELSE? WHO ELSE?
THAT I HAVE LIVED TO SEE THIS COME TO PASS —
MRS. "KWAKK WAKK" FINDS NAUGHT TO DISPUTE ITS AUTHENTICITY.
HAVE I, ALL THESE OFTEN YEARS, BEEN BLIND TO THE BEATITUDES OF THIS "MOUSE", HAS HE, AFTER ALL, A HEART — A HEART AKINDLE WITH KINDNESS? AH-H-ME.
"TWAS, INDEED, A SWEET CONCEIT, "KELLY" BAKING A "DOUGHNUT" FOR THAT "MOUSE" — FANCY YOU GOING IN FOR PASTRY —
PASTRY, MY NECK, COP, THAT WAS GOOD, SOLID, HARD BAKED CLAY — THE DOUGHNUT SHAPE WAS HIS IDEA.
POW
ZIP
YA-AAA HE BEAT ME — BUT —
JAIL
HIM, AND HIS "DOBIE DOUGHNUT" —
Copr. 1941, King Features Syndicate, Inc., World rights reserved.
HERRIMAN
5-11
WAIT HERE HE SAID.

ABOVE May 11, 1941.

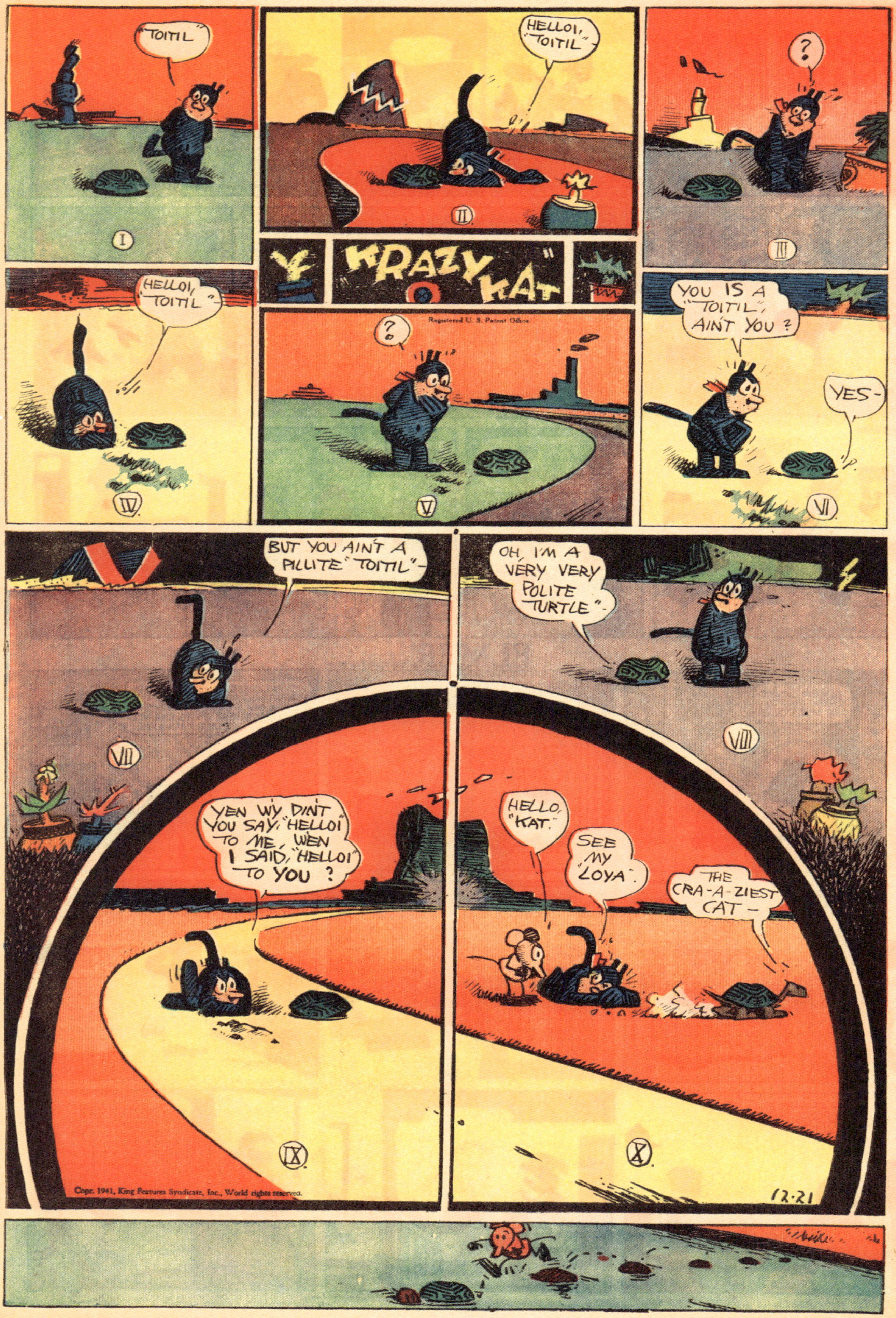
"TOITIL"
HELLOI, "TOITIL" -
?
"KRAZY KAT"
Registered U. S. Patent Office
HELLOI, "TOITIL" -
?
YOU IS A "TOITIL", AIN'T YOU ?
YES-
BUT YOU AIN'T A PILLITE "TOITIL" -
OH, I'M A VERY VERY POLITE TURTLE -
YEN WY DIN'T YOU SAY, "HELLOI" TO ME, WEN I SAID, "HELLOI" TO YOU ?
HELLO, "KAT."
SEE MY "LOYA".
THE CRA-A-ZIEST CAT -
Copr. 1941, King Features Syndicate, Inc., World rights reserved.
12-21

ABOVE December 21, 1941.

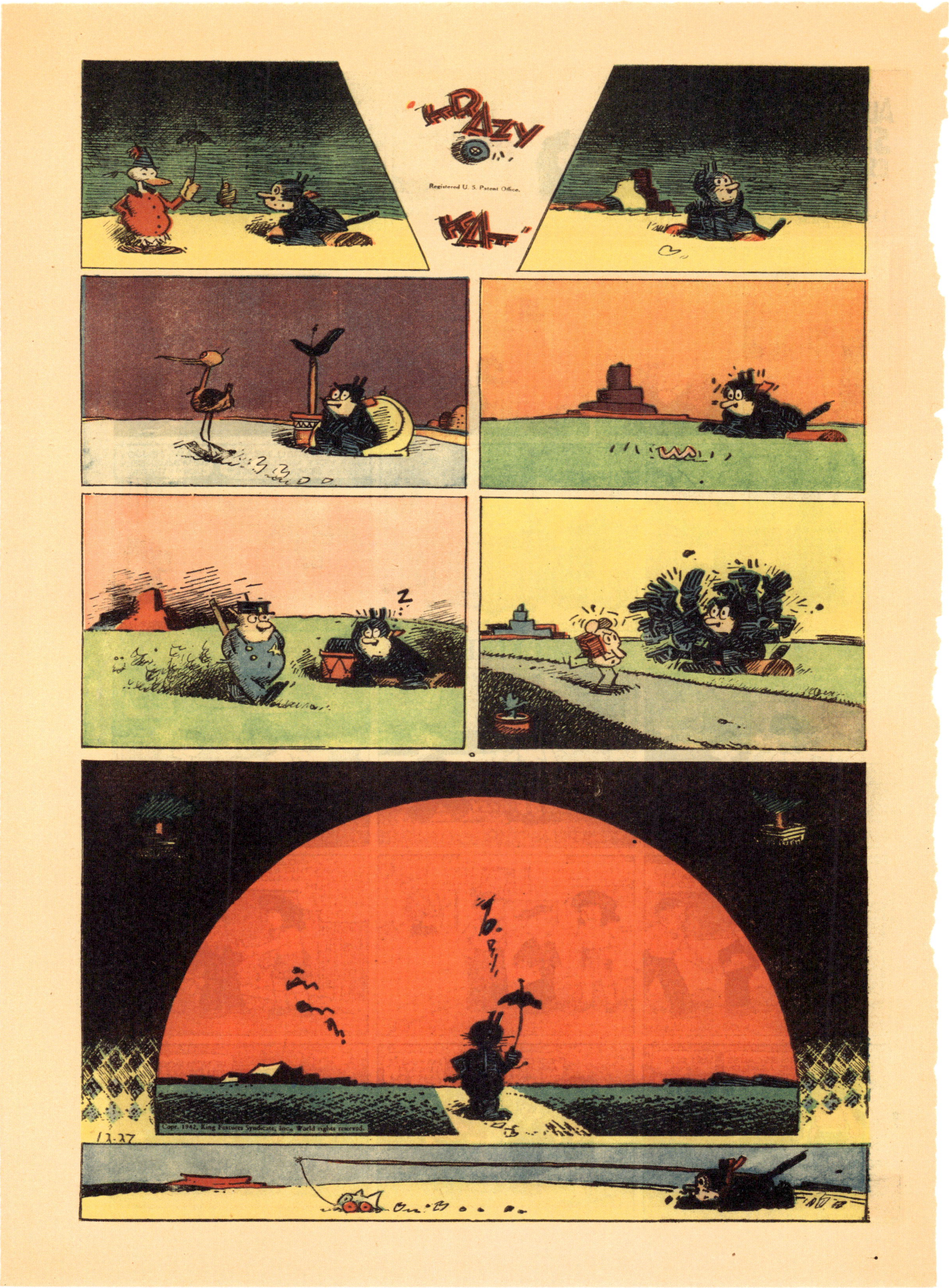
Krazy Kat
Registered U. S. Patent Office.
Copr. 1942, King Features Syndicate, Inc. World rights reserved.

ABOVE December 27, 1942.

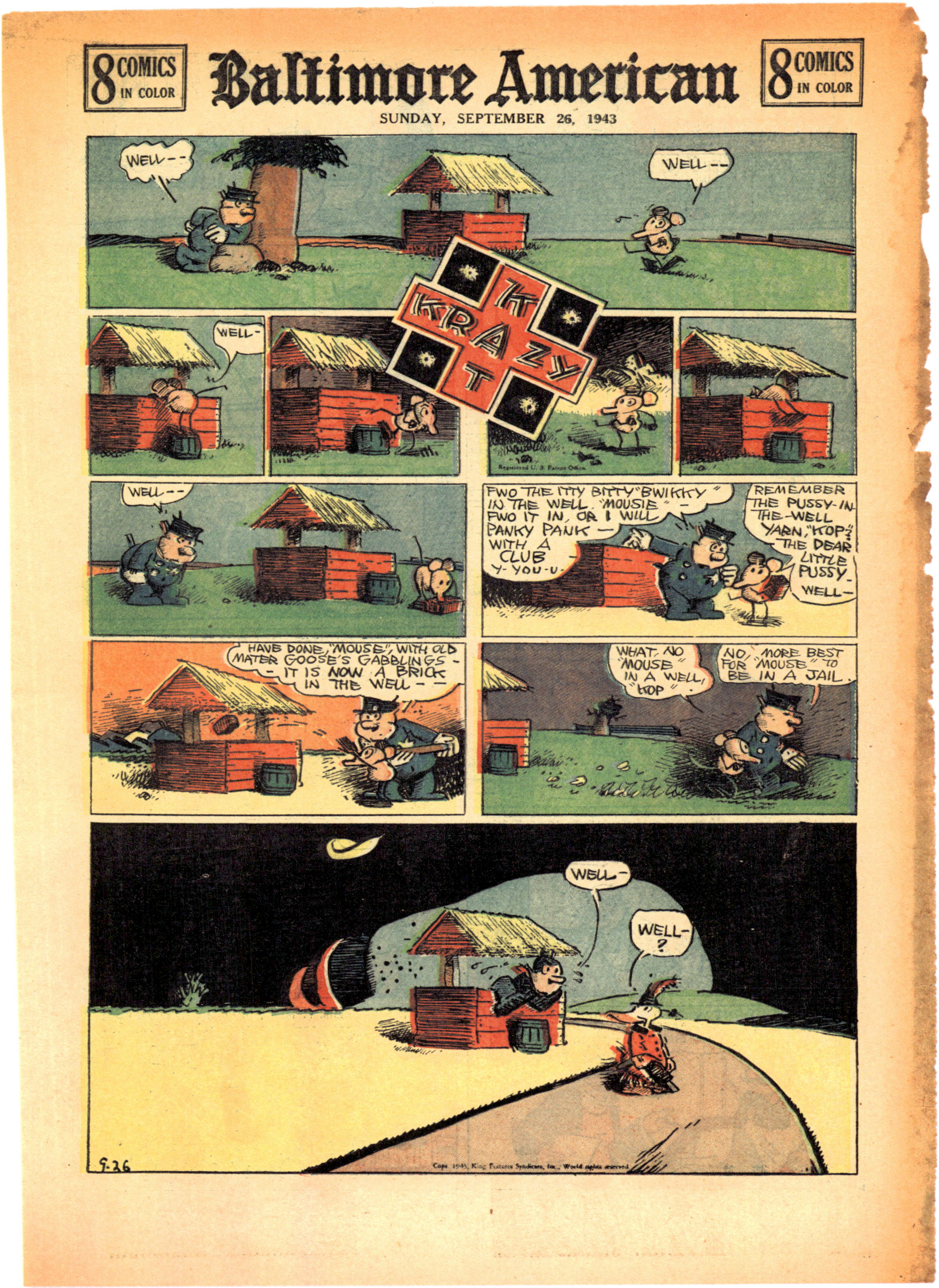
8 COMICS IN COLOR
Baltimore American
8 COMICS IN COLOR
SUNDAY, SEPTEMBER 26, 1943
WELL--
WELL --
KRAZY KAT
WELL-
Registered U. S. Patent Office
WELL--
FWO THE ITTY BITTY "BWIKKY" IN THE WELL, "MOUSIE" - FWO IT IN, OR I WILL PANKY PANK — WITH A CLUB Y-YOU-U.
REMEMBER THE PUSSY-IN-THE-WELL YARN, "KOP"? THE DEAR LITTLE PUSSY. WELL-
HAVE DONE, "MOUSE", WITH OLD MATER GOOSE'S GABBLINGS - - IT IS NOW A BRICK IN THE WELL - -
WHAT, NO "MOUSE" IN A WELL, "KOP".
NO, MORE BEST FOR "MOUSE" TO BE IN A JAIL.
WELL-
WELL-?
9-26
Copr. 1943, King Features Syndicate, Inc., World rights reserved

ABOVE September 26, 1943.

Warped with Fancy, Woofed with Dreams

by Harry L. Katz

"To become truly immortal, a work of art must escape all human limits: logic and common sense will only interfere. But once these barriers are broken, it will enter the realms of childhood visions and dreams."

—Giorgio de Chirico (1888–1978), Surrealist painter

So many cartoonists dream of becoming fine artists—ambitions tied to galleries and studios beyond the pages, their commercial careers studies in frustration, compromise, and creative sublimation. George Herriman never seemed to nurture that dream or feel that frustration. In fact, to the contrary, historical anecdotes suggest that many leading artists and writers were inspired by Herriman's work. As Ignatz Mouse muses on Coconino's "wolcennic" rock formations in a March 1943 Sunday page, Offissa Pupp exclaims, "He's just a 'mouse'—so how could he be 'esthetic'?" We might ask the same of Herriman. After all, he was just a cartoonist. Then how did he become so celebrated and accomplished; so literary, linguistic, artistic, and universally admired? What made *Krazy Kat* different from contemporary strips and, in 1922, according to oft-quoted critic Gilbert Seldes, "the most amusing and fantastic and satisfactory work of art produced in America today"?

In his celebrated essay, Seldes did not even use the words *comic strip*, referring rather to *Krazy Kat* as a "work of art" and to Herriman, by inference, as an artist. High praise for a working man cranking out two different daily strips each week plus full-page Sunday strips on the weekend. Yet Herriman was indeed a wonderful artist and brilliant writer, whose signature comic strip transcended the genre. He began his career in the margins of the cartooning industry in Southern California, the same way Krazy and Ignatz began theirs just outside the frame of a conventional daily strip called *The Dingbat Family/The Family Upstairs*. Born of mixed Creole parentage in New Orleans in 1880, Herriman got his start as a teenager working as an office boy at the *Los Angeles Herald*. He spent the first decade of the twentieth century, his twenties, creating comic panels and strips for a variety of newspapers and syndicates. In Los Angeles, he produced strips similar in style and content to the work of Bud Fisher, whose sensationally successful *Mutt and Jeff* strip debuted as the nation's first daily in San Francisco in 1908. No doubt Herriman and his publishers were mindful of Fisher's popularity and wished to capitalize on the formula he had created.

In 1910 Herriman settled in New York City, where he lived for twelve years working under contract exclusively for William Randolph Hearst. Just as Picasso

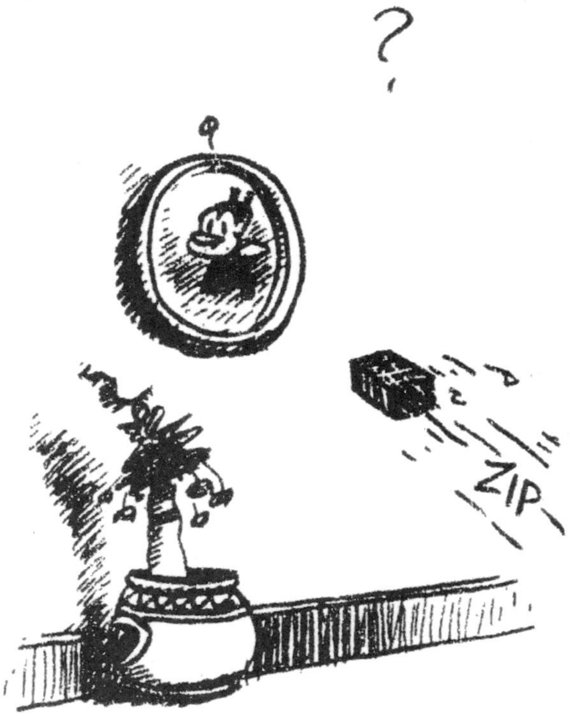
ZIP

learned to draw classically and picked up modernist theory from Cézanne and others before setting his own course toward abstraction, Herriman drew from his contemporaries in the cartooning milieu. Newspaper cartooning was little more than a decade old, and he found himself working alongside giants of the new industry: Jimmy Swinnerton, Gus Mager, Tad Dorgan, Harry Hershfield, Fred Opper, Winsor McCay, Rudolph Dirks, and Cliff Sterrett. Herriman fit in pretty well, as Dorgan suggested in a later published letter: "He brags about his favorites, Garge [Herriman's nickname] does, but never about himself. The violet imitated Garge when it assumed that attitude of shyness. He thinks he's the rottenest artist that ever got behind a pen, and no matter how many boosting letters he gets he's of the same opinion still. Of course, we know better." Dorgan noted that "Garge has three hobbies. They are Arizona Indians, chili con carne, and boxing gloves." Boxing was a marquee sport in America in 1910, but Indians and chili con carne were notably exotic back East, and George Herriman seemed so, too. He had light Creole skin and kinky hair hidden by a hat that seemed permanently perched atop his head. Herriman *was* different. They called him "the Greek" due to his dark complexion, but it was not his foreignness, suspect race, or ethnicity that set him apart. It was his creativity.

In 1910 America enjoyed unprecedented international peace and commercial prosperity. Rotund Republican William Howard Taft was president of the United States; the Woolworth Building, one of New York City's great early skyscrapers, rose from its foundation; the Wright Company began mass-producing airplanes, and the first passenger Zeppelin took to the air; the Mann Act passed, making interstate transport of women for immoral purposes illegal; the NAACP celebrated its first anniversary; at least sixty-seven black Americans were lynched; black boxer Jack Johnson knocked out white hope James Jeffries in fifteen rounds for the heavyweight crown; Cy Young won his five-hundredth game while the Phillies beat the Cubs in the World Series, and a baseball game was played under electric lights for the first time; Sigmund Freud published his analysis of Leonardo da Vinci's painting of the Virgin and St. Anne; music floated over the airwaves by wireless radio broadcast; Japan annexed Korea; Picasso and Braque continued their development of Cubism; Mark Twain died on April 21; and Zane Grey published *The Heritage of the Desert.* And, in the midst of all the action, on July 26, Ignatz Mouse flung the first object at Krazy Kat.

It was a time when changes in the funnies echoed those in technology, science, commerce, and the fine arts. In 1910 the world was rife with intellectual achievement. Winsor McCay and Lyonel Feininger were among the cartoonists who transformed the genre from a craft to an art form, pushing the formal and stylistic conventions of early comic strips. Gus Dirks and Jimmy Swinnerton added choreographed chaos and anamorphic magic to the mix, while cartoonists Gus Mager and Fred Opper were vaudeville funnymen supreme. Herriman learned from them all and, like modernists borrowing from Cézanne and African primitivism, created his own unique blend of manic comic art. Cartoonists, after all, were ahead of their time in bringing modern art precepts to the American people. Although the legendary Armory Show introduced European modern art to Americans in 1913, many were already familiar with it from the formal abstraction and conceptual playfulness evident in the comic pages from the century's first years.

Arizona, in 1910, was two years from statehood and a world away from the green mountains, golden prairies, and sultry southern skies familiar to most Americans. Settled safely only in the previous generation, the territory retained much of its natural mystery, innocence, and enchantment. Its indigenous inhabitants lent their own mystical spirituality to the landscape, as did the natural rock formations. If there was a land of dreams on Earth, it appeared to materialize in the deserts of Arizona. Herriman loved the remote Southwest, increasingly spending his summers at an outpost called Kayenta, near Monument Valley. In 1922 Herriman returned to Los Angeles with his family. The move facilitated his sojourns to the desert, where he found his creative and spiritual muse.

Herriman was not alone among his peers in the Great Southwest. Iconoclastic, adventurous, inspiration-seeking American artists had always been among the vanguard of those pushing the limits of civilization, following explorers, fur traders, and hunters into the wilderness to capture images of the unknown, unseen, and unimagined. During the nineteenth century, Albert Bierstadt and Thomas Moran produced stirring, majestic images of the West, creating an impetus for the western national parks and nascent federal conservation movement. Soon after 1900, such pioneering modernists as Georgia O'Keeffe, John Sloan, and others created an art community in Santa Fe and Taos, New Mexico, rendering the Southwest's desert scenes, flora, and native peoples with admiration, awe, respect, and contemporary formalism—reflecting the big themes and broad, worldly horizons envisioned by the avant-garde of the day.

Joined by Jimmy Swinnerton, Rudolph Dirks, and other cartooning pals in Arizona, Herriman found the mesas and arroyos of Coconino County and Monument Valley expressive of a larger yearning for space, freedom, and majesty far beyond the confines of a cartoon panel or newspaper page. As the decades passed, in a world ravaged by two world wars and a devastating global depression, the Southwest landscape seemed untouched, unsullied, pristine, and magical; an isolated world, apart and at peace.

Herriman's brain seems never to have been at peace, always in a creative and intellectual ferment. His bullpen buddy, Tad Dorgan, noted in an article published around 1920 that Krazy's creator "hangs around with a lot of painters, poets, and authors these days, but when I first saw him he still had grease from the box cars on his pants." For a Creole kid from New Orleans with an unrelenting mind, rubbing shoulders with the cognoscenti must have been an intellectual rush and release. Patrick McDonnell, creator of the comic strip *Mutts*, a true son of *Krazy Kat*, has written: "Herriman explores such unlikely comic-strip subjects as the forces of nature, the creation of art, the wonder of science, the magic of mysticism, and the power of spirituality. His pen line flows like handwriting: strong, personal, unselfconscious."

Flowing, unselfconscious, spiritual, and mystical, Herriman inspired the Beats, the modernists, and legions of loyal readers craving offbeat, intelligent creativity in the funnies. No other strip blended the arts, high and low, in such seamless fashion. Herriman stayed true to his origins as a comic strip artist, never straying, elevating the comic strip genre beyond its more pedestrian origins. He wrote text formed from vaudeville gags and Shakespeare, little ditties and lovely airs; drew gorgeous panels composed from increasingly sophisticated lines born of abstract conceptual musings. By the 1930s, he and Cliff Sterrett in their Sunday pages were producing some of the most contemporary, forward-looking art in the world, evoking the high-minded, easel-and-stretcher work of the Futurists and such Surrealists as Giorgio de Chirico.

Herriman's publisher, William Randolph Hearst, knew Krazy Kat was not for everybody, not for Everyman, but for all of the creative, yearning souls in our midst: the romantics and dreamers who, along with Herriman, believed against nature that a cat, a mouse, and a dog, united over decades in love, hate, and obsession, could, in fact, portray "the world's greatest trio in harmonics"—models of passion, fidelity, truth, and the innermost workings of the human heart.

Harry L. Katz is a former head curator in the Prints and Photographs Division at the Library of Congress. He is the editor of Cartoon America: Comic Art at the Library of Congress *and* Herblock: The Life and Work of the Great Political Cartoonist.

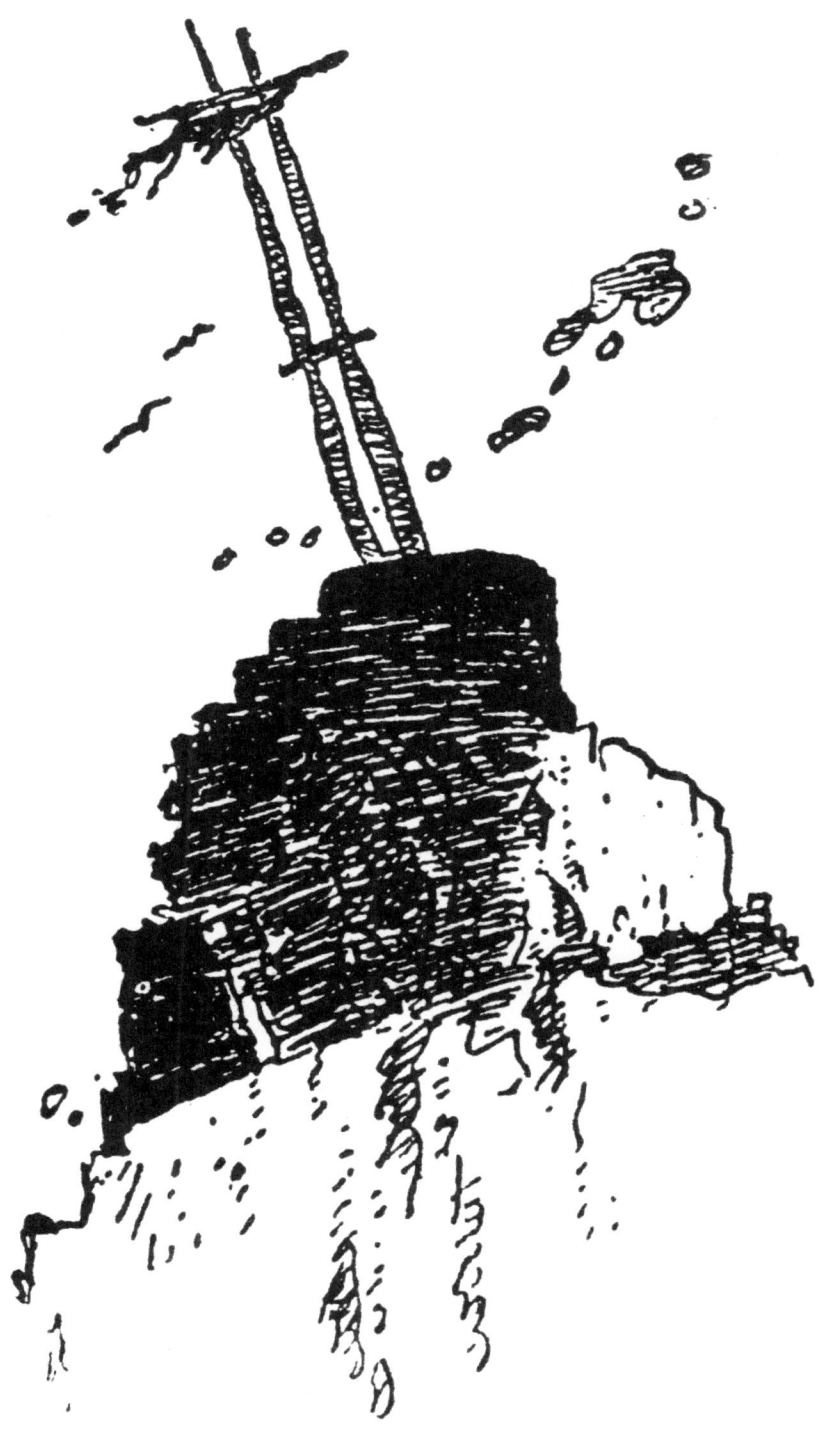

Oh, What a Gift!

As the poet Robert Burns said, what a gift it is "to see ourselves as others see us." George Herriman left us many deft doodles which reveal how he saw himself.

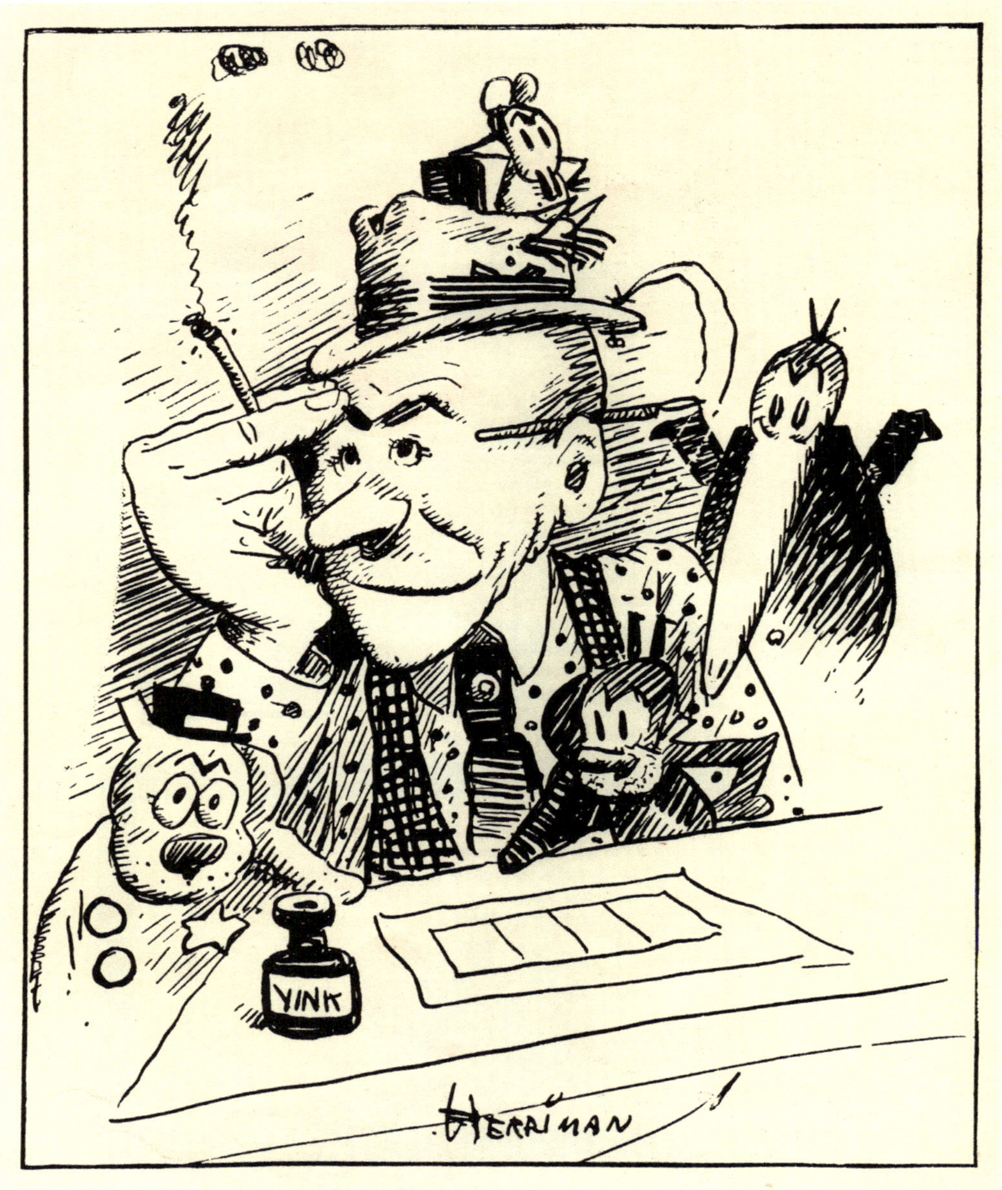
YINK
HERRIMAN

ABOVE George Herriman's self-portrait for the October 21, 1922, issue of *Judge* magazine.

OPPOSITE Comics fan John Boos used to send typed bios to his favorite cartoonists, asking them to autograph them. This is Herriman's, which the artist embellished with a self-portrait and the characters from *Krazy Kat*. February 10, 1936.

GEORGE HERRIMAN, who draws the delirious comic "Krazy Kat" for King Features Syndicate, Inc., and hundreds of thousands of enthusiastic readers, is a slight, gray-eyed, quiet man who always wears a hat, and never gets into the limelight if he can help it. On one occasion, after refusing to pose for a picture, on the ground that"the public doesn't care about my face," he was finally maneuvered to a drawing board. Then he graciously surrendered, complied with all requests, took off his coat, rolled up his sleeves, even sketched several large pictures of Krazy Kat. But he refused to pose without his hat. He did remove it for a moment "just to prove I have hair."

Herriman and the late "Tad", sports-cartoonist, were close friends, and Tad revealed this about him:

"His first name is George, but the boys call him Garge, because that's the way he pronounces it himself.

"No matter what happens Garge is always the same. You can steal his pens, but he only smiles. You can knock California, but he merely smiles. You can cut up rubber in his tobacco-pouch, and he'll smoke it to give you a laugh. He brags about his favorites, Garge does, but never about himself."

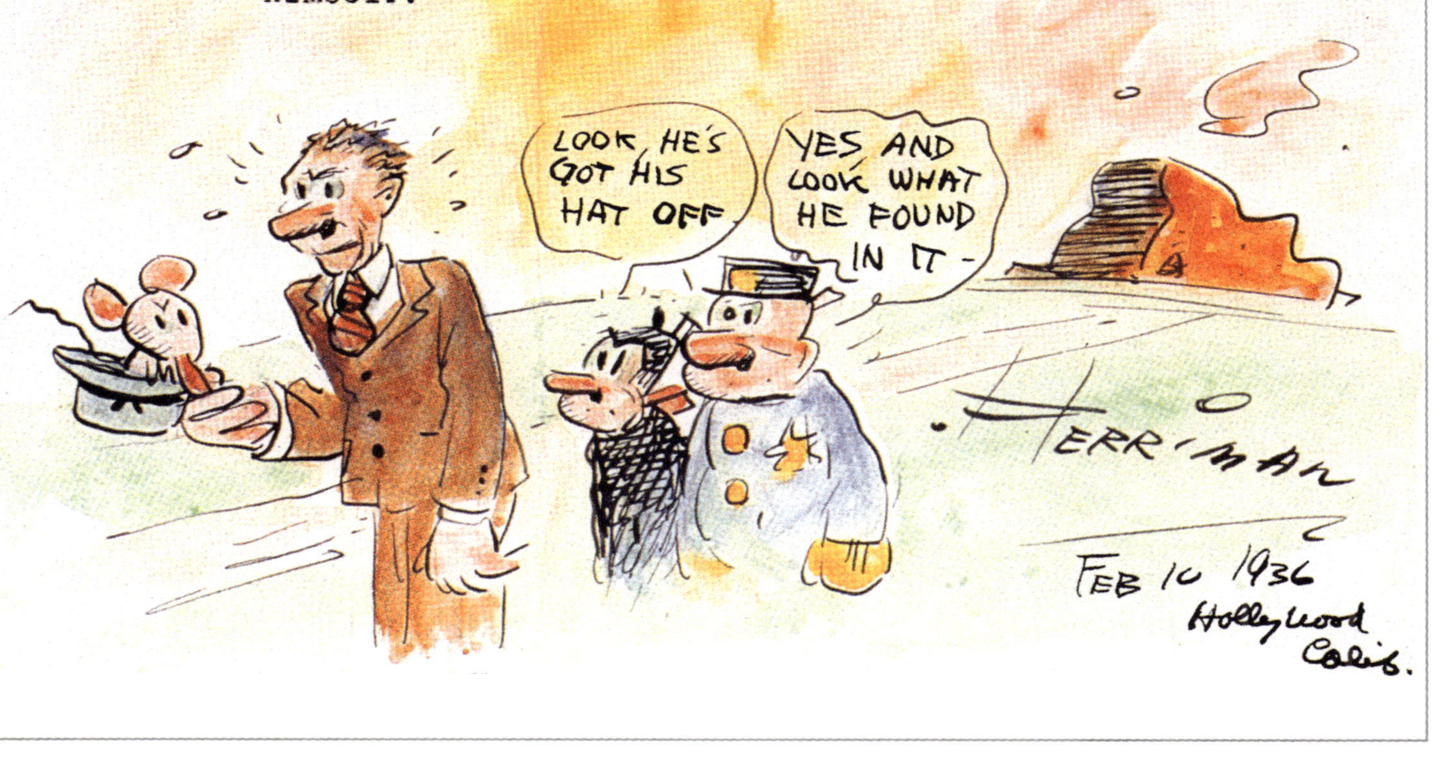
LOOK HE'S GOT HIS HAT OFF
YES AND LOOK WHAT HE FOUND IN IT -
HERRIMAN
FEB 10 1936
Hollywood Calif.

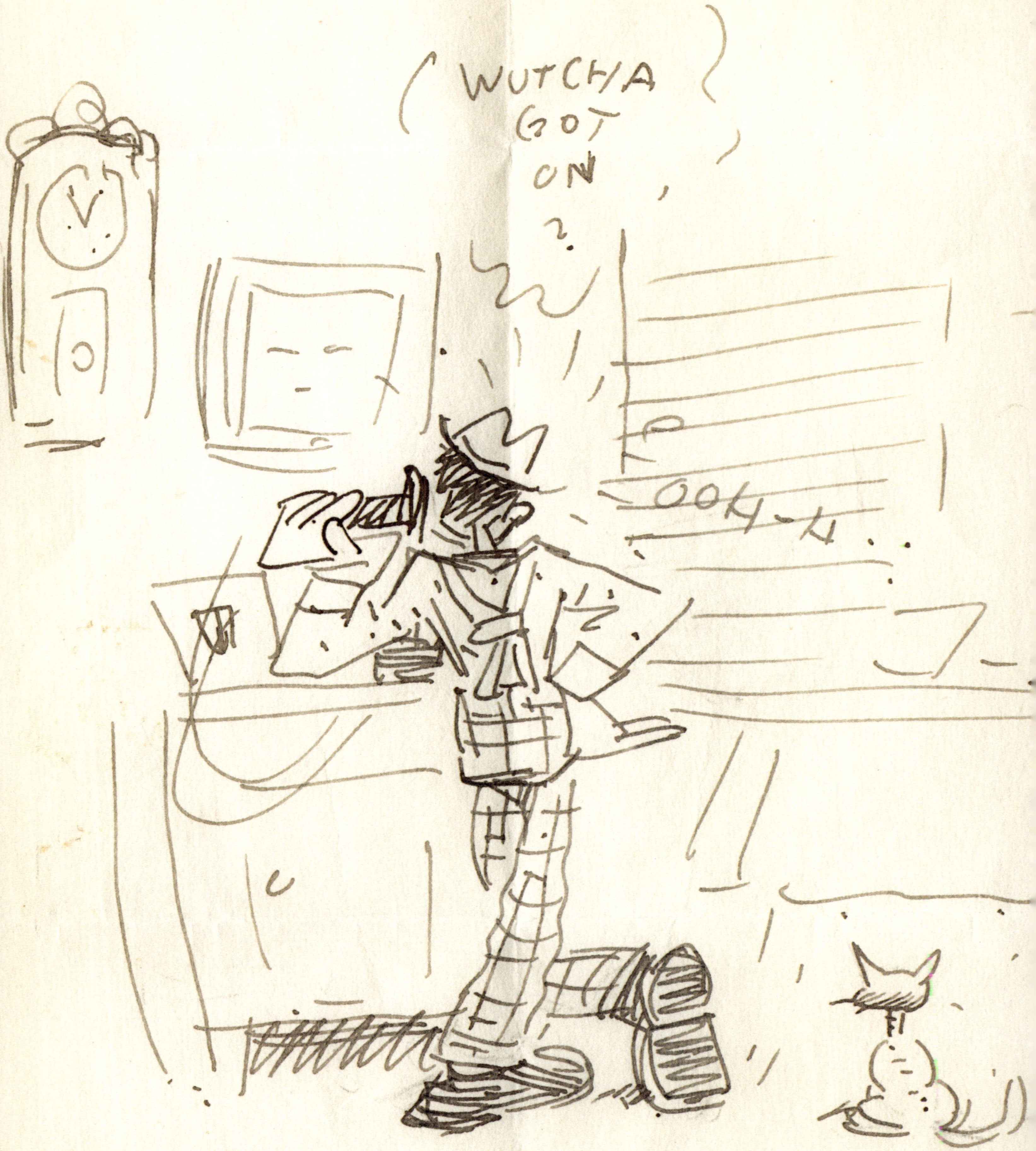
WUTCHA GOT ON ?
OOH-H..

thanks - for the
cheerful ones of
"Dorothy" and "R. DHU" -

She is a fine, upstanding gal -
and he is a "Braw Laddie" -

- my babies can go
set in the corner
and "ooze" -
"Oo.oo"
.. "Jee" ..

Ingabog:

Here's your
"pitcher" back -
and here's one
of me - doing
a much better
Jot of weeping -

and when I weep
the idea is
all my own -
I don't blame
nobody for
it.
thine
'ole Lachrymose
Herriman ..

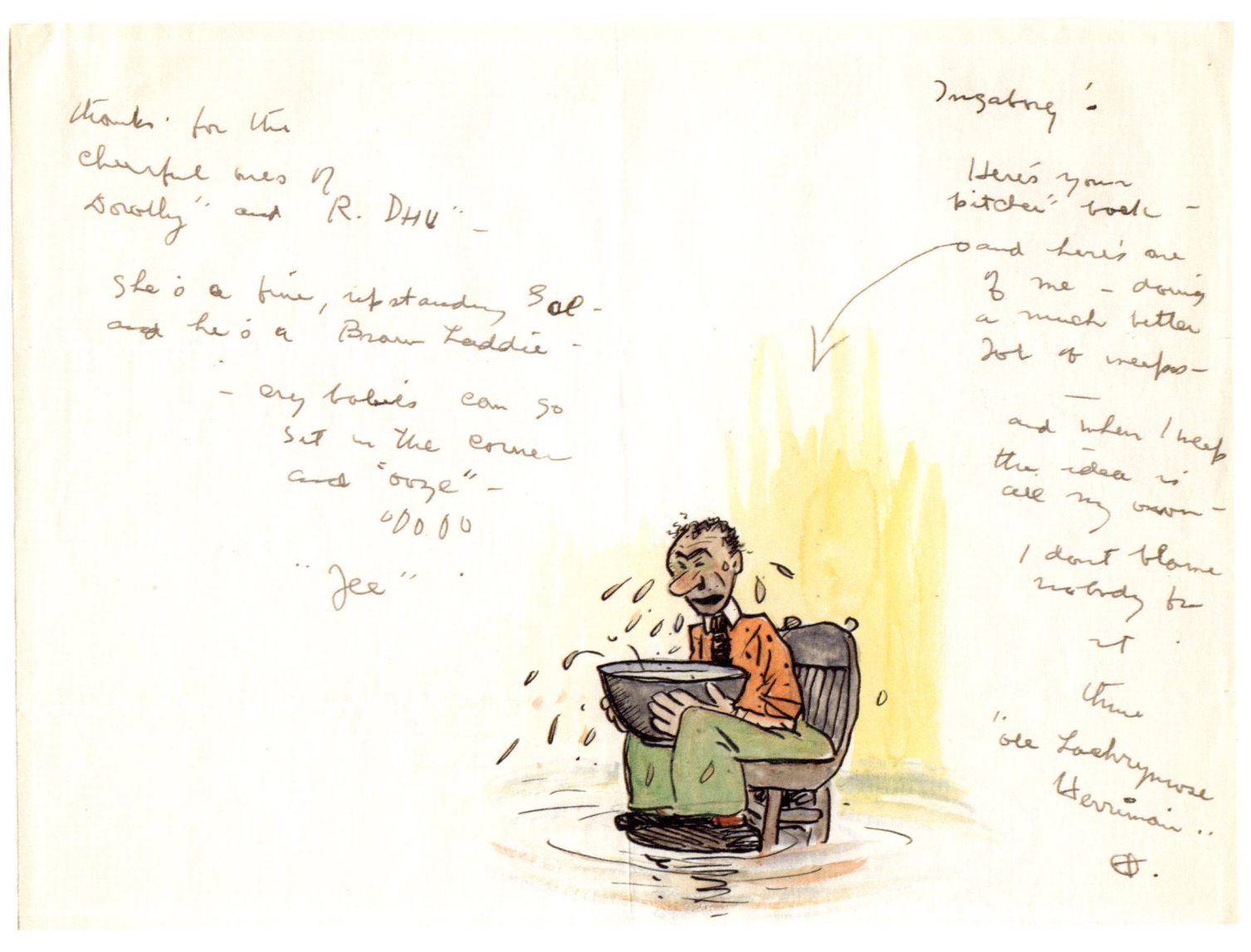

OPPOSITE After Herriman's wife passed away in 1931, the artist had an innocent, but sometimes humorously flirtatious, correspondence with Louise Swinnerton, cartoonist Jimmy Swinnerton's widow. Previously unpublished.

ABOVE Read them and weep. A light-hearted, lachrymose letter to Louise. 1930s. Previously unpublished.

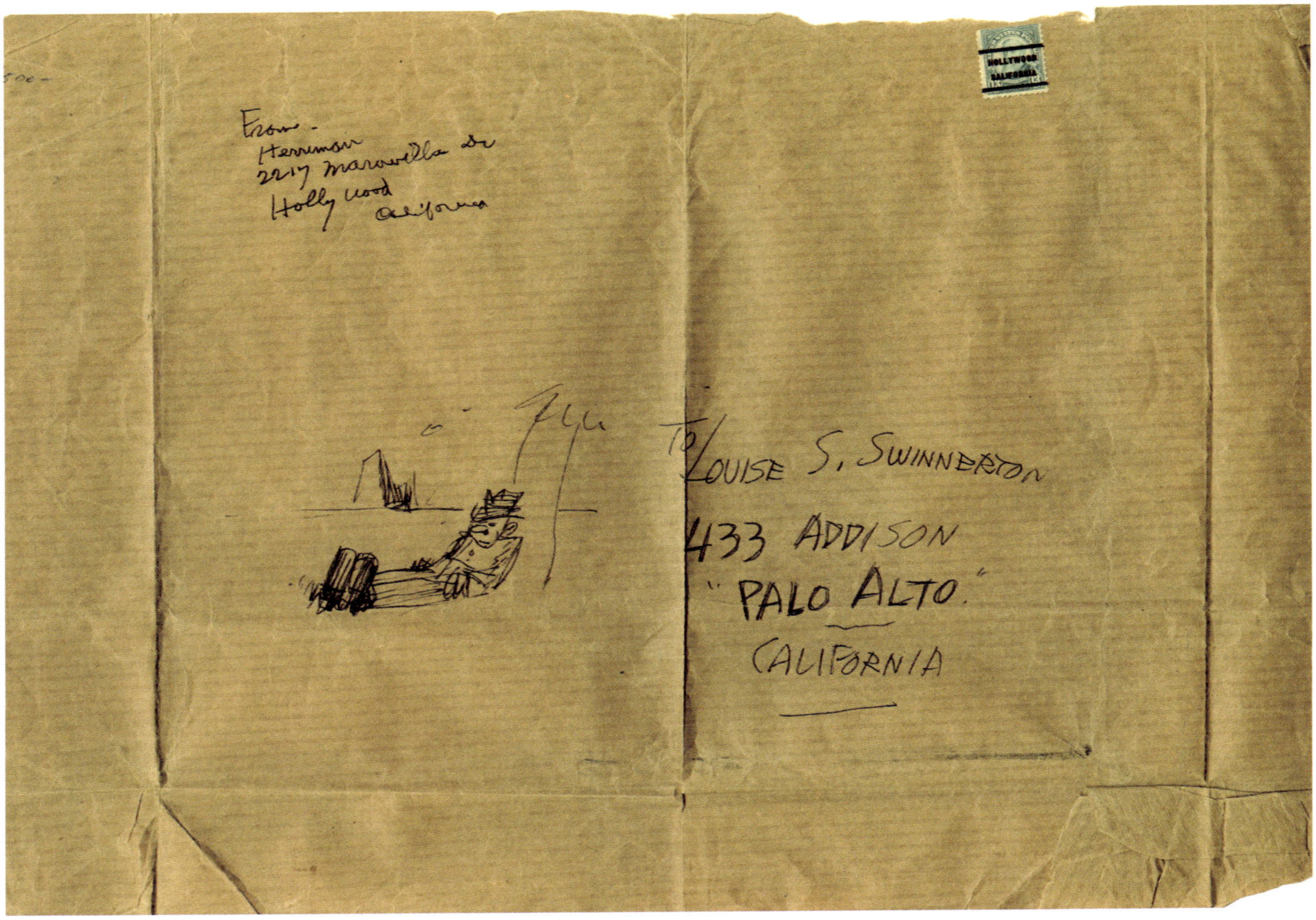
From -
Herriman
2217 Marawilla Dr
Hollywood
California
To/
Louise S. Swinnerton
433 Addison
"Palo Alto."
California

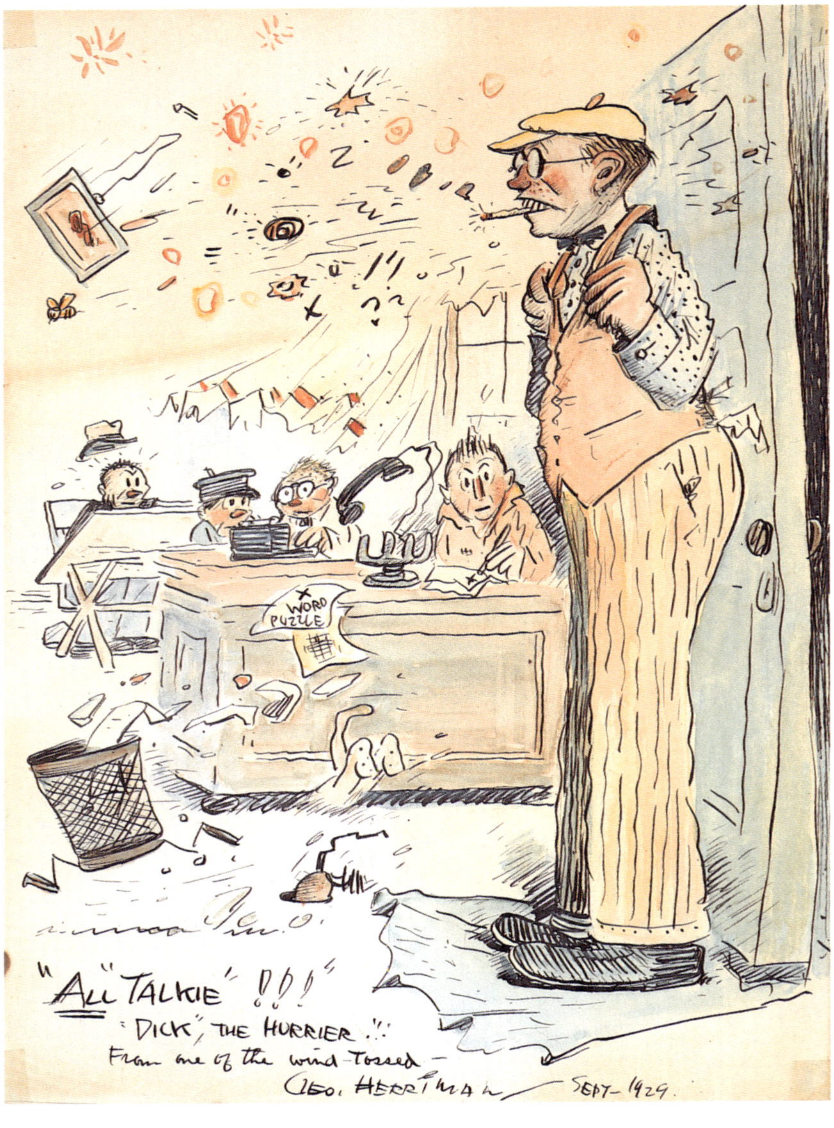
WORD PUZZLE
"ALL "TALKIE" !!!
"DICK", THE HURRIER."!
From one of the wind-Tossed -
GEO. HERRIMAN
SEPT- 1929.

ABOVE Siesta time. Illustrated envelope for a letter from Herriman to Louise Swinnerton.

RIGHT George Herriman pictures himself at the drawing board in the back, his hat flying. This is thought to be the only drawing picturing Herriman at Hal Roach Studios. The person in the foreground is Richard "Dick" Currier. At Hal Roach, Currier was an editor on many movies, such as *Another Fine Mess* (1930), starring Laurel and Hardy, and the Our Gang comedy *Bargain Day* (1931). The inscription reads, "All 'talkie'!!! 'Dick, the hurrier!' From one of the wind-tossed— Geo. Herriman." September 1929. Previously unpublished.

Mrs. Dingbat apparently oblivious of the "wink" but in reality aware of it.
Sounds of an eye winking; like a Kodak shutter
CLICK CLICK CLICK
Mr. D. not on at all.
you are indeed a hero
Note — WE BELIEVE, WITH OUR HUSBAND IN "GENTLE HUMOR," HENCE WE HAVE CUT OUT THE "BATTLE SCENE." TOO ROUGH, MUCH TOO ROUGH.
BUT, AS WE MAY NEVER HAVE ANOTHER CHANCE TO SAY IT, THE "OLD MAN" IS'NT REALLY ON THE LEVEL WITH THAT "GENTLE HUMOR" STUFF, Y'SHOULD SEE HOW HE BEHAVES "AT HOME" — "THE WRETCH."
as Mr. McNamara would say, "Goo-Bi";
Mrs. Geo. Herriman
RED
US
BOB.
"PEDRO"
OUR KAT.
TOOTS.
"THE OLE HOME AINT WHAT IT USED TO BE, SINCE "MA" HAS TOOK UP "ART" — "Us."

a Brick.
1.
2.
3.
Now, this is what I think Ignatz and Krazy should be — 4. Mrs. G.H.
CHEER UP, CHEER UP, I DON'T THINK OUR BOSS WILL EVER ASK THAT SHE DRAW YOU AGAIN —
A LITTLE CONSOLATION MEETING, BACK OF THE BARN AFTER THE ORDEAL. 5.

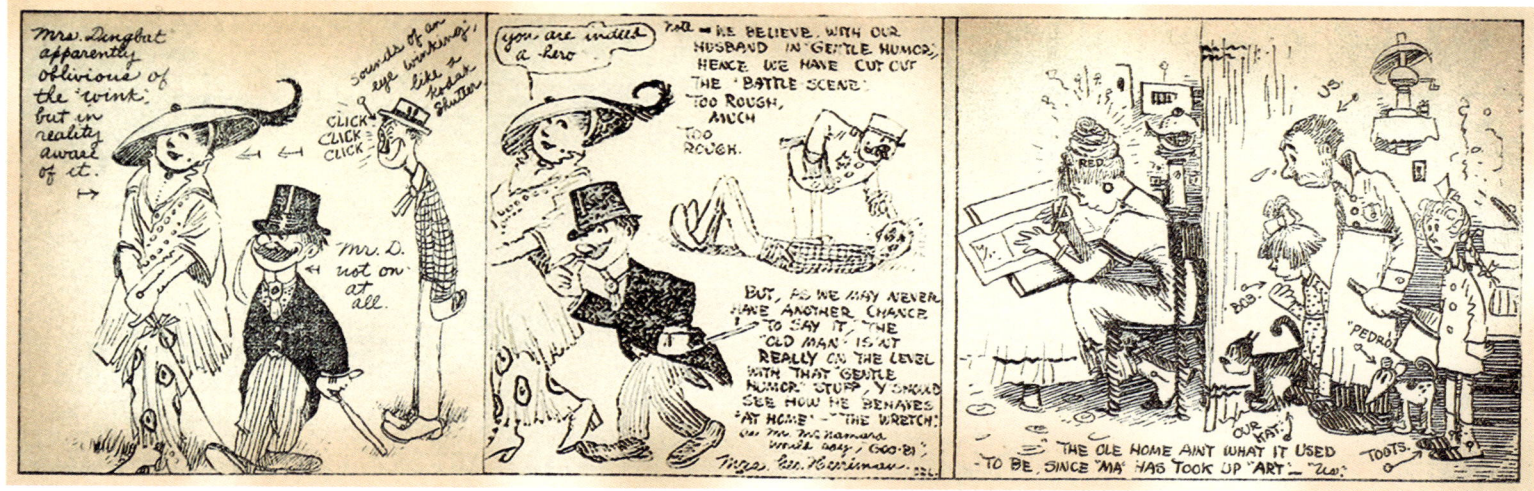

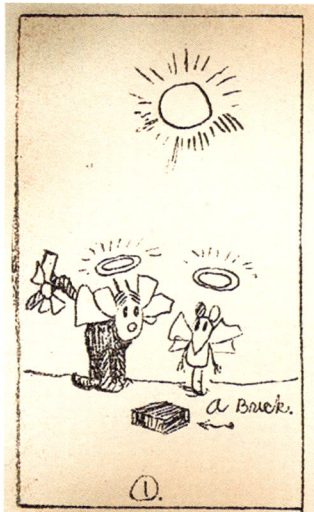

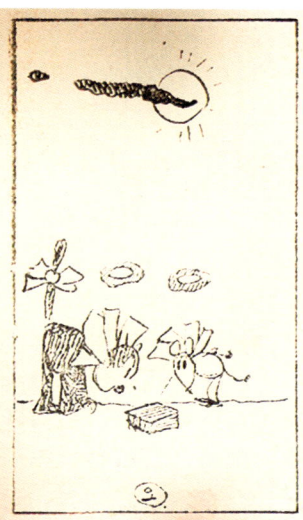

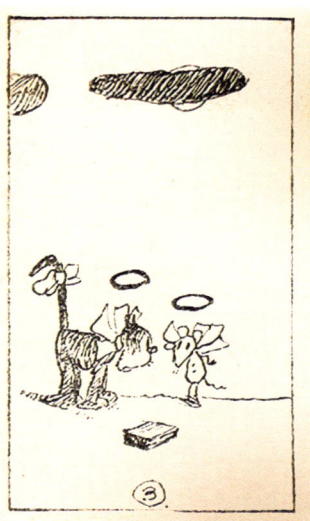

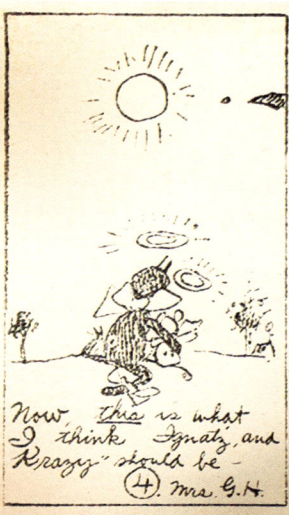

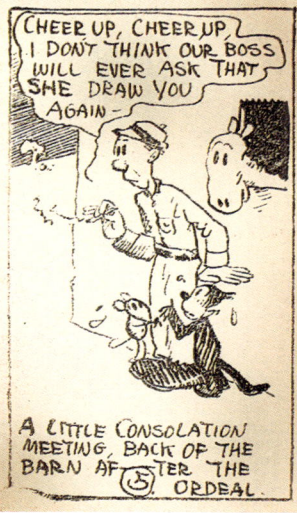

ABOVE On August 16, 1906, the Hearst papers published a stunt in which the cartoonists' wives ostensibly took over their husbands' strips. Participating were Mrs. George McManus, Mrs. Tom McNamara, Mrs. Harry Hershfield, and George Herriman's wife, Mabel. In reality the cartoonists drew the strips. Both Herriman's comics appeared in the papers. In the last panel of *The Dingbat Family,* Herriman drew himself and his clan. In *Krazy Kat,* George drew himself—commenting on the event—with Krazy and Ignatz, fearful of the whole idea, clinging to the cartoonist. This is the artist's only known full-figure appearance in *Krazy Kat* (his hand holding a pen was shown on at least one occasion). These strips have not been seen for over a hundred years.

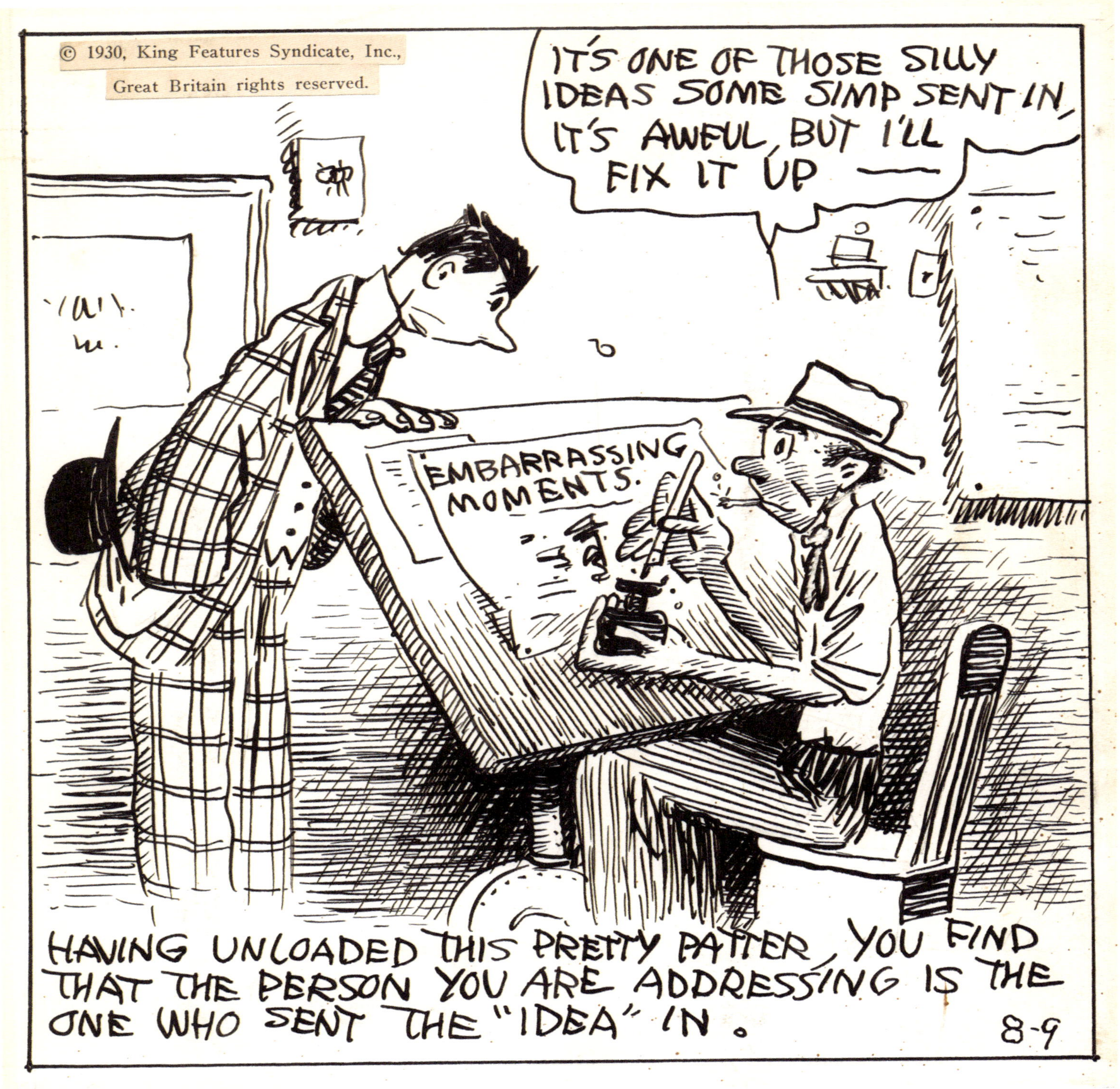
© 1930, King Features Syndicate, Inc.,
Great Britain rights reserved.
IT'S ONE OF THOSE SILLY IDEAS SOME SIMP SENT IN, IT'S AWFUL, BUT I'LL FIX IT UP —
EMBARRASSING MOMENTS.
HAVING UNLOADED THIS PRETTY PATTER, YOU FIND THAT THE PERSON YOU ARE ADDRESSING IS THE ONE WHO SENT THE "IDEA" IN.
8-9

ABOVE George Herriman self-portrait at the drawing board in his *Embarrassing Moments* panel. August 9, 1930.

The Krazy Kat That Walks by Himself
by Gilbert Seldes
This essay first appeared in *The Seven Lively Arts* (Harper & Brothers Publishers, 1924).

Krazy Kat, the daily comic strip of George Herriman is, to me, the most amusing and fantastic and satisfactory work of art produced in America today. With those who hold that a comic strip cannot be a work of art I shall not traffic. The qualities of *Krazy Kat* are irony and fantasy—exactly the same, it would appear, as distinguish *The Revolt of the Angels*; it is wholly beside the point to indicate a preference for the work of Anatole France, which is in the great line, in the major arts. It happens that in America irony and fantasy are practiced in the major arts by only one or two men, producing high-class trash; and Mr. Herriman, working in a despised medium, without an atom of pretentiousness, is day after day producing something essentially fine. It is the result of a naive sensibility rather like that of the *douanier* Rousseau; it does not lack intelligence, because it is a thought-out, constructed piece of work. In the second order of the world's art it is superbly first rate—and a delight! For ten years, daily and frequently on Sunday, Krazy Kat has appeared in America; in that time we have accepted and praised a hundred fakes from Europe and Asia—silly and trashy plays, bad painting, woeful operas, iniquitous religions, everything paste and brummagem, has had its vogue with us; and a genuine, honest native product has gone unnoticed until in the year of grace 1922 a ballet brought it a tardy and grudging acclaim.

Herriman is our great master of the fantastic and his early career throws a faint light on the invincible creation which is his present masterpiece. For all of his other things were comparative failures. He could not find, in the realistic framework he chose, an appropriate medium for his imaginings, or even for the strange draughtsmanship which is his natural mode of expression. *The Family Upstairs* seemed to the realist reader simply incredible; it failed to give him the pleasure of recognizing his neighbors in their more ludicrous moments. *The Dingbats*, hapless wretches, had the same defect. Another strip came nearer to providing the right tone: *Don Koyote and Sancho Pansy*; Herriman's mind has always been preoccupied with the mad knight of La Mancha, who reappears transfigured in *Krazy Kat*. And—although the inspirations are *never* literary—when it isn't Cervantes it is Dickens to whom he has the greatest affinity. The Dickens mode operated in *Baron Bean*—a figure half Micawber, half Charlie Chaplin as man of the world. I have noted, in writing of Chaplin, Mr. Herriman's acute and sympathetic appreciation of the first few moments of *The Kid*. It is only fair to say here that he had himself done the same thing in his medium. Baron Bean was always in rags, penniless, hungry; but he kept his man Grimes, and Grimes did his dirty work. Grimes was the Baron's outlet, and Grimes, faithful retainer, held by bonds of admiration and respect, helped the Baron in his one great love affair. Like all of Herriman's people, they lived on the enchanted mesa (pronounced: macey) by Coconino, near the town of Yorba Linda. The Baron was inventive; lacking the money to finance the purchase of a postage stamp, he entrusted a love letter to a carrier pigeon; and his "Go, my paloma," on that occasion, is immortal.

Some of these characters are reappearing in Herriman's latest work: *Stumble Inn*. Of this I have not seen enough to be sure. It is a mixture of fancy and realism; Mr. Stumble himself is the Dickens character again—the sentimental, endearing innkeeper who would rather lose his only patron than kill a favorite turkey cock for Thanksgiving. I have heard that recently a litter of pups has been found in the cellar of the inn; so I should judge that fantasy has won the day. For it is Herriman's bent to disguise what he has to say in creations of the animal world which are neither human nor animal, but each *sui generis*.

That is how the Kat started. The thought of a friendship between a cat and a mouse amused Herriman and one day he wrote them in as a footnote to *The Family Upstairs*. On their first appearance they played marbles while the family quarreled; and in the last picture the marble dropped through a hole in the bottom line. An office boy named Willie was the first to recognize the strange virtues of *Krazy Kat*. As surely as he was the greatest of office boys, so the greatest of editors, Arthur Brisbane, was the next to praise. He urged Herriman to keep the two characters in action; within a week they began a semi-independent existence in a strip an inch wide under the older strip. Slowly they were detached, were placed at one side, and naturally stepped into the full character of a strip when the *Family* departed. In time the Sundays appeared—three quarters of a page, involving the whole Krazy Kat and Ignatz families[1] and the flourishing town of Coconino—the flora and fauna of that enchanted region which Herriman created out of his memories of the Arizona desert he so dearly loves.

In one of his most metaphysical pictures Herriman presents Krazy as saying to Ignatz: "I ain't a Kat . . . and I ain't Krazy" (I put dots to indicate the lunatic shifting of background which goes on while these remarks are made; although the action is continuous and the characters motionless, it is in keeping with Herriman's method to have the backdrop in a continual state of agitation; you never know when a shrub will become a redwood, or a hut a church) . . . "it's wot's behind me that I am . . . it's the idea behind me, 'Ignatz' and that's wot I am." In an attitude of a contortionist Krazy points to the blank space behind him, and it is there that we must look for the "Idea." It is not far to seek. There is a plot and there is a theme—and considering that since 1913 or so there have been some three thousand strips, one may guess that the variations are infinite. The plot is that Krazy (androgynous, but according to his creator willing to be either) is in love with Ignatz Mouse; Ignatz, who is married, but vagrant, despises the Kat, and his one joy in life is to "Krease that Kat's bean with a brick" from the brickyard of Kolin Kelly. The fatuous Kat (Stark Young has found the perfect word for him: he is crack-brained) takes the brick, by a logic and a cosmic memory presently to be explained, as a symbol of love; he cannot, therefore, appreciate the efforts of Offissa B. Pupp to guard him and to entrammel the activities of Ignatz Mouse (or better, Mice). A deadly war is waged between Ignatz and Offissa Pupp—the latter is himself romantically in love with Krazy; and one often sees pictures in which Krazy and Ignatz conspire together to outwit the officer, both wanting the same thing, but with motives all at cross-purposes. This is the major plot; it is clear that the brick has little to do with the violent endings of other strips, for it is surcharged with emotions. It frequently comes not at the end, but at the beginning of an action; sometimes it does not arrive. It is a symbol.

The theme is greater than the plot. John Alden Carpenter has pointed out in the brilliant little foreword to his ballet, that Krazy Kat is a combination of Parsifal and Don Quixote, the perfect fool and the perfect knight. Ignatz is Sancho Panza and, I should say, Lucifer. He loathes the sentimental excursions, the philosophic ramblings of Krazy; he interrupts with a well-directed brick the romantic excesses of his companion. For example: Krazy blindfolded and with the scales of Justice in his hand declares: "Things is all out of perpotion, 'Ignatz.'" "In what way, fool?" inquires the Mice as the scene shifts to the edge of a pool in the middle of the desert. "In the way of 'ocean' for a instinct." "Well?" asks Ignatz. They are plunging head down into midsea, and only their hind legs, tails, and words are visible: "The ocean is so innikwilly distribitted." They appear, each prone on a mountain peak, above the clouds, and the Kat says casually across the chasm to Ignatz: "Take 'Denva, Kollorado,' and 'Tulsa, Okrahoma' they ain't got no

---

[1] I must hasten to correct an erroneous impression which may have caused pain to many of Krazy's admirers. The three children, Milton, Marshall, and Irving, are of Ignatz, not, as Mr. Stark Young says, of Krazy. Krazy is not an unmarried mother. For the sake of the record I may as well note here the names of the other principals: Offissa Bull Pupp; Mrs Ignatz Mice; Kristofer Kamel; Joe Bark the moon hater; Don Kiyoti, that inconsequential heterodox; Joe Stork, alias Jose Cigueno; Mock Duck; Kolin Kelly the brick merchant; Walter Cephus Austridge; and the Kat Klan: Aunt Tabby, Uncle Tom, Krazy Katbird, Osker Wildcat, Alec Kat, and the Krazy Katfish.

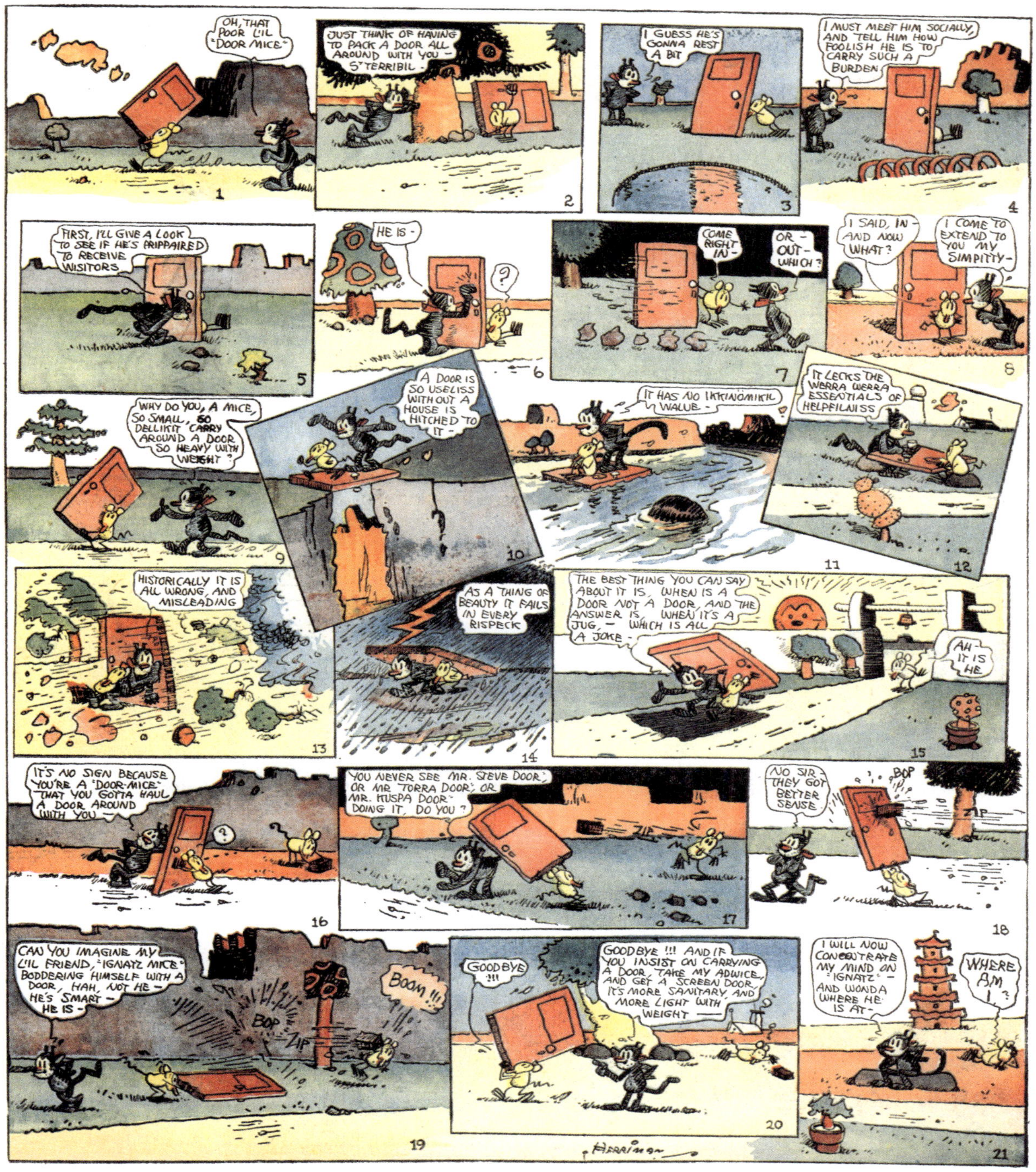
OH, THAT POOR L'IL "DOOR MICE"
JUST THINK OF HAVING TO PACK A DOOR ALL AROUND WITH YOU - S'TERRIBIL -
I GUESS HE'S GONNA REST A BIT
I MUST MEET HIM SOCIALLY, AND TELL HIM HOW FOOLISH HE IS TO CARRY SUCH A BURDEN
FIRST, I'LL GIVE A LOOK TO SEE IF HE'S PRIPPAIRED TO RECEIVE WISITORS
HE IS -
?
COME RIGHT IN -
OR - OUT - WHICH ?
I SAID, IN - AND NOW WHAT ?
I COME TO EXTEND TO YOU MY SIMPITTY -
WHY DO YOU, A MICE, SO SMALL, SO DELLIKIT CARRY AROUND A DOOR SO HEAVY WITH WEIGHT ?
A DOOR IS SO USELISS WITH OUT A HOUSE IS HITCHED TO IT -
IT HAS NO IKKINOMIKIL WALUE -
IT LECKS THE WERRA WERRA ESSENTIALS OF HELPFILNISS
HISTORICALLY IT IS ALL WRONG, AND MISLEADING
AS A THING OF BEAUTY IT FAILS IN EVERY RISPECK
THE BEST THING YOU CAN SAY ABOUT IT IS, WHEN IS A DOOR NOT A DOOR, AND THE ANSWER IS, WHEN IT'S A JUG, - WHICH IS ALL A JOKE -
AH - IT IS HE
IT'S NO SIGN BECAUSE YOU'RE A 'DOOR-MICE' THAT YOU GOTTA HAUL A DOOR AROUND WITH YOU -
?
YOU NEVER SEE MR. STEVE DOOR, OR MR TORRA DOOR, OR MR. HUSPA DOOR DOING IT, DO YOU ?
ZIP
NO SIR - THEY GOT BETTER SENSE
BOP
ZIP
CAN YOU IMAGINE MY L'IL FRIEND, "IGNATZ MICE" BODDERING HIMSELF WITH A DOOR, HAH, NOT HE - HE'S SMART - HE IS -
BOP
ZIP
BOOM !!!
GOODBYE !!!
GOODBYE !!! AND IF YOU INSIST ON CARRYING A DOOR, TAKE MY ADWICE, AND GET A SCREEN DOOR, IT'S MORE SANITARY, AND MORE LIGHT WITH WEIGHT ——
I WILL NOW CONCENTRATE MY MIND ON "IGNATZ" - AND WONDA WHERE HE IS AT -
WHERE AM I ?
HERRIMAN

ocean a tall—" (they are tossed by a vast sea, together in a packing-case) "while Sem Frencisco, Kellafornia, and Bostin, Messachoosit, has got more ocean than they can possibly use"—whereon Ignatz properly distributes a brick evenly on Krazy's noodle. Ignatz "has no time" for foolishness; he is a realist and Sees Things as They ARE. "I don't believe in Santa Claus," says he; "I'm too broad-minded and advanced for such nonsense."

But Mr. Herriman, who is a great ironist, understands pity. It is the destiny of Ignatz never to know what his brick means to Krazy. He does not enter into the racial memories of the Kat which go back to the days of Cleopatra, of the Bubastes, when Kats were held sacred. Then, on a beautiful day, a mouse fell in love with Krazy, the beautiful daughter of Kleopatra Kat; bashful, advised by a soothsayer to write his love, he carved a declaration on a brick and, tossing the "missive," was accepted, although he had nearly killed the Kat. "When the Egyptian day is done it has become the Romeonian custom to crease his lady's bean with a brick laden with tender sentiments . . . through the tide of dusty years" . . . the tradition continues. But only Krazy knows this. So at the end it is the incurable romanticist, the victim of acute Bovaryisme, who triumphs; for Krazy faints daily in full possession of his illusion, and Ignatz, stupidly hurling his brick, thinking to injure, fosters the illusion and keeps Krazy "heppy."

Not always, to be sure. Recently we beheld Krazy smoking an "eligint Hawanna cigar" and sighing for Ignatz [page 56]; the smoke screen he produced hid him from view when Ignatz passed, and before the Mice could turn back, Krazy had handed over the cigar to Offissa Pupp and departed, saying "Looking at 'Offissa Pupp' smoke himself up like a chimly is werra werra intrisking, but it is more wital that I find 'Ignatz'"—wherefore Ignatz, thinking the smoke screen a ruse, hurls his brick, blacks the officer's eye, and is promptly chased by the limb of the law. Up to this point you have the usual technique

ABOVE The January 21, 1922, Sunday that accompanied the original text of Seldes's essay.

of the comic strip, as old as Shakespeare. But note the final picture of Krazy beholding the pursuit, himself disconsolate, unbricked, alone, muttering: "Ah, there him is—playing tag with 'Offissa Pupp'—just like the boom compenions wot they is." It is this touch of irony and pity which transforms all of Herriman's work, which relates it, for all that the material is preposterous, to something profoundly true and moving. It isn't possible to retell these pictures; but that is the only way, until they are collected and published, that I can give the impression of Herriman's gentle irony, of his understanding of tragedy, of the *sancta simplicitas*, the innocent loveliness in the heart of a creature more like Pan than any other creation of our time.

Given the general theme, the variations are innumerable, the ingenuity never flags. I use haphazard examples from 1918 to 1923, for though the Kat has changed somewhat since the days when he was even occasionally feline, the essence is the same. Like Charlot, he was always living in a world of his own, and subjecting the commonplaces of actual life to the test of his higher logic. Does Ignatz say that "the bird is on the wing," Krazy suspects an error and after a careful scrutiny of bird life says that "from rissint obserwation I should say that the wing is on the bird." Or Ignatz observes that Don Kiyote is still running. Wrong, says the magnificent Kat: "he is either still or either running, but not both still and both running." Ignatz passes with a bag containing, he says, bird-seed. "Not that I doubt your word, Ignatz," says Krazy, "but could I give a look?" And he is astonished to find that it is bird-seed, after all, for he had all the time been thinking that birds grew from eggs. It is Ignatz who is impressed by a falling star; for Krazy "them that don't fall" are the miracle. I recommend Krazy to Mr. Chesterton, who, in his best moments, will understand. His mind is occupied with eternal oddities, with simple things to which his nature leaves him unreconciled. See him entering a bank and loftily writing a check for thirty million dollars. "You haven't that much money in

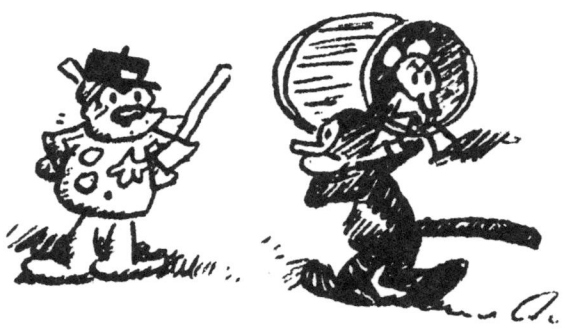

the bank," says the cashier. "I know it," replies Krazy; "have you?" There is a drastic simplicity about Krazy's movements; he is childlike, regarding with grave eyes the efforts of older people to be solemn, to pretend that things are what they seem; and like children he frightens us because none of our pretensions escapes him. A king to him is a "royal cootie." "Golla," says he, "I always had a ida they was grend, and megnifishint, and wondafil, and mejestic . . . but my goodniss! It ain't so." He should be given to the *enfant terrible* of Hans Andersen who knew the truth about kings.

He is, of course, blinded by love. Wandering alone in springtime, he suffers the sight of all things pairing off; the solitude of a lonesome pine worries him and when he finds a second lonesome pine he comes in the dead of night and transplants one to the side of the other, "so that in due course, Nature has her way." But there are moments when the fierce pang of an unrequited passion dies down. "In these blissfil hours my soul will know no strife," he confides to Mr. Bum Bill Bee, who, while the conversation goes on, catches sight of Ignatz with a brick, flies off, stings Ignatz from the field, and returns to hear: "In my Kosmis there will be no feeva of discord . . . all my immotions will function in hominy and kind feelings." Or we see him at peace with Ignatz himself. He has bought a pair of spectacles, and seeing that Ignatz has none, cuts them in two, so that each may have a monocle. He is gentle, and gentlemanly, and dear; and these divagations of his are among his loveliest moments; for when irony plays about him he is as helpless—as we are.

To put such a character into music was a fine thought, but Mr. Carpenter must have known that he was foredoomed to failure. It was a notable effort, for no other of our composers had seen the possibilities; most, I fear, did not care to "lower themselves" by the association. Mr. Carpenter caught much of the fantasy; it was exactly right for him to make the opening a parody—The Afternoon Nap of a Faun. The "Class A Fit," the Katnip Blues were also good. (There exists a Sunday *Krazy* of this very scene—it is 1919, I think, and shows hundreds of Krazy Kats in a wild abandoned revel in the Katnip field—a rout, a bacchanale, a satyr-dance, an erotic festival, with our own Krazy playing the viola in the corner, and Ignatz, who has been drinking, going to sign the pledge.) Mr. Carpenter almost missed one essential thing: the ecstasy of Krazy when the brick arrives at the end; certainly, as Mr. Bolm danced it one felt only the triumph of Ignatz, one did not feel the grand leaping up of Krazy's heart, the fulfillment of desire, as the brick fell upon him. The irony was missing. And it was a mistake for Bolm to try it, since it isn't Russian ballet Krazy requires; it is American dance. One man, one man only can do it right, and I publicly appeal to him to absent him from felicity awhile, and though he do it but once, though but a small number of people may see it, to pay tribute to his one compeer in America, to the one creation equaling his own—I mean, of course, Charlie Chaplin. He has been urged to do many things hostile to his nature; here is one thing he is destined to do. Until then the ballet ought to have Johnny and Ray Dooley for its creators. And I hope that Mr. Carpenter hasn't driven other composers off the subject. There is enough there for Irving Berlin and Deems Taylor to take up. Why don't they? The music it requires is a jazzed tenderness—as Mr. Carpenter knew. In their various ways Berlin and Taylor could accomplish it.

They may not be able to write profoundly in the private idiom of Krazy. I have preserved his spelling and the quotations have given some sense of his style. The accent is partly Dickens and partly Yiddish—and the rest is not to be identified, for it is Krazy. It was odd that in *Vanity Fair*'s notorious "rankings," Krazy tied with Doctor Johnson, to whom he owes much of his vocabulary. There is a real sense of the color of words and a high imagination in such passages as "the echoing cliffs of Kaibito" and "on the north side of 'wild-cat peak' the 'snow squaws' shake their winter blankets and bring forth a chill which rides the wind with goad and spur, hurling with an icy hand rime, and frost upon a dreamy land musing in the lap of Spring"; and there is the rhythm of wonder and excitement in "Ooy, 'Ignatz' it's awfil; he's got his legs cut off above his elbows, and he's wearing shoes, and he's standing on top of the water."

Nor, even with Mr. Herriman's help, will a ballet get quite the sense of his shifting backgrounds. He is alone in his freedom of movement; in his large pictures and small, the scene changes at will—it is actually our one work in the expressionistic mode. While Krazy and Ignatz talk they move from mountain to sea; or a tree stunted and flattened with odd ornaments of spots or design, grows suddenly long and thin; or a house changes into a church. The trees in this enchanted mesa are almost always set in flower pots with Coptic and Egyptian designs in the

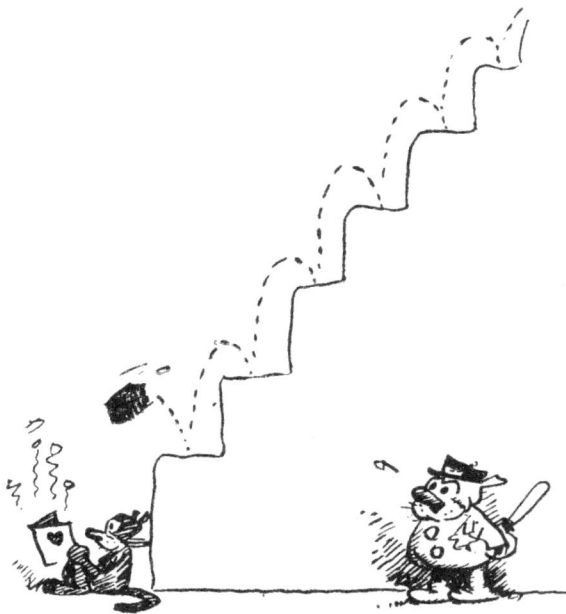

foliage as often as on the pot. There are adobe walls, fantastic cactus plants, strange fungus and growths. And they *compose designs*. For whether he be a primitive or an expressionist, Herriman is an artist; his works are built up; there is a definite relation between his theme and his structure, and between his lines, masses, and his page. His masterpieces in color show a new delight, for he is as naive and as assured with color as with line or black and white. The little figure of Krazy built around the navel, is amazingly adaptable, and Herriman economically makes him express all the emotions with a turn of the hand, a bending of that extraordinary starched bow he wears round the neck, or with a twist of his tail.

And he has had much to express for he has suffered much. I return to the vast enterprises of the Sunday pictures. There is one constructed entirely on the bias. Ignatz orders Krazy to push a huge rock off its base, then to follow it downhill. Down they go, crashing through houses, uprooting trees, tearing tunnels through mountains, the bowlder first, Krazy so intently after that he nearly crashes into it when it stops. He toils painfully back uphill. "Did it gather any moss?" asks Ignatz. "No." "That's what I thought." "L'il fillossiffa," comments Krazy, "always he seeks the truth, and always he finds it." There is the great day in which Krazy hears a lecture on the ectoplasm, how "it soars out into the limitless ether, to roam willy-nilly, unleashed, unfettered, and unbound" which becomes for him: "Just imegine having your 'ectospasm' running around, William and Nilliam, among the unlimitliss etha—golla, it's imbillivibil—" until a toy balloon, which looks like Ignatz, precipitates a heroic gesture and a tragedy. And there is the greatest of all, the epic, the Odyssean wanderings of the door:

Krazy beholds a dormouse, a little mouse with a huge door. It impresses him as being terrible that "a mice so small, so dellikit" should carry around a door so heavy with weight. (At this point their Odyssey begins; they use the door to cross a chasm.) "A door is so useless without a house is hitched to it." (It changes into a raft and they go down stream.) "It has no ikkinomikil value." (They dine off the door.) "It lecks the werra werra essentials of helpfilness." (It shelters them from a hailstorm.) "Historically it is all wrong and misleading." (It fends the lightning.) "As a thing of beauty it fails in every rispeck." (It shelters them from the sun.) And while Krazy goes on to deliver a lecture—"You never see Mr. Steve Door, or Mr. Torra Door, or Mr. Kuspa Door doing it, do you?" and "Can you imagine my li'l friends Ignatz Mice boddering himself with a door?"—his li'l friend Ignatz has appeared with the brick; unseen by Krazy he hurls it; it is intercepted by the door, rebounds, and strikes Ignatz down. Krazy continues his adwice until the dormouse sheers off, and then Krazy sits down to "concentrate his mind on Ignatz and wonda where he is at."

Such is our Krazy. Such is the work which America can pride itself on having produced, and can hastily set about to appreciate. It is rich with something we have too little of—fantasy. It is wise with pitying irony; it has delicacy, sensitiveness, and an unearthly beauty. The strange, unnerving, distorted trees, the language inhuman, un-animal, the events so logical, so wild, are all magic carpets and faery foam—all charged with unreality. Through them wanders Krazy, the most tender and the most foolish of creatures, a gentle monster of our new mythology.

George Herriman was one of the most endearing men I have ever known. Once, while he was living in New York, which was not where he wanted to be, he said he hoped to end his life on the mesa, lying down on a giant cactus leaf until he shriveled up and was blown away by the wind. He almost had his wish. Although he sounded rather sad the last time I talked to him, out West, he was approaching death as sweetly as he had approached life.

A collection of *Krazy Kat* daily and Sunday strips has been published, with an introduction by E. E. Cummings. The book is unfortunately not well-proportioned and the strips have been reduced a little too much, so that it isn't easy to read the text. But anyone who doubts the position I have given to Herriman can get an inkling, at least, from the collection.

Gilbert Seldes (January 3, 1893–September 29, 1970) was a writer and cultural critic. He was an associate editor of Collier's, and managing editor of the literary magazine the Dial.

Original Thoughts Daily

Herriman drew thousands of daily comic strips in his career, sometimes working on more than one title concurrently. The original art for most of these has been lost to the ages, but a number have survived, as printed on the following pages.

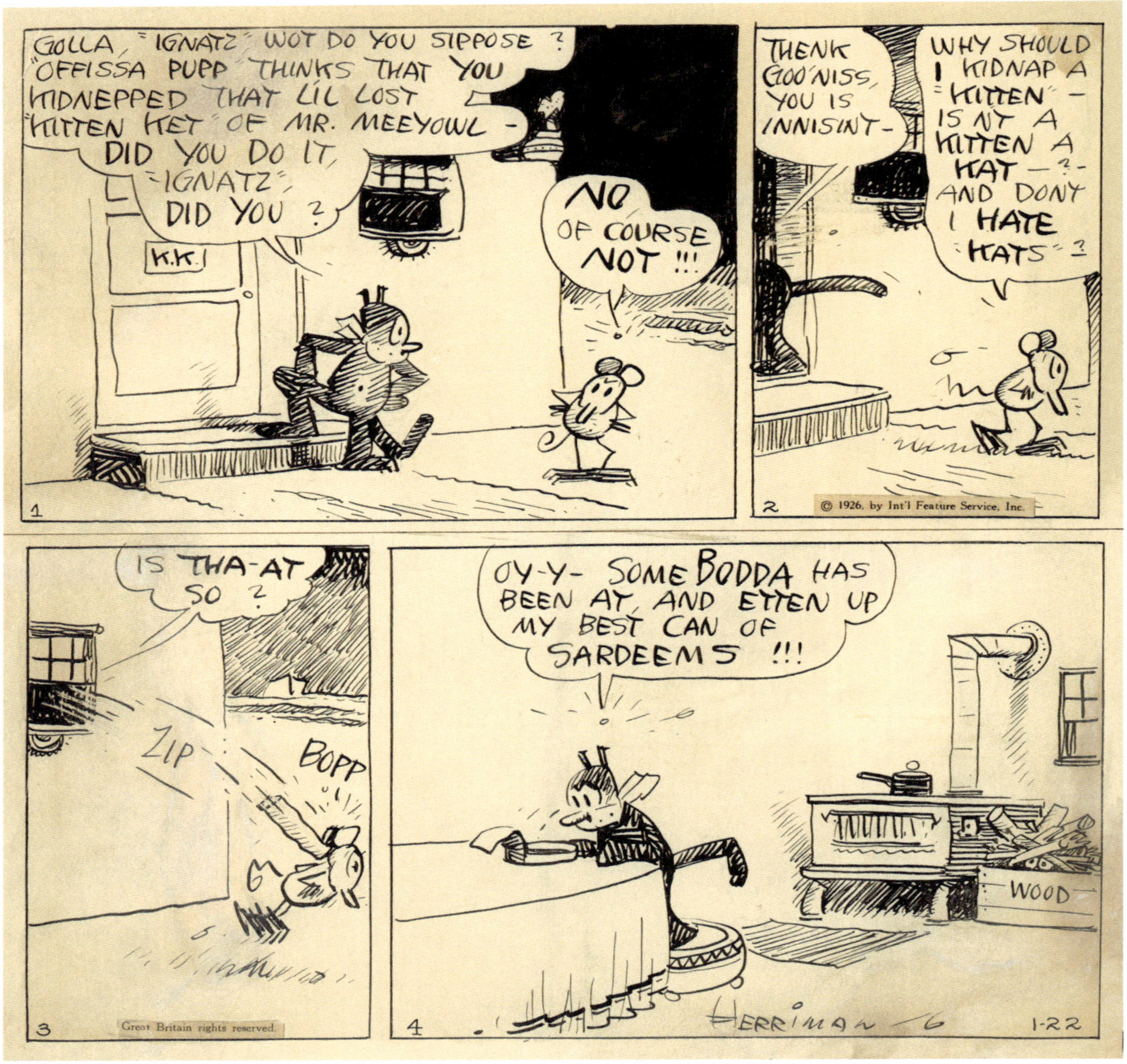
GOLLA, "IGNATZ" WOT DO YOU SIPPOSE ? "OFFISSA PUPP" THINKS THAT YOU KIDNEPPED THAT LIL LOST "KITTEN" KET OF MR. MEEYOWL - DID YOU DO IT, "IGNATZ" DID YOU ?
K.K.
NO OF COURSE NOT !!!
1
THENK GOO'NISS, YOU IS INNISINT -
WHY SHOULD I KIDNAP A "KITTEN" - IS NT A KITTEN A KAT -?- AND DONT I HATE KATS ?
2
© 1926, by Int'l Feature Service, Inc.
IS THA-AT SO ?
ZIP
BOPP
3
Great Britain rights reserved.
OY-Y- SOME BODDA HAS BEEN AT, AND ETTEN UP MY BEST CAN OF SARDEEMS !!!
WOOD
4
HERRIMAN
1-22

ABOVE A daily that has been cut and "stacked" to run in some papers, à la later *Peanuts* strips. January 22, 1926.

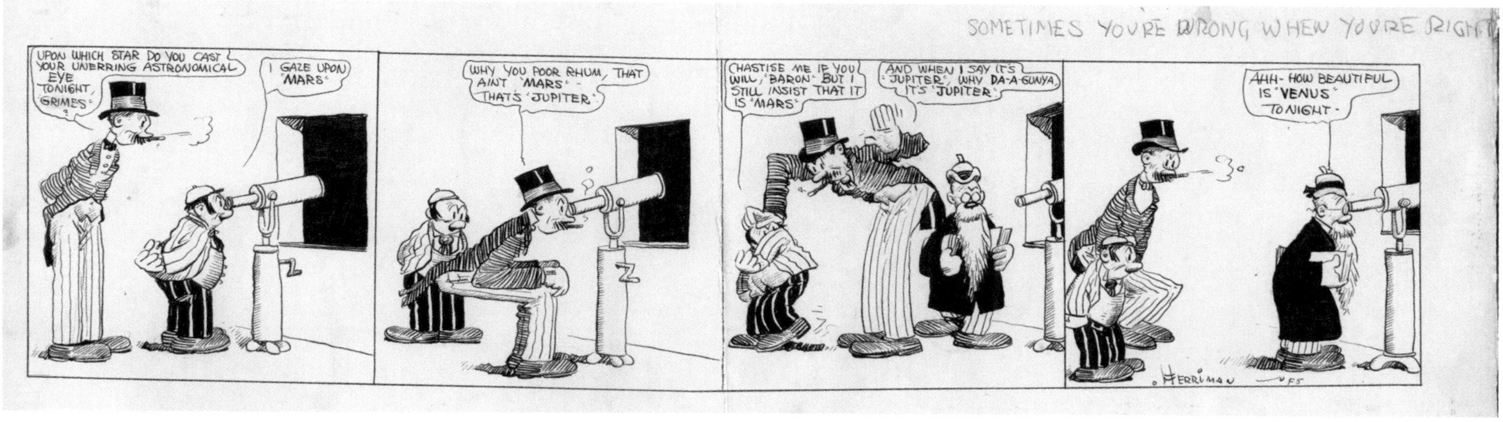
SOMETIMES YOU'RE WRONG WHEN YOU'RE RIGHT
UPON WHICH STAR DO YOU CAST YOUR UNERRING ASTRONOMICAL EYE TONIGHT, "GRIMES"?
I GAZE UPON "MARS"
WHY YOU POOR RHUM, THAT AINT "MARS" - THAT'S "JUPITER"
CHASTISE ME IF YOU WILL, "BARON" BUT I STILL INSIST THAT IT IS "MARS"
AND WHEN I SAY IT'S "JUPITER", WHY DA-A-GUNYA, IT'S "JUPITER"
AHH- HOW BEAUTIFUL IS "VENUS" TONIGHT -
HERRIMAN

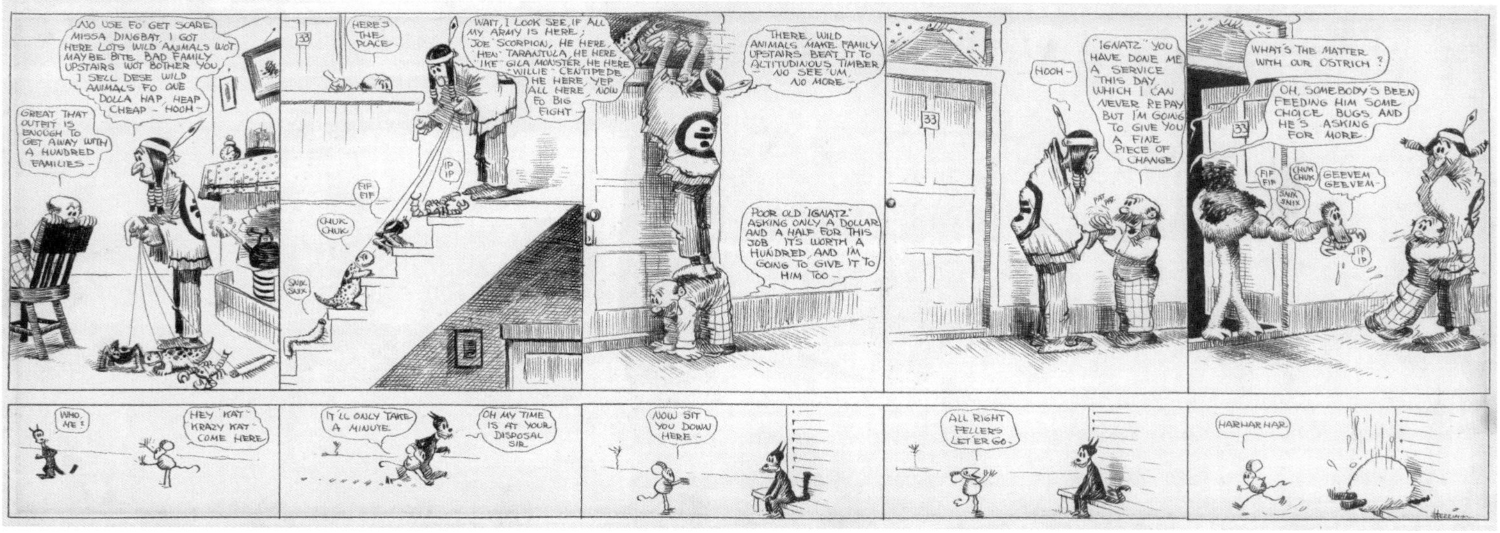
NO USE FO' GET SCARE MISSA DINGBAT, I GOT HERE LOTS WILD ANIMALS WOT MAYBE BITE BAD FAMILY UPSTAIRS WOT BOTHER YOU, I SELL DESE WILD ANIMALS FO ONE DOLLA HAP, HEAP CHEAP - HOOH -
GREAT THAT OUTFIT IS ENOUGH TO GET AWAY WITH A HUNDRED FAMILIES -
HERE'S THE PLACE
WAIT, I LOOK SEE, IF ALL MY ARMY IS HERE; "JOE" SCORPION, HE HERE, "HEN" TARANTULA, HE HERE "IKE" GILA MONSTER, HE HERE "WILLIE" CENTIPEDE HE HERE, YEP ALL HERE, NOW FO BIG FIGHT -
IP IP
FIF FIF
CHUK CHUK
SNIK SNIX
THERE, WILD ANIMALS MAKE FAMILY UPSTAIRS BEAT IT TO ALTITUDINOUS TIMBER NO SEE UM, NO MORE -
POOR OLD "IGNATZ" ASKING ONLY A DOLLAR AND A HALF FOR THIS JOB, IT'S WORTH A HUNDRED, AND I'M GOING TO GIVE IT TO HIM TOO -
HOOH -
"IGNATZ" YOU HAVE DONE ME A SERVICE THIS DAY WHICH I CAN NEVER REPAY BUT I'M GOING TO GIVE YOU A FINE PIECE OF CHANGE
PAT PAT
WHAT'S THE MATTER WITH OUR OSTRICH ?
OH, SOMEBODY'S BEEN FEEDING HIM SOME CHOICE BUGS, AND HE'S ASKING FOR MORE -
FIF FIF
CHUK CHUK
SNIK SNIX
GEEVEM GEEVEM -
IP IP
WHO, ME!
HEY KAT KRAZY KAT COME HERE
IT'LL ONLY TAKE A MINUTE
OH MY TIME IS AT YOUR DISPOSAL SIR
NOW SIT YOU DOWN HERE -
ALL RIGHT FELLERS LET'ER GO -
HARHARHAR

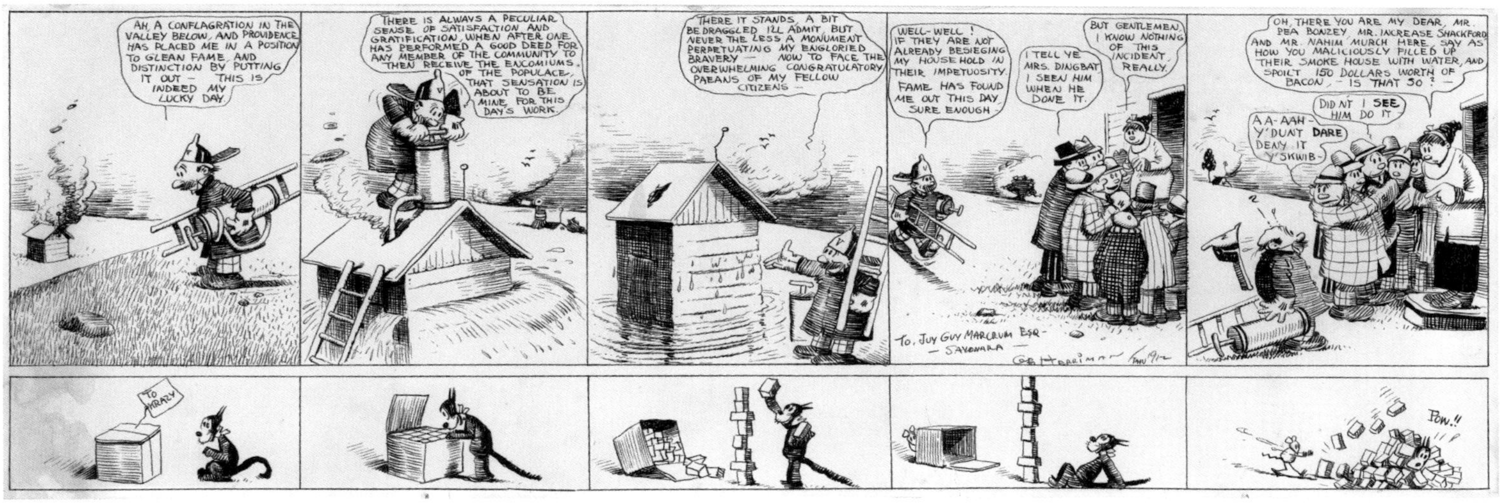
AH, A CONFLAGRATION IN THE VALLEY BELOW, AND PROVIDENCE HAS PLACED ME IN A POSITION TO GLEAN FAME AND DISTINCTION BY PUTTING IT OUT - THIS IS INDEED MY LUCKY DAY.
THERE IS ALWAYS A PECULIAR SENSE OF SATISFACTION AND GRATIFICATION, WHEN AFTER ONE HAS PERFORMED A GOOD DEED FOR ANY MEMBER OF THE COMMUNITY TO THEN RECEIVE THE ENCOMIUMS OF THE POPULACE, THAT SENSATION IS ABOUT TO BE MINE FOR THIS DAY'S WORK.
THERE IT STANDS, A BIT BEDRAGGLED I'LL ADMIT, BUT NEVER THE LESS A MONUMENT PERPETUATING MY ENGLORIED BRAVERY - NOW TO FACE THE OVERWHELMING CONGRATULATORY PAEANS OF MY FELLOW CITIZENS -
WELL- WELL! IF THEY ARE NOT ALREADY BESIEGING MY HOUSE HOLD IN THEIR IMPETUOSITY. FAME HAS FOUND ME OUT THIS DAY SURE ENOUGH -
I TELL YE MRS. DINGBAT I SEEN HIM WHEN HE DONE IT.
BUT GENTLEMEN I KNOW NOTHING OF THIS INCIDENT. REALLY.
TO. JUY GUY MARCREUM ESQR — SAYONARA
OH, THERE YOU ARE MY DEAR, MR. PEA BONZEY, MR. INCREASE SHACKFORD AND MR. NAHIM MURCH HERE, SAY AS HOW YOU MALICIOUSLY FILLED UP THEIR SMOKE HOUSE WITH WATER, AND SPOILT 150 DOLLARS WORTH OF BACON, - IS THAT SO ? -
DID NT I SEE HIM DO IT
A A-AAH - Y'DUNT DARE DENY IT Y'SKWIB -
TO KRAZY
POW!!

TOP A *Baron Bean* daily titled "Sometimes You're Wrong When You're Right." The strip is undated, but Herriman drew this feature between January 15, 1916, and January 22, 1919.

MIDDLE *The Family Upstairs*—titled "Their Ostrich Has a Feast at Dingbat's Expense." The name of the Native American is Ignatz. At the bottom, the early antics of our cat and mouse. Early 1910s.

BOTTOM *The Dingbat Family* strip, inscribed in panel four, "To Juy Guy Marcreum, Esq.—Sayonara—January, 1912."

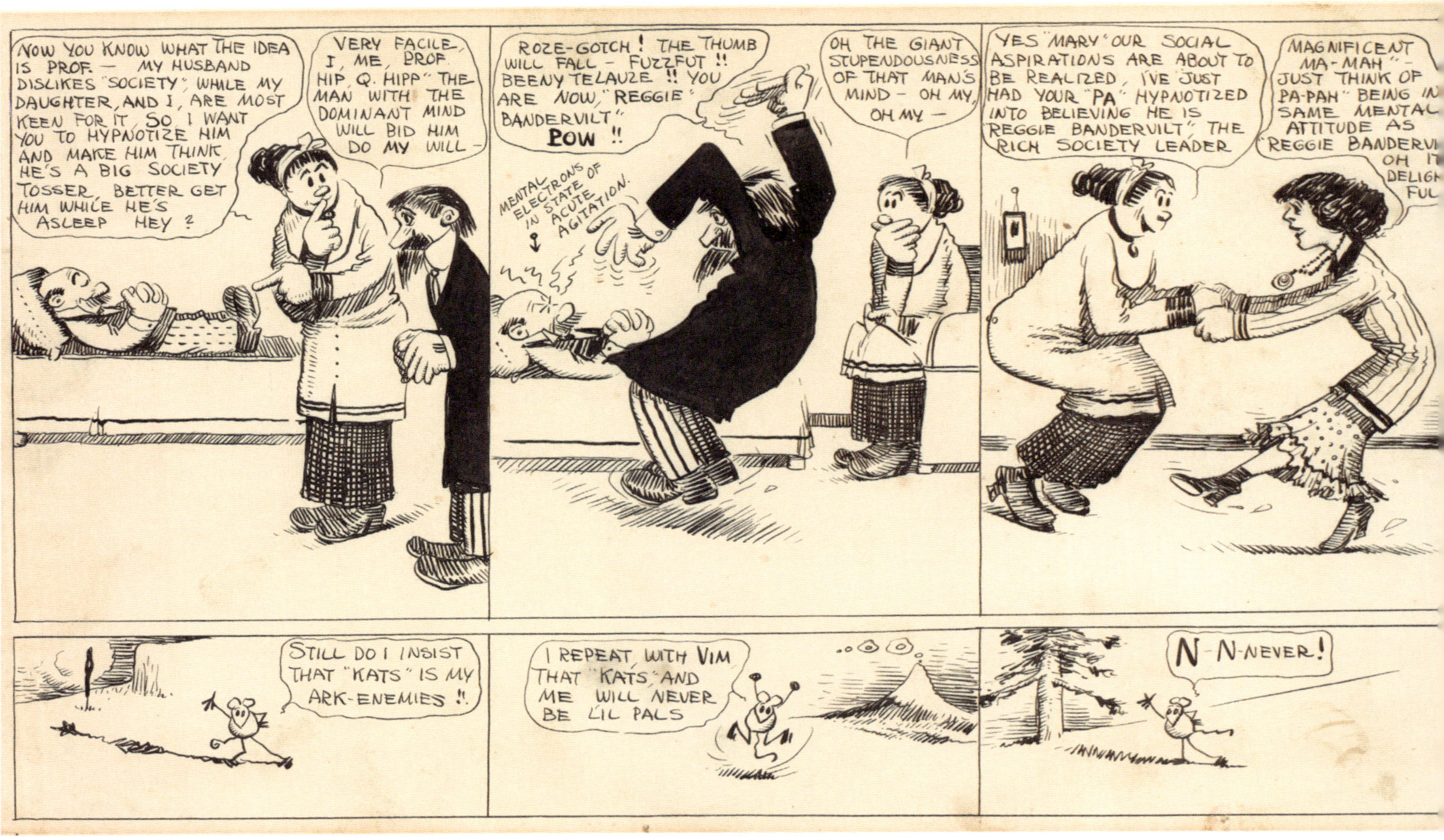
NOW YOU KNOW WHAT THE IDEA IS PROF — MY HUSBAND DISLIKES "SOCIETY", WHILE MY DAUGHTER, AND I, ARE MOST KEEN FOR IT, SO I WANT YOU TO HYPNOTIZE HIM AND MAKE HIM THINK HE'S A BIG SOCIETY TOSSER, BETTER GET HIM WHILE HE'S ASLEEP HEY ?
VERY FACILE, I, ME, PROF. HIP. Q. HIPP" THE MAN WITH THE DOMINANT MIND WILL BID HIM DO MY WILL —
ROZE-GOTCH! THE THUMB WILL FALL - FUZZFUT!! BEENY TELAUZE!! YOU ARE NOW, "REGGIE BANDERVILT" POW!!
MENTAL ELECTRONS IN STATE OF ACUTE AGITATION.
OH THE GIANT STUPENDOUSNESS OF THAT MAN'S MIND - OH MY, OH MY —
YES "MARY" OUR SOCIAL ASPIRATIONS ARE ABOUT TO BE REALIZED, I'VE JUST HAD YOUR "PA" HYPNOTIZED INTO BELIEVING HE IS "REGGIE BANDERVILT", THE RICH SOCIETY LEADER
MAGNIFICENT MA-MAH" - JUST THINK OF "PA-PAH" BEING IN SAME MENTAL ATTITUDE AS "REGGIE BANDERV OH IT DELIGH FUL
STILL DO I INSIST THAT "KATS" IS MY ARK-ENEMIES !!.
I REPEAT WITH VIM THAT "KATS" AND ME WILL NEVER BE LIL PALS
N-N-NEVER!

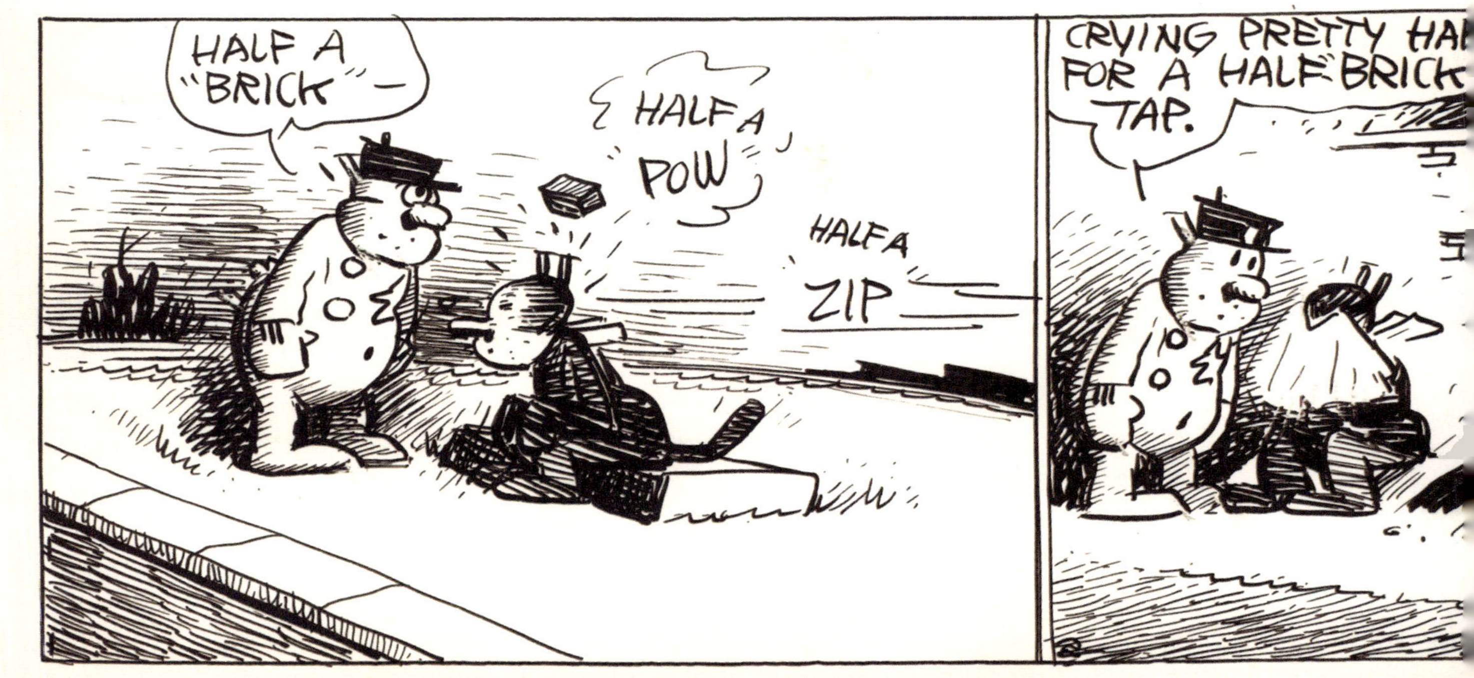
HALF A "BRICK" —
HALF A POW
HALF A ZIP
CRYING PRETTY HA FOR A HALF BRICK TAP.

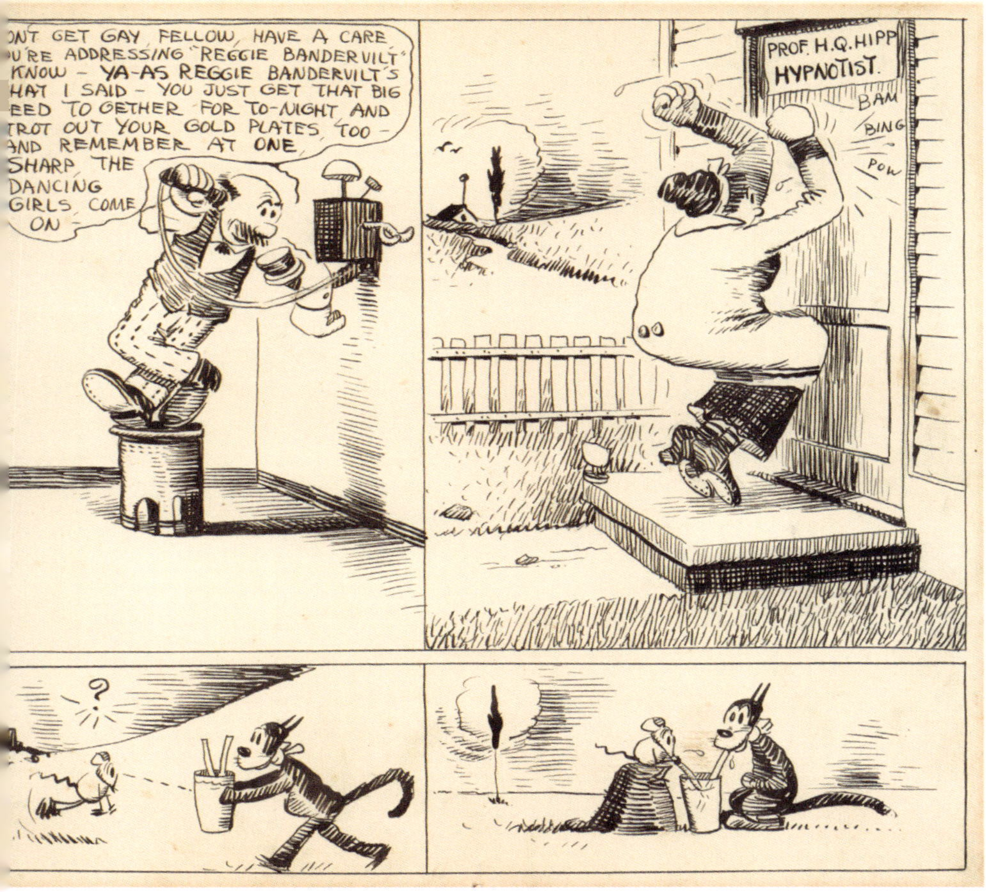
ONT GET GAY, FELLOW, HAVE A CARE
OU'RE ADDRESSING "REGGIE BANDERVILT"
KNOW - YA-AS REGGIE BANDERVILT'S
HAT I SAID - YOU JUST GET THAT BIG
EED TO GETHER FOR TO-NIGHT AND
TROT OUT YOUR GOLD PLATES, TOO
AND REMEMBER AT ONE
SHARP THE
DANCING
GIRLS COME
ON
PROF. H.Q. HIPP
HYPNOTIST.
BAM
BING
POW
?

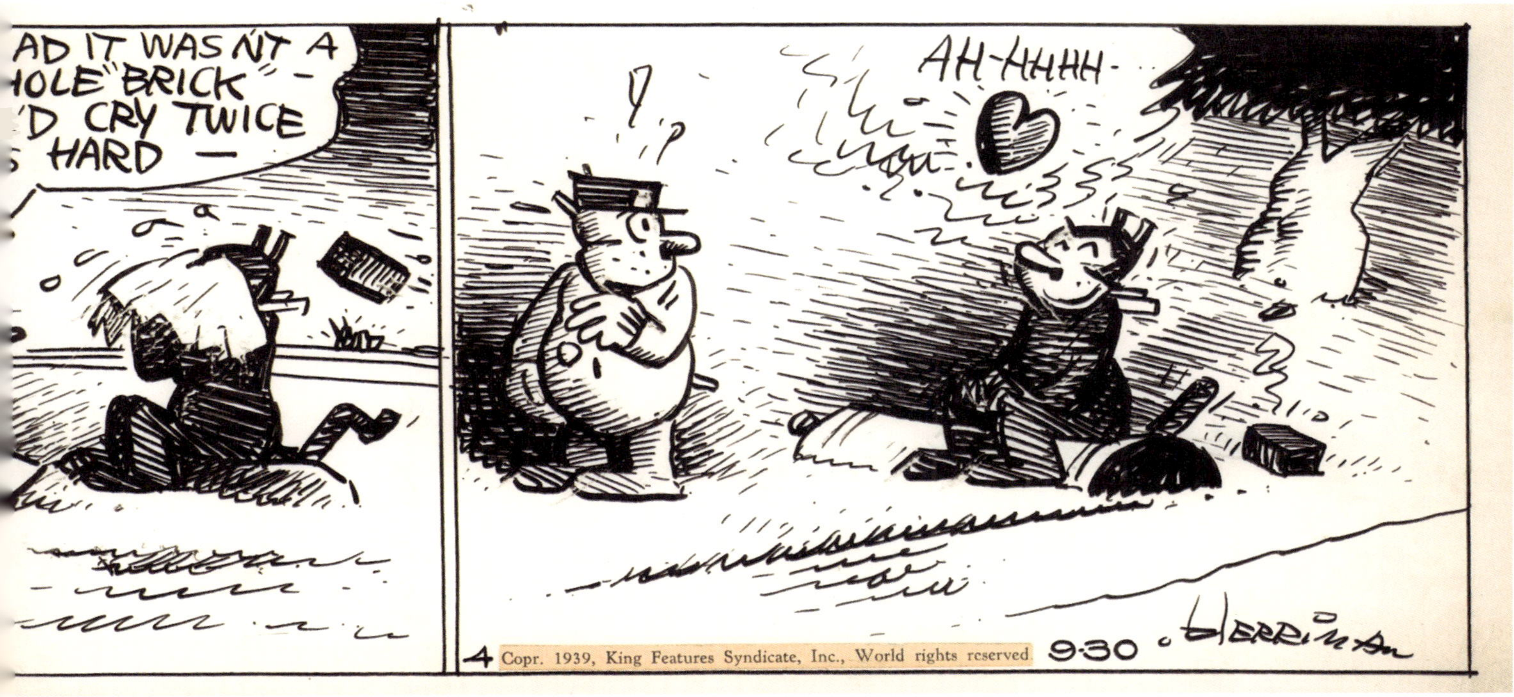
AD IT WAS N'T A
HOLE BRICK -
'D CRY TWICE
S HARD —
AH-HHHH-
4 Copr. 1939, King Features Syndicate, Inc., World rights reserved
9-30
HERRIMAN

TOP *The Dingbat Family,* undated.

BOTTOM A *Krazy Kat* daily. September 30, 1939.

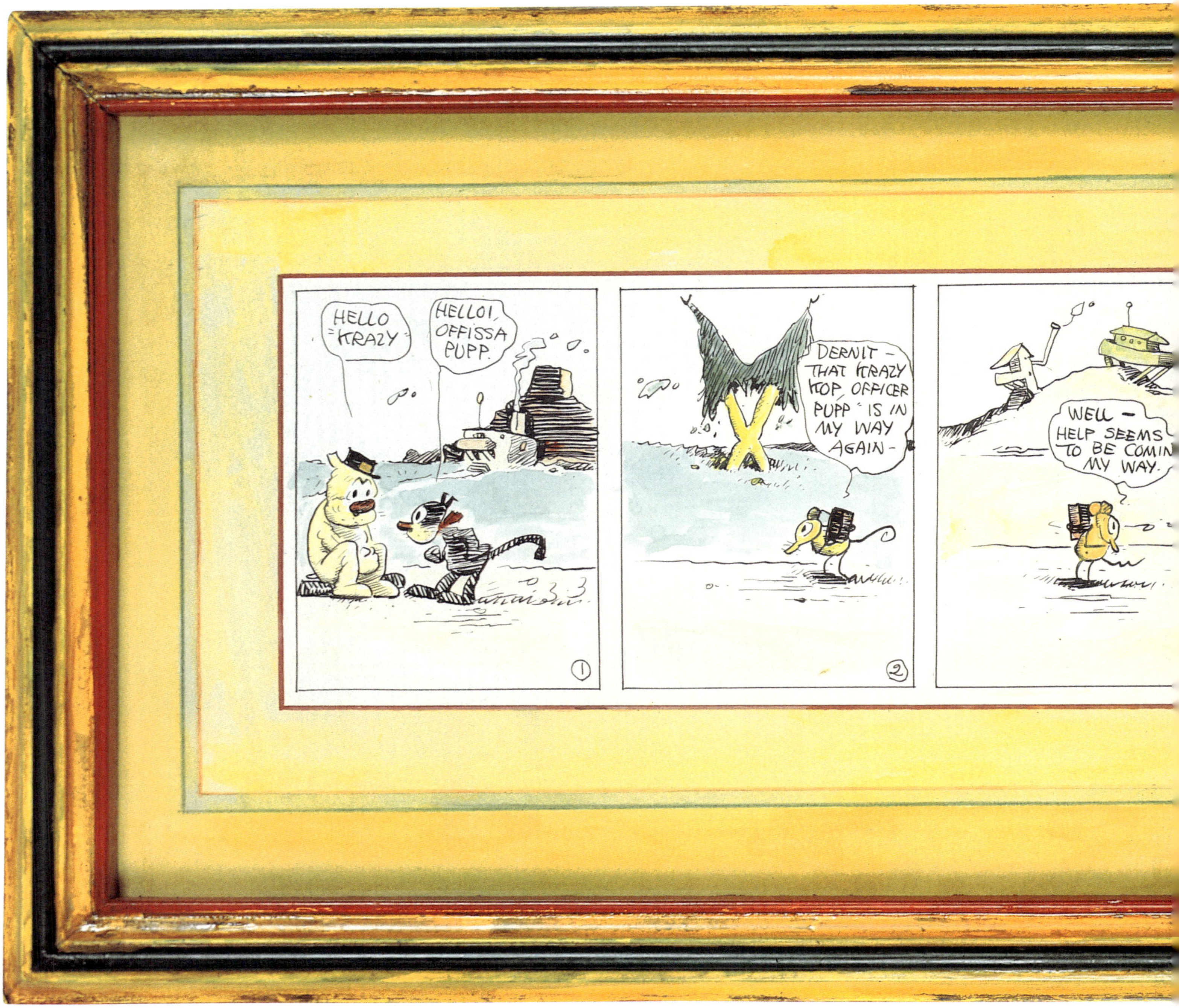
HELLO KRAZY
HELLO!, OFFISSA PUPP.
DERNIT - THAT KRAZY KOP, OFFICER PUPP IS IN MY WAY AGAIN -
WELL - HELP SEEMS TO BE COMIN MY WAY.

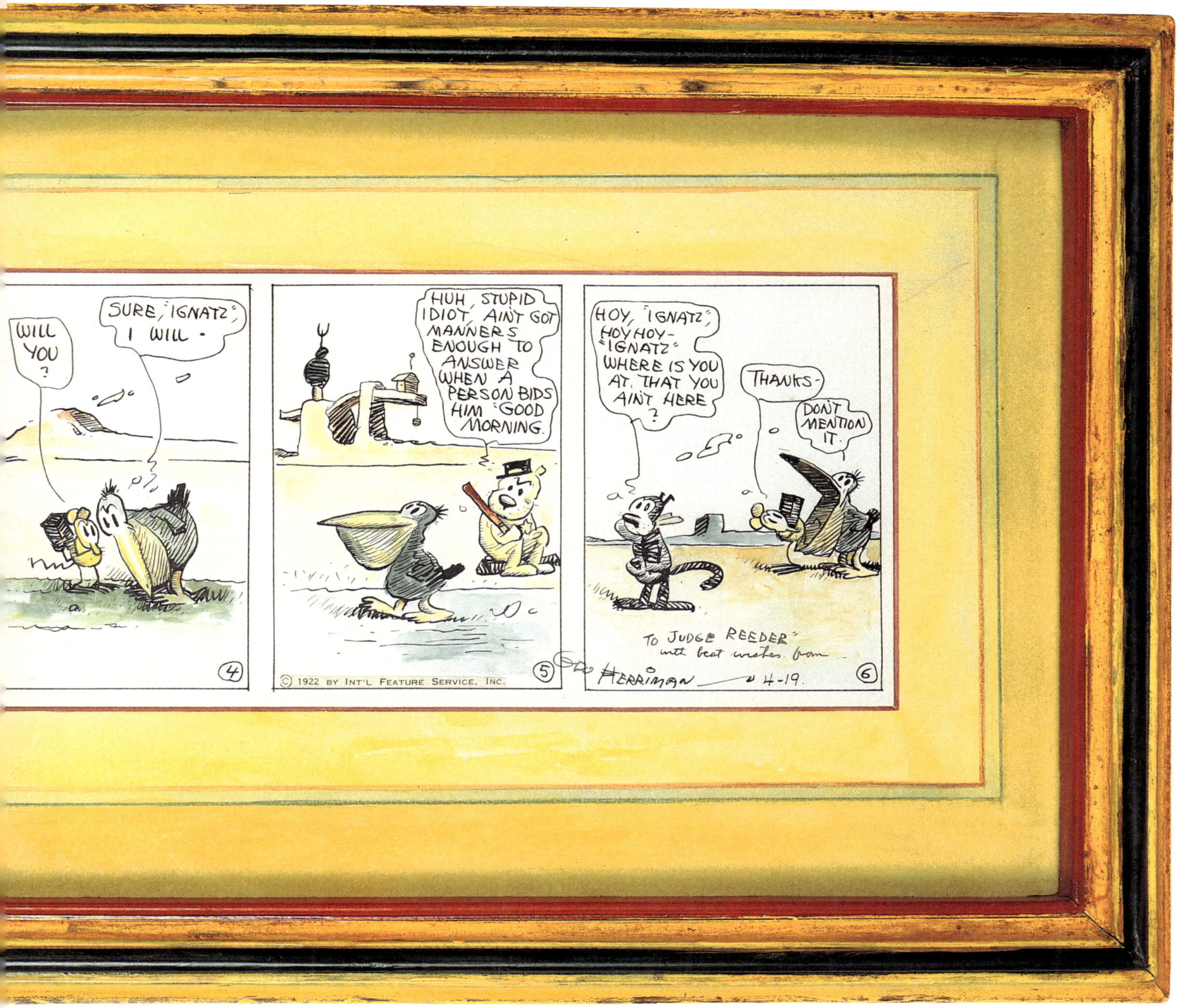
WILL YOU ?
SURE, IGNATZ, I WILL -
4
HUH, STUPID IDIOT, AIN'T GOT MANNERS ENOUGH TO ANSWER WHEN A PERSON BIDS HIM "GOOD MORNING."
© 1922 BY INT'L FEATURE SERVICE, INC.
5
HOY, IGNATZ, HOY HOY - "IGNATZ" WHERE IS YOU AT, THAT YOU AIN'T HERE ?
THANKS -
DON'T MENTION IT.
To JUDGE REEDER with best wishes from
Geo HERRIMAN 4-19.
6

ABOVE A hand-colored daily from April 19, 1922, inscribed, "To Judge Reeder with best wishes." It is said this original was framed by Herriman himself. Previously unpublished in this hand-colored version.

NOW, I'LL SCRUB MY WALK — AN' THEN ALL MY SCRUBBING WILL BE DONE.
© 1932, King Features Syndicate, Inc., Great Britain rights reserv
R

HERE IT IS "JENUERY" AGAIN —
YES —
AND IT IS ALSO 1918.
YES —
IT'S A NEW YEAR AINT IT ?
YES —
THEN WHY DUNT WE HAVE A NEW MONTH INSTEAD OF THE SAME OLD JENUERY EVERY YEAR.
POW
ZIP
HERRIMAN

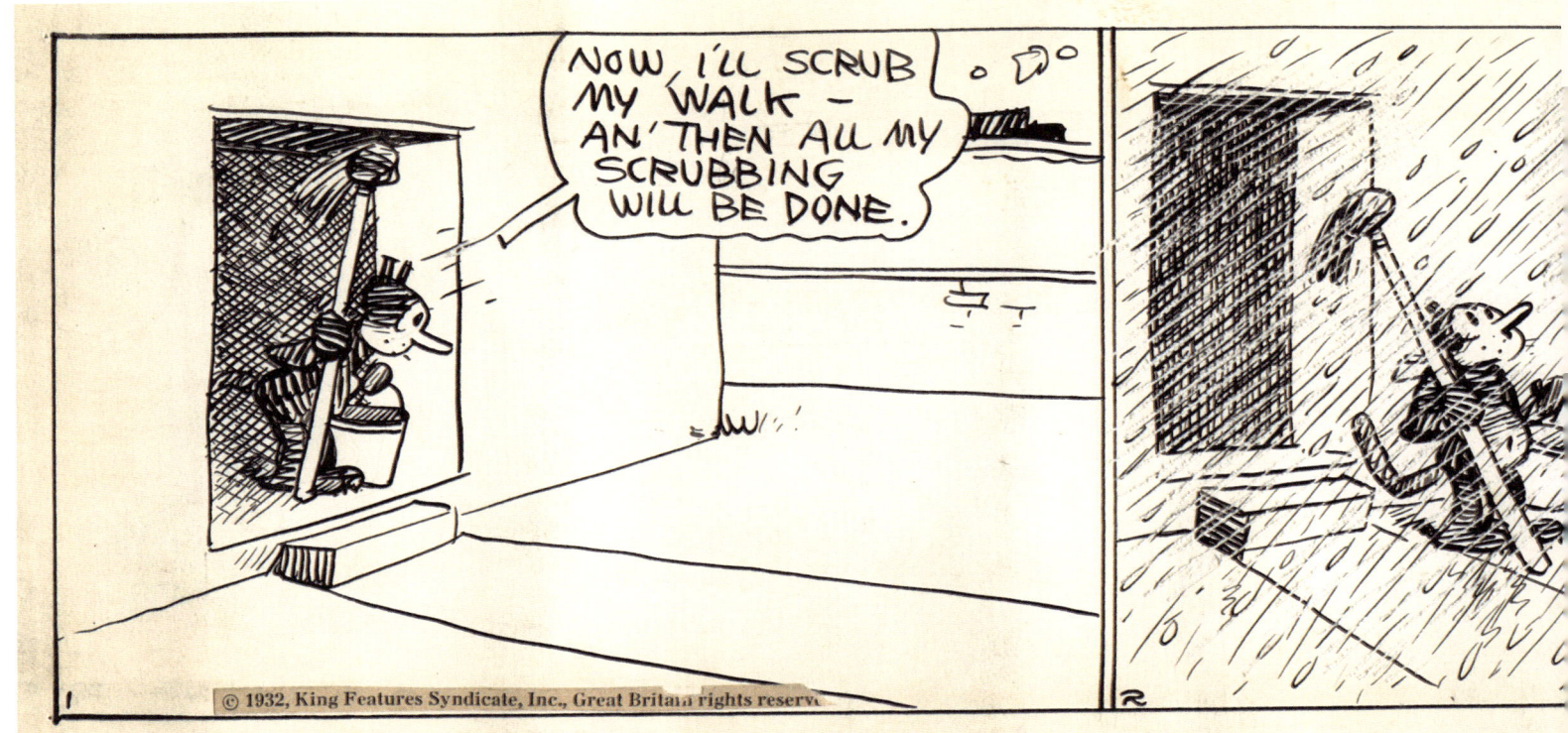

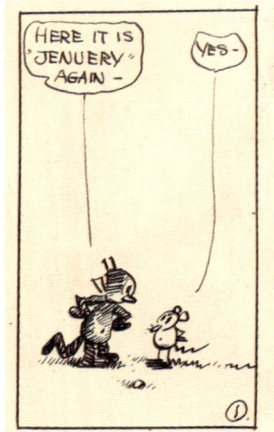

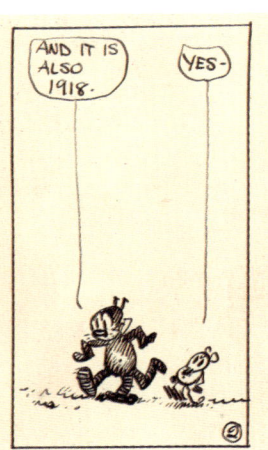

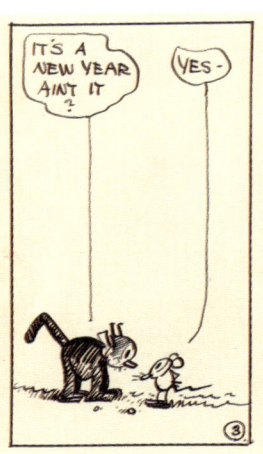

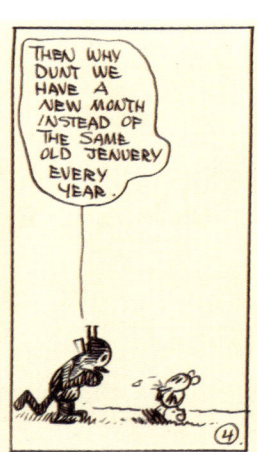

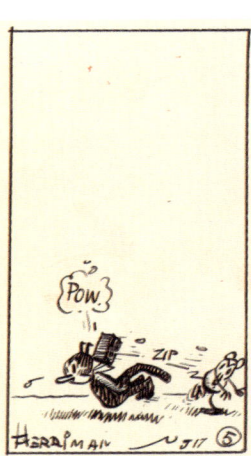

TOP A *Krazy Kat* daily from June 18, 1932. Herriman often used a razor blade to scratch the India-inked paper for a textural effect. Here the technique is gloriously used to delineate the rain.

BOTTOM An early *Krazy Kat* daily from January 17, 1918.

OPPOSITE A stacked daily from July 6, 1936. This is from the famed *Tiger Tea* sequence, Herriman's only extended "adventure narrative."

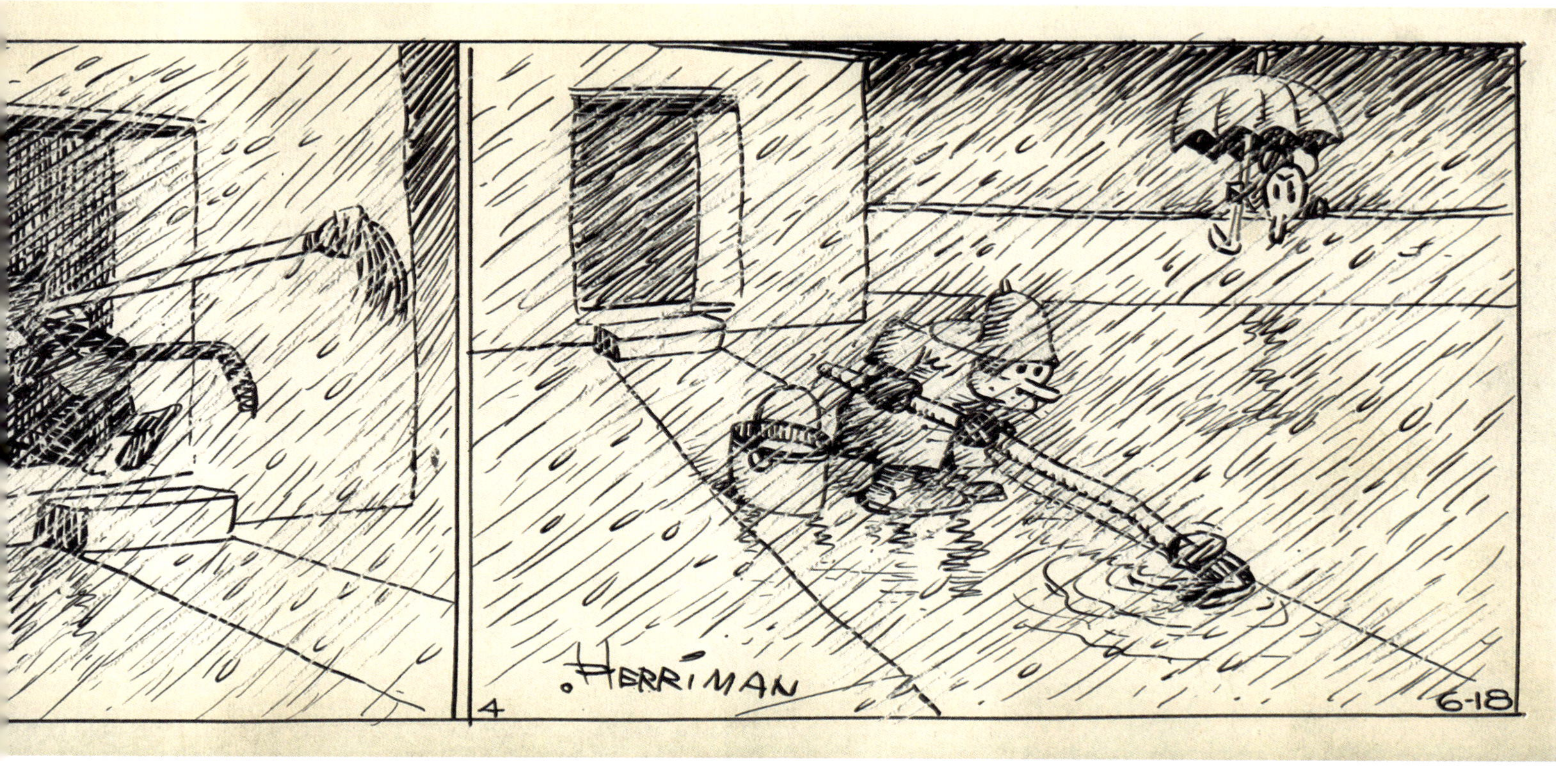
4
HERRIMAN
6-18

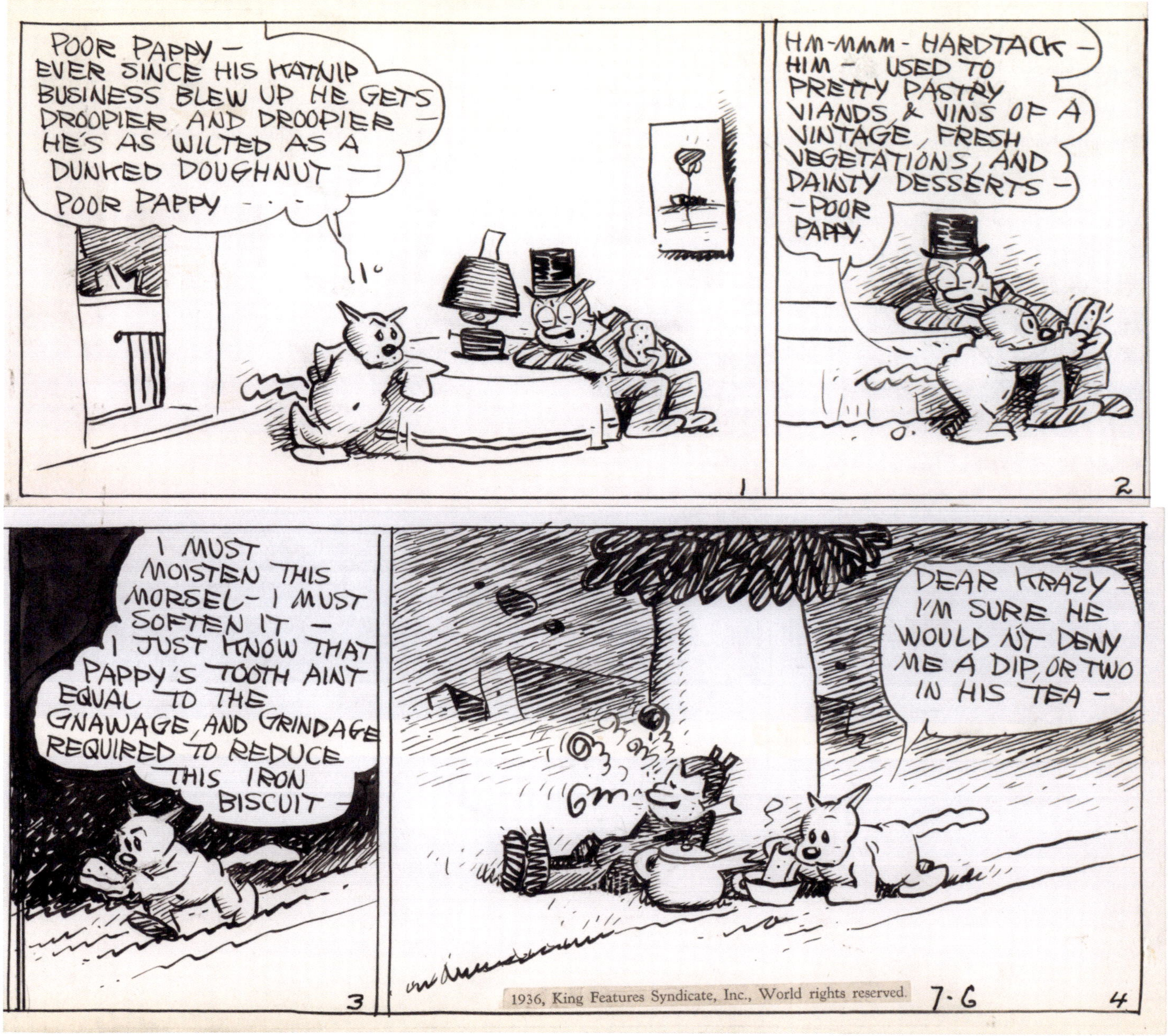
POOR PAPPY — EVER SINCE HIS KATNIP BUSINESS BLEW UP HE GETS DROOPIER AND DROOPIER HE'S AS WILTED AS A DUNKED DOUGHNUT — POOR PAPPY - - -
1
HM-MMM- HARDTACK — HIM — USED TO PRETTY PASTRY VIANDS & VINS OF A VINTAGE, FRESH VEGETATIONS, AND DAINTY DESSERTS — —POOR PAPPY
2
I MUST MOISTEN THIS MORSEL — I MUST SOFTEN IT — I JUST KNOW THAT PAPPY'S TOOTH AINT EQUAL TO THE GNAWAGE, AND GRINDAGE REQUIRED TO REDUCE THIS IRON BISCUIT —
3
DEAR KRAZY — I'M SURE HE WOULD N'T DENY ME A DIP, OR TWO IN HIS TEA —
7-6
4

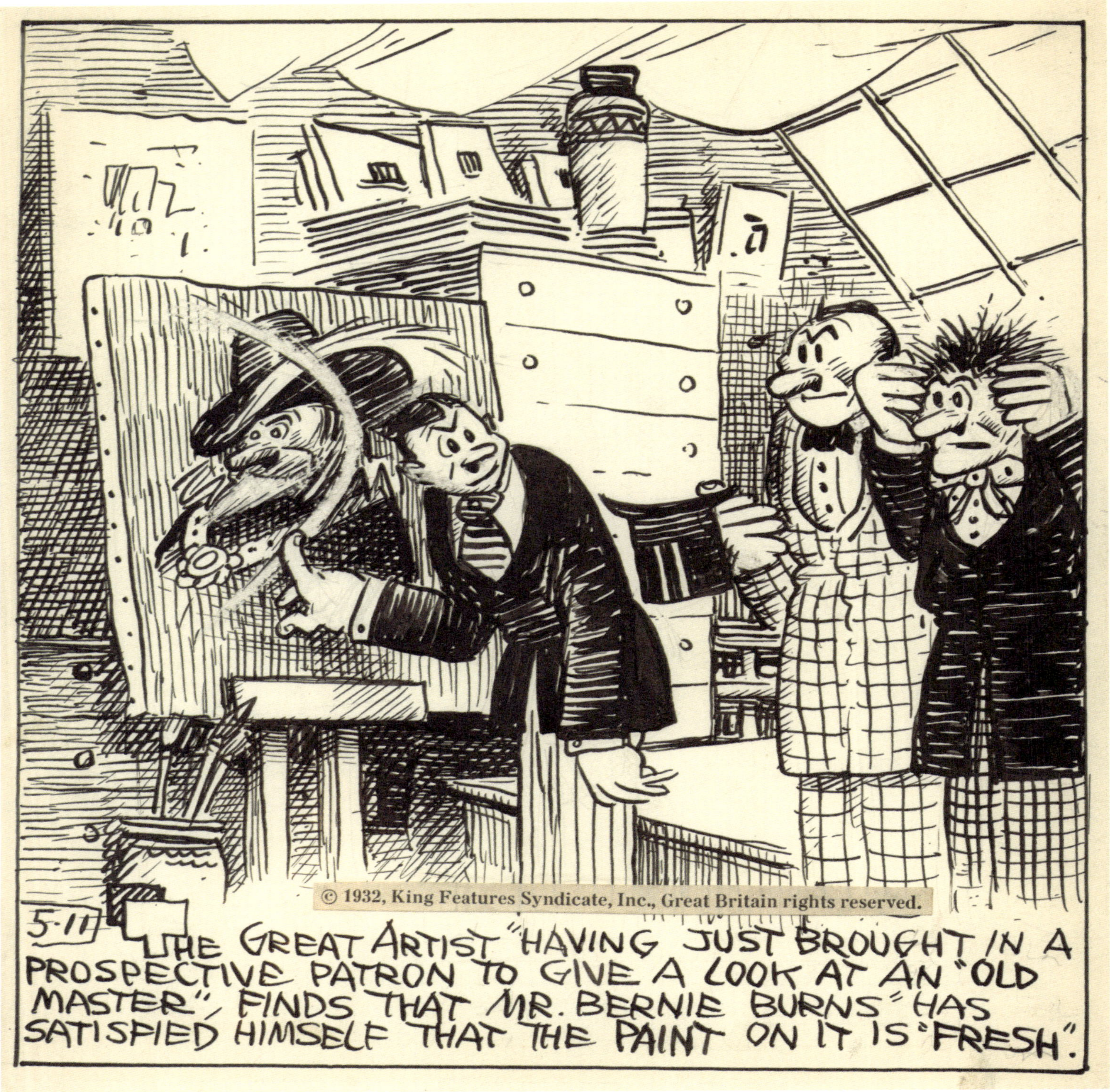

© 1932, King Features Syndicate, Inc., Great Britain rights reserved.
5-11
THE GREAT ARTIST "HAVING JUST BROUGHT IN A PROSPECTIVE PATRON TO GIVE A LOOK AT AN "OLD MASTER", FINDS THAT MR. BERNIE BURNS HAS SATISFIED HIMSELF THAT THE PAINT ON IT IS "FRESH".

ABOVE An artsy daily *Bernie Burns* panel, formerly *Embarrassing Moments*. May 11, 1932.

Krazy Kat

by E. E. Cummings

This essay was initially written as the introduction to *Krazy Kat*, the first collection of the strip in book form (Henry Holt, 1946), published two years after George Herriman's passing.

Twenty years ago, a celebration happened—the celebration of Krazy Kat by Gilbert Seldes. It happened in a book called *The Seven Lively Arts*, and it happened so wisely, so lovingly, so joyously, that recelebrating Krazy would be like teaching penguins to fly. Penguins (as a lot of people don't realize) do fly—not through the sea of the sky but through the sky of the sea—and my present ambition is merely, with our celebrated friend's assistance, to show how their flying affects every nonpenguin.

What concerns me fundamentally is a meteoric burlesk melodrama, born of the immemorial adage *love will find a way*. This frank frenzy (encouraged by a strictly irrational landscape in perpetual metamorphosis) generates three protagonists and a plot. Two of the protagonists are easily recognized as a cynical brick-throwing mouse and a sentimental policeman-dog. The third protagonist—whose ambiguous gender doesn't disguise the good news that here comes our heroine—may be described as a humbly poetic, gently clownlike, supremely innocent, and illimitably affectionate creature (slightly resembling a child's drawing of a cat, but gifted with the secret grace and obvious clumsiness of a penguin on terra firma) who is never so happy as when egoist-mouse, thwarting altruist-dog, hits her in the head with a brick. Dog hates mouse and worships "cat," mouse despises "cat" and hates dog, "cat" hates no one and loves mouse.

Ignatz Mouse and Offissa Pupp are opposite sides of the same coin. Is Offissa Pupp kind? Only in so far as Ignatz Mouse is cruel. If you're a twofisted, spineless progressive (a mighty fashionable stance nowadays) Offissa Pupp, who forcefully asserts the will of socalled society, becomes a cosmic angel; while Ignatz Mouse, who forcefully defies society's socalled will by asserting his authentic own, becomes a demon of anarchy and a fiend of chaos. But if—whisper it—you're a 100% hidebound reactionary, the foot's in the other shoe. Ignatz Mouse then stands forth as a hero, pluckily struggling to keep the flag of free-will flying; while Offissa Pupp assumes the monstrous mien of a Goliath, satanically bullying a tiny but indomitable David. Well, let's flip the coin—so: and lo! Offissa Pupp comes up. That makes Ignatz Mouse "tails." Now we have a hero whose heart has gone to his head and a villain whose head has gone to his heart.

This hero and this villain no more understand Krazy Kat than the mythical denizens of a twodimensional realm understand some threedimensional intruder. The world of Offissa Pupp and Ignatz Mouse is a knowledgeable power-world, in terms of which our unknowledgeable heroine is powerlessness personified. The sensical law of this world is *might makes right*, the nonsensical law of our heroine is *love con-*

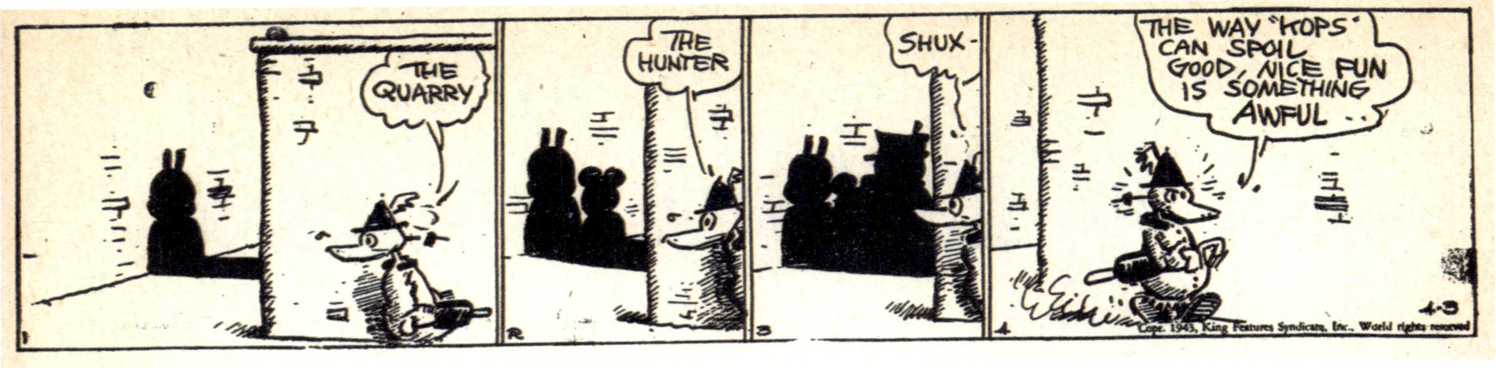
THE QUARRY
THE HUNTER
SHUX-
THE WAY "KOPS" CAN SPOIL GOOD, NICE FUN IS SOMETHING AWFUL..
4-3
Copr. 1943, King Features Syndicate, Inc., World rights reserved

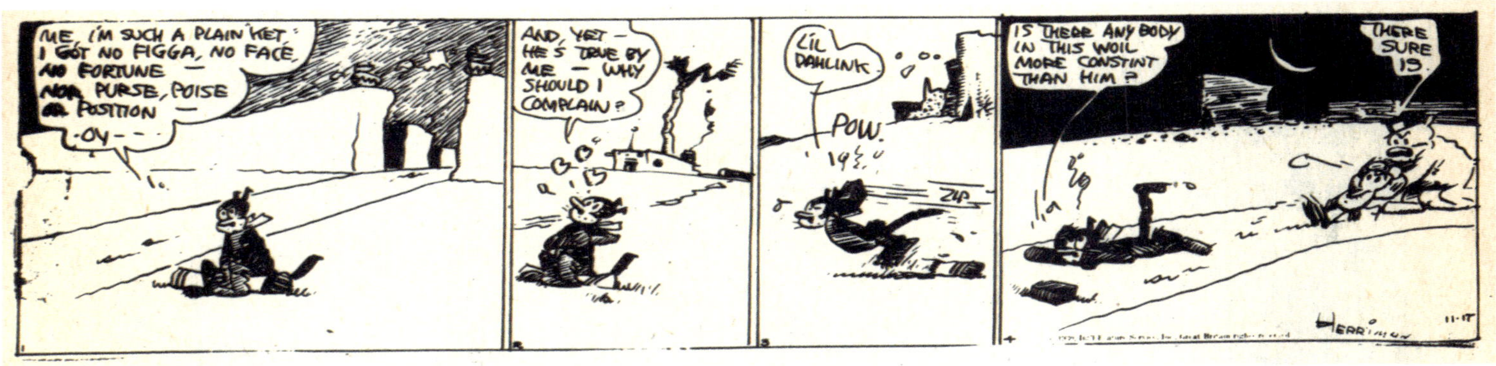
ME, I'M SUCH A PLAIN KET. I GOT NO FIGGA, NO FACE, NO FORTUNE — NOR PURSE, POISE OR POSITION —
-OY- - -
AND, YET — HE'S TRUE BY ME — WHY SHOULD I COMPLAIN?
LIL DAHLINK
POW.
ZIP
IS THERE ANY BODY IN THIS WOIL MORE CONSTINT THAN HIM?
THERE SURE IS.
HERRIMAN
11-17

quers all. To put the oak in the acorn: Ignatz Mouse and Offissa Pupp (each completely convinced that his own particular brand of might makes right) are simpleminded—Krazy isn't—therefore, to Offissa Pupp and Ignatz Mouse, Krazy is. But if both our hero and our villain don't and can't understand our heroine, each of them can and each of them does misunderstand her differently. To our softheaded altruist, she is the adorably helpless incarnation of saintliness. To our hardhearted egoist, she is the puzzlingly indestructible embodiment of idiocy. The benevolent overdog sees her as an inspired weakling. The malevolent undermouse views her as a born target. Meanwhile Krazy Kat, through this double misunderstanding, fulfills her joyous destiny.

Let's make no mistake about Krazy. A lot of people "love" because, and a lot of people "love" although, and a few individuals love. Love is something illimitable; and a lot of people spend their limited lives trying to prevent anything illimitable from happening to them. Krazy, however, is not a lot of people. Krazy is herself. Krazy is illimitable—she loves. She loves in the only way anyone can love: illimitably. She isn't morbid and she isn't longsuffering; she doesn't "love" someone because he hurts her and she doesn't "love" someone although he hurts her. She doesn't, moreover, "love" someone who hurts her. Quite the contrary: she loves someone who gives her unmitigated joy. How? By always trying his limited worst to make her unlove him, and always failing—not that our heroine is insensitive (for a more sensitive heroine never existed), but that our villain's every effort to limit her love with his unlove ends by a transforming of his limitations into her illimitability. If you're going to pity anyone, the last anyone to pity is our loving heroine, Krazy Kat. You might better pity that doggedly idolatrous imbecile, our hero; who policemanfully strives to protect his idol from catastrophic desecration at the paws of our iconoclastic villain—never suspecting that this very desecration becomes, through our transcending heroine, a consecration; and that this consecration reveals the ultimate meaning of existence. But the person to really pity (if really pity you must) is Ignatz. Poor villain! All his malevolence turns to beneficence at contact with Krazy's head. By profaning the temple of altruism, alias law and order, he worships (entirely against his will) at the shrine of love.

I repeat: let's make no mistake about Krazy. Her helplessness, as we have just seen, is merely sensical—nonsensically she's a triumphant, not to say invincible, phenomenon. As for this invincible phenomenon's supposed idiocy, it doesn't even begin to fool nonsensical you and me. Life, to a lot of people, means either the triumph of mind over matter or the triumph of matter over mind; but you and I aren't a lot of people. We understand that, just as there is something—love—infinitely more significant than brute force, there is something—wisdom—infinitely more significant than mental prowess. A remarkably developed intelligence impresses us about as much as sixteen-inch biceps. If we know anything, we know that a lot of people can learn knowledge (which is the same thing as unlearning ignorance) but that no one can learn wisdom. Wisdom, like love, is a spiritual gift. And Krazy happens to be extraordinarily gifted. She has not only the gift of love, but the gift of wisdom as well.

ABOVE AND OPPOSITE Dailies from April 3, 1943, November 17, 1939, and November 6, 1930, that accompanied the first publication of Cummings's essay.

Her unknowledgeable wisdom blossoms in almost every episode of our meteoric burlesk melodrama; the supreme blossom, perhaps, being a tribute to Offissa Pupp and Ignatz Mouse—who (as she observes) are playing a little game together. Right! The game they're playing, willy nilly, is the exciting democratic game of *cat loves mouse,* the game which a lot of highly moral people all over the socalled world consider uncivilized. I refer (of course) to those red-brown-and-black-shirted Puritans who want us all to scrap democracy and adopt their modernized version of *follow the leader*—a strictly ultraprogressive and superbenevolent affair which begins with the liquidation of Ignatz Mouse by Offissa Pupp. But (objects Krazy, in her innocent democratic way) Ignatz Mouse and Offissa Pupp are having fun. Right again! And—from the Puritan point of view—nothing could be worse. Fun, to Puritans, is something wicked: an invention of The Devil Himself. That's why all these superbenevolent collectivists are so hyperspinelessly keen on having us play their ultraprogressive game. The first superbenevolent rule of their ultraprogressive game is *thou shalt not play.*

If only the devilish game of democracy were exclusively concerned with such mindful matters as ignorance and knowledge, crime and punishment, cruelty and kindness, collectivists would really have something on the ball. But it so happens that democracy involves the spiritual values of wisdom, love, and joy. Democracy isn't democracy because or although Ignatz Mouse and Offissa Pupp are fighting a peaceful war. Democracy is democracy in so far as our villain and our hero—by having their fun, by playing their brutal little game—happen (despite their worst and best efforts) to be fulfilling our heroine's immeasurable destiny. Joy is her destiny: and joy comes through Ignatz—via Offissa Pupp; since it's our villain's loathing for law which gives him the strength of ten when he hurls his blissyielding brick. Let's not forget that. And let's be perfectly sure about something else. Even if Offissa Pupp should go crazy and start chasing Krazy, and even if Krazy should go crazy and start chasing Ignatz, and even if crazy Krazy should swallow crazy Ignatz and crazy Offissa Pupp should swallow crazy Krazy and it was the millennium—there'd still be the brick. And (having nothing else to swallow) Offissa Pupp would then swallow the brick. Whereupon, as the brick hit Krazy, Krazy would be happy.

Alas for sensical reformers! Never can they realize that penguins do fly; that Krazy's idiocy and helplessness in terms of a world—any world—are as nothing to the *n*th power, by comparison with a world's—any world's—helplessness and idiocy in terms of Krazy. Yet the truth of truth lies here and nowhere else. Always (no matter what's real) Krazy is no mere reality. She is a living ideal. She is a spiritual force, inhabiting a merely real world—and the realer a merely real world happens to be, the more this living ideal becomes herself. Hence—needless to add—the brick. Only if, and whenever, that kind of reality (cruelly wielded by our heroic villain, Ignatz Mouse, in despite of our villainous hero, Offissa Pupp) smites Krazy—fairly and squarely—does the joyous symbol of Love Fulfilled appear above our triumphantly unknowledgeable heroine. And now do we understand the meaning of democracy? If we don't, a poet-painter called George Herriman most certainly cannot be blamed. Democracy, he tells us again and again and again, isn't some ultraprogressive myth of a superbenevolent World As Should Be. The meteoric burlesk melodrama of democracy is a struggle between society (Offissa Pupp) and the individual (Ignatz Mouse) over an ideal (our heroine)—a struggle from which, again and again and again, emerges one stupendous fact: namely, that the ideal of democracy fulfills herself only if, and whenever, society fails to suppress the individual.

Could anything possibly be clearer?

Nothing—unless it's the kindred fact that our illimitably affectionate Krazy has no connection with the oldfashioned heroine of common or garden melodrama. The prosaically "virtuous" puppet couldn't bat a decorously "innocent" eyelash without immediately provoking some utterly estimable Mr. Righto to liquidate some perfectly wicked Mr. Wrongo. In her hyperspineless puritanical simplicity, she desires nothing quite so much as an ultraprogressive and superbenevolent substitute for human nature. Democracy's merciful leading lady, on the other hand, is a fundamentally complex being who demands the whole mystery of life. Krazy Kat—who, with every mangled word and murdered gesture, translates a mangling and murdering world into Peace And Goodwill—is the only original and authentic revolutionary protagonist. All blood-and-thunder Worlds As Should Be cannot comprise this immeasurably generous heroine of the strictly unmitigated future.

She has no fear—even of a mouse.

E. E. Cummings (October 14, 1894–September 3, 1962) was a preeminent poet of the twentieth century. He drew and painted in addition to composing nearly three thousand poems, two autobiographical books, and essays like this one on Krazy Kat.

IT'S NO USE — NOT EVEN IN THE STILL WATCHES OF THE NIGHT —
JAIL

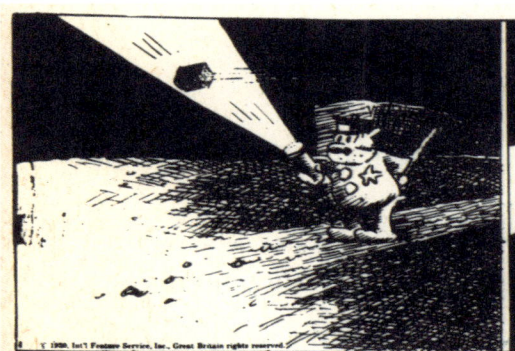

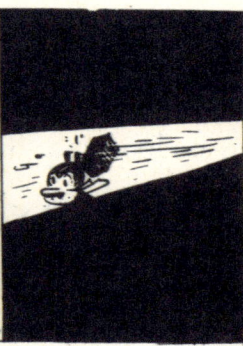

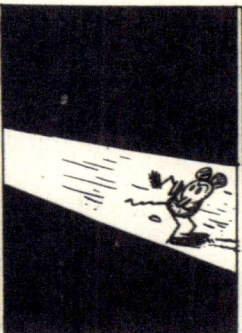

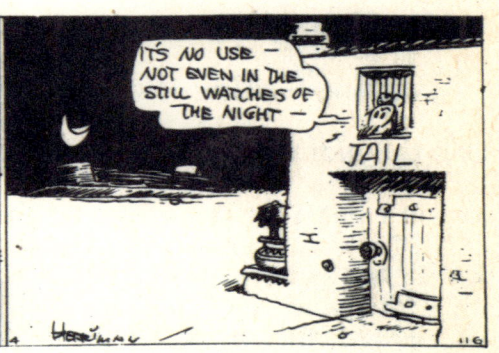

A Month of Sundays. Years, Even!

When the Sunday comics pages were as big as king-size sheets and every cartoonist had his own full page, Herriman found his most spectacular showcase. To see the original art from which the newspapers were printed heightens the experience even more. A number of the surviving original Sundays were subsequently hand-colored, and sometimes framed and matted, by the artist as gifts for friends and admirers. Most of the artwork presented here has never been published in this form before.

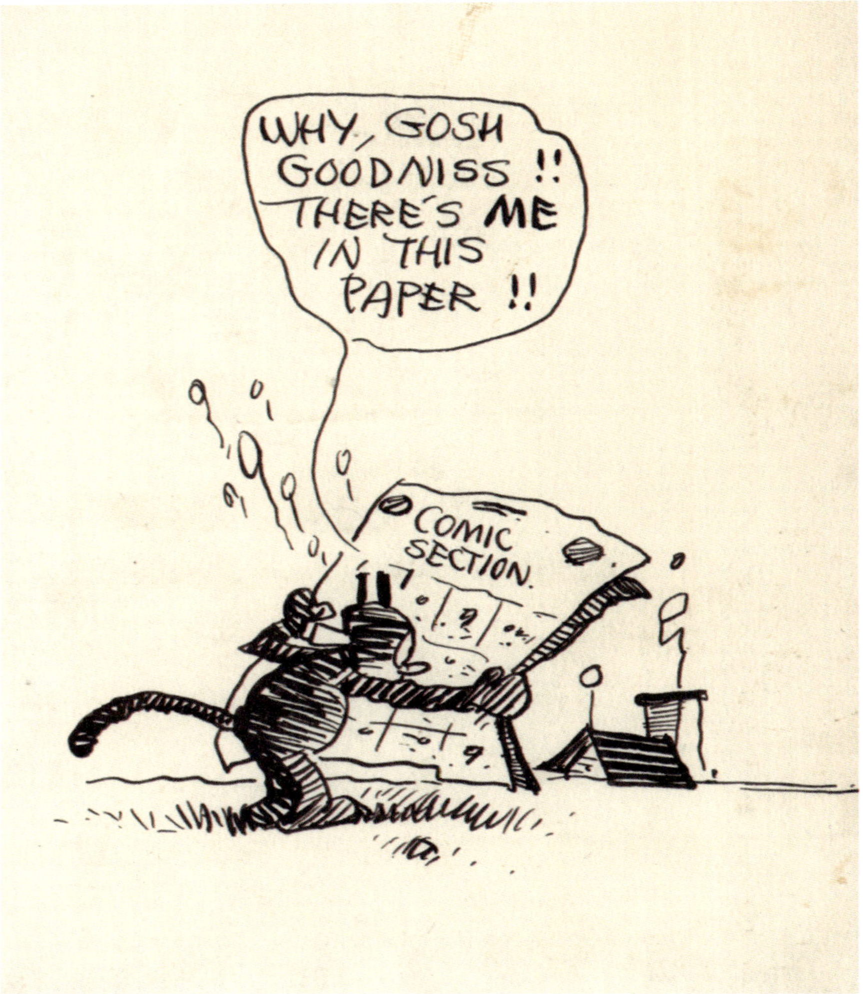
WHY, GOSH GOODNISS !! THERE'S ME IN THIS PAPER !!
COMIC SECTION

ABOVE Detail (panel four) from one of Herriman's most famous and surreal strips, in which Krazy Kat reads about himself in the Sunday paper. The full strip is reproduced on page 68. April 16, 1922.

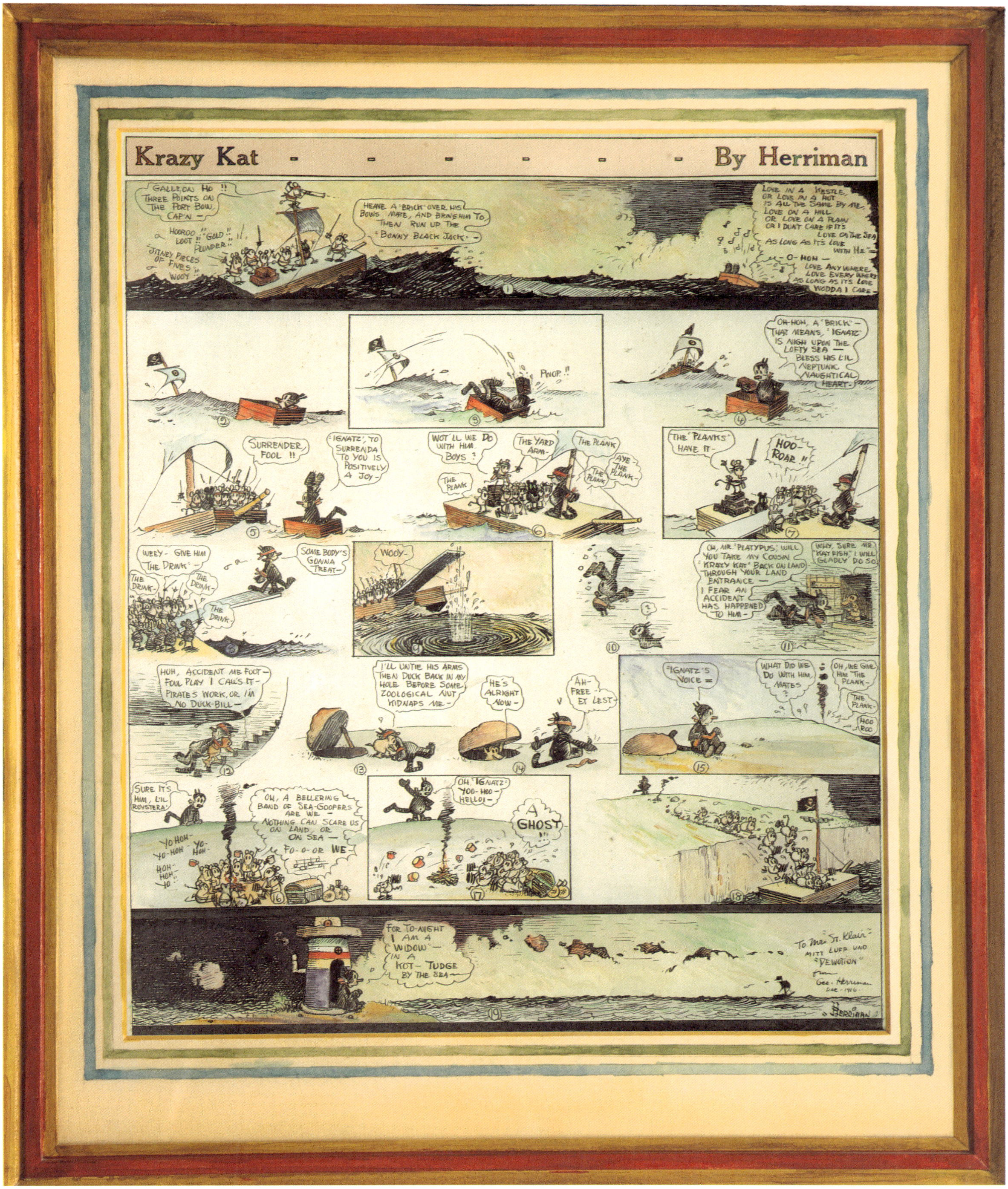
Krazy Kat - - - - - - By Herriman
GALLEON HO !! THREE POINTS ON THE PORT BOW, CAP'N -
HOOROO !! LOOT !!
"GOLD !!"
PLUNDER !!
"JITNEY PIECES OF FIVES" WOOY !!
HEAVE A "BRICK" OVER HIS BOWS MATE, AND BRING HIM TO. THEN RUN UP THE "BONNY BLACK JACK" -
LOVE IN A KESTLE, OR LOVE IN A HUT IS ALL THE SAME BY ME, LOVE ON A HILL OR LOVE ON A PLAIN OR I DON'T CARE IF IT'S LOVE ON THE SEA AS LONG AS IT'S LOVE WITH HE" -
- O - HOH -
LOVE ANY WHERE LOVE EVERY WHERE AS LONG AS IT'S LOVE WODDA I CARE -
PWOP !!
OH-HOH, A "BRICK" - THAT MEANS, "IGNATZ" IS NIGH UPON THE LOFTY SEA - BLESS HIS L'IL NEPTUNIC NAUGHTICAL HEART -
SURRENDER, FOOL !!
"IGNATZ", TO SURRENDA TO YOU IS POSITIVELY 4 JOY -
WOT'LL WE DO WITH HIM BOYS ?
THE YARD ARM -
THE PLANK
THE PLANK
THE PLANK
AYE - THE PLANK -
THE "PLANKS" HAVE IT -
HOO-ROAR !!
WEEY - GIVE HIM THE DRINK -
THE DRINK -
THE DRINK -
THE DRINK -
SOME BODY'S GONNA TREAT -
WOOY -
OH, MR. "PLATYPUS," WILL YOU TAKE MY COUSIN "KRAZY KAT" BACK ON LAND THROUGH YOUR LAND ENTRANCE - I FEAR AN ACCIDENT HAS HAPPENED TO HIM -
WHY, SURE MR. "KAT FISH," I WILL GLADLY DO SO.
HUH, ACCIDENT ME FOOT - FOUL PLAY I CALL'S IT - PIRATE'S WORK, OR I'M NO DUCK-BILL -
I'LL UNTIE HIS ARMS THEN DUCK BACK IN MY HOLE BEFORE SOME ZOOLOGICAL NUT KIDNAPS ME -
HE'S ALRIGHT NOW -
AH - FREE ET LEST -
"IGNATZ'S VOICE" =
WHAT DID WE DO WITH HIM, MATES ?
OH, WE GIVE HIM THE PLANK -
THE PLANK -
HOO ROO
SURE IT'S HIM, L'IL ROYSTERA'
YO HOH - YO-HOH - YO-HOH -
HOH-HOH-HO !!
OH, A BELLERING BAND OF SEA-GOOFERS ARE WE - NOTHING CAN SCARE US ON LAND, OR ON SEA - FO-O-OR WE -
OH, "IGNATZ" YOO-HOO - HELLO! -
A GHOST - !!!
FOR TO-NIGHT I AM A "WIDOW" - IN A KOT - TUDGE BY THE SEA -
To Mrs "St. Klair" - mitt luff und "Dewotion" from Geo. Herriman Dec - 1916 -
HERRIMAN

ABOVE The dedication reads "To Mrs. 'St. Klair'—mitt luff und 'Dewotion' from Geo. Herriman. Dec. 1916."

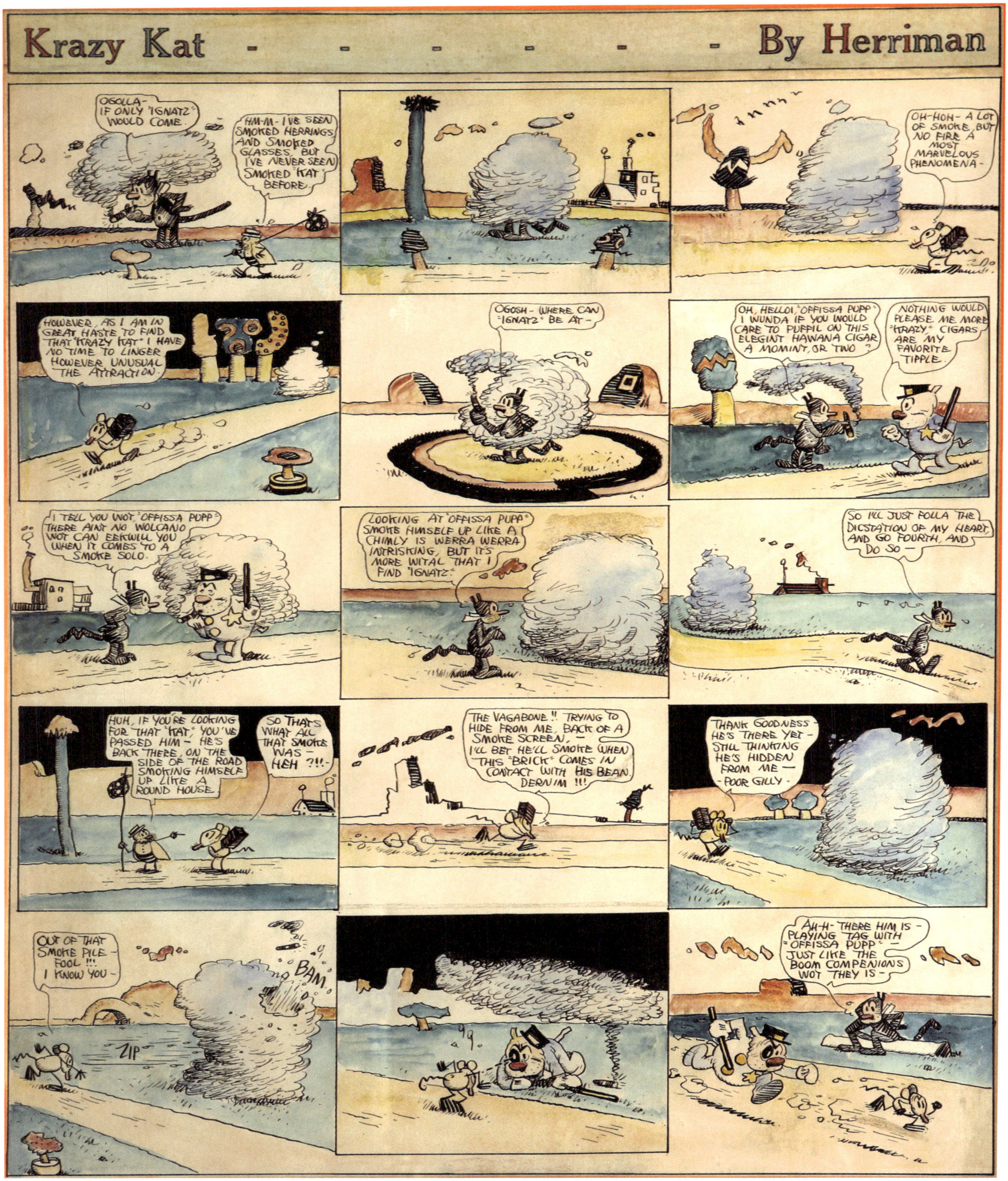
Krazy Kat - - - - - - By Herriman
OGOLLA - IF ONLY "IGNATZ" WOULD COME.
HM-M - I'VE SEEN SMOKED HERRINGS AND SMOKED GLASSES, BUT I'VE NEVER SEEN SMOKED "KAT" BEFORE.
OH-HOH - A LOT OF SMOKE, BUT NO FIRE - A MOST MARVELOUS PHENOMENA -
HOWEVER, AS I AM IN GREAT HASTE TO FIND THAT "KRAZY KAT" I HAVE NO TIME TO LINGER HOWEVER UNUSUAL THE ATTRACTION.
OGOSH - WHERE CAN "IGNATZ" BE AT -
OH, HELLO! "OFFISSA PUPP" I WUNDA IF YOU WOULD CARE TO PUFFIL ON THIS ELEGINT HAWANA CIGAR A MOMINT, OR TWO ?
NOTHING WOULD PLEASE ME MORE "KRAZY" CIGARS ARE MY FAVORITE TIPPLE.
I TELL YOU WOT, "OFFISSA PUPP" THERE AIN'T NO WOLCANO WOT CAN EEKWULL YOU WHEN IT COMES TO A SMOKE SOLO.
LOOKING AT "OFFISSA PUPP" SMOKE HIMSELF UP LIKE A CHIMLY IS WERRA WERRA INTRISTING, BUT IT'S MORE WITAL THAT I FIND "IGNATZ".
SO I'LL JUST FOLLA THE DICSTATION OF MY HEART, AND GO FOURTH, AND DO SO -
HUH, IF YOU'RE LOOKING FOR THAT "KAT" YOU'VE PASSED HIM - HE'S BACK THERE, ON THE SIDE OF THE ROAD SMOKING HIMSELF UP LIKE A ROUND HOUSE.
SO THAT'S WHAT ALL THAT SMOKE WAS - HEH ?!! -
THE VAGABONE !! TRYING TO HIDE FROM ME, BACK OF A SMOKE SCREEN, - I'LL BET HE'LL SMOKE WHEN THIS "BRICK" COMES IN CONTACT WITH HIS BEAN DERNIM !!!
THANK GOODNESS - HE'S THERE YET - STILL THINKING HE'S HIDDEN FROM ME - POOR GILLY -
OUT OF THAT SMOKE PILE - FOOL !!! I KNOW YOU -
ZIP
BAM
AH-H - THERE HIM IS - PLAYING TAG WITH "OFFISSA PUPP" - JUST LIKE THE BOOM COMPENIONS WOT THEY IS -

ABOVE This page was cited by Gilbert Seldes as having a "touch of irony and pity which transform all of Herriman's work, which relates it, for all that the material is preposterous, to something profoundly true and moving." March 11, 1922.

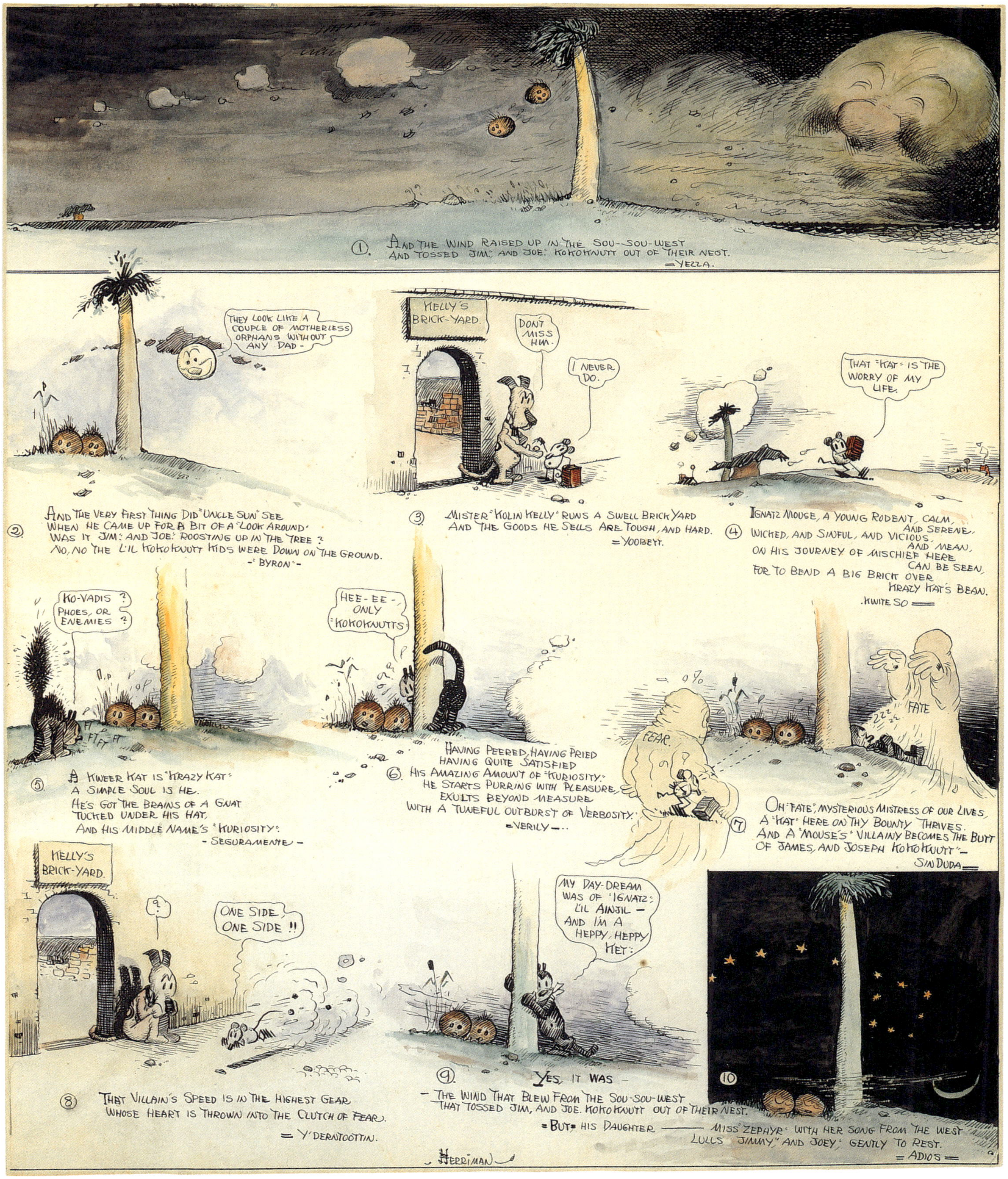
(1). And the wind raised up in the Sou--Sou-West and tossed "Jim" and "Joe" Kokoknutt out of their nest. =Yezza.
They look like a couple of motherless orphans without any dad-
(2). And the very first thing did "Uncle Sun" see when he came up for a bit of a "look around" was it "Jim" and "Joe" roosting up in the tree? No, no the l'il Kokoknutt kids were down on the ground. -"Byron"-
Kelly's Brick-Yard.
Don't miss him.
I never do.
(3). Mister "Kolin Kelly" runs a swell brick yard and the goods he sells are tough, and hard. =Yoobett.
That "Kat" is the worry of my life.
(4). Ignatz Mouse, a young rodent, calm, and serene, wicked, and sinful, and vicious, and mean, on his journey of mischief here can be seen, for to bend a big brick over Krazy Kat's bean. .Kwite so
Ko-vadis? Phoes, or enemies?
(5). A kweer kat is "Krazy Kat" a simple soul is he. He's got the brains of a gnat tucked under his hat, and his middle name's "Kuriosity". - Seguramente -
Hee-ee- only "Kokoknutts"
(6). Having peered, having pried having quite satisfied his amazing amount of "Kuriosity" he starts purring with pleasure, exults beyond measure with a tuneful outburst of verbosity. =Verily-..
Fear.
Fate
(7). Oh "Fate", mysterious mistress of our lives, a "Kat" here on thy bounty thrives. And a "Mouse's" villainy becomes the butt of James, and Joseph Kokoknutt"- Sin Duda
Kelly's Brick-Yard.
?
One side, one side!!
(8). That villain's speed is in the highest gear whose heart is thrown into the clutch of fear. = Y'derntoottin.
My day-dream was of "Ignatz" l'il ainjil - and I'm a heppy, heppy Kat.
(9). Yes, it was - - The wind that blew from the Sou-sou-west that tossed Jim, and Joe. Kokoknutt out of their nest.
(10). =But= his daughter ——— Miss "Zephyr" with her song from the west lulls "Jimmy," and Joey, gently to rest. = Adios =
Herriman

ABOVE A hand-colored Sunday from July 2, 1916.

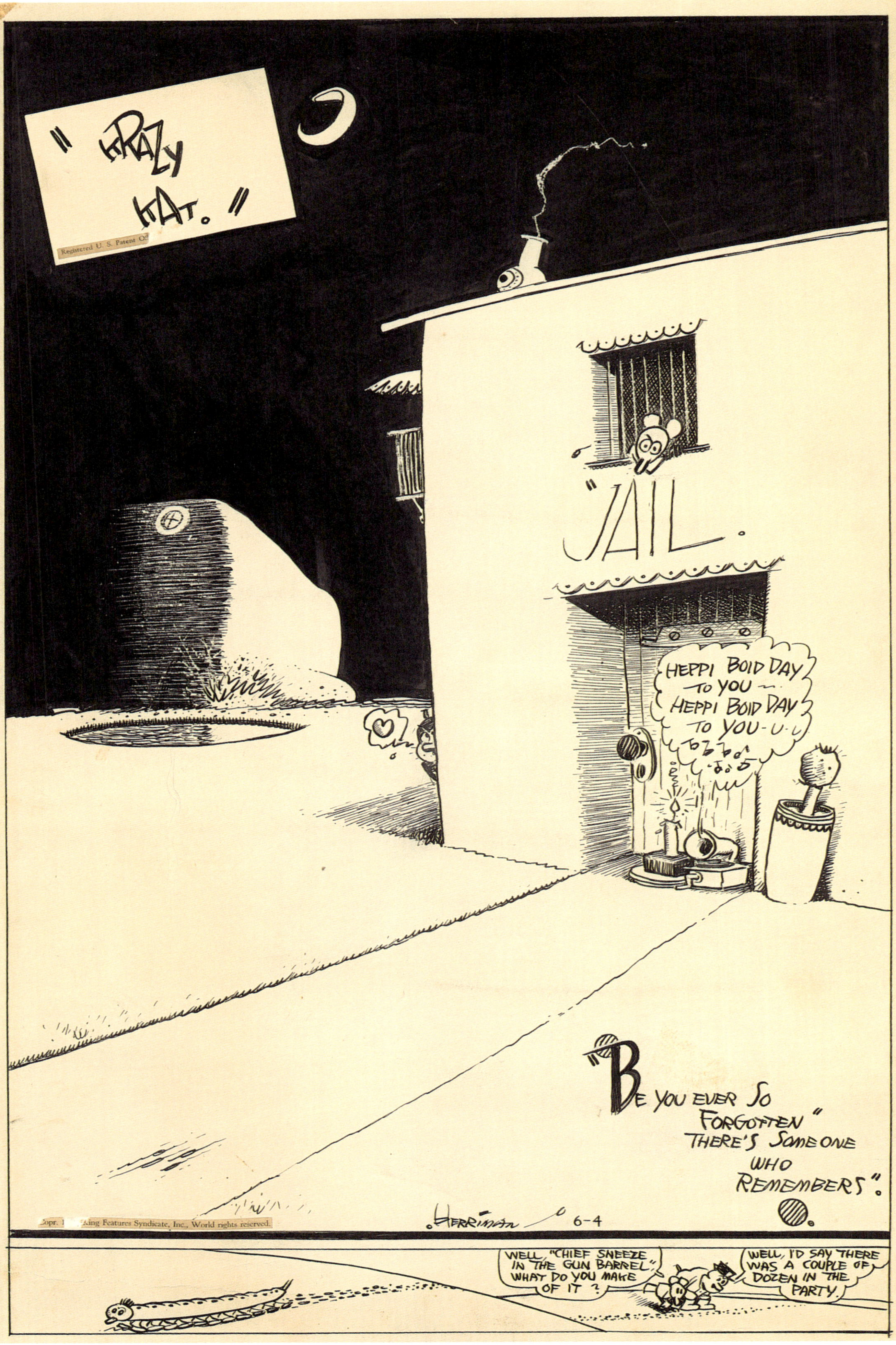
"KRAZY KAT."
Registered U. S. Patent O.
"JAIL.
HEPPI BOID DAY TO YOU — HEPPI BOID DAY TO YOU-U-U
"BE YOU EVER SO FORGOTTEN" THERE'S SOME ONE WHO REMEMBERS".
Copr. 19 King Features Syndicate, Inc., World rights reserved.
HERRIMAN 6-4
WELL, "CHIEF SNEEZE IN THE GUN BARREL", WHAT DO YOU MAKE OF IT ?
WELL, I'D SAY THERE WAS A COUPLE OF DOZEN IN THE PARTY.

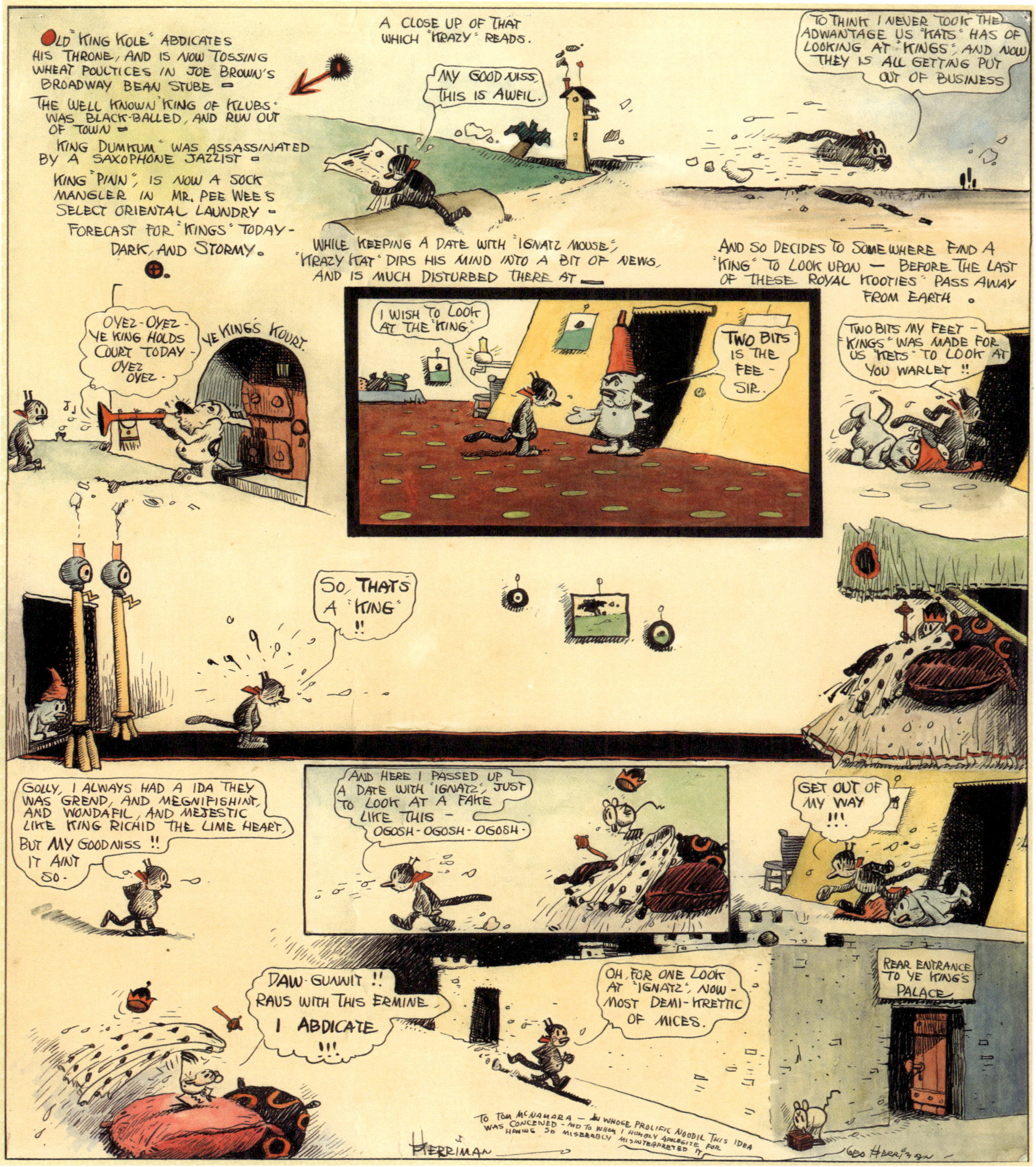
OLD "KING KOLE" ABDICATES HIS THRONE, AND IS NOW TOSSING WHEAT POULTICES IN JOE BROWN'S BROADWAY BEAN STUBE =
THE WELL KNOWN "KING OF KLUBS" WAS BLACK-BALLED, AND RUN OUT OF TOWN =
"KING DUMKUM" WAS ASSASSINATED BY A SAXOPHONE JAZZIST =
"KING "PINN", IS NOW A SOCK MANGLER IN MR. PEE WEE'S SELECT ORIENTAL LAUNDRY =
FORECAST FOR "KINGS" TODAY - DARK AND STORMY.
A CLOSE UP OF THAT WHICH "KRAZY" READS.
MY GOOD NISS. THIS IS AWFIL.
WHILE KEEPING A DATE WITH "IGNATZ MOUSE", "KRAZY KAT" DIPS HIS MIND INTO A BIT OF NEWS, AND IS MUCH DISTURBED THERE AT —
TO THINK I NEVER TOOK THE ADWANTAGE US "KATS" HAS OF LOOKING AT "KINGS", AND NOW THEY IS ALL GETTING PUT OUT OF BUSINESS
AND SO DECIDES TO SOME WHERE FIND A "KING" TO LOOK UPON — BEFORE THE LAST OF THESE ROYAL "KOOTIES" PASS AWAY FROM EARTH.
OYEZ - OYEZ - YE KING HOLDS COURT TODAY - OYEZ OYEZ -
YE KING'S KOURT.
I WISH TO LOOK AT THE "KING"
TWO BITS IS THE FEE SIR.
TWO BITS MY FEET - "KINGS" WAS MADE FOR US "KATS" TO LOOK AT YOU WARLET !!
SO, THAT'S A "KING" !!
GOLLY, I ALWAYS HAD A IDA THEY WAS GREND, AND MEGNIFISHINT, AND WONDAFIL, AND MEJESTIC LIKE KING RICHID THE LIME HEART. BUT MY GOODNISS !! IT AINT SO.
AND HERE I PASSED UP A DATE WITH "IGNATZ", JUST TO LOOK AT A FAKE LIKE THIS - OGOSH - OGOSH - OGOSH.
GET OUT OF MY WAY !!!
DAW-GUNNIT !! RAUS WITH THIS ERMINE I ABDICATE !!!
OH, FOR ONE LOOK AT "IGNATZ", NOW - MOST DEMI-KRETTIC OF MICES.
REAR ENTRANCE TO YE KING'S PALACE
TO TOM McNAMARA — IN WHOSE PROLIFIC NOODIL THIS IDEA WAS CONCEIVED - AND TO WHOM I HUMBLY APOLOGIZE FOR HAVING SO MISERABLY MISINTERPRETED IT
HERRIMAN
GEO HERRIMAN

OPPOSITE June 4, 1939.

ABOVE A *Krazy Kat* Sunday, inscribed, "To Tom McNamara—in whose prolific noodil this idea was conceived—and to whom I humbly apologize for having so miserably misinterpreted it." November 17, 1918.

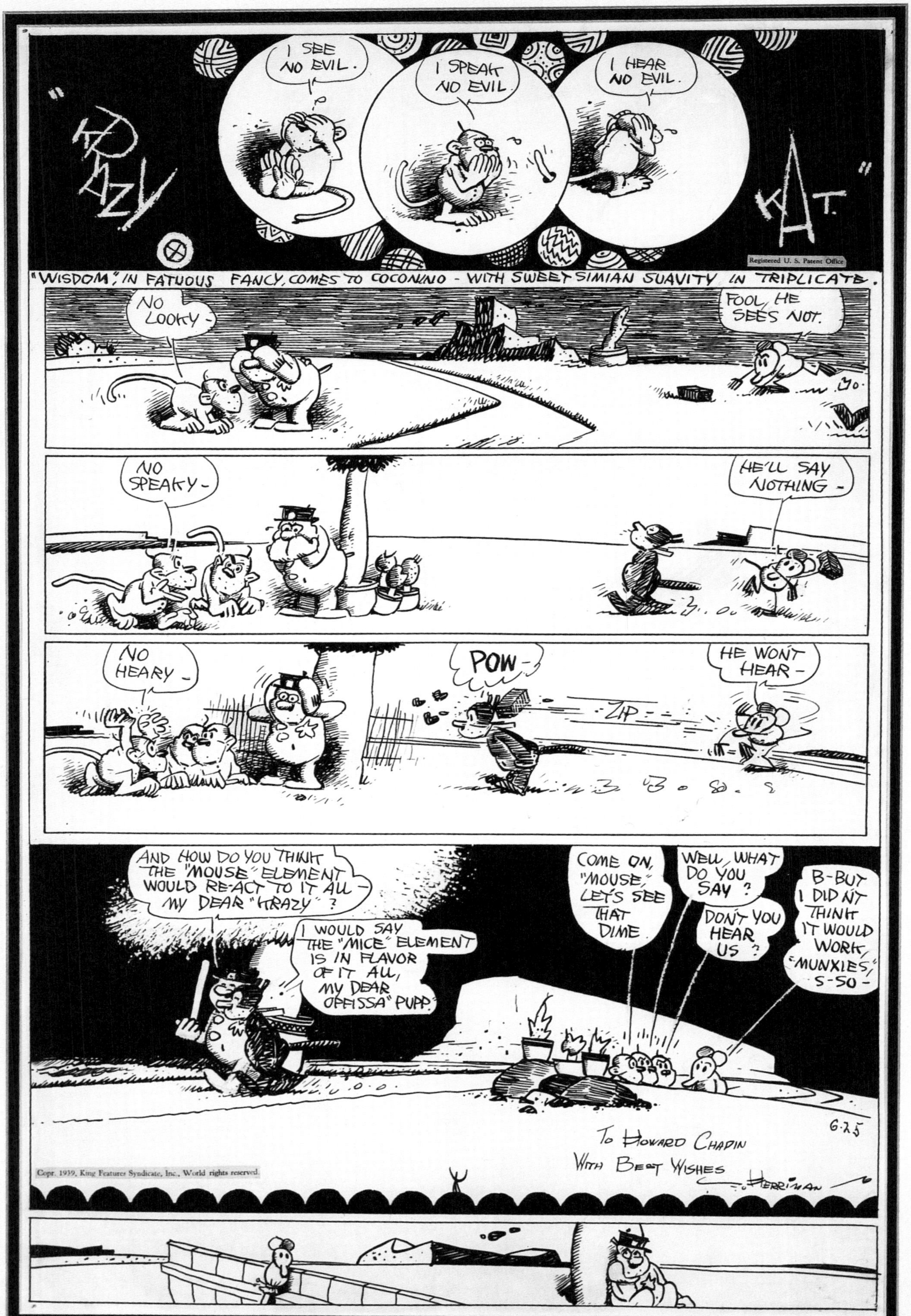
"KRAZY KAT."
I SEE NO EVIL.
I SPEAK NO EVIL
I HEAR NO EVIL.
Registered U. S. Patent Office
"WISDOM," IN FATUOUS FANCY, COMES TO COCONINO - WITH SWEET SIMIAN SUAVITY IN TRIPLICATE.
NO LOOKY -
FOOL, HE SEES NOT.
NO SPEAKY -
HE'LL SAY NOTHING -
NO HEARY -
POW -
ZIP
HE WON'T HEAR -
AND HOW DO YOU THINK THE "MOUSE" ELEMENT WOULD RE-ACT TO IT ALL - MY DEAR "KRAZY" ?
I WOULD SAY THE "MICE" ELEMENT IS IN FLAVOR OF IT ALL, MY DEAR "OFFISSA" PUPP.
COME ON, "MOUSE," LET'S SEE THAT DIME
WELL, WHAT DO YOU SAY ?
DON'T YOU HEAR US ?
B-BUT I DID N'T THINK IT WOULD WORK, "MUNXIES," S-SO -
6.25
TO HOWARD CHAPIN
WITH BEST WISHES
HERRIMAN
Copr. 1939, King Features Syndicate, Inc., World rights reserved.

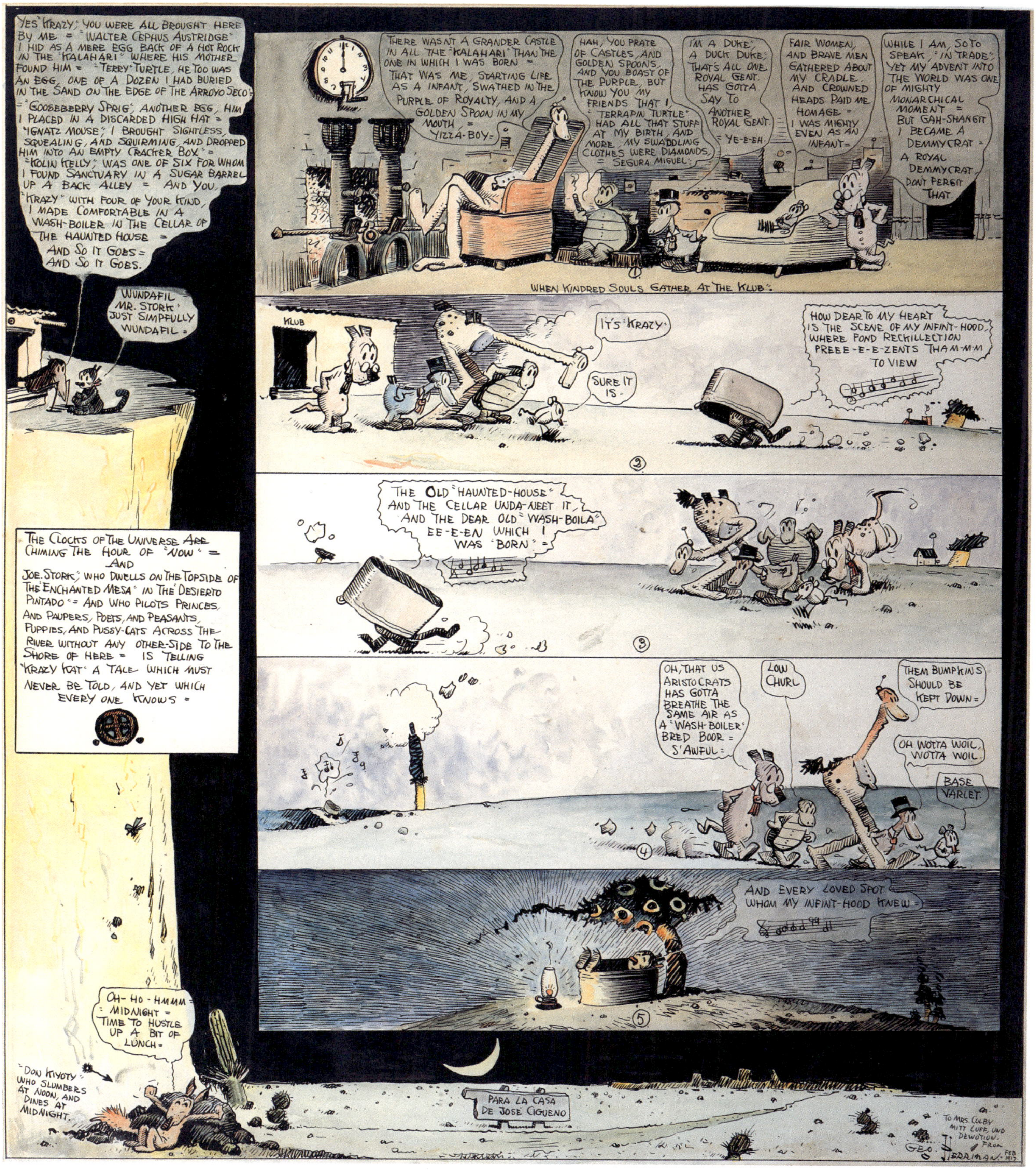
YES "KRAZY," YOU WERE ALL BROUGHT HERE BY ME = "WALTER CEPHUS AUSTRIDGE" I HID AS A MERE EGG BACK OF A HOT ROCK IN THE "KALAHARI" WHERE HIS MOTHER FOUND HIM = "TERRY" TURTLE, HE TOO WAS AN EGG, ONE OF A DOZEN I HAD BURIED IN THE SAND ON THE EDGE OF THE ARROYO SECO = "GOOSEBERRY SPRIG," ANOTHER EGG, HIM I PLACED IN A DISCARDED HIGH HAT = "IGNATZ MOUSE," I BROUGHT SIGHTLESS, SQUEALING, AND SQUIRMING, AND DROPPED HIM INTO AN EMPTY CRACKER BOX = "KOLIN KELLY," WAS ONE OF SIX FOR WHOM I FOUND SANCTUARY IN A SUGAR BARREL UP A BACK ALLEY = AND YOU, "KRAZY" WITH FOUR OF YOUR KIND, I MADE COMFORTABLE IN A WASH-BOILER IN THE CELLAR OF THE HAUNTED HOUSE = AND SO IT GOES = AND SO IT GOES.
WUNDAFIL MR. STORK: JUST SIMPFULLY WUNDAFIL =
THERE WASN'T A GRANDER CASTLE IN ALL THE "KALAHARI" THAN THE ONE IN WHICH I WAS BORN = THAT WAS ME, STARTING LIFE AS A INFANT, SWATHED IN THE PURPLE OF ROYALTY, AND A GOLDEN SPOON IN MY MOUTH, = YIZZA-BOY =
HAH, YOU PRATE OF CASTLES, AND GOLDEN SPOONS, AND YOU BOAST OF THE PURPLE, BUT KNOW YOU MY FRIENDS THAT I, "TERRAPIN TURTLE" HAD ALL THAT STUFF AT MY BIRTH, AND MORE, MY SWADDLING CLOTHES WERE DIAMONDS, = SEGURA MIGUEL:
I'M A DUKE, A DUCK DUKE, THAT'S ALL ONE ROYAL GENT. HAS GOTTA SAY TO ANOTHER ROYAL GENT. = YE-E-EH.
FAIR WOMEN, AND BRAVE MEN GATHERED ABOUT MY CRADLE. AND CROWNED HEADS PAID ME HOMAGE = I WAS MIGHTY EVEN AS AN INFANT =
WHILE I AM, SO TO SPEAK, "IN TRADE," YET MY ADVENT INTO THE WORLD WAS ONE OF MIGHTY MONARCHICAL MOMENT = BUT GAH-SHANGIT I BECAME A DEMMYCRAT = A ROYAL DEMMYCRAT, DON'T FERGIT THAT.
WHEN KINDRED SOULS GATHER AT THE KLUB".
KLUB
IT'S "KRAZY"
SURE IT IS -
HOW DEAR TO MY HEART IS THE SCENE OF MY INFINT-HOOD, WHERE FOND RECKILLECTION PREEE-E-E-ZENTS THAM-M-M TO VIEW
THE OLD "HAUNTED-HOUSE" AND THE CELLAR UNDA-NEET IT, AND THE DEAR OLD "WASH-BOILA" EE-E-EN WHICH I WAS "BORN" =
THE CLOCKS OF THE UNIVERSE ARE CHIMING THE HOUR OF "NOW" = AND JOE. STORK, WHO DWELLS ON THE TOPSIDE OF THE "ENCHANTED MESA" IN THE "DESIERTO PINTADO" = AND WHO PILOTS PRINCES, AND PAUPERS, POETS, AND PEASANTS, PUPPIES, AND PUSSY-CATS ACROSS THE RIVER WITHOUT ANY OTHER-SIDE TO THE SHORE OF HERE = IS TELLING "KRAZY KAT" A TALE WHICH MUST NEVER BE TOLD, AND YET WHICH EVERY ONE KNOWS =
OH, THAT US ARISTOCRATS HAS GOTTA BREATHE THE SAME AIR AS A "WASH-BOILER" BRED BOOR = S'AWFUL =
LOW CHURL
THEM BUMPKINS SHOULD BE KEPT DOWN =
OH WOTTA WOIL, WOTTA WOIL.
BASE VARLET.
AND EVERY LOVED SPOT WHOM MY INFINT-HOOD KNEW =
OH-HO-HMMM = MIDNIGHT = TIME TO HUSTLE UP A BIT OF LUNCH =
"DON KIYOTY" WHO SLUMBERS AT NOON, AND DINES AT MIDNIGHT.
PARA LA CASA DE JOSÉ CIGUENO
TO MRS. COLBY MITT LUFF, UND DEWOTION. FROM GEO. HERRIMAN. FEB 1917.

OPPOSITE This Sunday is inscribed, "To Howard Chapin with best wishes. Herriman." June 25, 1939.

ABOVE This Sunday is inscribed, "To Mrs. Colby mitt luff, und dewotion, from Geo. Herriman. Feb. 1917." February 11, 1917.

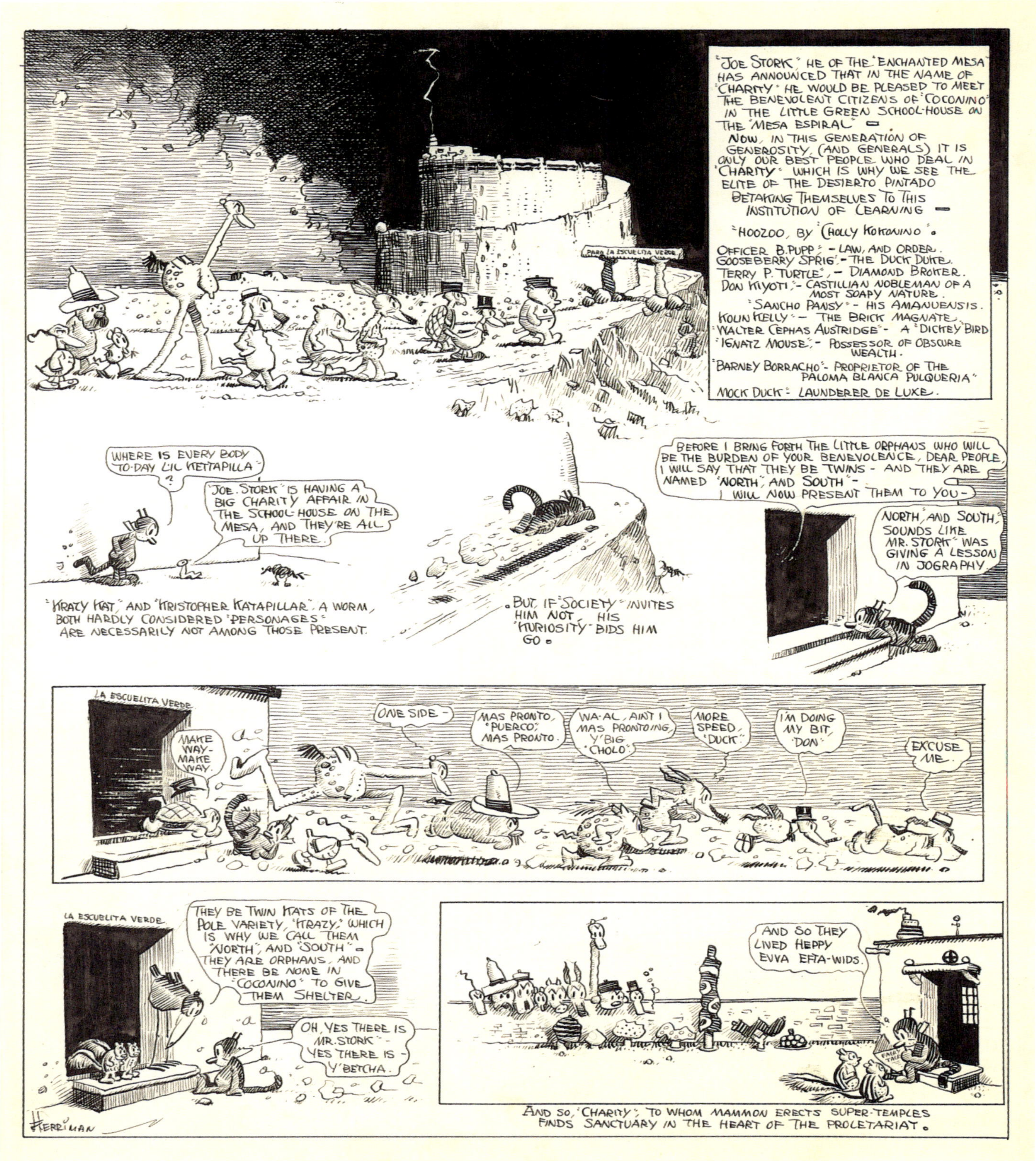

"JOE STORK," HE OF THE "ENCHANTED MESA" HAS ANNOUNCED THAT IN THE NAME OF "CHARITY" HE WOULD BE PLEASED TO MEET THE BENEVOLENT CITIZENS OF "COCONINO" IN THE LITTLE GREEN SCHOOL-HOUSE ON THE "MESA ESPIRAL" —
NOW, IN THIS GENERATION OF GENEROSITY, (AND GENERALS) IT IS ONLY OUR BEST PEOPLE WHO DEAL IN "CHARITY" WHICH IS WHY WE SEE THE ELITE OF THE DESIERTO PINTADO BETAKING THEMSELVES TO THIS INSTITUTION OF LEARNING —
"HOOZOO, BY CHOLLY KOKONINO."
OFFICER B. PUPP - LAW, AND ORDER.
GOOSEBERRY SPRIG - THE DUCK DUKE.
TERRY P. TURTLE - DIAMOND BROKER.
DON KIYOTI - CASTILLIAN NOBLEMAN OF A MOST SOAPY NATURE.
"SANCHO PANSY" - HIS AMANUENSIS.
KOLIN KELLY - THE BRICK MAGNATE.
WALTER CEPHAS AUSTRIDGE - A "DICKEY" BIRD
IGNATZ MOUSE - POSSESSOR OF OBSCURE WEALTH.
"BARNEY BORRACHO" - PROPRIETOR OF THE PALOMA BLANCA PULQUERIA"
MOCK DUCK - LAUNDERER DE LUXE.
PARA LA ESCUELITA VERDE
WHERE IS EVERY BODY TO-DAY L'IL KETTAPILLA ?
"JOE. STORK" IS HAVING A BIG CHARITY AFFAIR IN THE SCHOOL-HOUSE ON THE MESA, AND THEY'RE ALL UP THERE.
"KRAZY KAT," AND "KRISTOPHER KATAPILLAR" A WORM, BOTH HARDLY CONSIDERED "PERSONAGES" ARE NECESSARILY NOT AMONG THOSE PRESENT.
BUT, IF "SOCIETY" INVITES HIM NOT, HIS "KURIOSITY" BIDS HIM GO.
BEFORE I BRING FORTH THE LITTLE ORPHANS WHO WILL BE THE BURDEN OF YOUR BENEVOLENCE, DEAR PEOPLE, I WILL SAY THAT THEY BE TWINS - AND THEY ARE NAMED "NORTH," AND SOUTH" - I WILL NOW PRESENT THEM TO YOU -
"NORTH," AND SOUTH," SOUNDS LIKE MR. STORK WAS GIVING A LESSON IN JOGRAPHY
LA ESCUELITA VERDE
MAKE WAY - MAKE WAY.
ONE SIDE -
MAS PRONTO, "PUERCO," MAS PRONTO.
WA-AL, AINT I MAS PRONTOING, Y' BIG "CHOLO"
MORE SPEED, "DUCK"
I'M DOING MY BIT, "DON"
EXCUSE ME.
LA ESCUELITA VERDE
THEY BE TWIN KATS OF THE POLE VARIETY, "KRAZY," WHICH IS WHY WE CALL THEM "NORTH," AND "SOUTH". THEY ARE ORPHANS, AND THERE BE NONE IN "COCONINO" TO GIVE THEM SHELTER.
OH, YES THERE IS MR. STORK - YES THERE IS - Y' BETCHA.
HERRIMAN
AND SO THEY LIVED HEPPY EVVA EFTA-WIDS.
FAIRY TALES
AND SO, "CHARITY," TO WHOM MAMMON ERECTS SUPER-TEMPLES FINDS SANCTUARY IN THE HEART OF THE PROLETARIAT.

ABOVE May 5, 1918.

OPPOSITE November 4, 1917.

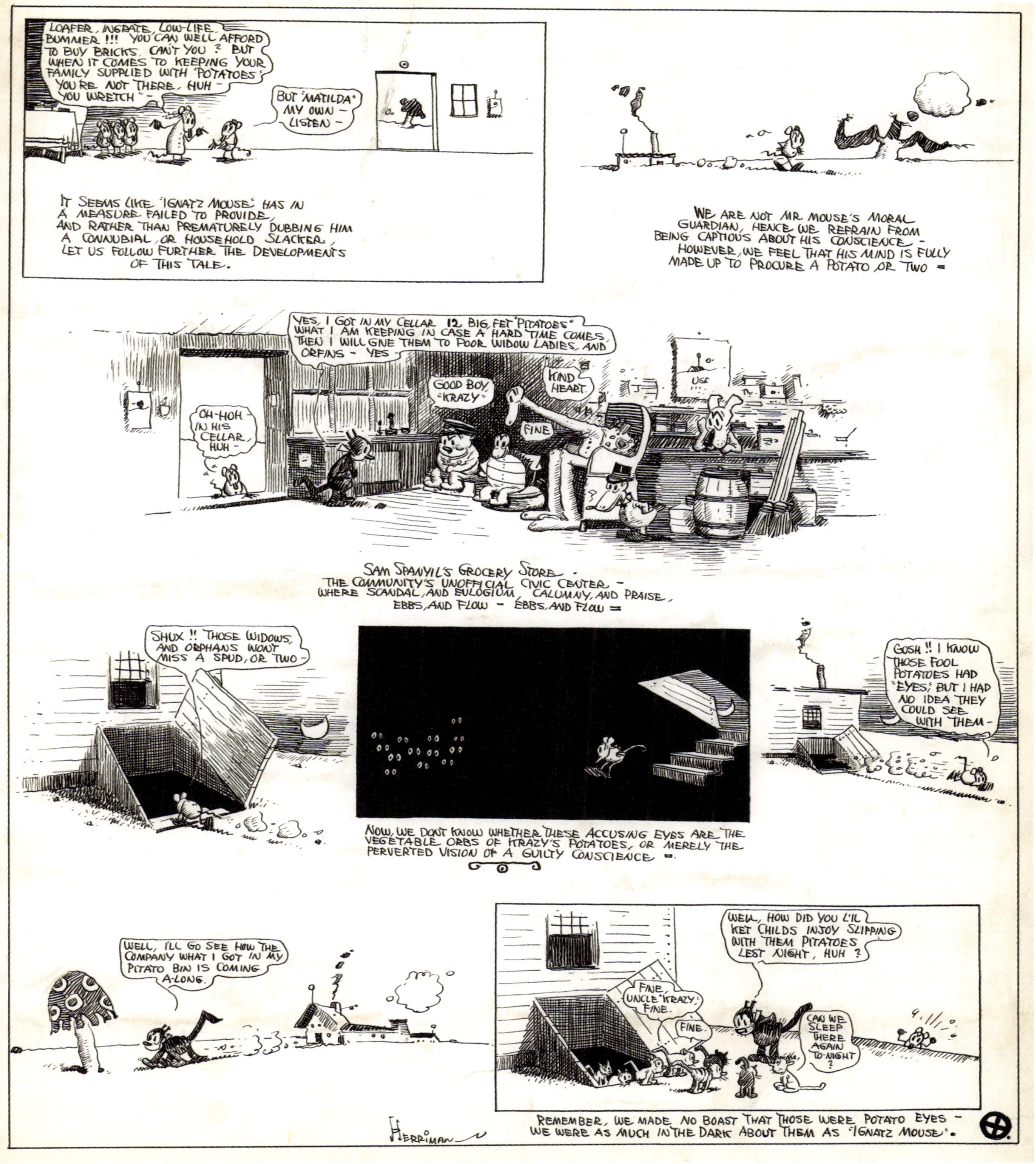
LOAFER, INGRATE, LOW-LIFE BUMMER !!! YOU CAN WELL AFFORD TO BUY BRICKS, CAN'T YOU ? BUT WHEN IT COMES TO KEEPING YOUR FAMILY SUPPLIED WITH 'POTATOES' YOU'RE NOT THERE, HUH — YOU WRETCH —
BUT 'MATILDA' MY OWN — LISTEN —
IT SEEMS LIKE 'IGNATZ MOUSE' HAS IN A MEASURE FAILED TO PROVIDE, AND RATHER THAN PREMATURELY DUBBING HIM A CONNUBIAL, OR HOUSEHOLD SLACKER, LET US FOLLOW FURTHER THE DEVELOPMENTS OF THIS TALE.
WE ARE NOT MR. MOUSE'S MORAL GUARDIAN, HENCE WE REFRAIN FROM BEING CAPTIOUS ABOUT HIS CONSCIENCE — HOWEVER, WE FEEL THAT HIS MIND IS FULLY MADE UP TO PROCURE A POTATO OR TWO =
YES, I GOT IN MY CELLAR 12 BIG, FET 'PITATOES' WHAT I AM KEEPING IN CASE A HARD TIME COMES THEN I WILL GIVE THEM TO POOR WIDOW LADIES, AND ORFINS — YES —
GOOD BOY, 'KRAZY'
KIND HEART.
FINE
OH-HOH IN HIS CELLAR, HUH —
SAM SPANYIL'S GROCERY STORE — THE COMMUNITY'S UNOFFICIAL CIVIC CENTER — WHERE SCANDAL, AND EULOGIUM, CALUMNY, AND PRAISE, EBBS, AND FLOW — EBBS, AND FLOW =
SHUX !! THOSE WIDOWS AND ORPHANS WONT MISS A SPUD, OR TWO —
NOW, WE DONT KNOW WHETHER THESE ACCUSING EYES ARE THE VEGETABLE ORBS OF KRAZY'S POTATOES, OR MERELY THE PERVERTED VISION OF A GUILTY CONSCIENCE =
GOSH !! I KNOW THOSE FOOL POTATOES HAD 'EYES,' BUT I HAD NO IDEA THEY COULD SEE WITH THEM —
WELL, I'LL GO SEE HOW THE COMPANY WHAT I GOT IN MY PITATO BIN IS COMING A-LONG.
WELL, HOW DID YOU L'IL KET CHILDS INJOY SLIPPING WITH THEM PITATOES LEST NIGHT, HUH ?
FINE, UNCLE 'KRAZY' FINE.
FINE.
CAN WE SLEEP THERE AGAIN TO-NIGHT ?
HERRIMAN
REMEMBER, WE MADE NO BOAST THAT THOSE WERE POTATO EYES — WE WERE AS MUCH IN THE DARK ABOUT THEM AS 'IGNATZ MOUSE'.

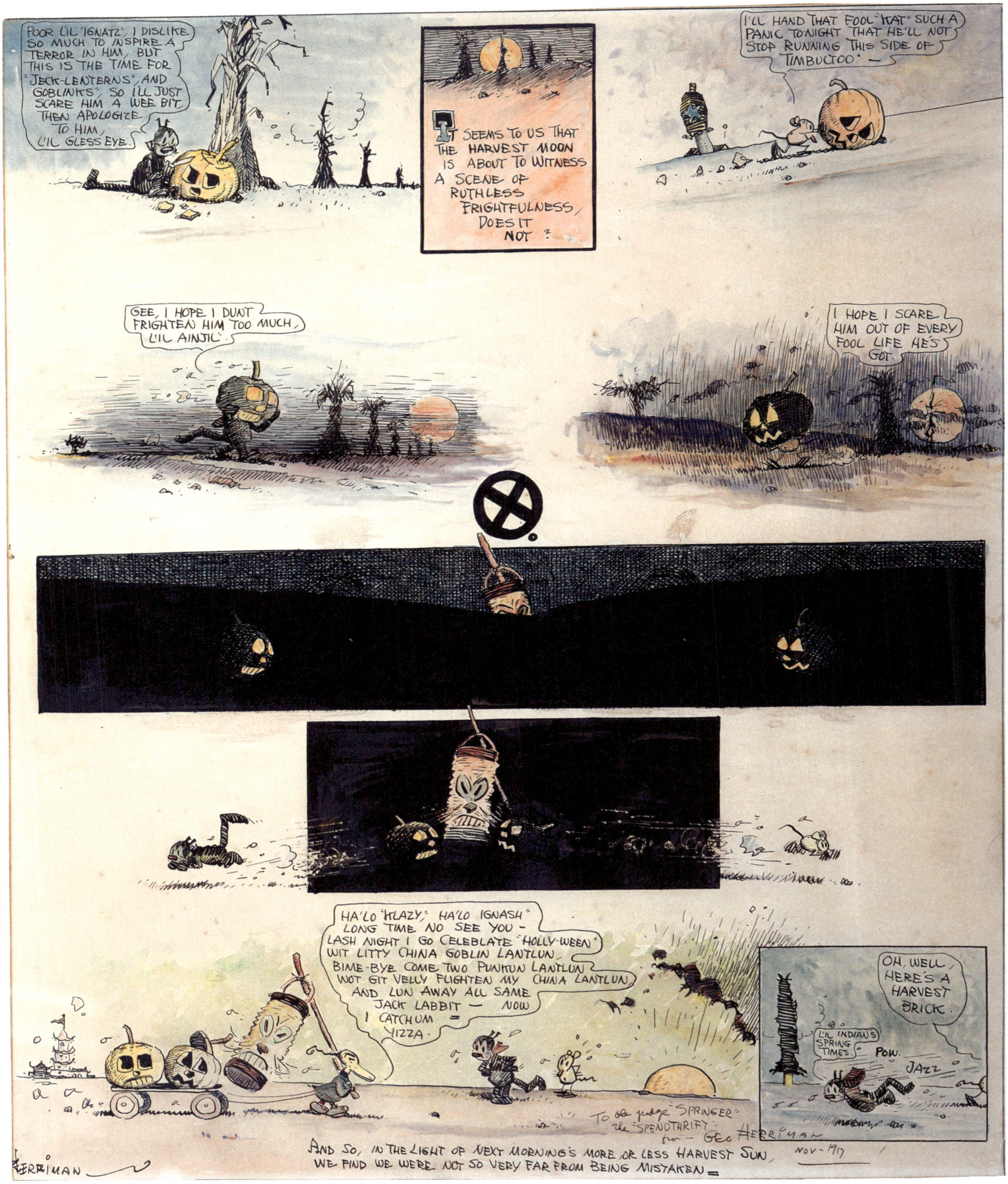

POOR LI'L 'IGNATZ', I DISLIKE SO MUCH TO INSPIRE A TERROR IN HIM, BUT THIS IS THE TIME FOR "JECK-LENTERNS", AND GOBLINKS", SO I'LL JUST SCARE HIM A WEE BIT, THEN APOLOGIZE TO HIM, LI'L GLESS EYE.
IT SEEMS TO US THAT THE HARVEST MOON IS ABOUT TO WITNESS A SCENE OF RUTHLESS FRIGHTFULNESS, DOES IT NOT ?
I'LL HAND THAT FOOL "KAT" SUCH A PANIC TONIGHT THAT HE'LL NOT STOP RUNNING THIS SIDE OF TIMBUCTOO" —
GEE, I HOPE I DUNT FRIGHTEN HIM TOO MUCH, LI'L AINJIL'
I HOPE I SCARE HIM OUT OF EVERY FOOL LIFE HE'S GOT.
HA'LO "KLAZY," HA'LO IGNASH" LONG TIME NO SEE YOU — LASH NIGHT I GO CELEBLATE "HOLLY-WEEN" WIT LITTY CHINA GOBLIN LANTLUN, BIME-BYE COME TWO PUNKUN LANTLUN WOT GIT VELLY FLIGHTEN MY CHINA LANTLUN AND LUN AWAY ALL SAME JACK LABBIT — NOW I CATCHUM = YIZZA.
OH, WELL HERE'S A HARVEST BRICK
LI'L INDIAN'S SPRING TIMES.
POW.
JAZZ
AND SO, IN THE LIGHT OF NEXT MORNING'S MORE OR LESS HARVEST SUN, WE FIND WE WERE NOT SO VERY FAR FROM BEING MISTAKEN =
To ole judge "SPRINGER" the "SPENDTHRIFT" from — GEO HERRIMAN
NOV - 1917
HERRIMAN

ABOVE This Sunday is inscribed, "To ole Judge 'Springer' the 'spendthrift' from Geo. Herriman. Nov. 1917." October 28, 1917.

OPPOSITE July 25, 1936.

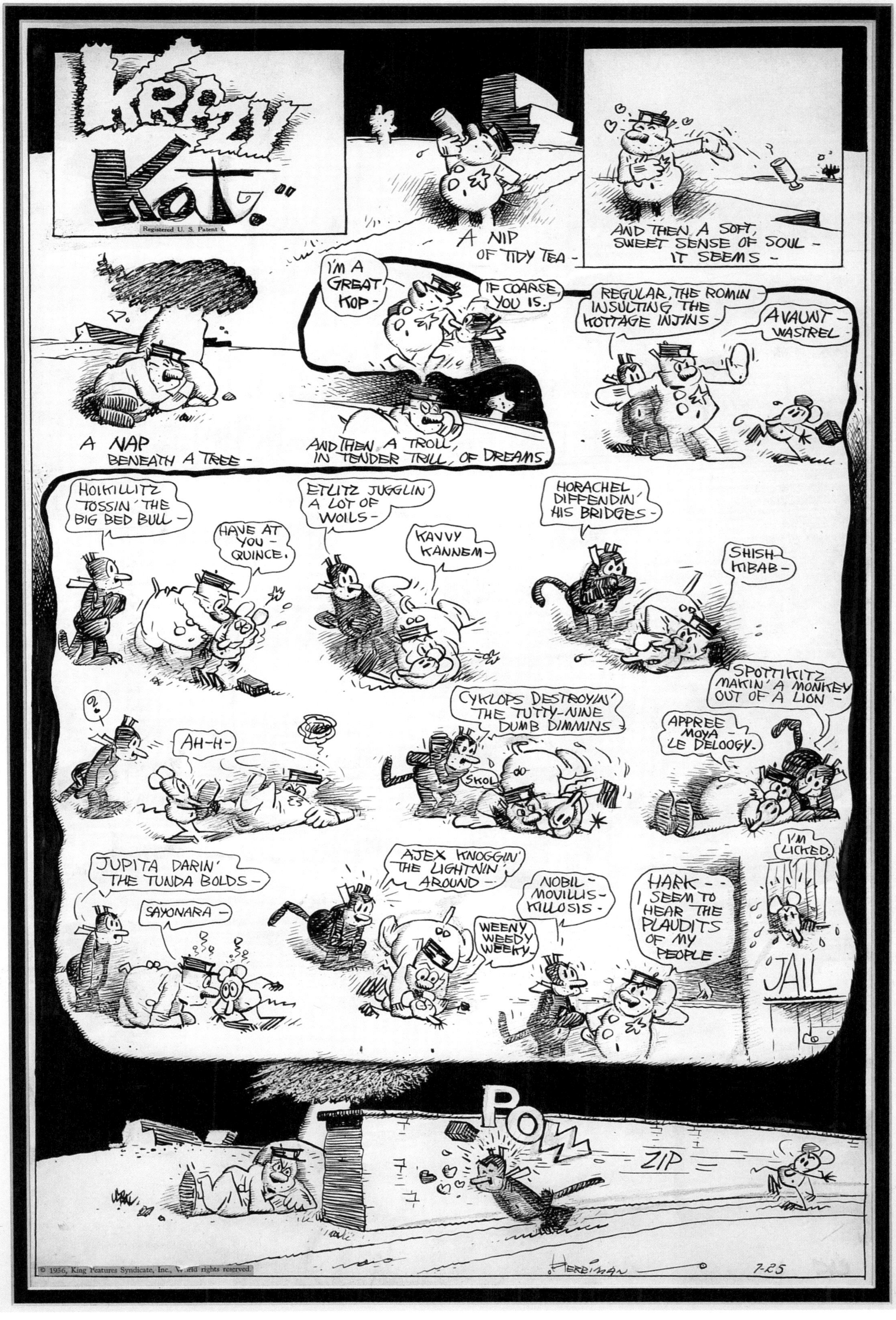
Krazy Kat
Registered U. S. Patent
A NIP OF TIDY TEA -
AND THEN A SOFT, SWEET SENSE OF SOUL - IT SEEMS -
A NAP BENEATH A TREE -
I'M A GREAT KOP -
IF COARSE, YOU IS.
AND THEN A TROLL, IN TENDER TRILL, OF DREAMS.
REGULAR, THE ROMIN INSULTING THE KOTTAGE INJINS -
AVAUNT - WASTREL -
HOIKILLITZ TOSSIN' THE BIG BED BULL -
HAVE AT YOU - QUINCE.
ETLITZ JUGGLIN' A LOT OF WOILS -
KAVVY KANNEM -
HORACHEL DIFFENDIN' HIS BRIDGES -
SHISH KIBAB -
AH-H-
CYKLOPS DESTROYIN' THE TUTTY-NINE DUMB DIMMINS
SKOL
SPOTTIKITZ MAKIN' A MONKEY OUT OF A LION -
APPREE MOYA - LE DELOOGY.
JUPITA DARIN' THE TUNDA BOLDS -
SAYONARA -
AJEX KNOGGIN' THE LIGHTNIN' AROUND -
WEENY WEEDY WEEKY.
NOBIL - MOVILLIS - KILLOSIS -
HARK - I SEEM TO HEAR THE PLAUDITS OF MY PEOPLE -
I'M LICKED.
JAIL
POW
ZIP
HERRIMAN
7-25

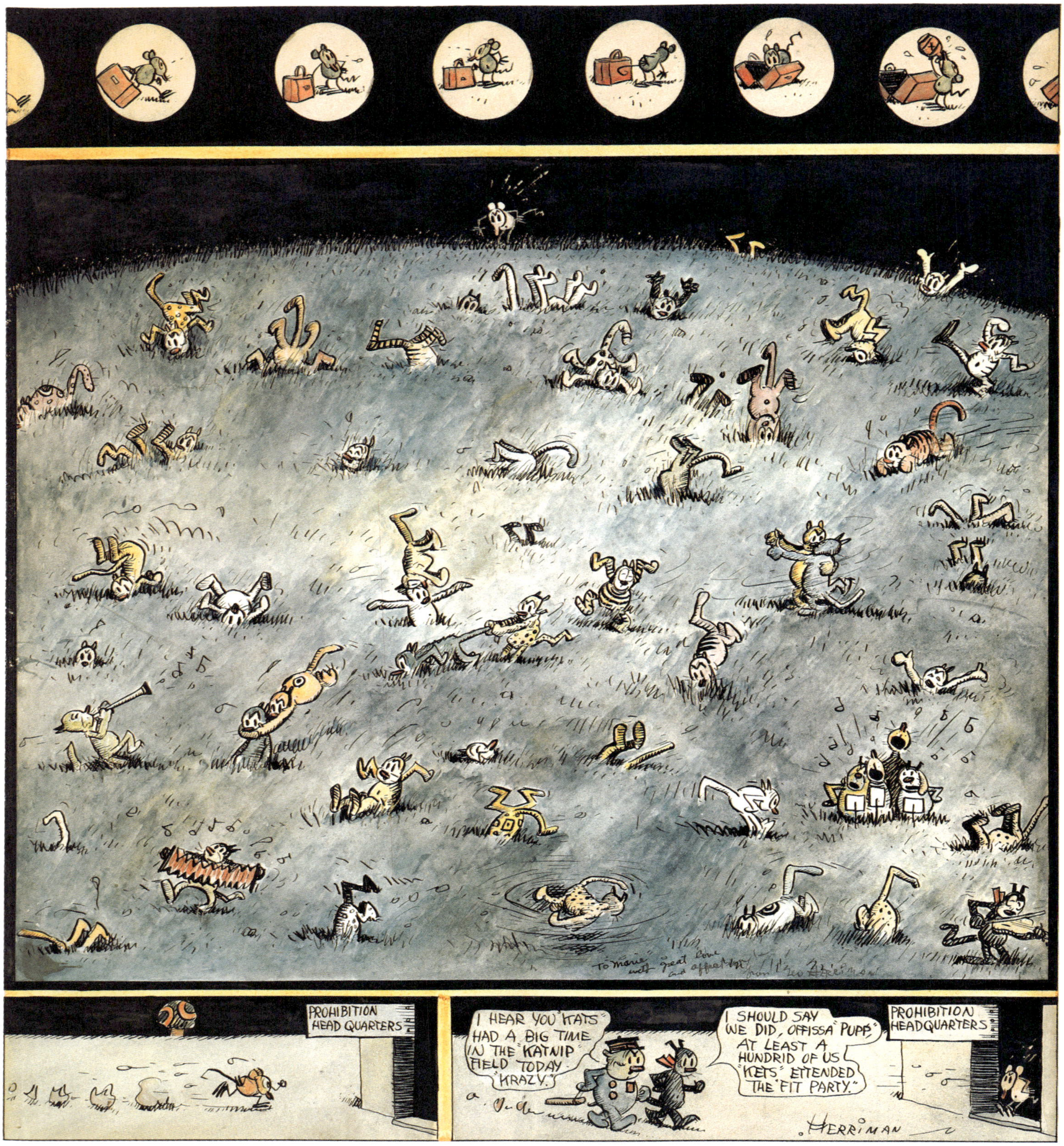
PROHIBITION HEAD QUARTERS
I HEAR YOU "KATS" HAD A "BIG TIME" IN THE "KATNIP" FIELD TODAY "KRAZY."
I SHOULD SAY WE DID, "OFFISSA" "PUPP" AT LEAST A HUNDRID OF US "KETS" ETTENDED THE "FIT PARTY."
PROHIBITION HEADQUARTERS
HERRIMAN

ABOVE May 18, 1919.

OPPOSITE June 30, 1918.

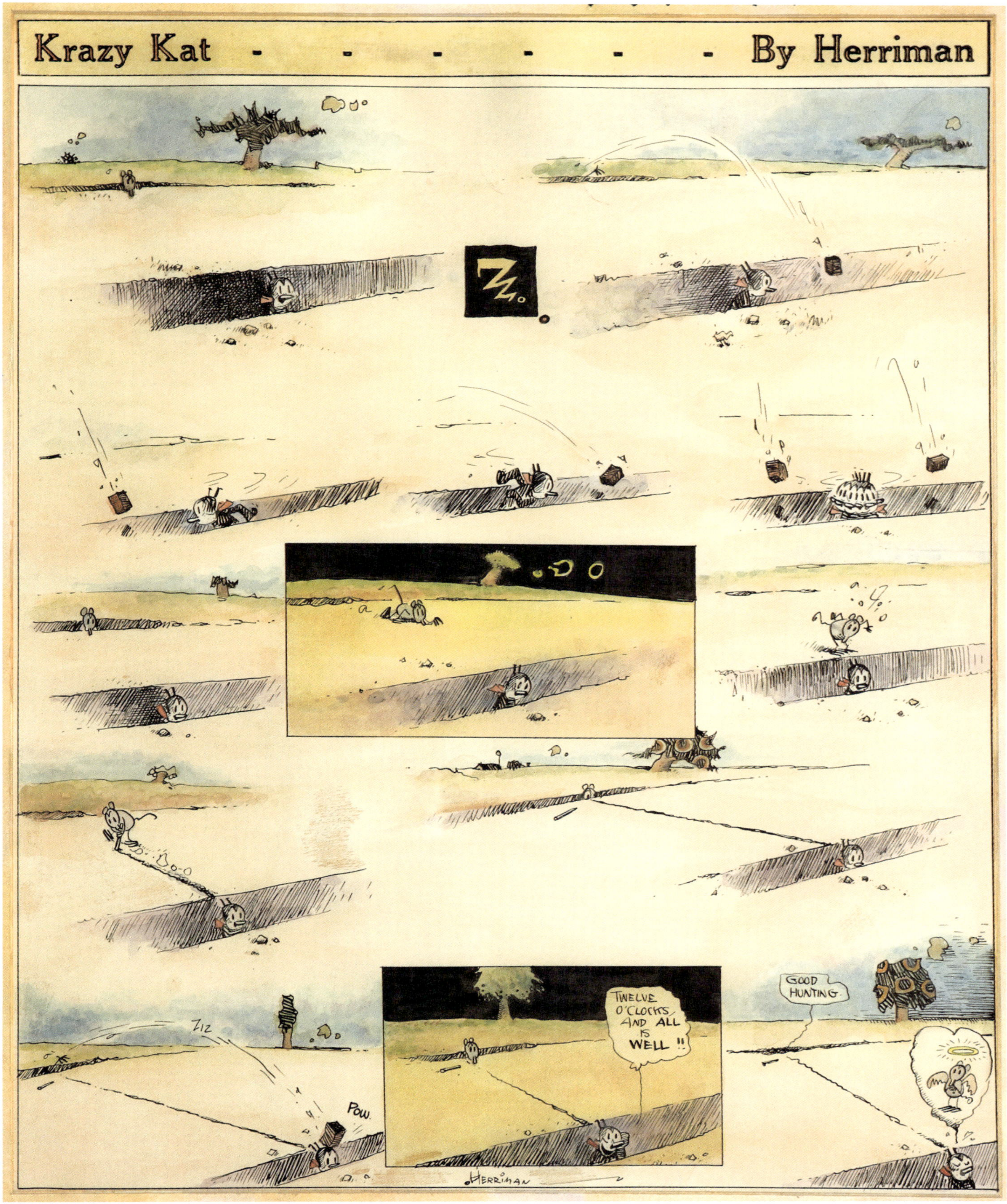
Krazy Kat - - - - - - By Herriman
Zz
ZIZ
POW.
TWELVE O'CLOCKS AND ALL IS WELL !!
GOOD HUNTING.
HERRIMAN

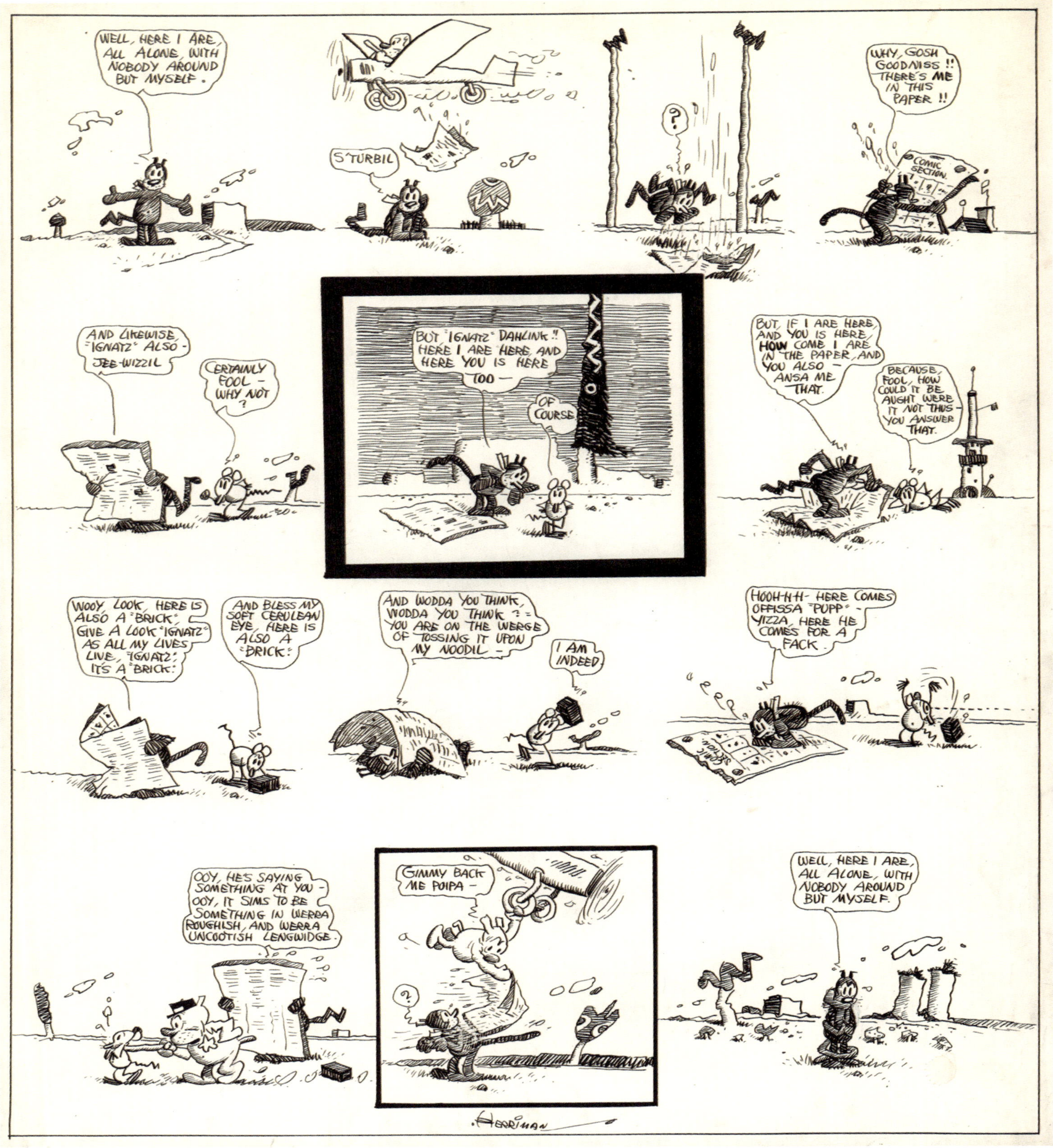
WELL, HERE I ARE, ALL ALONE, WITH NOBODY AROUND BUT MYSELF.
S'TURBIL
?
WHY, GOSH GOODNISS!! THERE'S ME IN THIS PAPER!!
COMIC SECTION
AND LIKEWISE, "IGNATZ" ALSO - JEE-WIZZIL
CERTAINLY FOOL - WHY NOT?
BUT "IGNATZ" DAHLINK!! HERE I ARE HERE, AND HERE YOU IS HERE TOO -
OF COURSE
BUT, IF I ARE HERE, AND YOU IS HERE, HOW COME I ARE IN THE PAPER, AND YOU ALSO - ANSA ME THAT.
BECAUSE, FOOL, HOW COULD IT BE AUGHT WERE IT NOT THUS YOU ANSWER THAT.
WOOY, LOOK, HERE IS ALSO A "BRICK", GIVE A LOOK "IGNATZ" AS ALL MY LIVES LIVE, "IGNATZ", IT'S A "BRICK".
AND BLESS MY SOFT CERULEAN EYE, HERE IS ALSO A "BRICK".
AND WODDA YOU THINK, WODDA YOU THINK?? YOU ARE ON THE WERGE OF TOSSING IT UPON MY NOODIL -
I AM INDEED
HOOH-H-H- HERE COMES OFFISSA "PUPP" - YIZZA, HERE HE COMES FOR A FACK.
COMIC SECTION
OOY, HE'S SAYING SOMETHING AT YOU - OOY, IT SIMS TO BE SOMETHING IN WERRA ROUGHISH, AND WERRA UNCOOTISH LENGWIDGE.
GIMMY BACK ME POIPA -
?
WELL, HERE I ARE, ALL ALONE, WITH NOBODY AROUND BUT MYSELF.
HERRIMAN

ABOVE April 16, 1922.

OPPOSITE December 25, 1932.

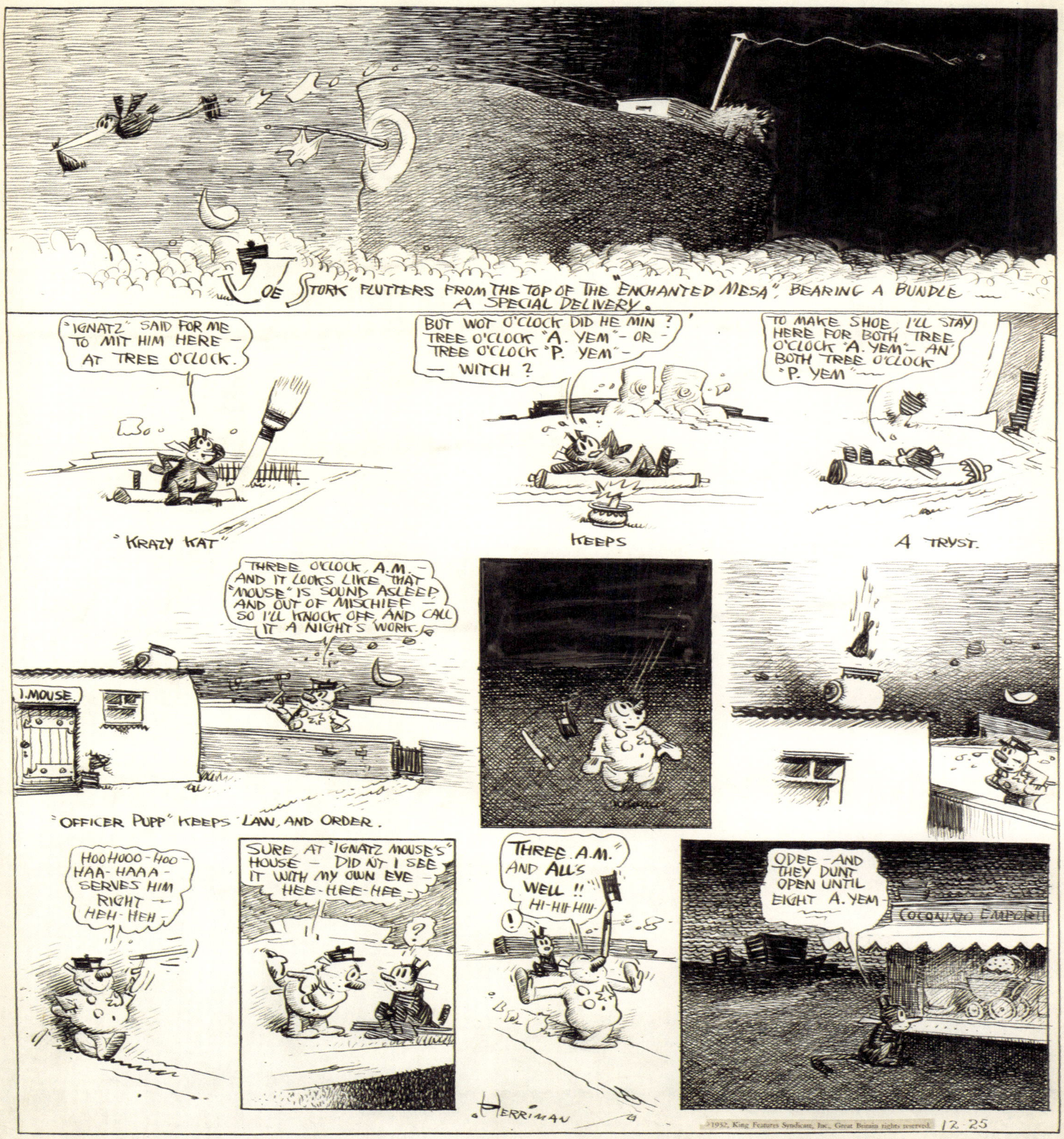
"JOE STORK" FLUTTERS FROM THE TOP OF THE "ENCHANTED MESA", BEARING A BUNDLE — A SPECIAL DELIVERY.
"IGNATZ" SAID FOR ME TO MIT HIM HERE — AT TREE O'CLOCK.
BUT WOT O'CLOCK DID HE MIN? TREE O'CLOCK "A. YEM" — OR — TREE O'CLOCK "P. YEM" — WITCH?
TO MAKE SHOE, I'LL STAY HERE FOR BOTH TREE O'CLOCK "A. YEM" — AN' BOTH TREE O'CLOCK "P. YEM"
"KRAZY KAT" KEEPS A TRYST.
THREE O'CLOCK, A.M. — AND IT LOOKS LIKE THAT "MOUSE" IS SOUND ASLEEP, AND OUT OF MISCHIEF — SO I'LL KNOCK OFF, AND CALL IT A NIGHT'S WORK.
I. MOUSE
"OFFICER PUPP" KEEPS LAW, AND ORDER.
HOO HOOO - HOO — HAA - HAAA — SERVES HIM RIGHT — HEH - HEH —
SURE AT "IGNATZ MOUSE'S" HOUSE — DID N'T I SEE IT WITH MY OWN EYE — HEE - HEE - HEE —
?
THREE A.M. AND ALL'S WELL!! HI-HII-HIII-
!
ODEE — AND THEY DUNT OPEN UNTIL EIGHT A. YEM —
COCONINO EMPORI
HERRIMAN
©1932, King Features Syndicate, Inc., Great Britain rights reserved.
12-25

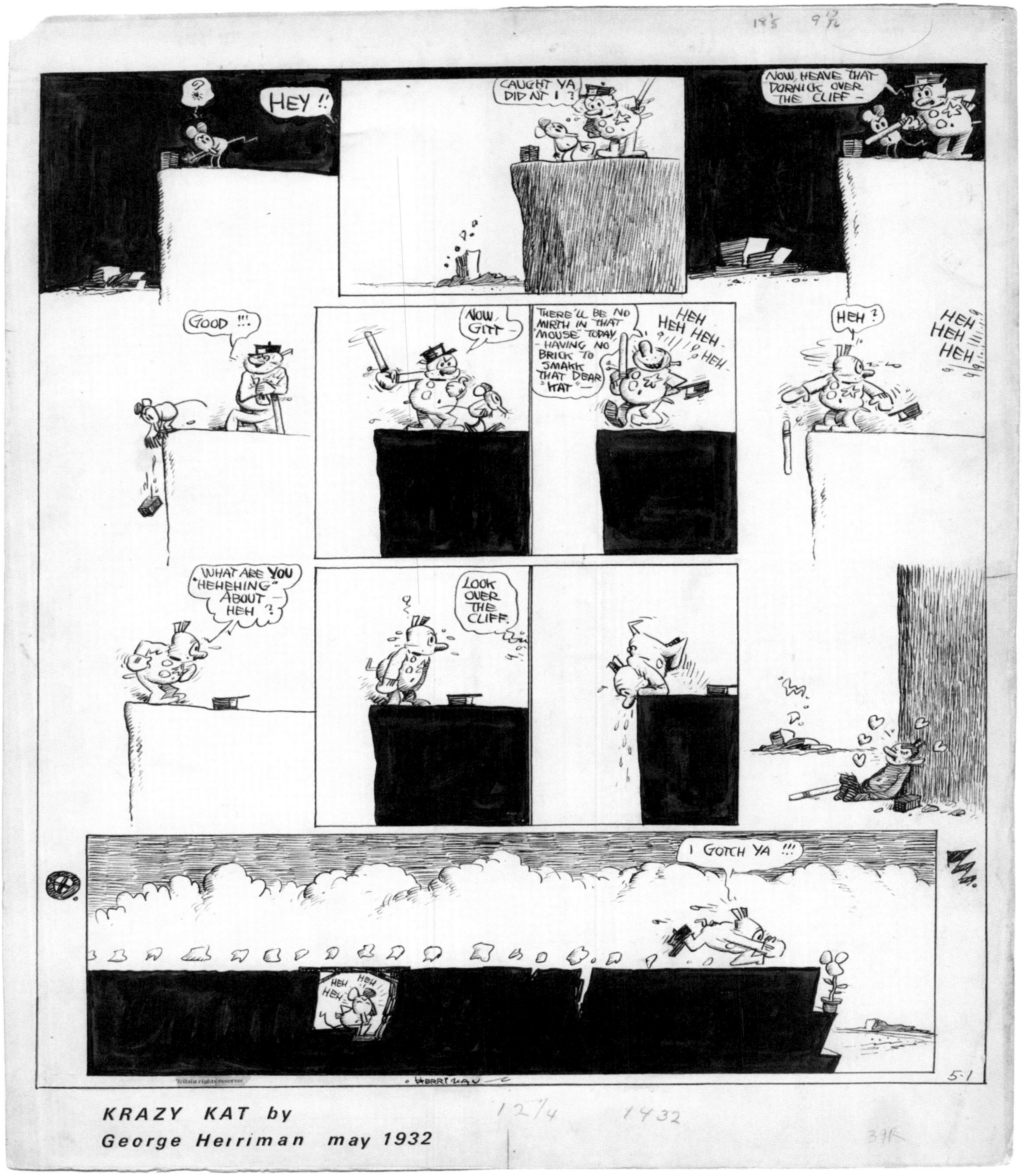
HEY !!
CAUGHT YA DIDN'T I ?
NOW, HEAVE THAT DORNICK OVER THE CLIFF -
GOOD !!!
NOW, GITT -
THERE'LL BE NO MIRTH IN THAT "MOUSE" TODAY, - HAVING NO BRICK TO SMAKK THAT DEAR "KAT" -
HEH HEH HEH - HEH
HEH ?
HEH HEH HEH
WHAT ARE YOU "HEHEHING" ABOUT - HEH ?
LOOK OVER THE CLIFF.
I GOTCH YA !!!
HEH HEH HEH
HERRIMAN
5-1
KRAZY KAT by
George Herriman may 1932

ABOVE May 1, 1932.

OPPOSITE Inscribed, "To Kelly from 'Kelly'—et al—mit luff—Herriman." June 5, 1938.

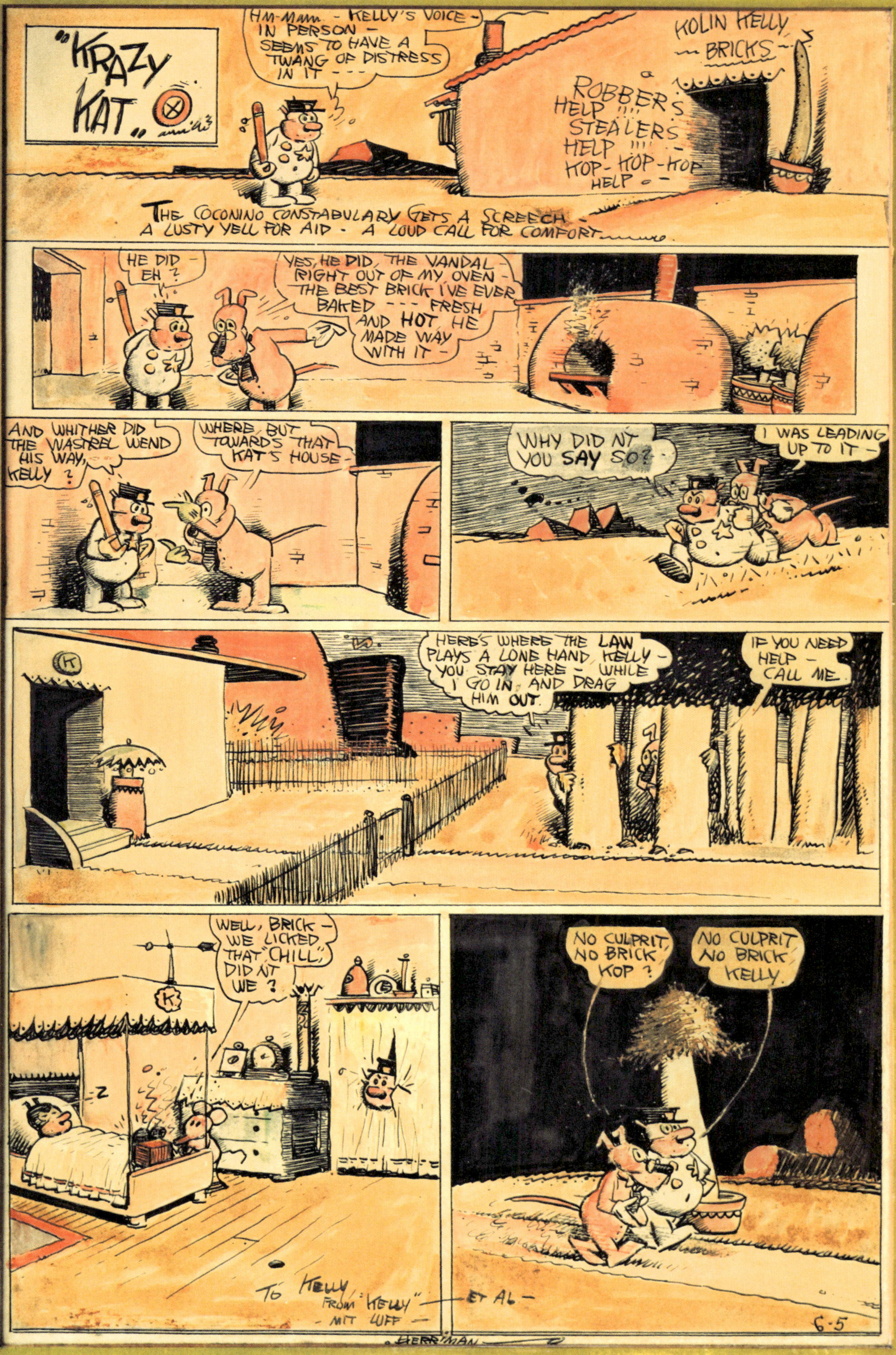
"KRAZY KAT"
HM-MMM - KELLY'S VOICE - IN PERSON - SEEMS TO HAVE A TWANG OF DISTRESS IN IT ---
KOLIN KELLY BRICKS
ROBBERS HELP !!!! STEALERS HELP !!!! HOP-HOP-HOP HELP
THE COCONINO CONSTABULARY GETS A SCREECH - A LUSTY YELL FOR AID - A LOUD CALL FOR COMFORT
HE DID - EH ?
YES, HE DID, THE VANDAL RIGHT OUT OF MY OVEN - THE BEST BRICK I'VE EVER BAKED --- FRESH AND HOT HE MADE WAY WITH IT -
AND WHITHER DID THE WASTREL WEND HIS WAY, KELLY ?
WHERE BUT TOWARDS THAT KAT'S HOUSE -
WHY DID NT YOU SAY SO?
I WAS LEADING UP TO IT -
HERE'S WHERE THE LAW PLAYS A LONE HAND, KELLY - YOU STAY HERE - WHILE I GO IN AND DRAG HIM OUT.
IF YOU NEED HELP - CALL ME.
WELL, BRICK - WE LICKED THAT "CHILL," DID NT WE ?
Z
NO CULPRIT, NO BRICK KOP ?
NO CULPRIT NO BRICK KELLY
TO KELLY FROM "KELLY" - ET AL -
- MIT LUFF -
6-5
HERRIMAN

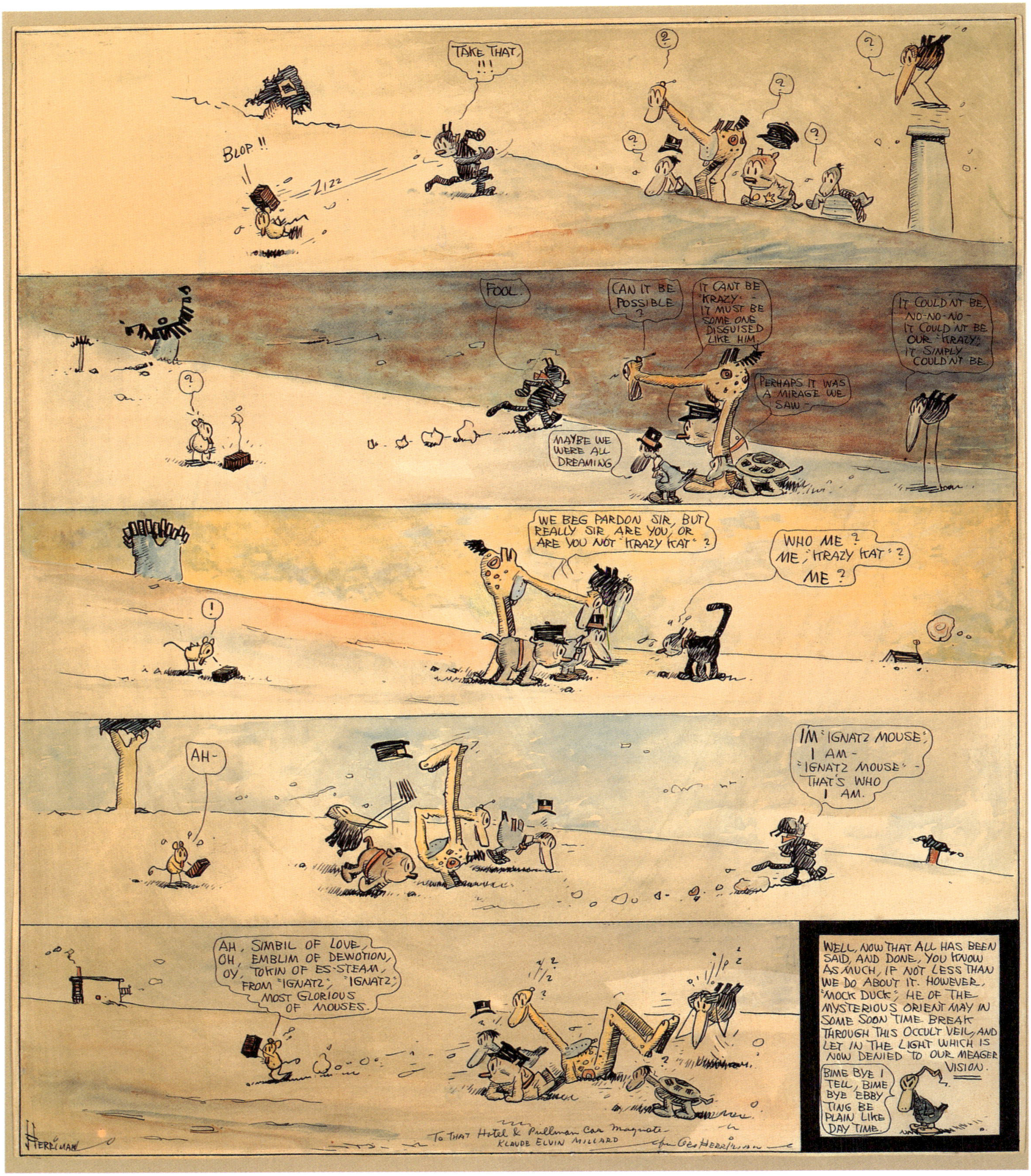
BLOP !!
ZIZZ
TAKE THAT !!!
FOOL.
CAN IT BE POSSIBLE ?
IT CANT BE "KRAZY" - IT MUST BE SOME ONE DISGUISED LIKE HIM.
PERHAPS IT WAS A MIRAGE WE SAW -
MAYBE WE WERE ALL DREAMING
IT COULD N'T BE, NO-NO-NO - IT COULD N'T BE OUR "KRAZY", IT SIMPLY COULD N'T BE.
WE BEG PARDON SIR, BUT REALLY SIR, ARE YOU, OR ARE YOU NOT "KRAZY KAT" ?
WHO ME ? ME, "KRAZY KAT" ? ME ?
AH-
I'M "IGNATZ MOUSE", I AM - "IGNATZ MOUSE" - THAT'S WHO I AM.
AH, SIMBIL OF LOVE, OH, EMBLIM OF DEWOTION, OY, TOKIN OF ES-STEAM, FROM "IGNATZ", "IGNATZ" MOST GLORIOUS OF MOUSES.
WELL, NOW THAT ALL HAS BEEN SAID, AND DONE, YOU KNOW AS MUCH, IF NOT LESS THAN WE DO ABOUT IT. HOWEVER, "MOCK DUCK", HE OF THE MYSTERIOUS ORIENT MAY IN SOME SOON TIME BREAK THROUGH THIS OCCULT VEIL, AND LET IN THE LIGHT WHICH IS NOW DENIED TO OUR MEAGER VISION.
BIME BYE I TELL, BIME BYE EBBY TING BE PLAIN LIKE DAY TIME.
HERRIMAN
To that Hotel & Pullman Car magnate KLAUDE ELVIN MILLARD fm Geo Herriman

ABOVE *Zizz—Blop!!* Turnabout is fair play. In the opening panel, Krazy throws a brick at Ignatz. "Take that!!" he exclaims. The inscription reads, "To that hotel & Pullman car magnate—Klaude Elvin Millard. From Geo. Herriman." September 9, 1917.

OPPOSITE June 4, 1944.

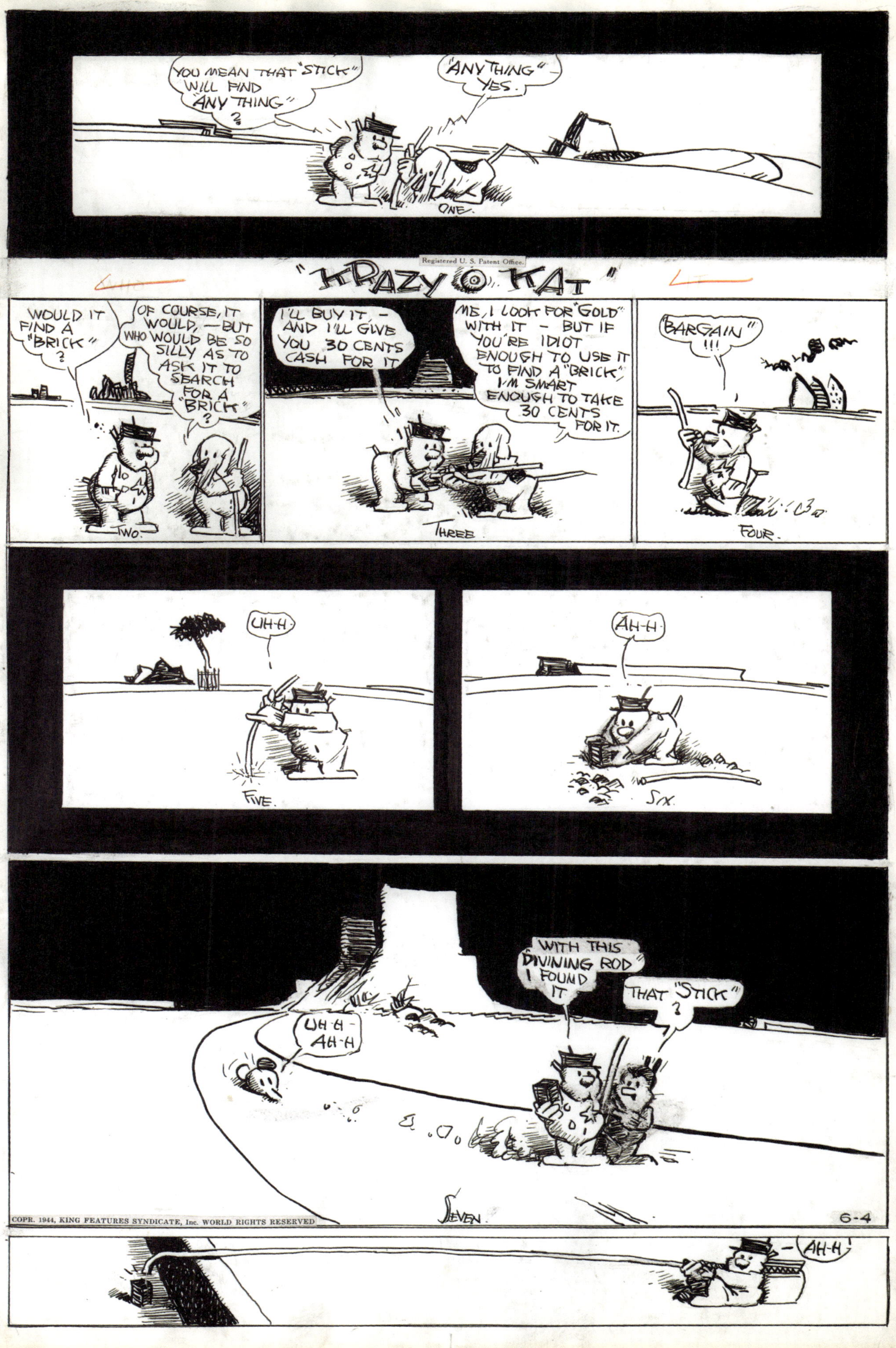
YOU MEAN THAT "STICK" WILL FIND "ANY THING" ?
"ANY THING" — YES.
ONE.
Registered U. S. Patent Office.
"KRAZY KAT"
WOULD IT FIND A "BRICK" ?
OF COURSE, IT WOULD, — BUT WHO WOULD BE SO SILLY AS TO ASK IT TO SEARCH FOR A "BRICK" ?
TWO.
I'LL BUY IT — AND I'LL GIVE YOU 30 CENTS CASH FOR IT
ME, I LOOK FOR "GOLD" WITH IT — BUT IF YOU'RE IDIOT ENOUGH TO USE IT TO FIND A "BRICK", I'M SMART ENOUGH TO TAKE 30 CENTS FOR IT.
THREE.
"BARGAIN" !!!
FOUR.
UH-H
FIVE.
AH-H
SIX.
WITH THIS "DIVINING ROD" I FOUND IT
THAT "STICK" ?
UH-H AH-H
SEVEN.
COPR. 1944, KING FEATURES SYNDICATE, Inc. WORLD RIGHTS RESERVED
6-4
AH-H

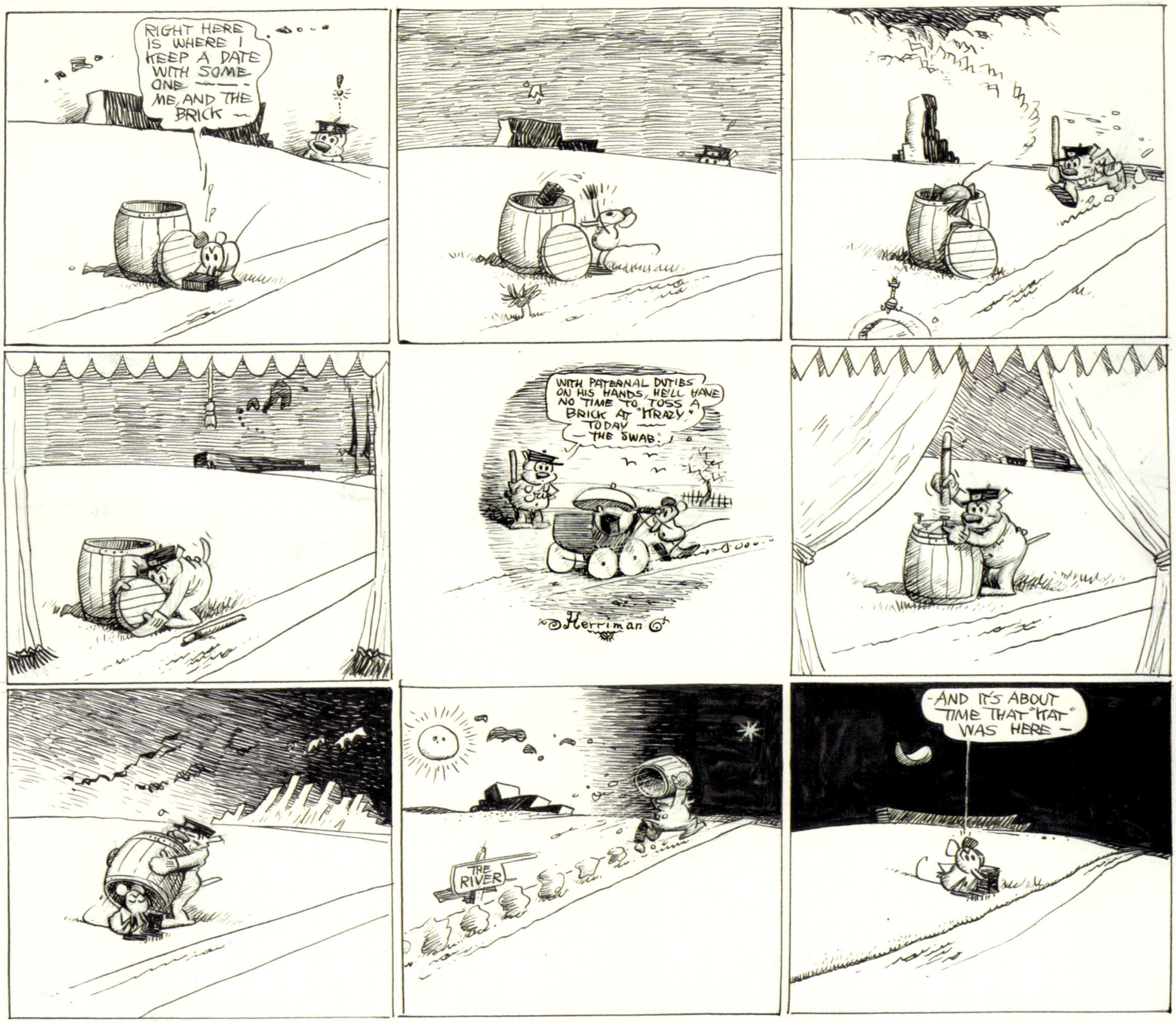
RIGHT HERE IS WHERE I KEEP A DATE WITH SOME ONE —— ME, AND THE BRICK —
WITH PATERNAL DUTIES ON HIS HANDS, HE'LL HAVE NO TIME TO TOSS A BRICK AT "KRAZY" TODAY — — THE SWAB.
Herriman
THE RIVER
AND IT'S ABOUT TIME THAT "KAT" WAS HERE —

ABOVE A number of comics art scholars concur that this undated piece is previously unpublished.

It's Krazy, I Tell You. KRAZY!
by Craig McCracken

To me the kraziest thing about George Herriman's comic masterpiece *Krazy Kat* is that it even exists in the first place. Sure I've spent countless hours staring at the dynamic compositions and energetic line work, asking myself, "How did he do this?" But the real question is: How did this happen? How did this shy, humble genius of a man get the freedom to sit holed up in the hills of Hollywood and unpretentiously create one of the most pure, sincere, and individual works of art in one of the most mainstream commercial media ever?

It's Krazy, I tell you. KRAZY!

I was asked, as an animator, to write down my thoughts on *Krazy Kat*. This was a bit tough as I can't really tell where the animator in me ends and the cartoonist begins. And the world is chock-full of cartoonists singing the praises of Herriman. You just say "Krazy Kat" to a cartoonist and we all bow our heads and sigh in humble reverence. So I figured I could tackle this thing by looking at it not as an animator/cartoonist, but as someone who works in another, very commercial medium: television.

TV is no different than most businesses. The goal is to get everyone to buy what you're selling and *not* buy what the other guy is selling. The same can be said about the comics section of the newspaper, especially in Herriman's time. The comics page was one of the main visual entertainment media of the day, and it was the cartoonist's job to move as many rags as they could. The more relatable, accessible, and sellable a strip was, the more papers you sold and the more money was made. Just like TV is today. The game's the same, just the technology is different.

In an industry where money and art are far apart, how did this very noncommercial, incredibly artistic strip get produced without an ounce of creative compromise? Like TV executives today, the editors and publishers had a hand in the strips they were paying for. For instance, a one-off character in *Thimble Theatre* steps in, says, "Ja think I'm a cowboy?" and *POW*, he connected with the readers so hard that editors had to give top billing to Popeye the Sailor. To help boost readership in a strip about cars, an editor suggested that Walt Wallet find an orphaned baby on his doorstep and *Gasoline Alley* was never the same again. Even when good ol' Sparky Schulz wanted to call his li'l folks *Li'l Folks,* an editor said nuts to that and (good grief) called it *Peanuts*. And in 1916 when an animated *Krazy Kat* made its debut on the silver screen, it was changed to be more like the popular

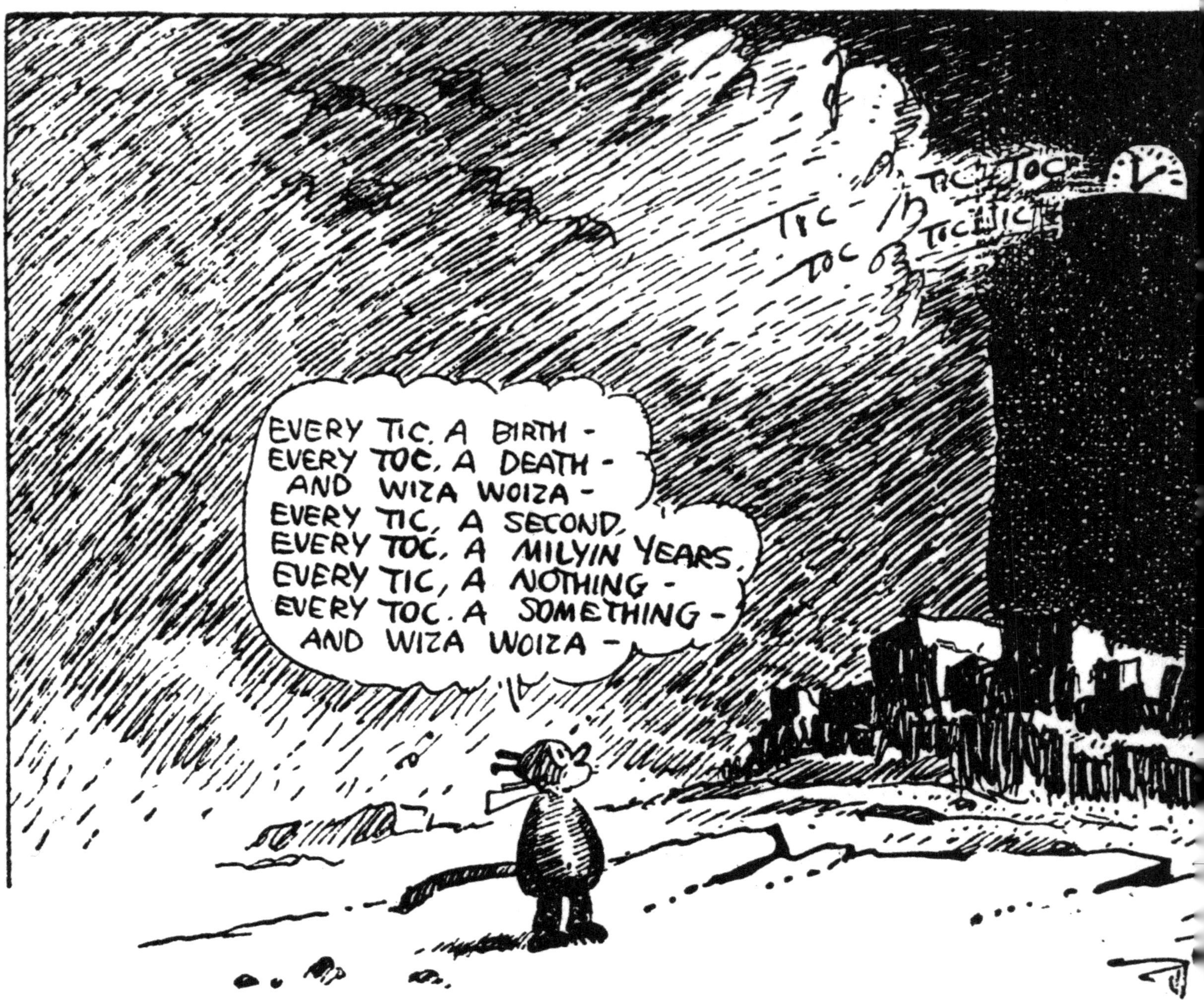
TIC TOC
TIC TIC
TOC
EVERY TIC, A BIRTH -
EVERY TOC, A DEATH -
AND WIZA WOIZA -
EVERY TIC, A SECOND,
EVERY TOC, A MILYIN YEARS,
EVERY TIC, A NOTHING -
EVERY TOC. A SOMETHING -
AND WIZA WOIZA -

animated fare of the day than the strip that shares its name.

How did *Krazy* the comic strip not get krazy notes?

Was it because it was recognized by editors and the public as a brilliant and groundbreaking graphic mantra on life and love?

No. From everything I've read on the subject, most people didn't get it. Truth be told, one hundred years later some people still don't get it. Here was a weird strip that repeated the same joke over and over. It went from day to night and back to day all in a matter of three panels. He turns into she and she into he. Cacti keep coming and going. And aul da weerd poetik lengwage wuz spelld aul wrung. *Krazy* konfused a lot of people and in turn frustrated a lot of editors, who wanted to kancel the strip entirely.

But luckily not everyone felt this way. As the story goes, the strip got a lot of praise from highfalutin artistic types, which made Herriman's boss, William Randolph Hearst, feel highfalutin and artistic, too. So he gave Herriman a lifetime contract.

That's KRAZY!

Can you imagine that happening today? In a world where creative success is determined in a matter of days or even over a weekend, the thought of a TV or movie executive giving an artist a lifetime contract just because *some* of the people liked the artist's stuff is unheard of. It just doesn't happen. But fortunately for George Herriman, and most fortunately for us, it did.

Like I said in the beginning, the kraziest thing about *Krazy Kat* is that it exists in the first place. For thirty-plus years ol' man Herriman got to do what he wanted to do as he doodled down the daily dealings of the denizens who dwelled in dear ol' Coconino County, without the fear of being dumped.

So let's hear it for George Herriman, the patron saint of kartoonists! Whether he realized it or not,

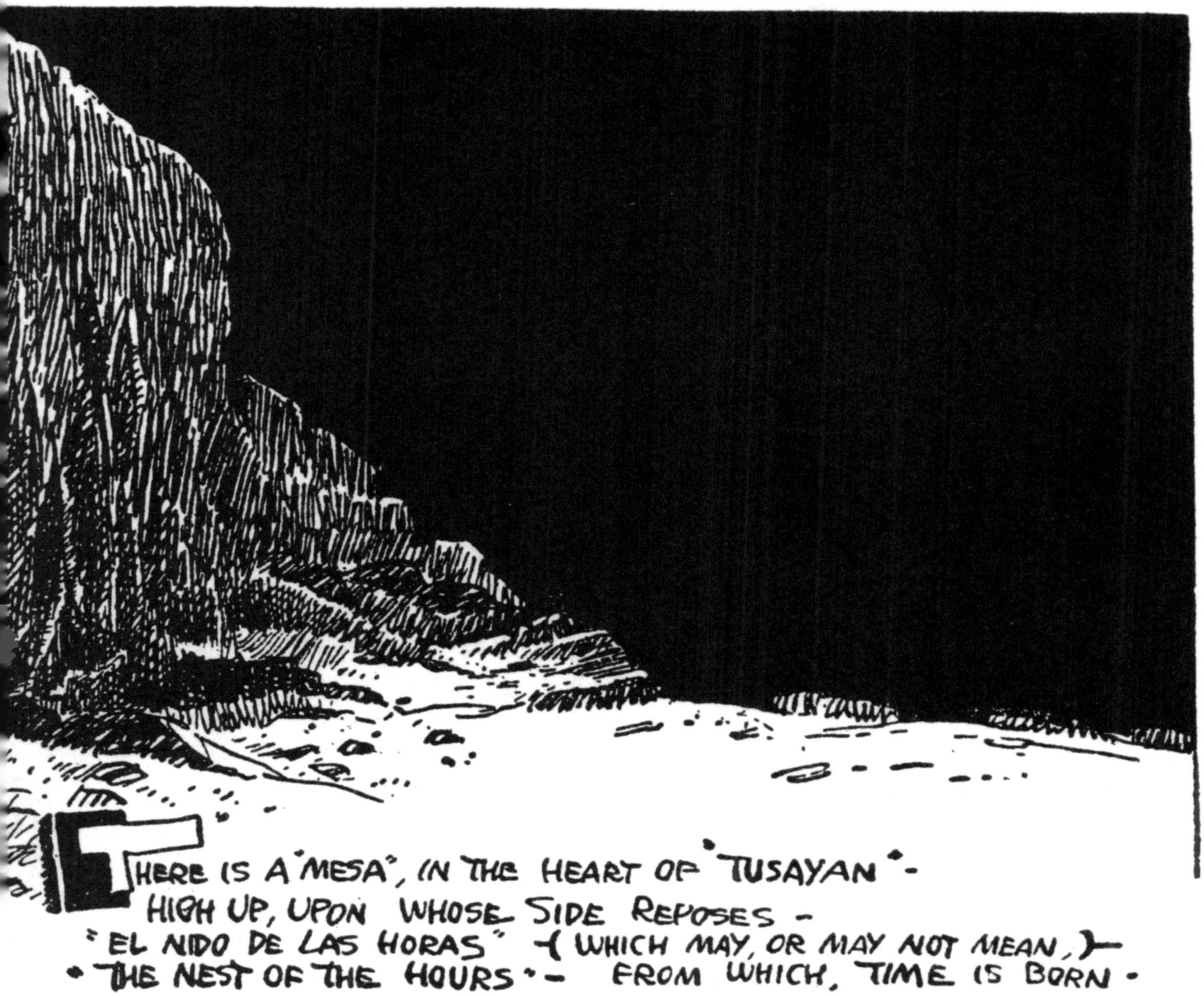
THERE IS A "MESA", IN THE HEART OF "TUSAYAN" -
HIGH UP, UPON WHOSE SIDE REPOSES -
"EL NIDO DE LAS HORAS" -(WHICH MAY, OR MAY NOT MEAN,)-
"THE NEST OF THE HOURS" - FROM WHICH, TIME IS BORN.

this modest and unassuming artist, with pen in hand, totally took down and slayed the Man! He beat the system, and kreated something so kool, so klever, so unkompromised that whenever you kome in kontact with it, it'll hit you like a ton of bricks!

Craig McCracken is the Emmy Award–winning creator/producer of the Cartoon Network series The Powerpuff Girls *and* Foster's Home for Imaginary Friends. *He lives in the Hollywood Hills with his wife, Lauren Faust, two dogs, one cat, fifteen fish, and one amazing view of George Herriman's house.*

Kat-Toons

Krazy Kat had many incarnations in the field of animation. Silent shorts were produced in the 1910s by Hearst's International Film Service (IFS) and then taken over by John Bray. In the mid-1920s, Bill Nolan animated a version of Krazy Kat that looked like the justly popular Felix the Cat. These cartoons, distributed by Margaret J. Winkler, were later produced by her husband, Charles B. Mintz, for Paramount and, later, Columbia Pictures. By this time in the 1930s, Krazy Kat looked more like Mickey Mouse, both in his appearance and personality.

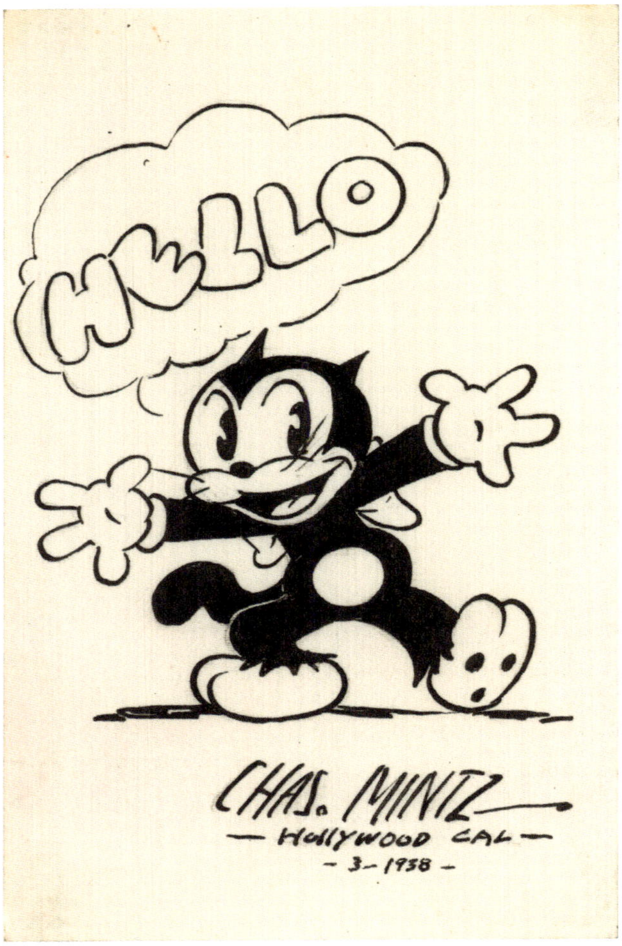
HELLO
CHAS. MINTZ
— HOLLYWOOD CAL —
- 3-1938 -

ABOVE A previously unpublished specialty drawing dated March 1938 and signed by Charles Mintz, although probably drawn by one of his animators.

OPPOSITE, TOP LEFT Packaging, not drawn by Herriman, for two 16mm *Krazy Kat* short animated cartoons.

OPPOSITE, TOP RIGHT A trade advertisement for M. J. Winkler's animated series. The artwork is attributed to Jack King. 1925.

OPPOSITE, BOTTOM; OVERLEAF Film industry ads for the Columbia Pictures *Krazy Kat* cartoons. Circa 1929.

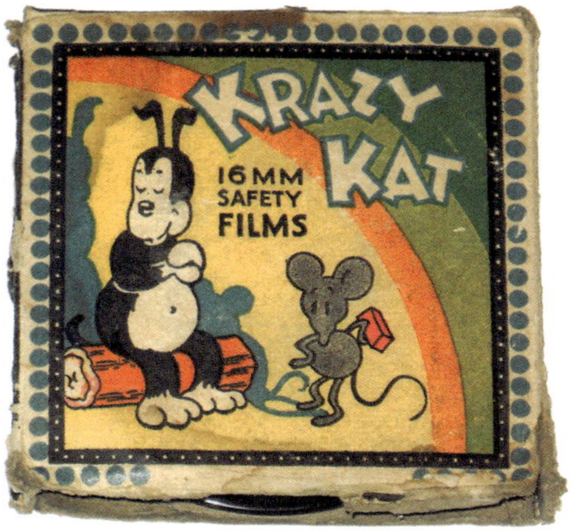
KRAZY KAT
16MM SAFETY FILMS

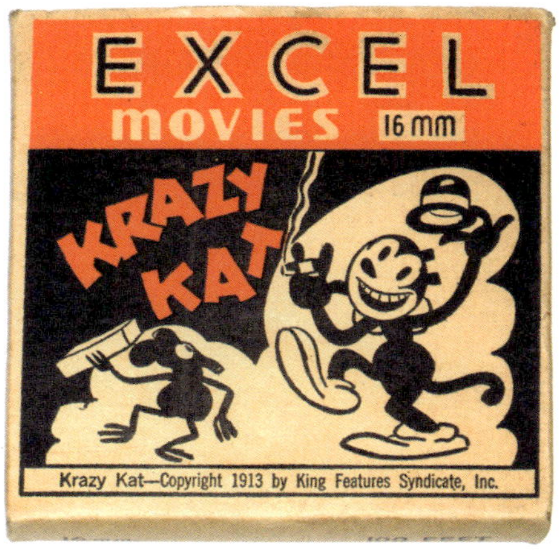
EXCEL
movies 16mm
KRAZY KAT
Krazy Kat—Copyright 1913 by King Features Syndicate, Inc.

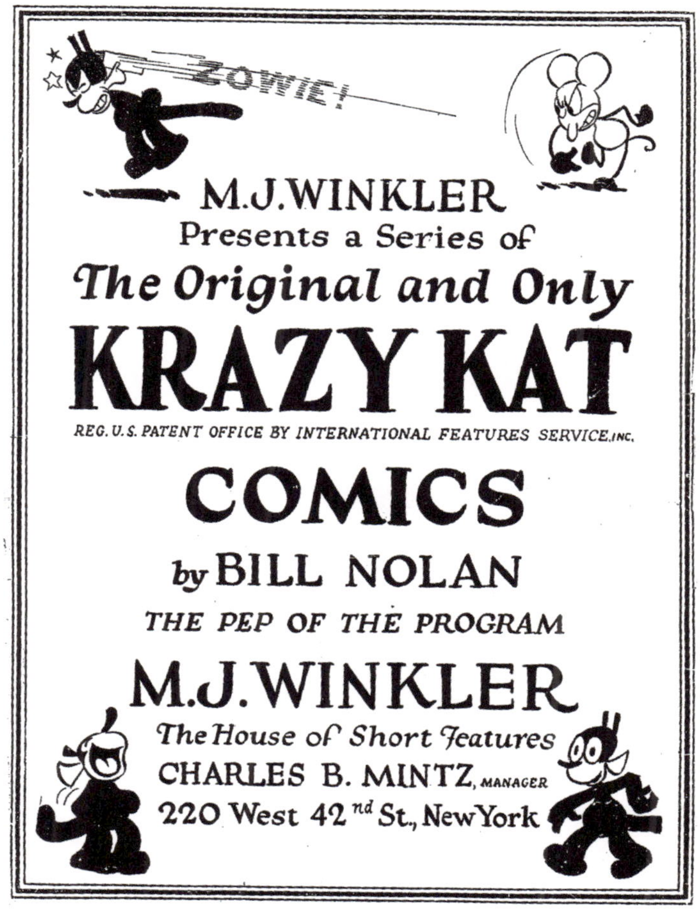
ZOWIE!
M.J.WINKLER
Presents a Series of
The Original and Only
KRAZY KAT
REG. U.S. PATENT OFFICE BY INTERNATIONAL FEATURES SERVICE, INC.
COMICS
by BILL NOLAN
THE PEP OF THE PROGRAM
M.J.WINKLER
The House of Short Features
CHARLES B. MINTZ, MANAGER
220 West 42nd St., New York

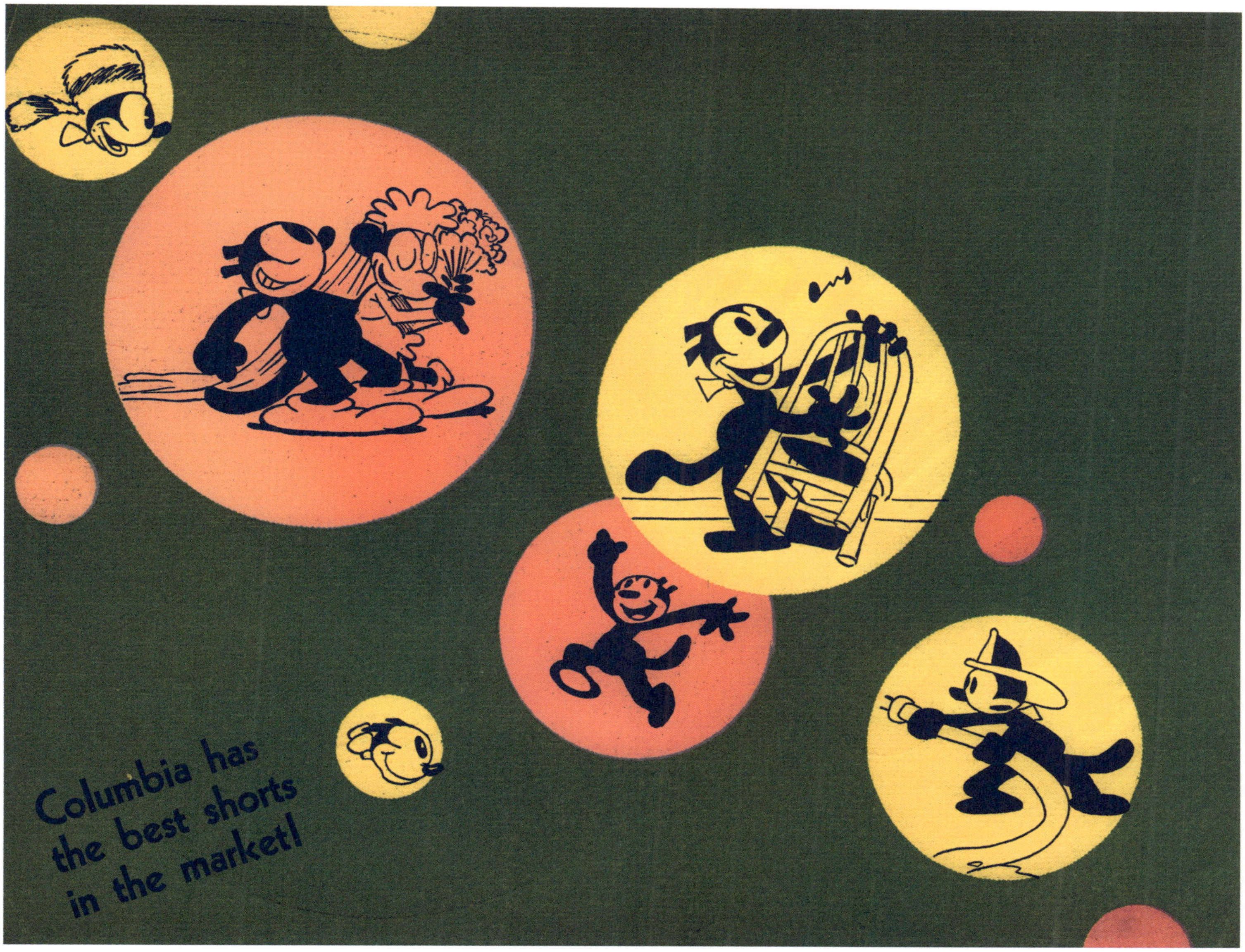
Columbia has the best shorts in the market!

13 KRAZY KAT

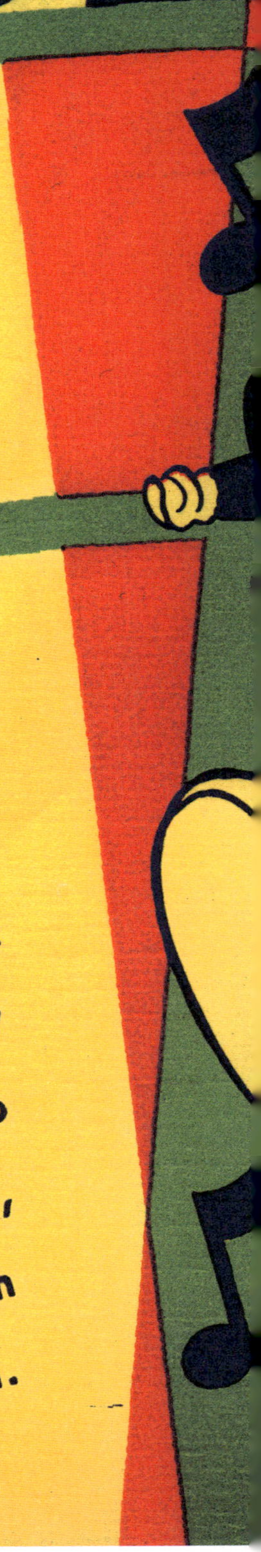

The Columbia short subject line-up would hardly be complete without Krazy Kat, a prime favorite among the rabid followers of the talking cartoons. Different from Mickey Mouse and the Silly Symphonies in technique, but no less novel and entertaining, Krazy Kat is a sure enough box-office attraction.

A Winkler Product

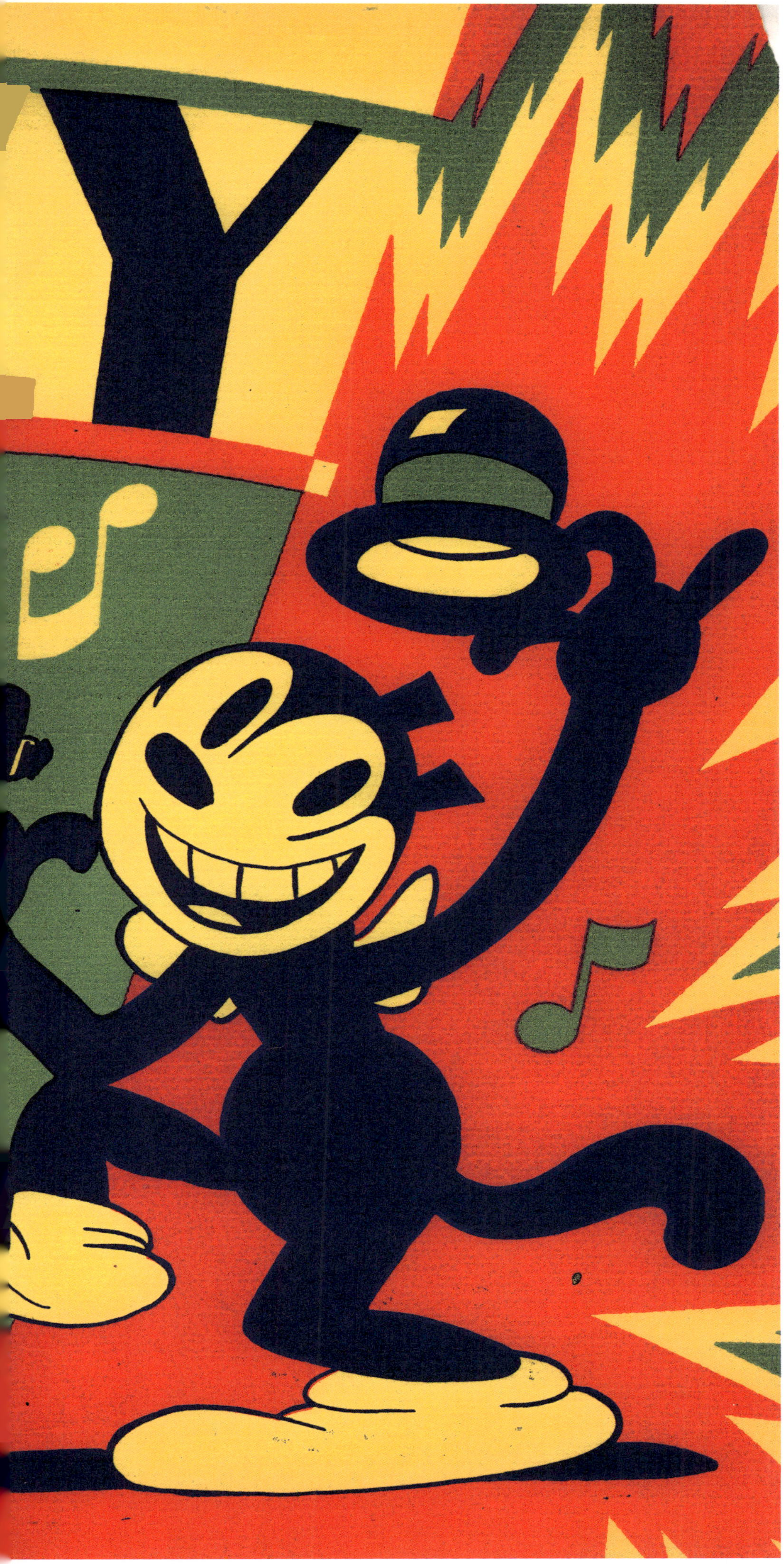

LEFT This Kat is smokin'! More Felix or Mickey than Krazy, but fascinating and charming nonetheless.

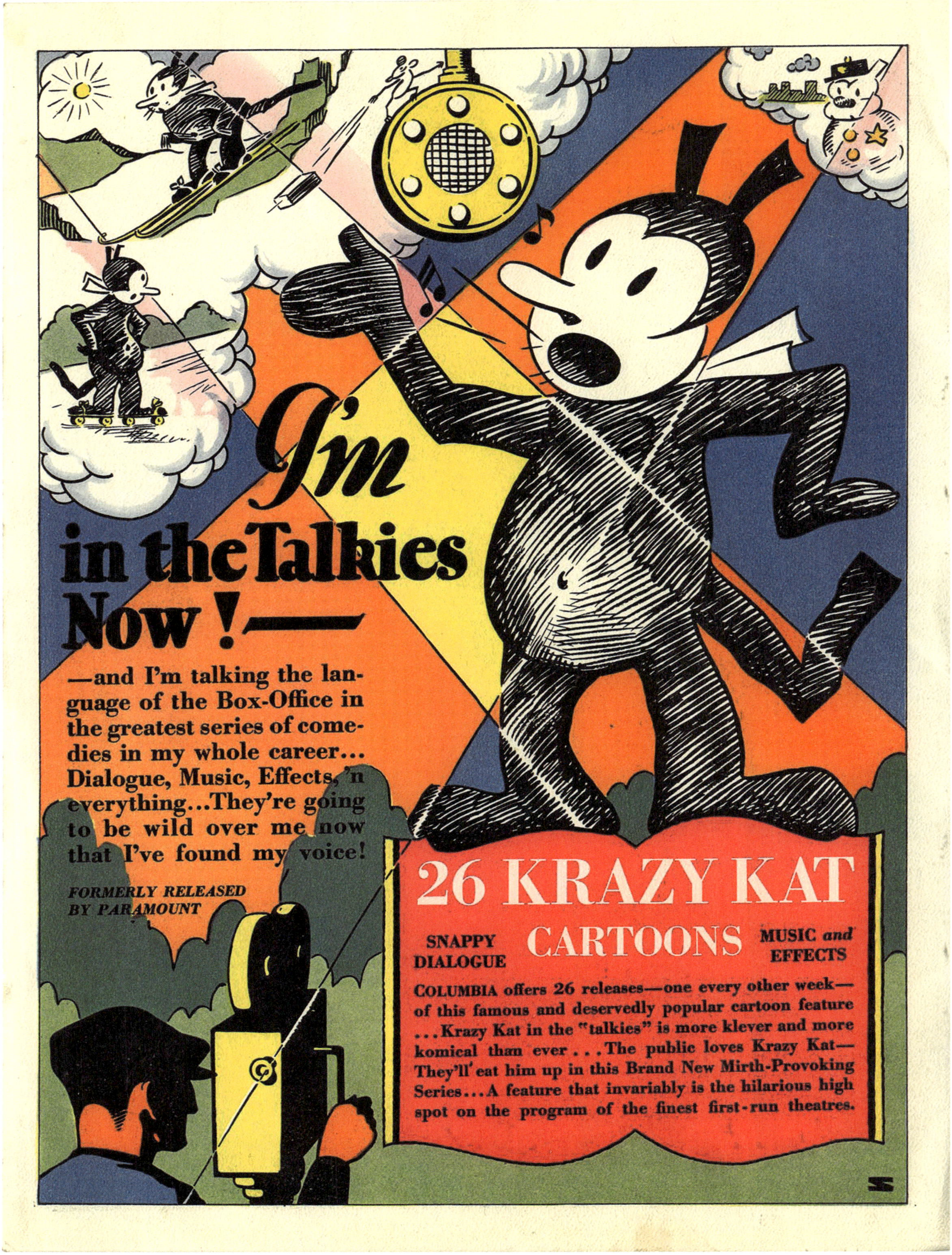
I'm in the Talkies Now!—
—and I'm talking the language of the Box-Office in the greatest series of comedies in my whole career... Dialogue, Music, Effects, 'n everything...They're going to be wild over me now that I've found my voice!
FORMERLY RELEASED BY PARAMOUNT
26 KRAZY KAT CARTOONS
SNAPPY DIALOGUE
MUSIC and EFFECTS
COLUMBIA offers 26 releases—one every other week—of this famous and deservedly popular cartoon feature ...Krazy Kat in the "talkies" is more klever and more komical than ever...The public loves Krazy Kat—They'll eat him up in this Brand New Mirth-Provoking Series...A feature that invariably is the hilarious high spot on the program of the finest first-run theatres.

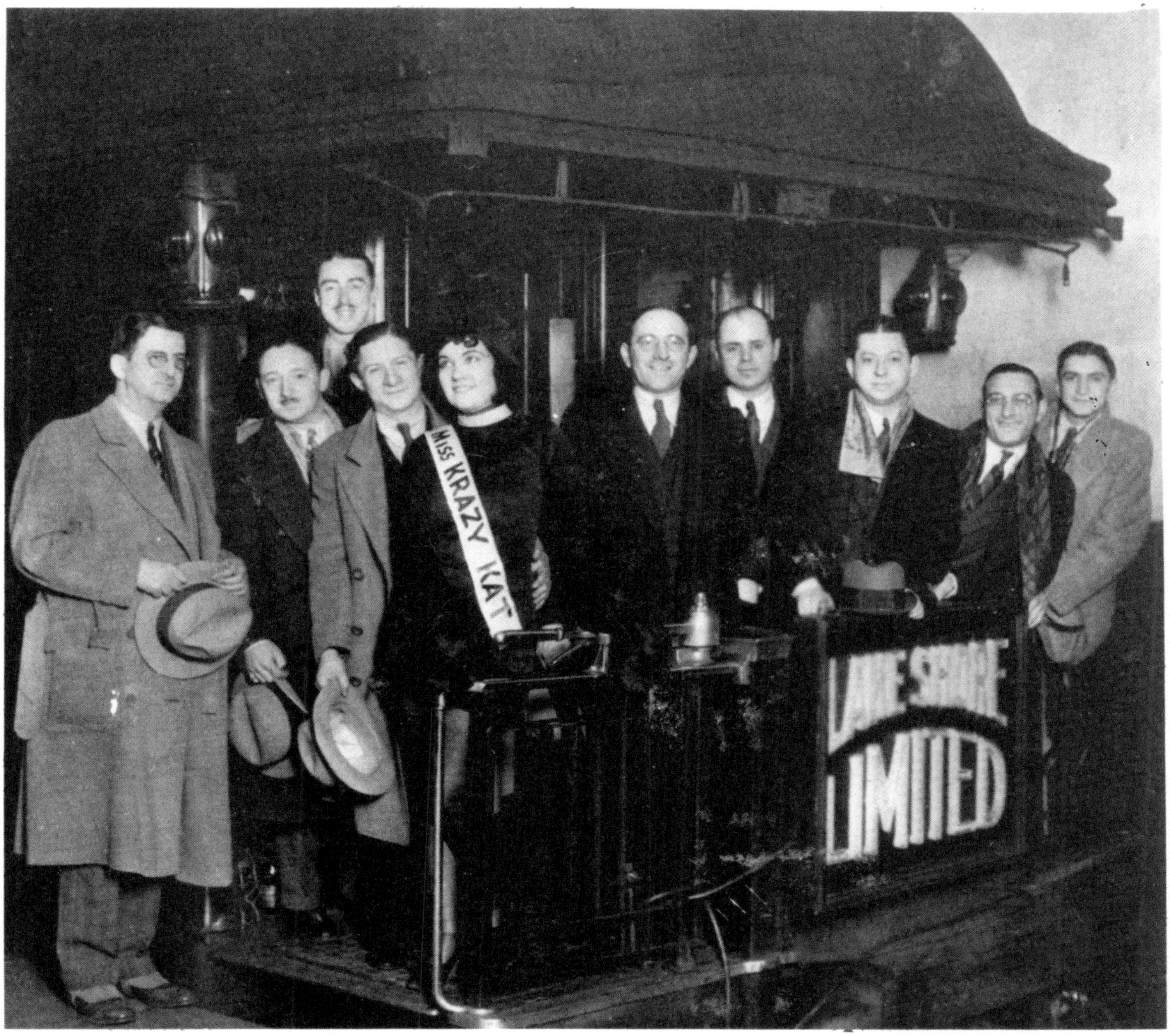
Miss KRAZY KAT
LAKE SHORE
LIMITED

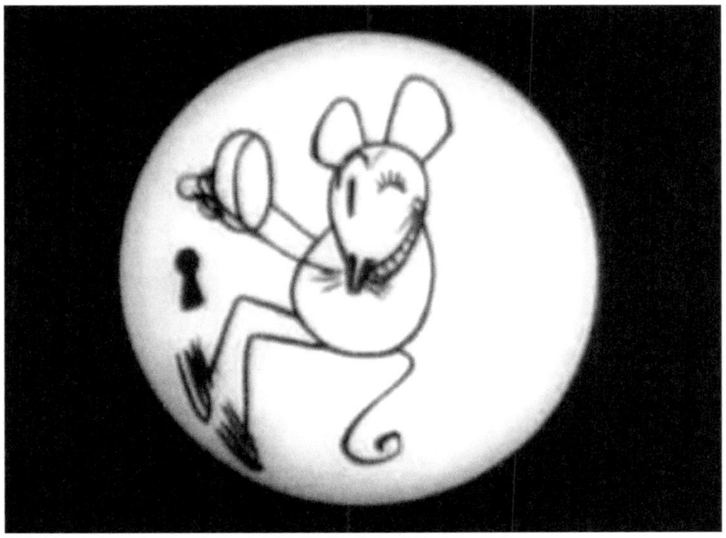

OPPOSITE This industry ad by Columbia showcases a much more Herriman-looking Krazy Kat. 1930s.

ABOVE The staff of the Charles Mintz Studio leaving New York to go to California in 1930. From left to right: Charles Mintz, Al Rose, Jack Carr, Jimmy Bronis, Miss Krazy Kat, Ben Harrison, Art Davis, Manny Gould, Joe DeNat, and Harry Love.

LEFT A screenshot from *At the Circus,* 1916.

OVERLEAF A poster for the cartoon *Krazy Kat in Wedding Bells*, 1932.

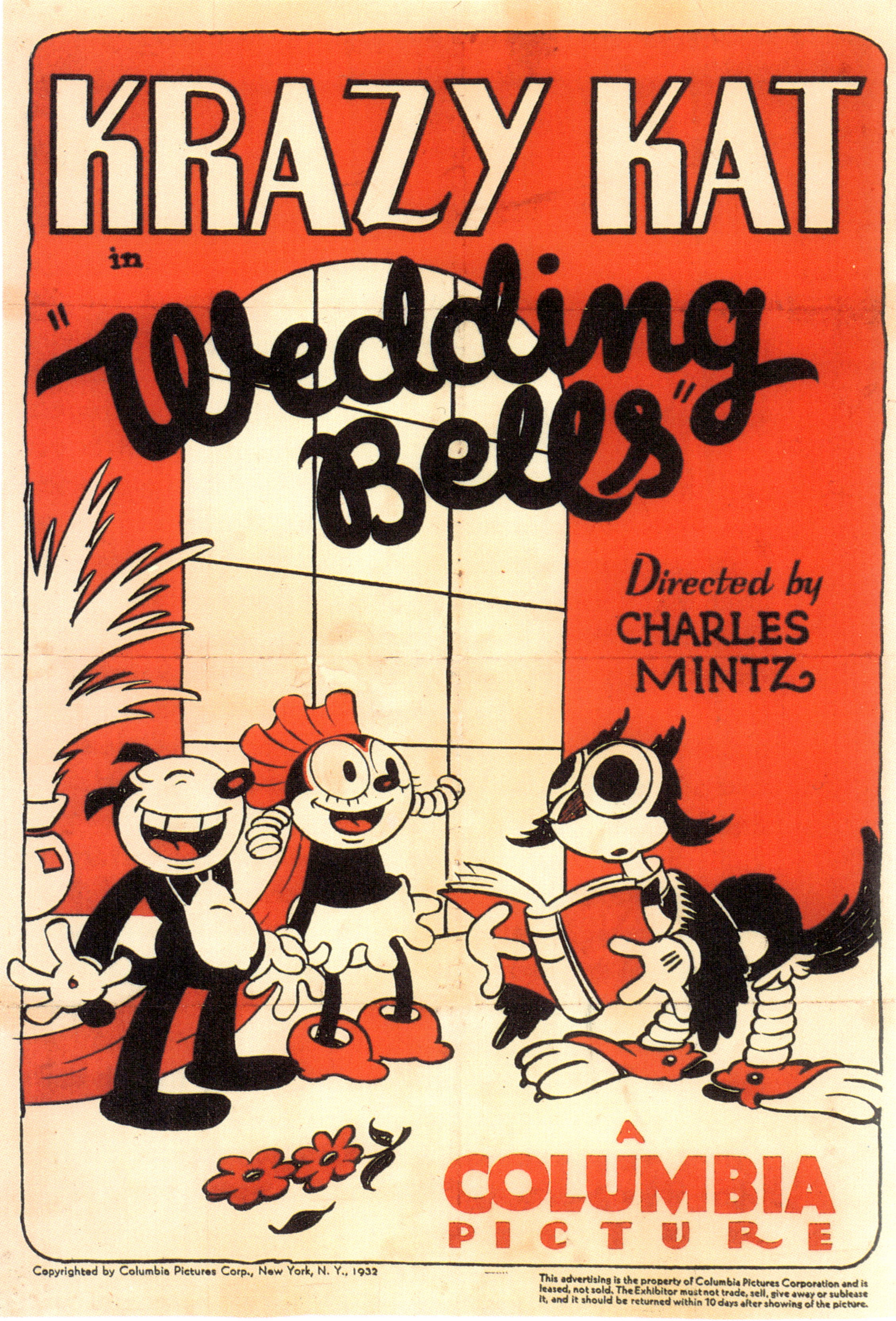
KRAZY KAT
in
"Wedding Bells"
Directed by
CHARLES MINTZ
A
COLUMBIA
PICTURE
Copyrighted by Columbia Pictures Corp., New York, N. Y., 1932
This advertising is the property of Columbia Pictures Corporation and is leased, not sold. The Exhibitor must not trade, sell, give away or sublease it, and it should be returned within 10 days after showing of the picture.

KKKKRRRAaaaAZZZEEEEE!
An Appreciation of Krazy Kat by Someone Who Doesn't Know What He's Talking About

by Richard Thompson

Krazy Kat himself is made of inky hatched zigzags, like comic black electricity, that are barely contained by his outline. His tail, or "caudal appendage," twitches with the nervous energy of a cat, curling and hooking and straightening to show his mood, or hanging at a lazy angle to balance his cantilevered, curious posture. The little bits of ribbon that stand behind his bent ears are like residual antennae. Krazy's face is a rubbery clown's mask. Unless he's in full voice or singing, his mouth is hidden under his blunt muzzle and little peg nose. His eyes are two expressive ink slashes that regard the unfolding astonishments of his world with wonder and also a kind of grave trust.

Ignatz Mouse is pinched together out of two lumps of ugly pink putty. His limbs, which had started out long and spidery then gradually shortened, are made of wiry scratches. Likewise his hairless tail. The little egg of his head with its sausage nose is like a clenched fist that's giving you the finger. His furious little eyes are set close together. This lessens his depth perception but doesn't seem to affect his aim, and may help him focus his monomania.

Offissa Pupp is solid, built of bricks and mortar like his jail. Like Krazy, his face is a simple mask, jowlier and thicker, most often registering bafflement, disapprobation, and the loyalty and devotion of his kind. His cop's uniform and little white gloves are part of his pelt, and he removes his cap mostly to scratch his head. He has a little bellybuttoned potbelly, as do Krazy and Ignatz, but while theirs give them just enough ballast for gravity to hold onto, his is fatter and gives him real weight. His tail isn't much but he does have a little truncheon, which works well for flourishing and gesturing and for clubbing heads, specifically Ignatz's.

George Herriman renders this trio with all the vivacity and sympathy his virtuoso pen can muster. Herriman was a quiet man who must have watched the world closely and listened carefully. His eye was sharp and his ear was unerring, but his drawing hand was sublime. A hugely prolific cartoonist, Herriman produced quantities of drawings for the various papers that employed him: editorial illustrations, caricatures, dingbats, comic panels, one-shot strips, and finally, daily strips, of which he launched several dozen. He worked very much in the bigfoot style of the day, with casts of characters drawn from racetracks, saloons, Dickens, vaudeville, and the stereotypes common to the early 1900s.

This was the early morning of the newspaper cartoon, especially the comic strip, where vast fields of newsprint were there for the filling, and editors let a

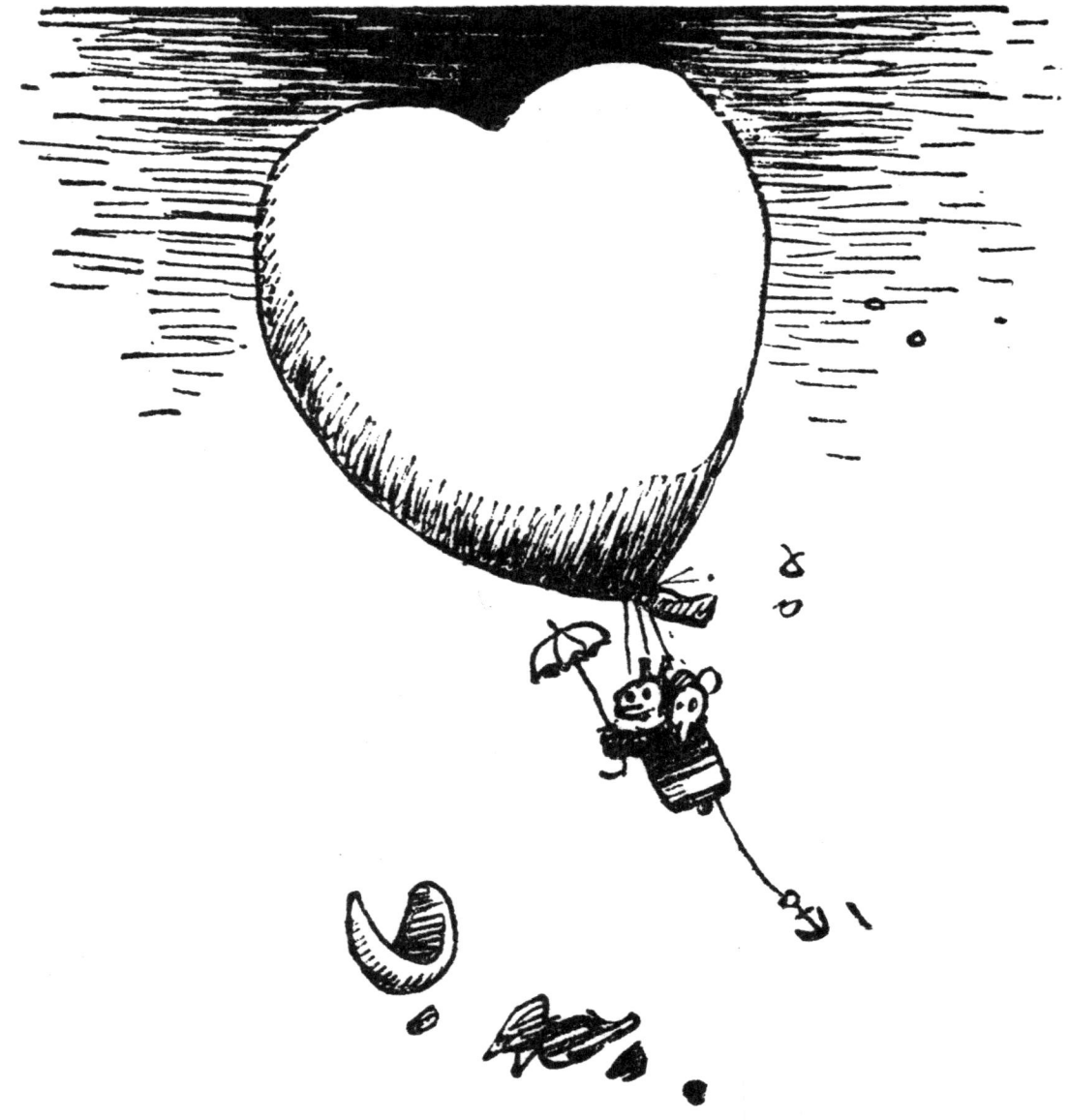

cartoonist loose on the page to fill it the best he could. Experimentation must've been easier then, with so much unexplored territory. In the same way that a silent film comedian could take a ladder, a bucket, a few stooges, and a likely notion onto a set and produce in an afternoon a one-reeler of ingenious split-second slapstick, a cartoonist working his eight-hour day in a newspaper bullpen could let his imagination run riot over his bristol board and produce something just as ingenious. If the comic showed promise or popularity it might win a daily spot on the page.

Krazy Kat is a wonder of improvisation. Some comic strips are launched more or less fully formed, their premise and characters obvious from the first strip published, and the gradual and inevitable changes wrought over the years only bring them into greater focus. When a proto-Shermy, after our first glimpse of Charlie Brown, says, "How I hate him," you have some idea of what *Peanuts* is about, and expect the worst for poor Charlie. Or when Calvin first catches his tiger with a tuna fish sandwich, you get the feeling it's the beginning of a beautiful friendship. Other strips grow almost by accident, leaving a paper trail and showing their work, evolving by the natural spontaneity of a cartoonist's imagination.

Krazy is much the latter. It started small under the Dingbat family's floorboards as an afterthought, a tangential doodle, a little piece of absurdity. A runty mouse throws a rock at an innocent cat who looks surprised. The little long-faced beribboned cat's appearance underfoot at the Dingbats' was not his first bow on the comics page. Herriman had drawn him several times before, here and there, and the cat must've spent some time in the wings of Herriman's mind awaiting a more fulfilling role. *The Dingbat Family* was Herriman's first venture into the domestic strip, and the cast is enjoyable but also easily upstaged, first by their strange and unseen neighbors upstairs and then by the cat and mouse who show up to torment him. It's almost axiomatic of comic strips that a sufficiently engaging talking animal will unbalance a strip and upstage any character who is merely human. Let loose a good-talking cat or self-aware dog and no one's safe. And this Kat talks like no one else, and everybody else at the same time, an endless mishmash of phoneticisms, slang, and whole slews of regional patois.

Herriman gradually assembled his little cast of mouse, cat, and dog and with offhanded ingenuity plotted the fraught and ironic tensions of their relationships. The cat, the free spirit, loves the mouse, the cynical anarchist, and the proper, bourgeois dog loves the cat and violently disapproves of the mouse, who violently disapproves of the cat's affections. This tightly wound paradox is a lovely conceit for a daily strip. Few media are as amenable to repetition as a daily comic strip, where familiarity breeds affection. The cat, dog, and mouse form a triangle whose asymmetry propels the strip, fueled by the trajectory of the brick. The brick, Ignatz's precious projectile, is a symbol of love, probably, but only Krazy recognizes that. To Pupp it's an illegal weapon that Ignatz had better drop right now, and to Ignatz it's an expression of contempt, which is his great tragedy. He'll never know, materialistic little realist that he is, why Krazy is so ecstatic to see that brick in flight toward his head.

Like a patient nature photographer who places his camera in some remote spot, Herriman catches the behavior of these shy species. They are always shown full-figure, center stage in the panel. Having simplified his essential plot, Herriman simplifies his drawings. *Krazy Kat* is often described as surreal, but it's closer to abstraction. Herriman's beloved Coconino County is rendered in patterns and vast areas of black, all deftly balanced among the panels without darkening the tone of the strip. If the cast shadows tell right, the sun shines most brightly on Coconino when the sky is inkiest black.

Herriman's inked line has a spring and tensile strength and character that delights the eye no end. It slides across the page with the grace of an art deco decoration, then develops a comic wiggle, bends and multiplies into combs and lattices of crosshatching. It describes a horizon line, a ragged fluff of clouds and, making the air visible, the trajectory of a brick or the radiation of Ignatz's frustration. And best of all it wraps around the strange oblongs and rhomboids of his ever posturing characters. Yet for all its grace and control, Herriman's line has enough offhanded scratchiness to it to suggest that the focus is several inches deep into the paper's surface, and to remind you that ink is a liquid medium.

With the characters carefully placed at center, the surroundings suddenly spring to life. From panel to panel, mesas erode and reform as houses, trees spring up from pots, bristle into cacti, then lengthen into broomsticks, and on and on. Most all of nature comes to antic life in the strip's unfolding; the moon flies overhead in various phases, night falls in a shower of window shades, and the wild weather that blows across the desert possesses a personality. For all the depth of focus and the roads that disappear into the horizon, the landscape also has the feel of an interior; the distant mesas and mountains are just a bit of fringe and a chintz pattern away from becoming some of the lumpier contemporary furniture. To push the tension between the natural and artificial even further, *Krazy Kat* will suddenly display the accoutrements of theater: curtains part, scrims descend, and footlights rise up, then a deliriously unnecessary "Intermission" sign appears in an ornate frame.

Finally, of course, the whole form of the strip itself quickens to life. Panels shake loose of the grid and wander at will, piling up here and there or dropping in where they're least wanted, like one of Joe Stork's babies. For all the seeming randomness and whimsicality, Herriman's pages hold together with the sturdiness of beautiful brickwork. His playful virtuosity in juggling these elements and keeping things coherent and moving at speed is his greatest accomplishment. With it he ties together all the parts of his strip, drawing, character, language, and theme, and made *Krazy Kat* the greatest comic strip yet created.

Richard Thompson draws the daily syndicated comic strip Cul de Sac *and the weekly cartoon* Richard's Poor Almanack. *He wrote and drew a comic strip introduction to* Barney Google: Gambling, Horse Races, and High Toned Women! *(IDW/Yoe Books, 2010). As much as Thompson loves* Krazy Kat, *he had trouble writing an essay that didn't contain the word* poetry, *but in the end he managed it.*

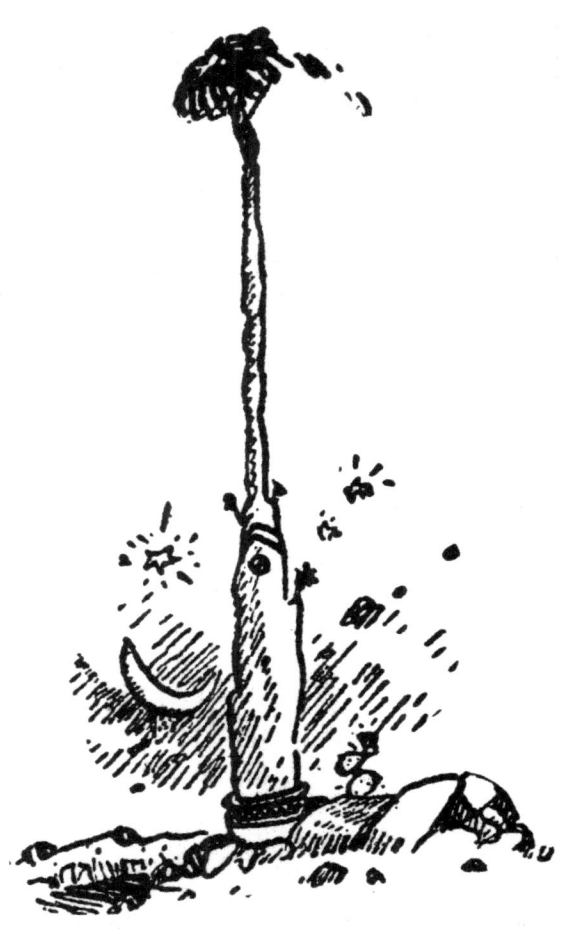

The Fine Art of Cartooning

Herriman created beautiful ink-and-watercolor paintings to be given as gifts, sometimes handmaking the mats and frames himself.

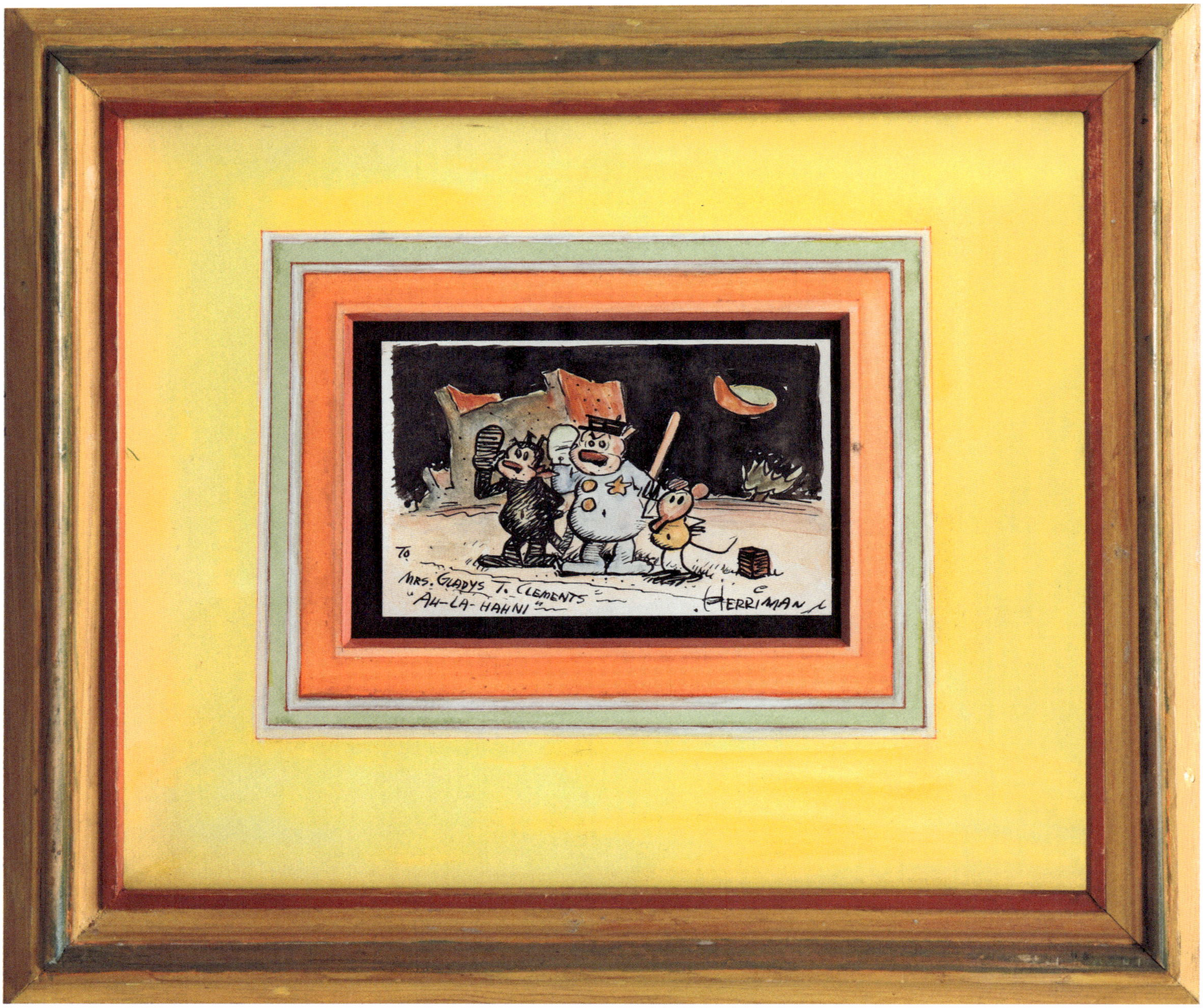
To
Mrs. Gladys T. Clements
"Ah-La-Hahni"
Herriman

ABOVE Ink and watercolor inscribed, "To Mrs. Gladys T. Clements 'Ah-La-Hahni.'"

OPPOSITE Herriman's largest known painting, created on a window shade. It measures approximately 30 inches by 44 inches.

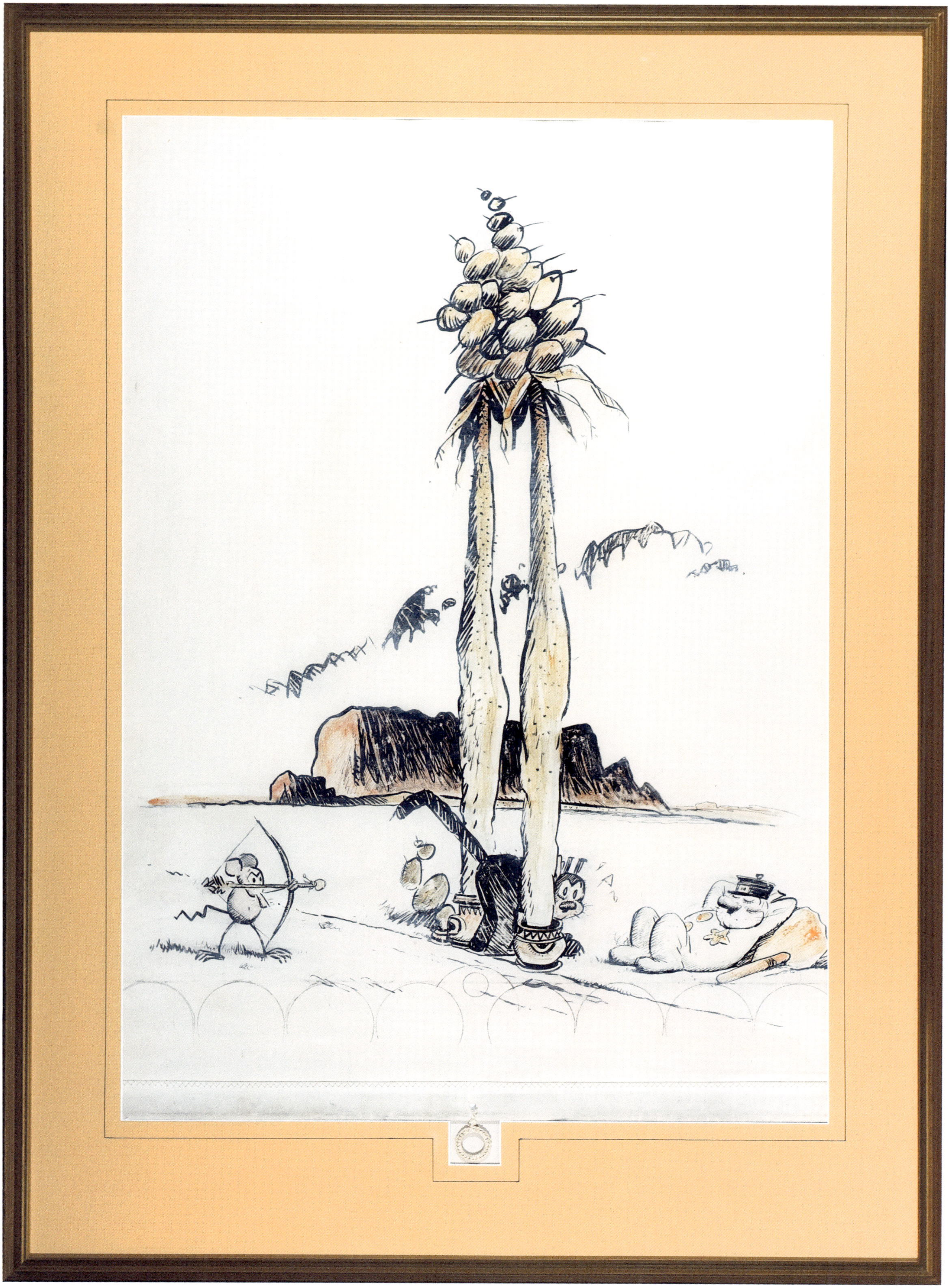

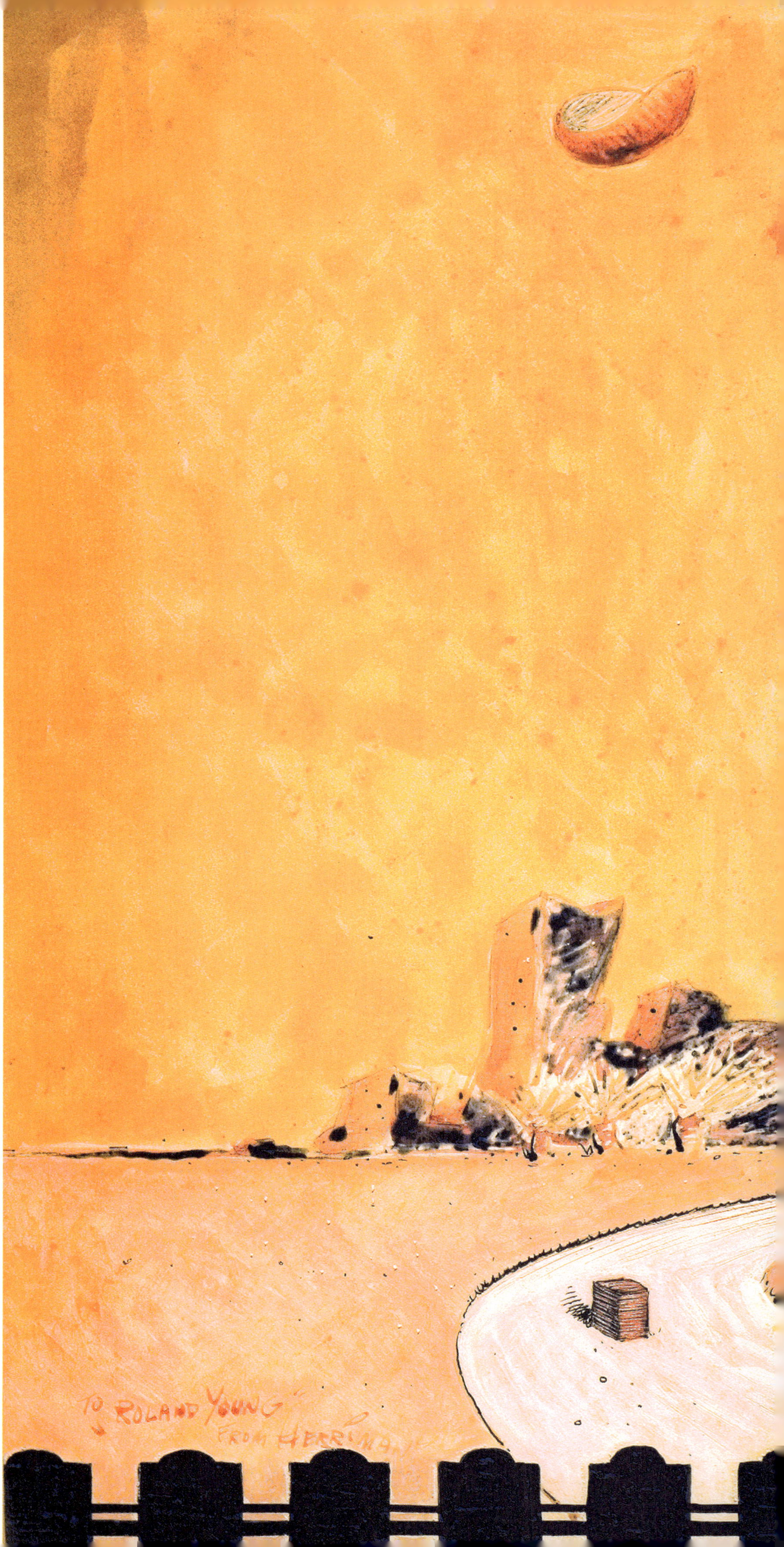
TO ROLAND YOUNG
FROM HERRIMAN

RIGHT A previously unpublished painting George Herriman created for his friend Roland Young, who starred in the *Topper* movies.

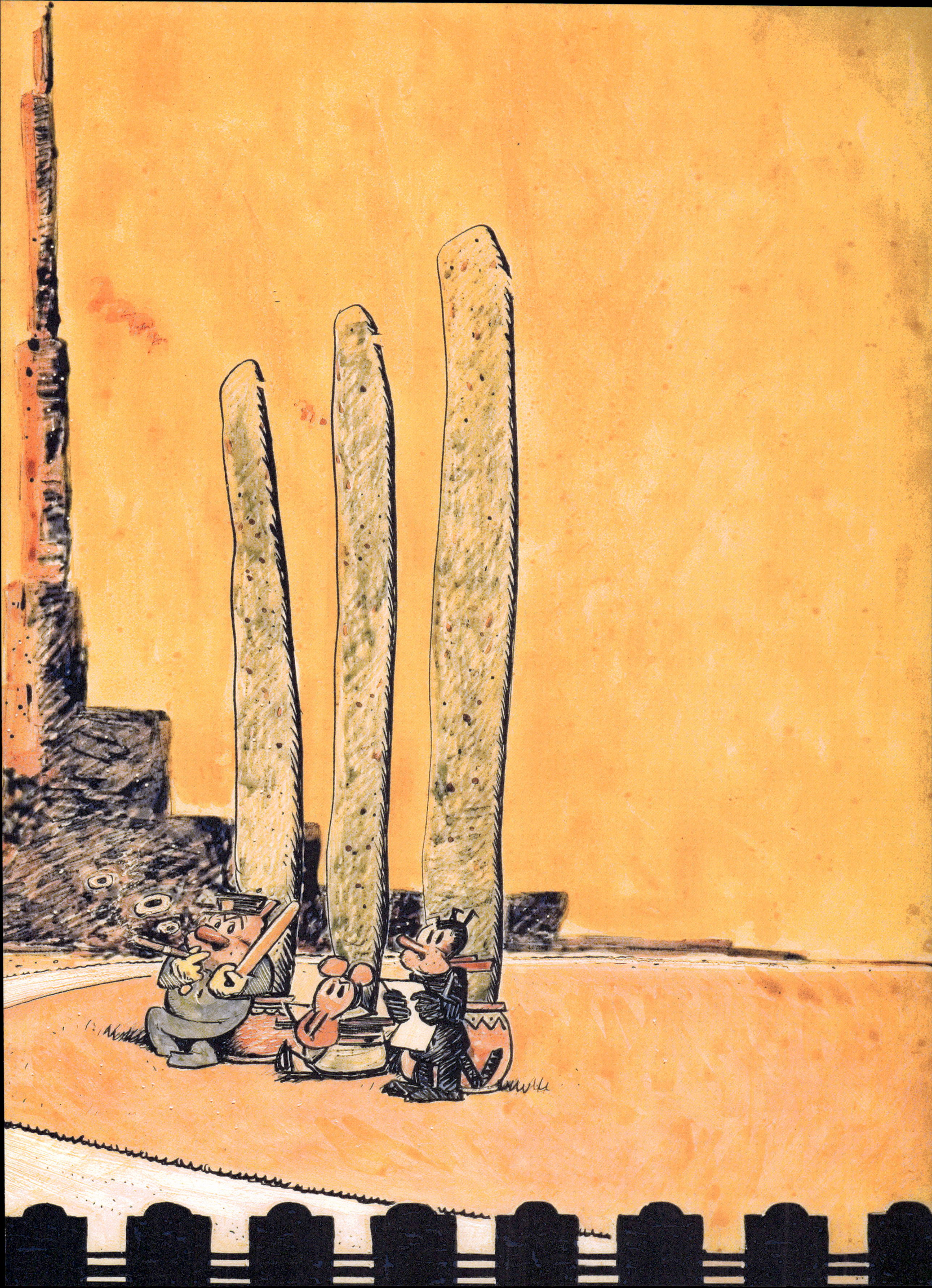

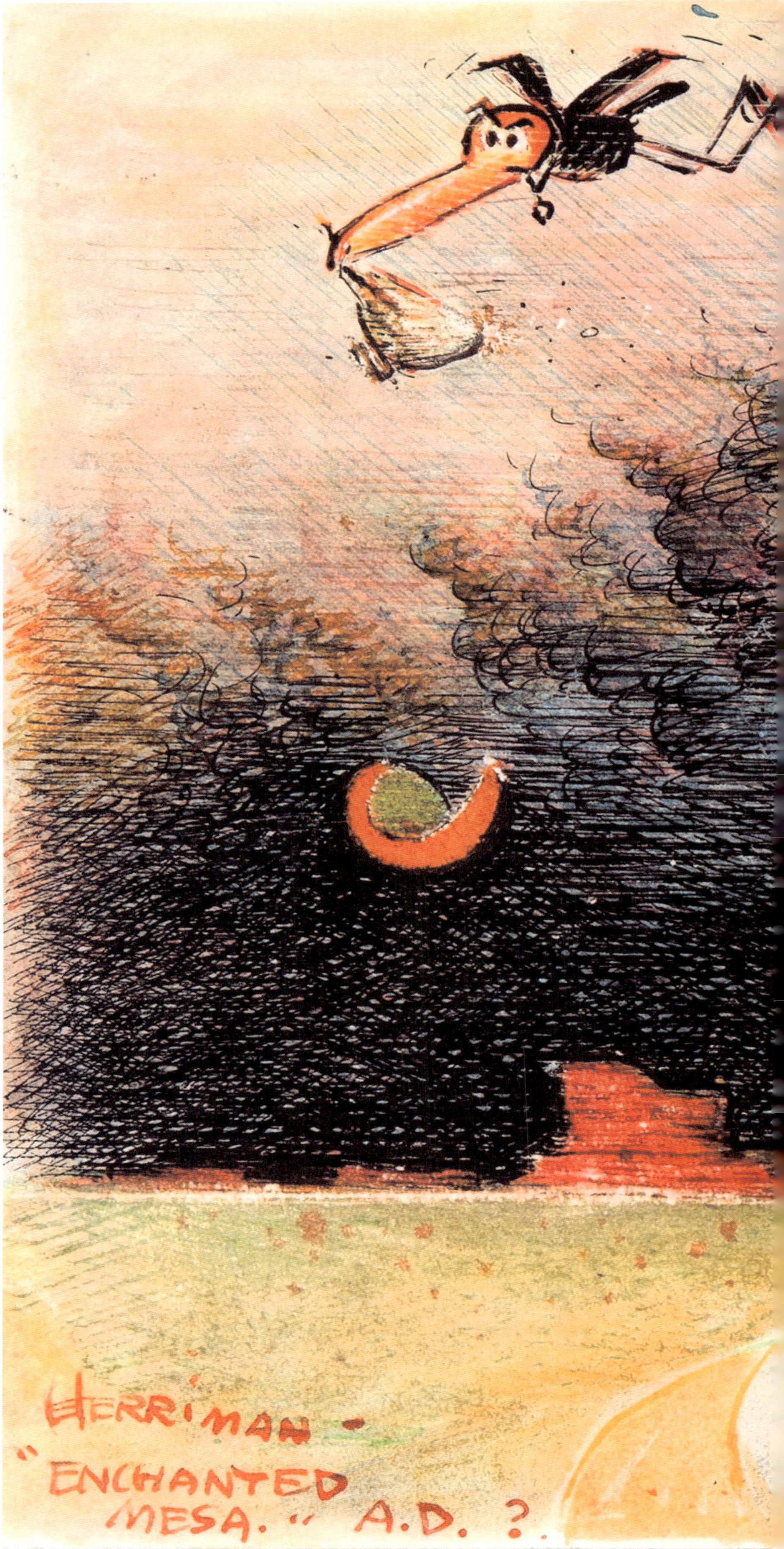
HERRIMAN -
"ENCHANTED
MESA." A.D. ?.

RIGHT A blue velour-covered book was presented to William Randolph Hearst by the artists of the King Features Syndicate in honor of his 79th birthday. The artists included Alex Raymond (*Flash Gordon*), Hal Foster (*Prince Valiant*), Chic Young (*Blondie*), and George Herriman. Herriman's dedication reads, "Could be our boss. Could be our chief. Could be our friend. Could BE.—Herriman, 'Enchanted Mesa.' A.D.?" April 29, 1942. Previously unpublished.

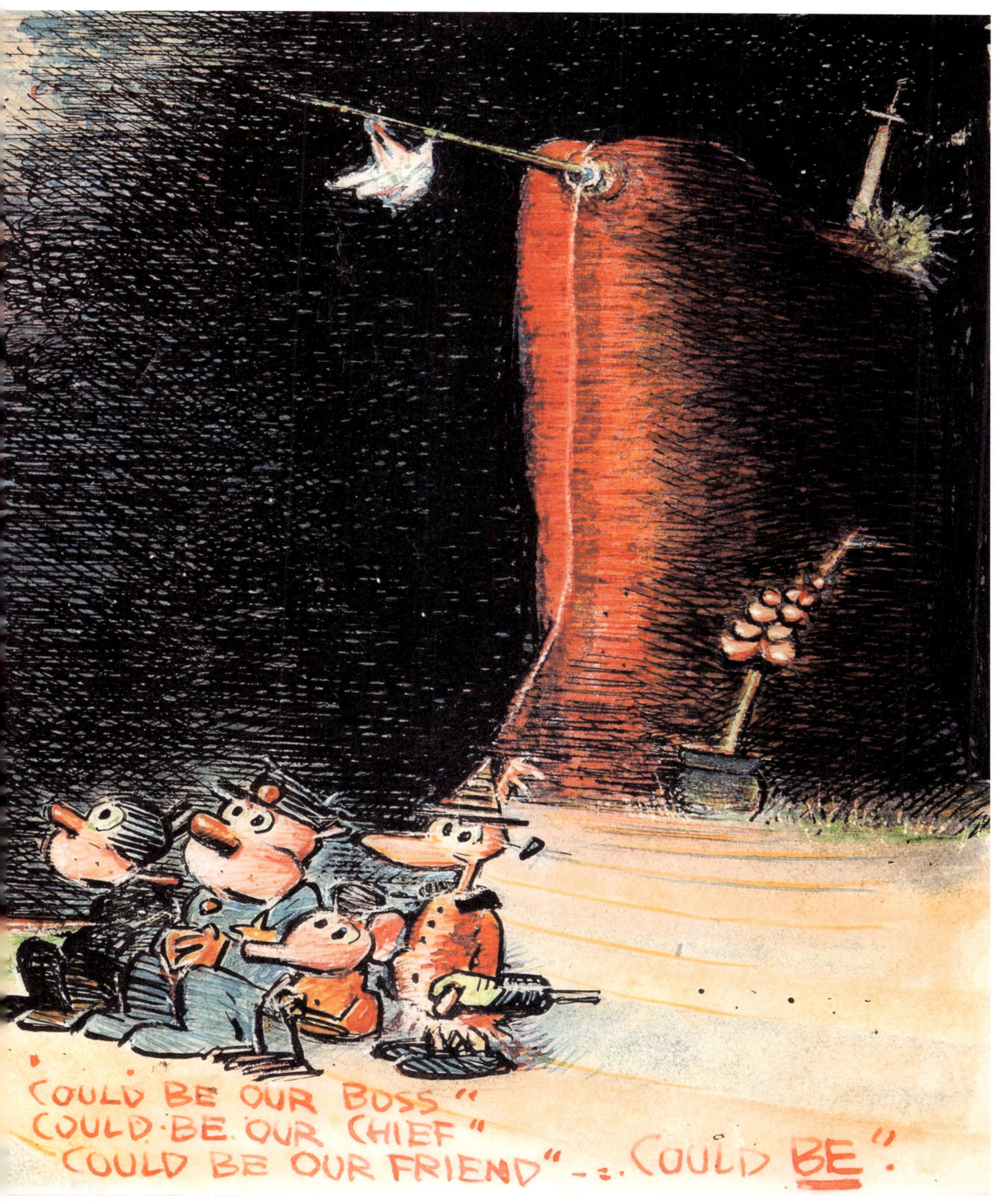

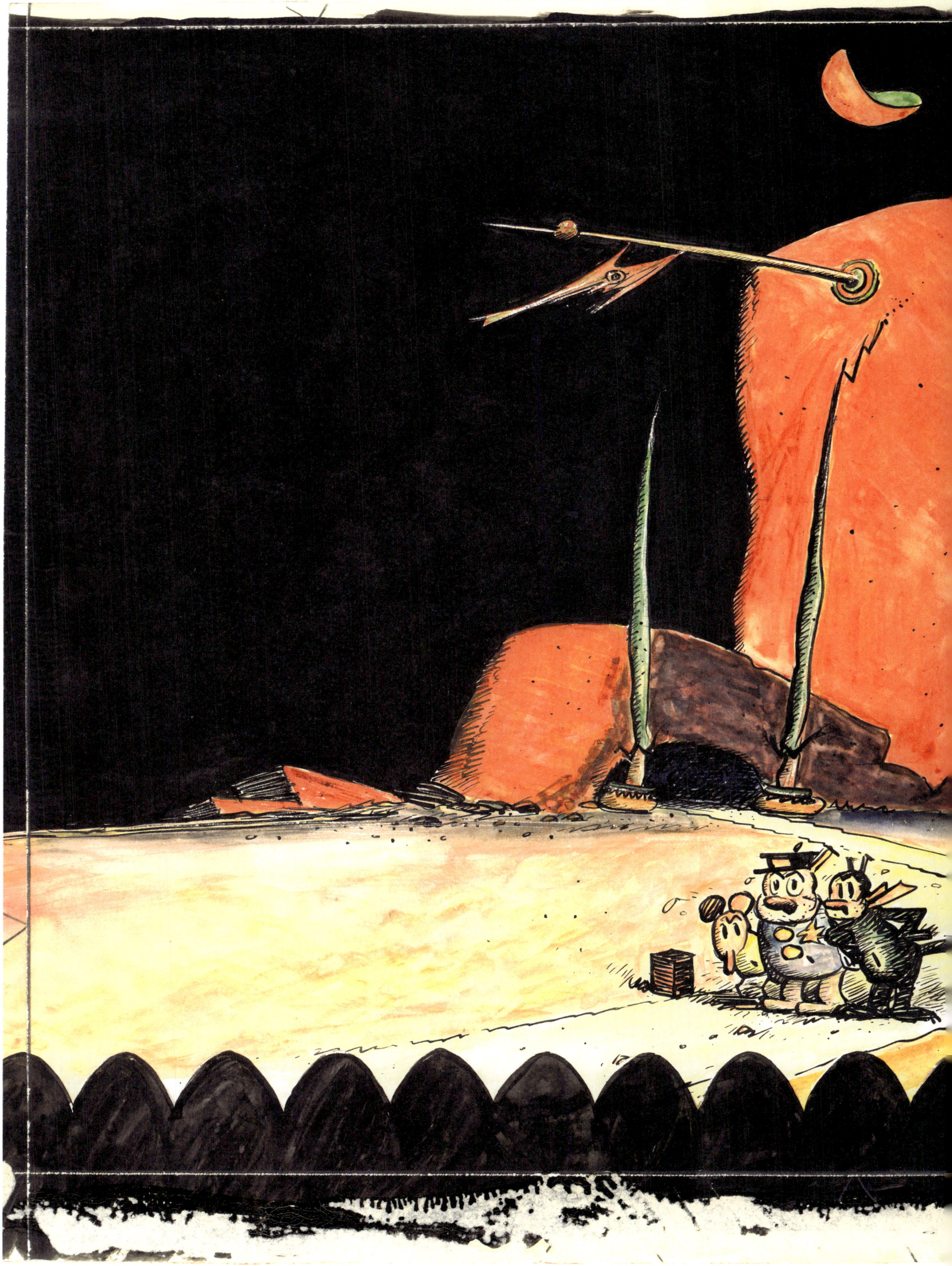

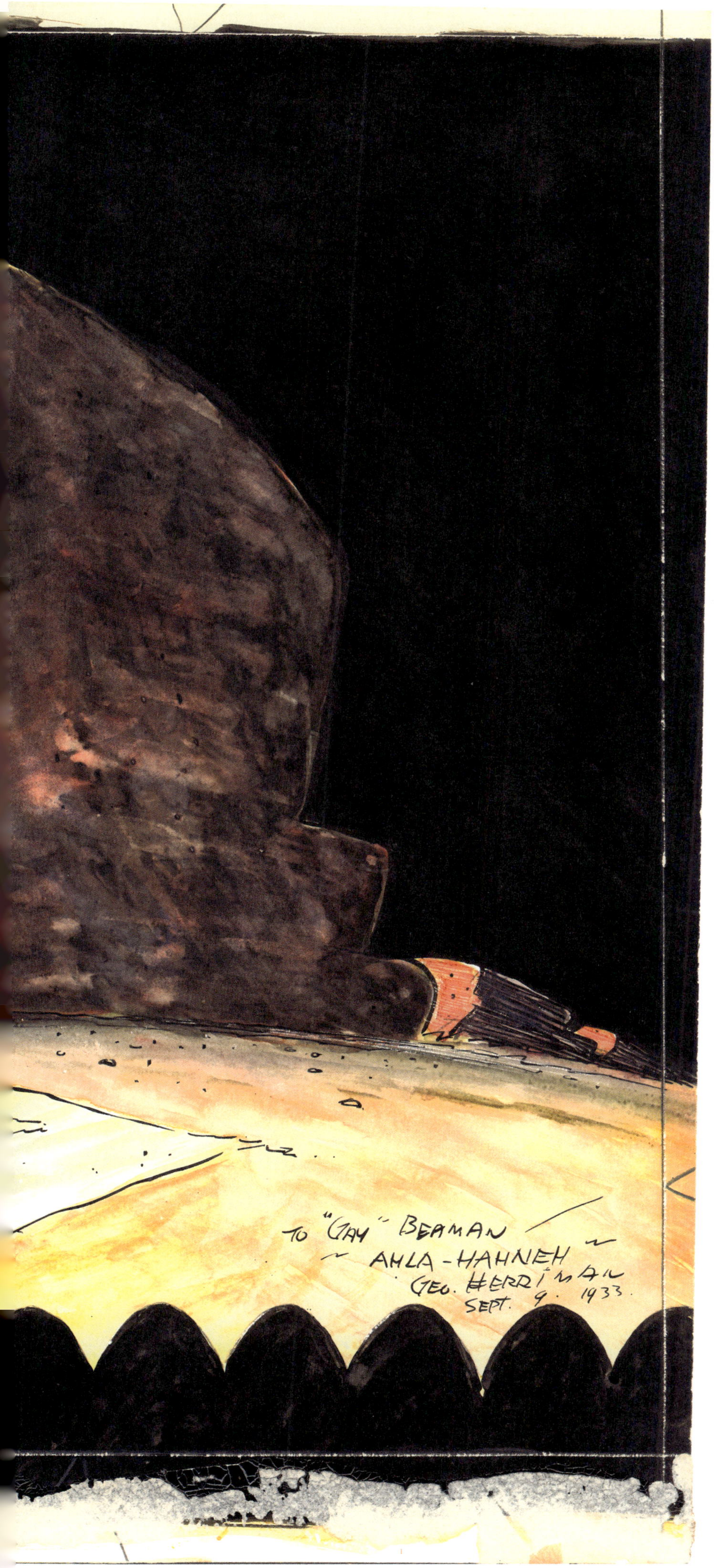
TO "GAY" BEAMAN
~ AHLA-HAHNEH ~
GEO. HERRIMAN
SEPT. 9. 1933

LEFT The inscription reads, "To 'Gay' Beaman—Ahla-Hahneh—Geo. Herriman Sept. 9, 1933."

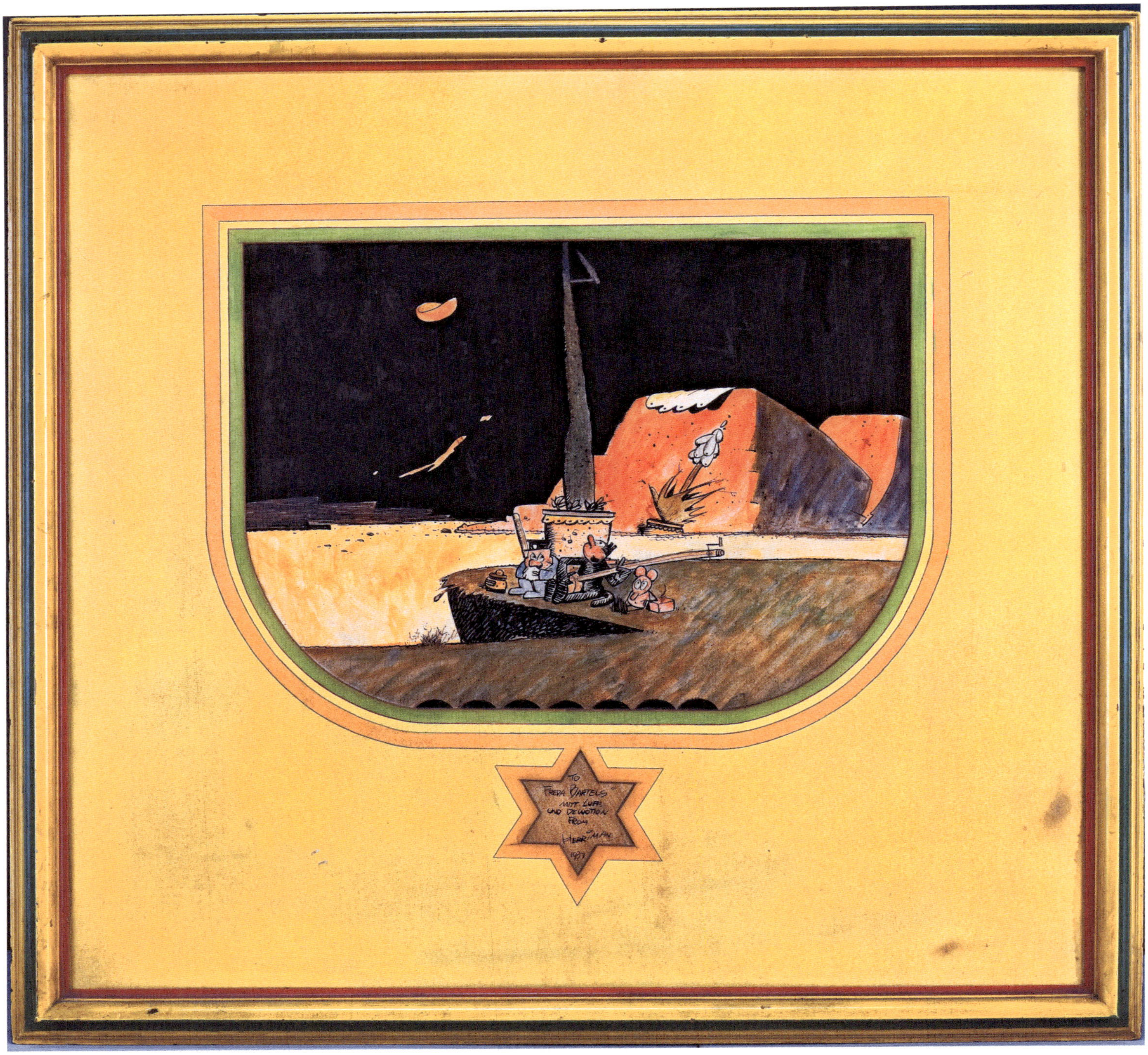
"TO
FREDA BARTELS"
MITT LUFF,
UND DEWOTION
FROM
HERRIMAN
1937

ABOVE The inscription reads, "To 'Freda Bartels' mitt luff, und dewotion from Herriman, 1937."

OPPOSITE In this wonderful painting, Herriman depicts Dorothea Lange and Maynard Dixon. Lange became famous for her compelling photographs of the Great Depression, including the *Migrant Mother*. She is portrayed here holding her camera. Dixon was a fine artist, and is pictured painting his favorite subject, the American West. The inscription reads, "To Mr. & Mrs. Maynard Dixon—recalling a pleasant little *pasear* in that dear *disierto pintado*—Aug. 1922—Herriman." Previously unpublished.

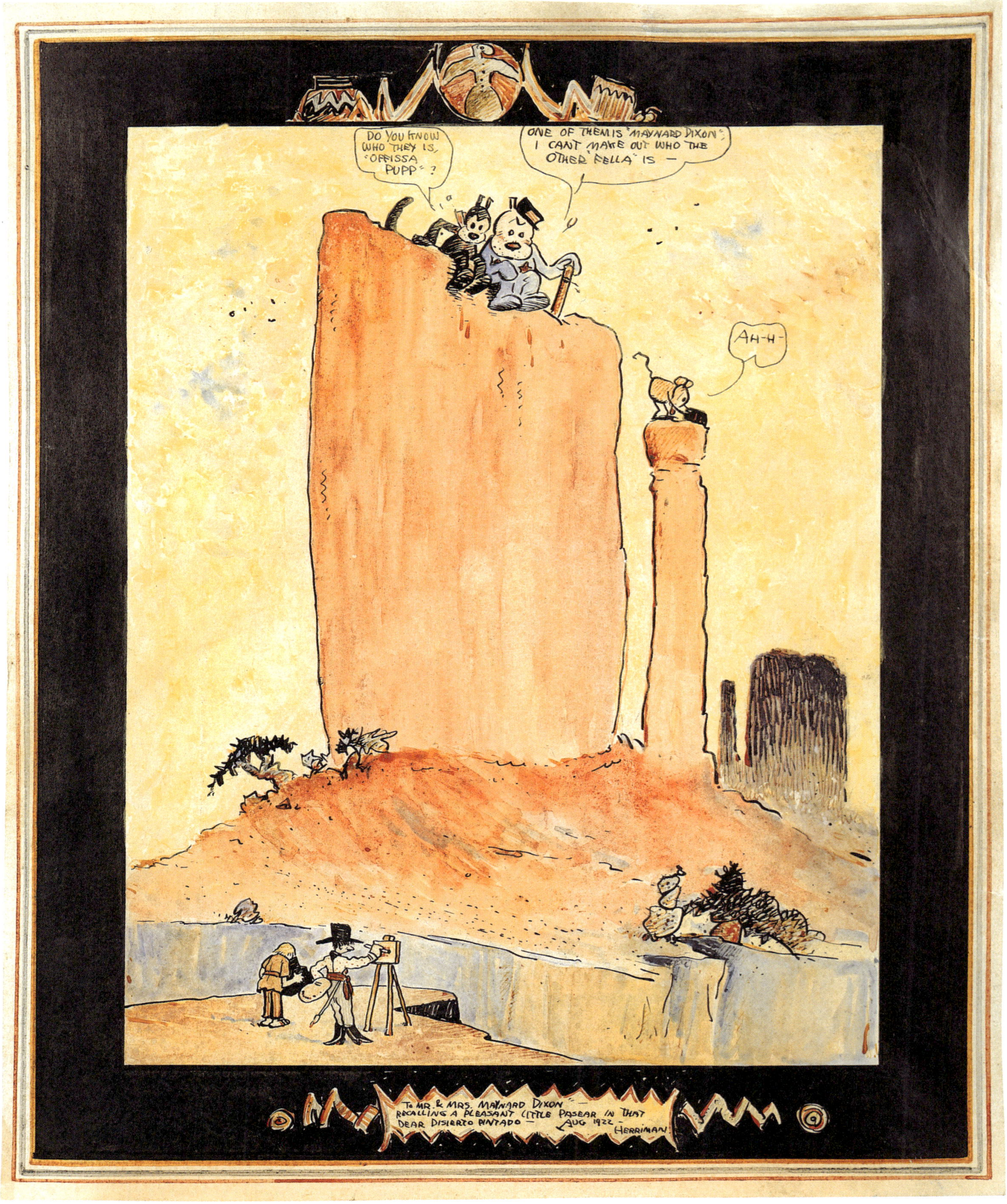
DO YOU KNOW WHO THEY IS, "OFFISSA PUPP"?
ONE OF THEM IS "MAYNARD DIXON"; I CANT MAKE OUT WHO THE OTHER "FELLA" IS —
AH-H-
TO MR. & MRS. MAYNARD DIXON — RECALLING A PLEASANT LITTLE PASEAR IN THAT DEAR DISIERTO PINTADO — AUG 1922 — HERRIMAN.

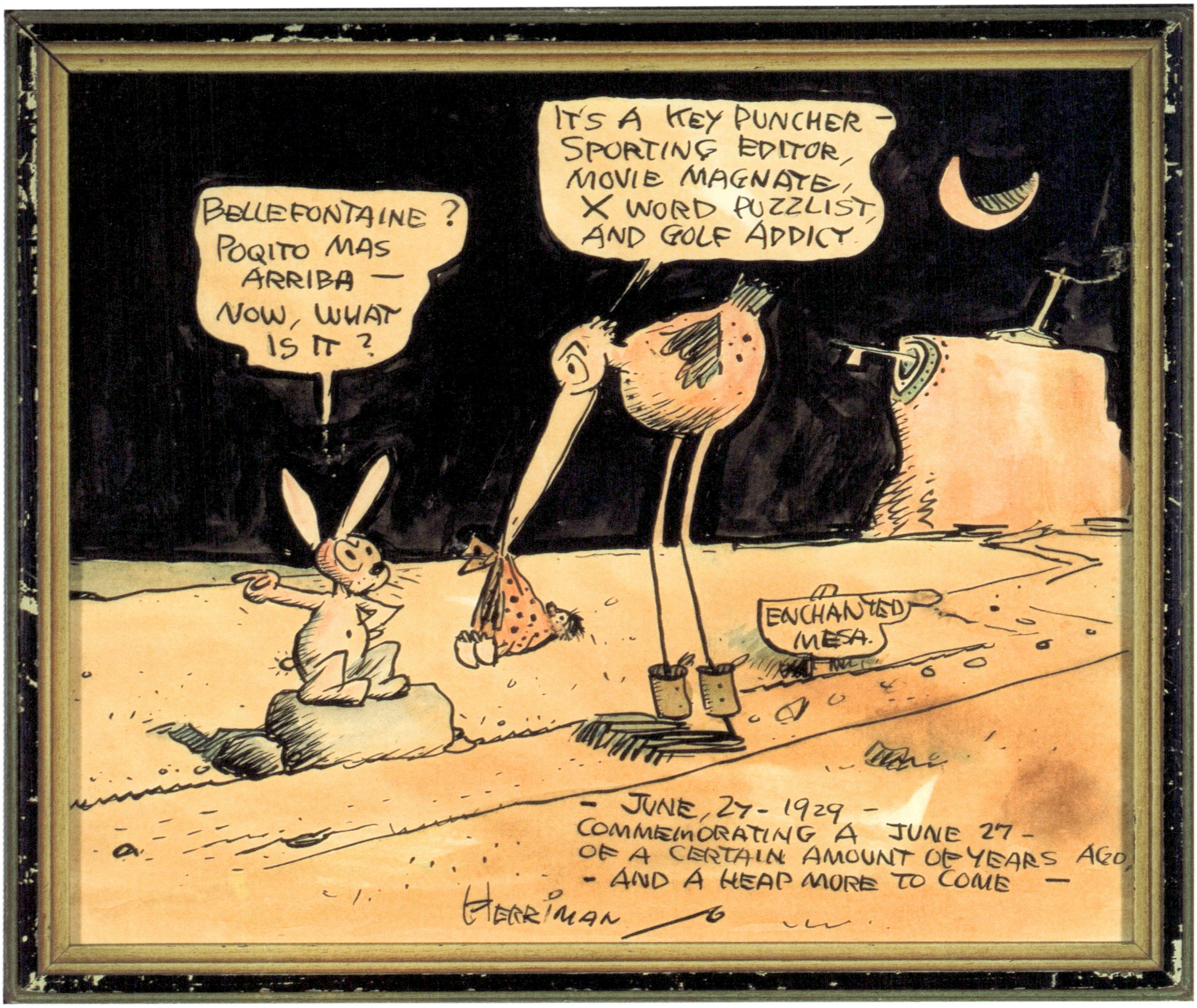
BELLEFONTAINE? POQITO MAS ARRIBA — NOW, WHAT IS IT?
IT'S A KEY PUNCHER — SPORTING EDITOR, MOVIE MAGNATE, X WORD PUZZLIST, AND GOLF ADDICT
ENCHANTED MESA.
- JUNE, 27 - 1929 -
COMMEMORATING A JUNE 27 -
OF A CERTAIN AMOUNT OF YEARS AGO,
- AND A HEAP MORE TO COME -
HERRIMAN

ABOVE The inscription reads, "June, 27—1929—commemorating a June 27 of a certain amount of years ago—and a heap more to come—Herriman."

OPPOSITE The inscription reads, "To Marion Pollard from 'ole man' Herriman, mit luff 'und dewotion.'" Previously unpublished.

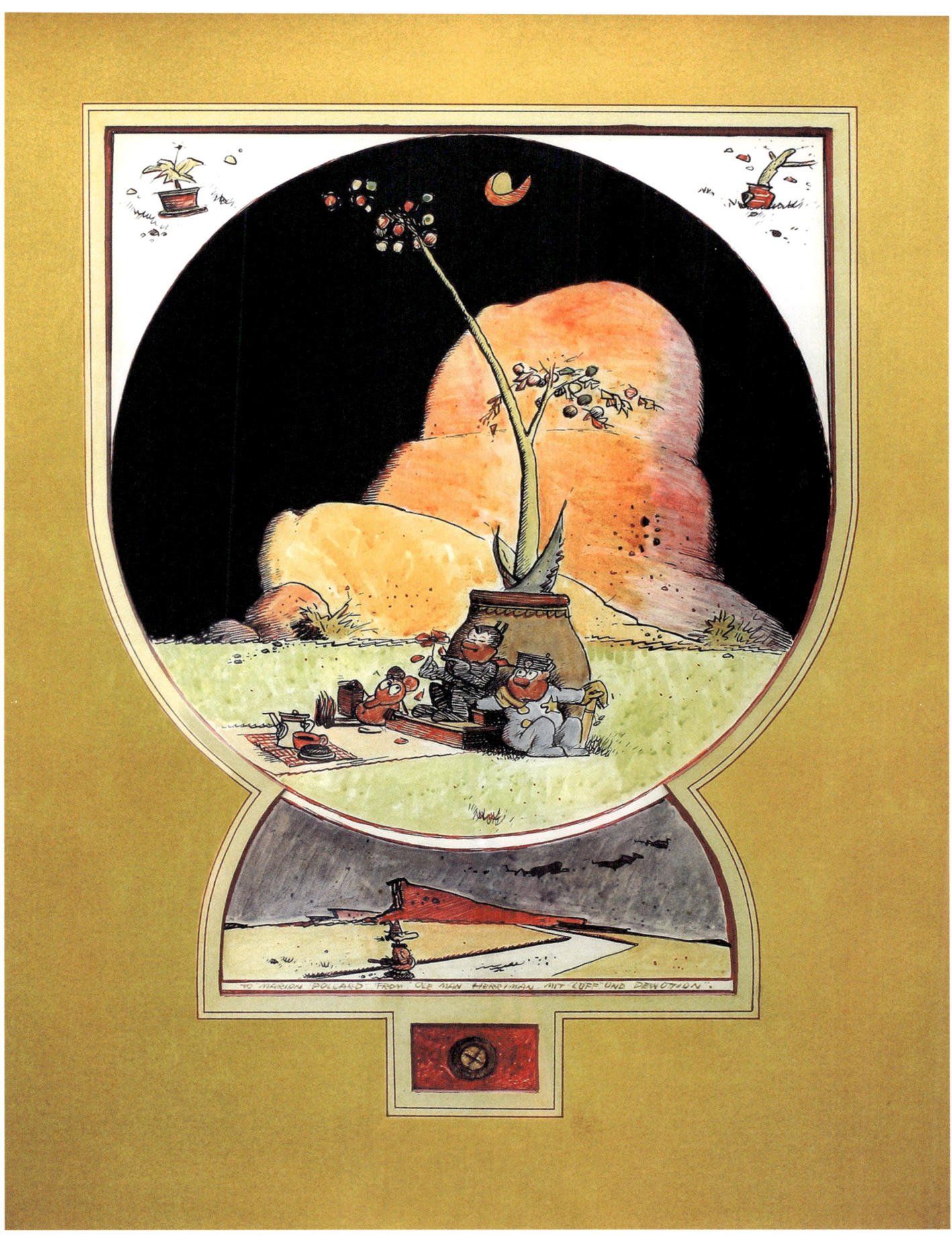

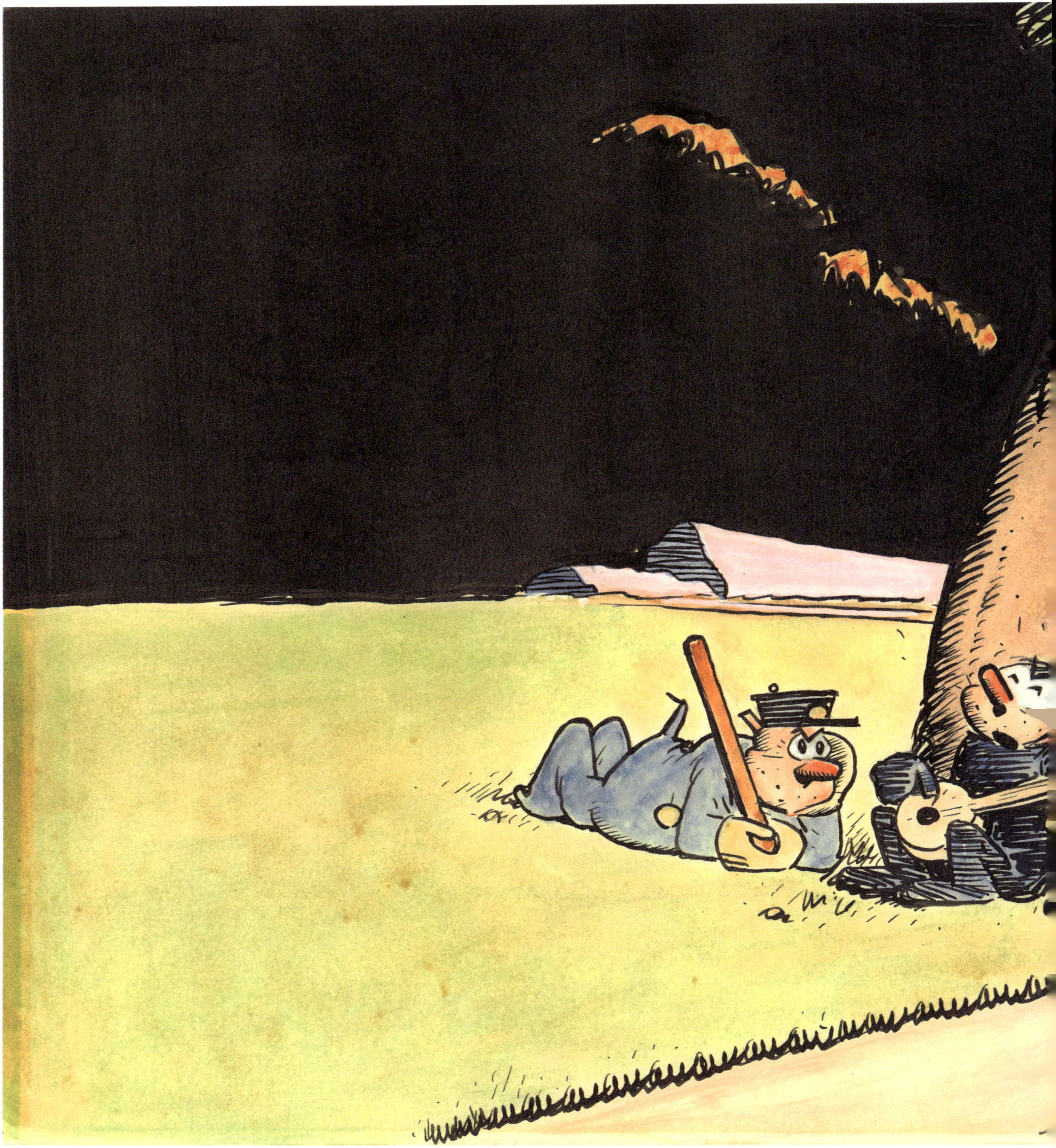

ABOVE The inscription reads, "To Morris Weiss—from Herriman—1936." Morris Weiss is a cartoonist who created the character Margie for Timely Comics.

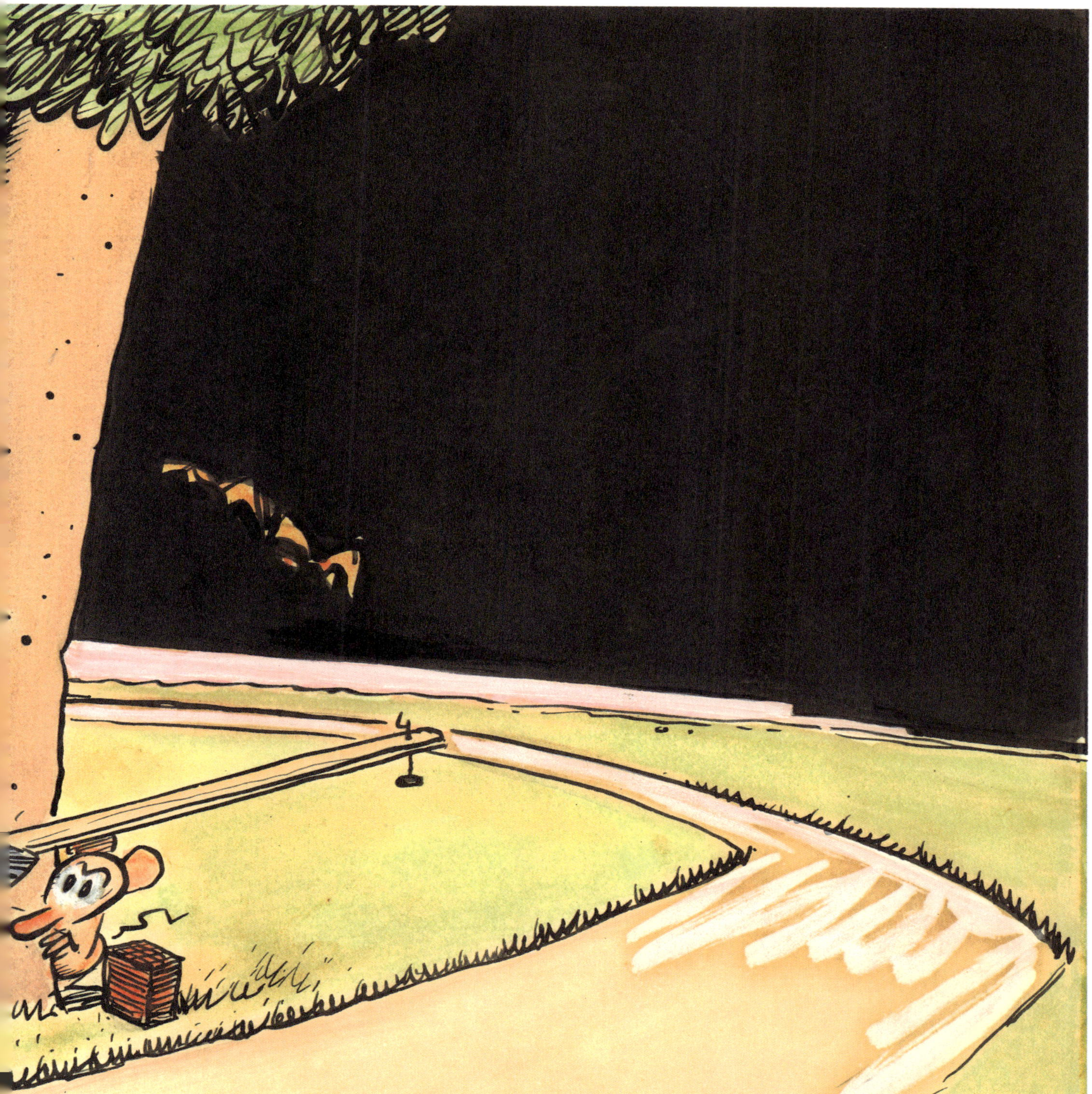
TO MERRIS WEISS -
FROM HERRIMAN 1936.

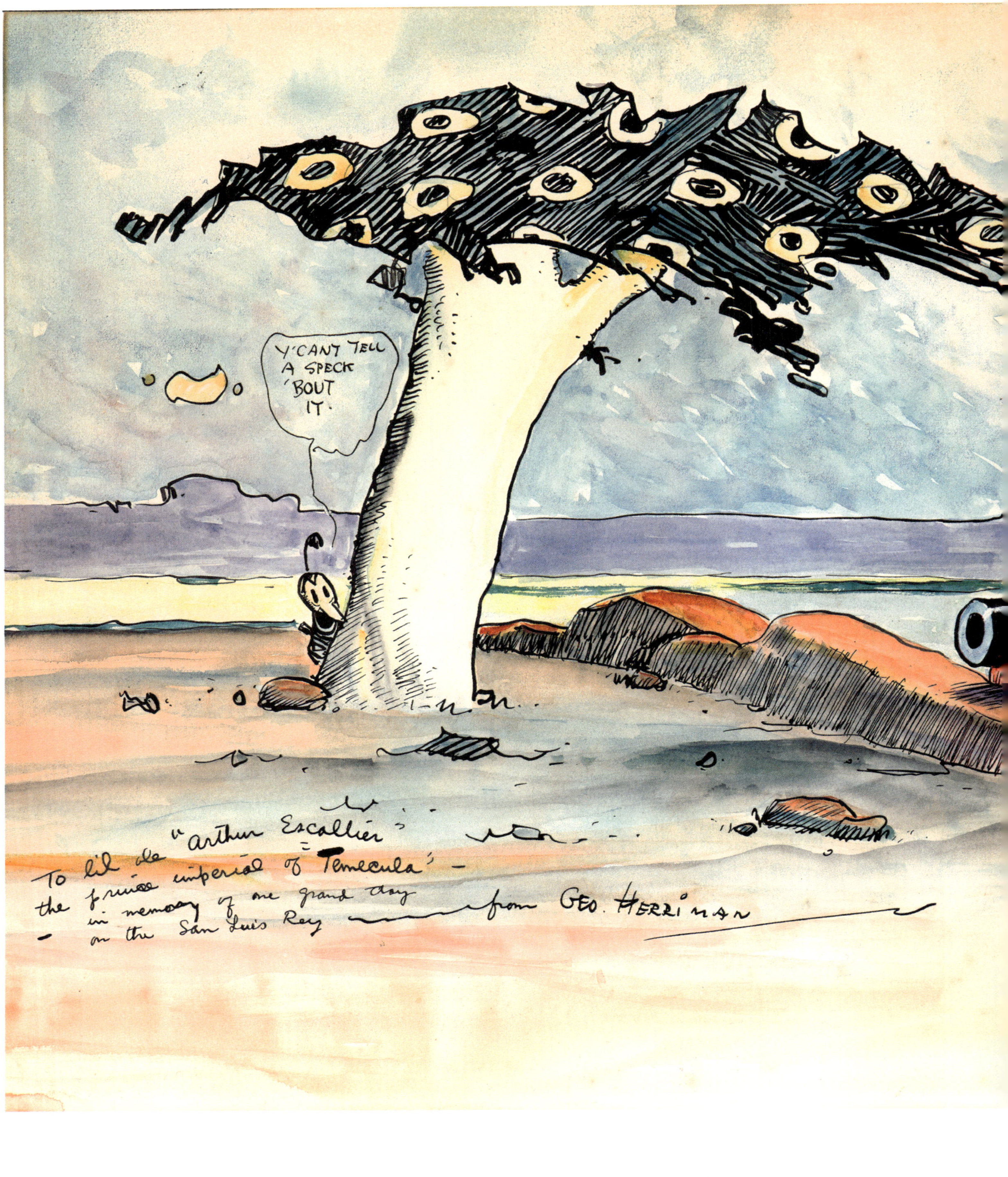
Y'CAN'T TELL A SPECK 'BOUT IT.
To lil ole "arthur Escallier" the prince imperial of Temecula - in memory of one grand day on the San Luis Rey from Geo. Herriman

ABOVE The inscription reads, "To lil ole 'Arthur Escallier' the prince imperial of Temecula—in memory of one grand day on the San Luis Rey—from Geo. Herriman." 1930s.

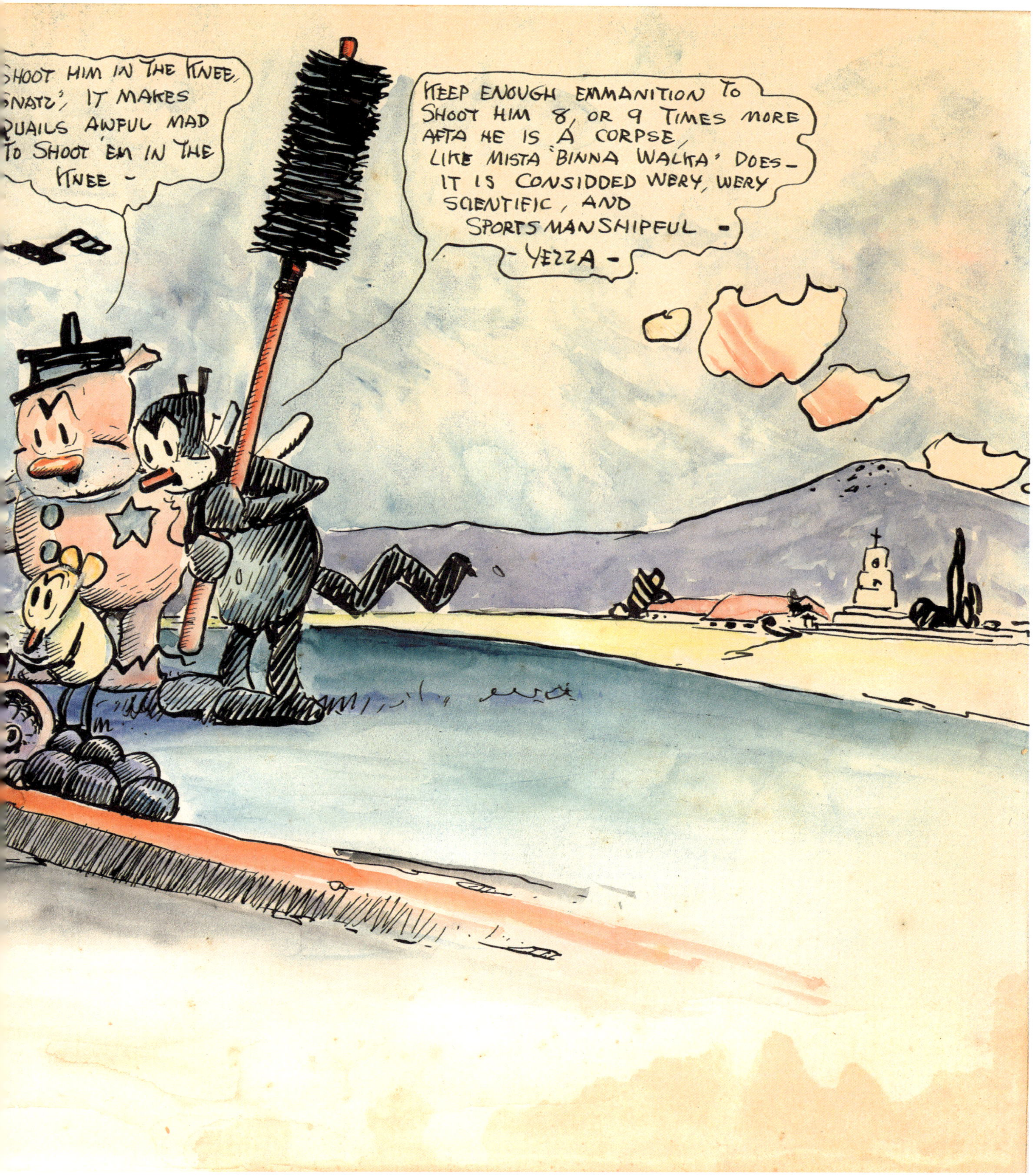
SHOOT HIM IN THE KNEE, SNATZ; IT MAKES QUAILS AWFUL MAD TO SHOOT 'EM IN THE KNEE -
KEEP ENOUGH EMMANITION TO SHOOT HIM 8, OR 9 TIMES MORE AFTA HE IS A CORPSE, LIKE MISTA 'BINNA WALKA' DOES - IT IS CONSIDDED WERY, WERY SCIENTIFIC, AND SPORTSMANSHIPFUL - - YEZZA -

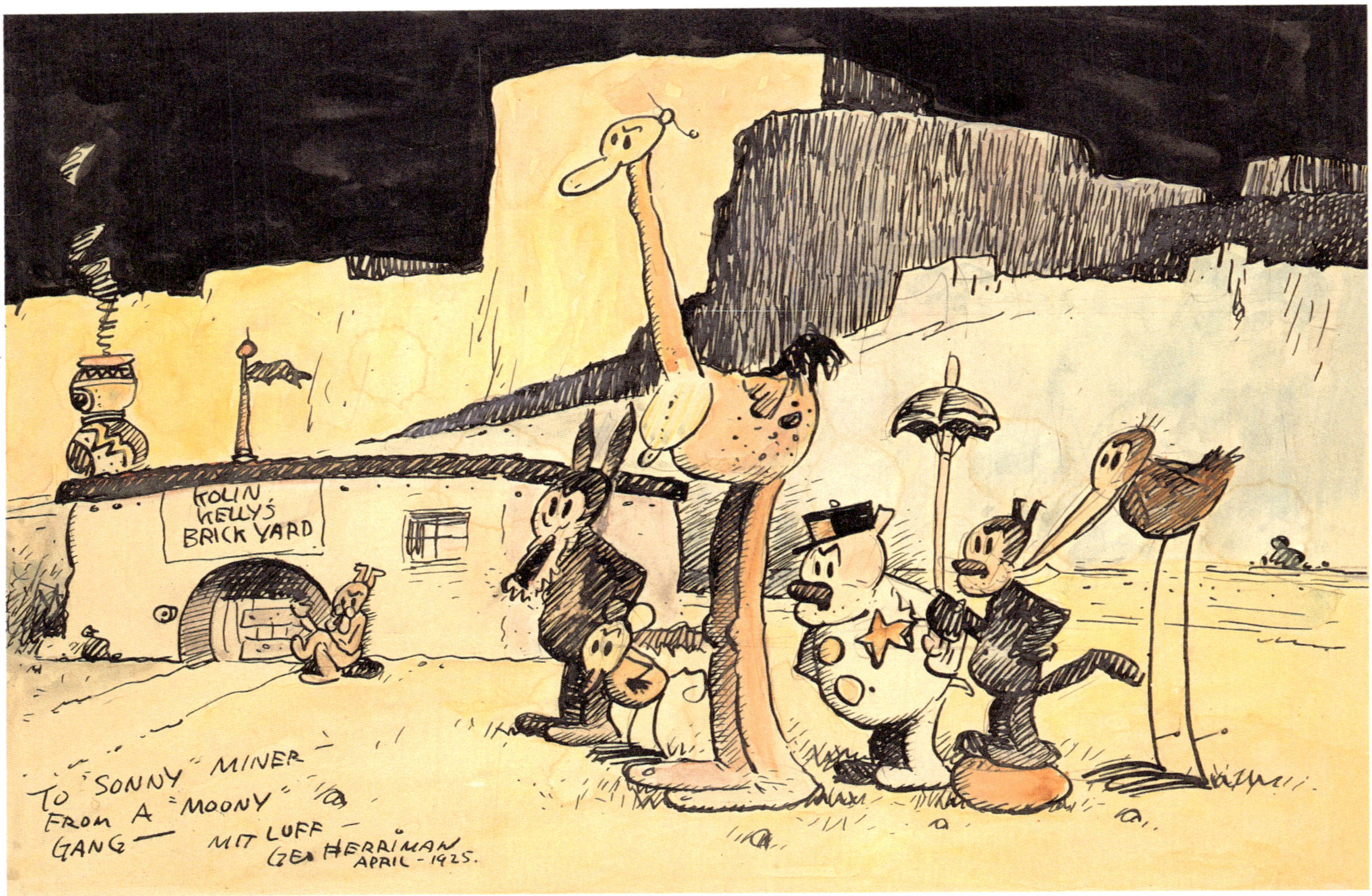
KOLIN KELLY'S BRICK YARD
TO "SONNY" MINER — FROM A "MOONY" GANG — MIT LUFF — GEO HERRIMAN APRIL - 1925.

ABOVE The denizens of Coconino County standing in front of the famed Kolin Kelly's Brick Yard. The inscription reads, "To 'Sonny' Miner—from a 'moony' gang—mit luff—Geo. Herriman, April 1925."

OPPOSITE The inscription reads, "To Sir Michael, Master of the Hounds, to Their Graces the Duke & Duchess of Wellington, the respects of K. Kat et al.—per Geo. Herriman, Apr. 12, 1921."

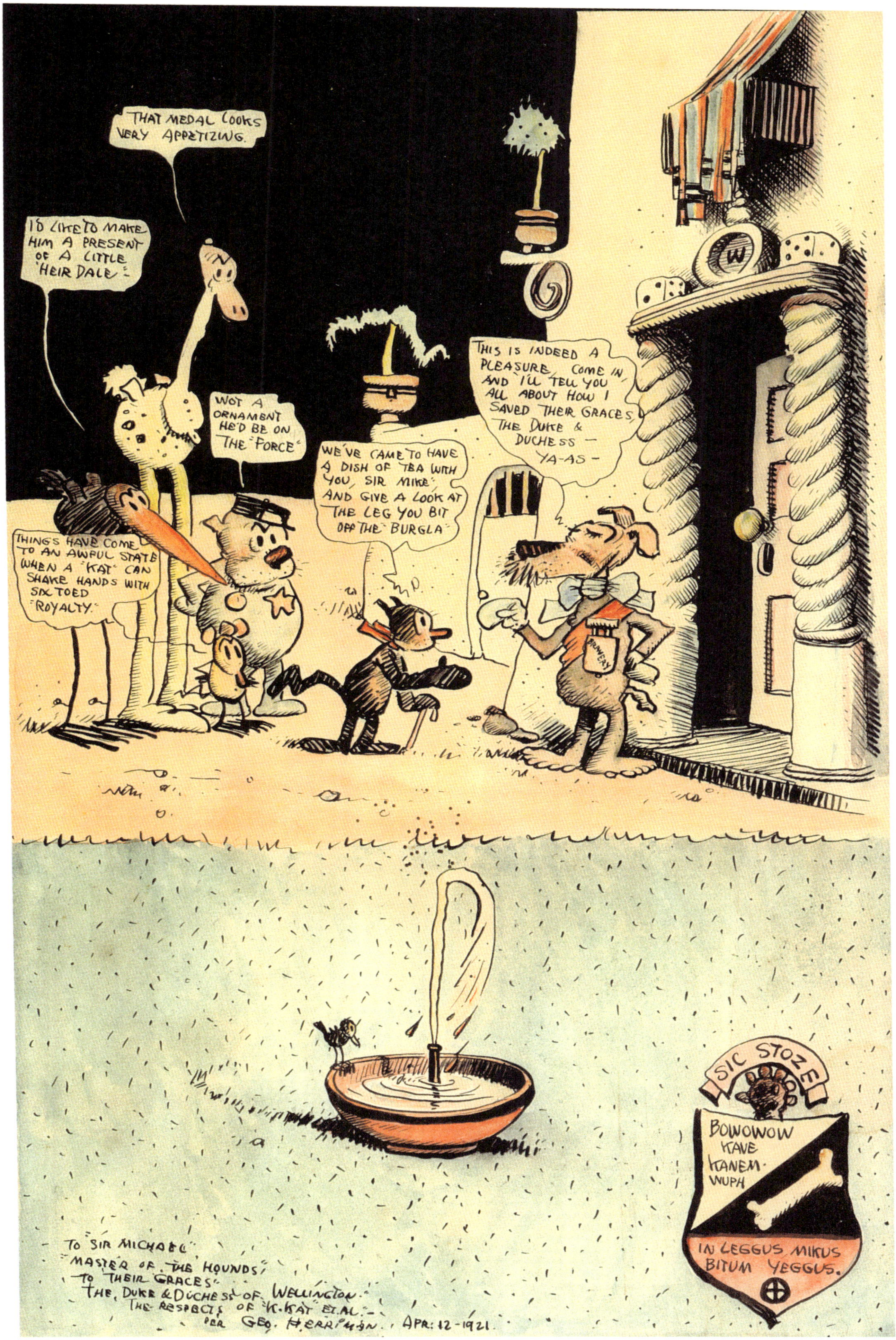
THAT MEDAL LOOKS VERY APPETIZING.
ID LIKE TO MAKE HIM A PRESENT OF A LITTLE "HEIR DALE"–
WOT A ORNAMENT HE'D BE ON THE "FORCE"
THINGS HAVE COME TO AN AWFUL STATE WHEN A "KAT" CAN SHAKE HANDS WITH SIX TOED "ROYALTY."
WE'VE CAME TO HAVE A DISH OF TEA WITH YOU, SIR MIKE" AND GIVE A LOOK AT THE LEG YOU BIT OFF THE "BURGLA"
THIS IS INDEED A PLEASURE, COME IN AND I'LL TELL YOU ALL ABOUT HOW I SAVED THEIR GRACES THE DUKE & DUCHESS – YA-AS –
W
SIC STOZE
BOWOWOW KAVE KANEM WUPH
IN LEGGUS MIKUS BITUM YEGGUS.
TO SIR MICHAEL"
MASTER OF THE HOUNDS
TO THEIR GRACES
THE DUKE & DUCHESS OF WELLINGTON.
THE RESPECTS OF "K. KAT" ET. AL.–
PER GEO. HERRIMAN. APR: 12-1921.

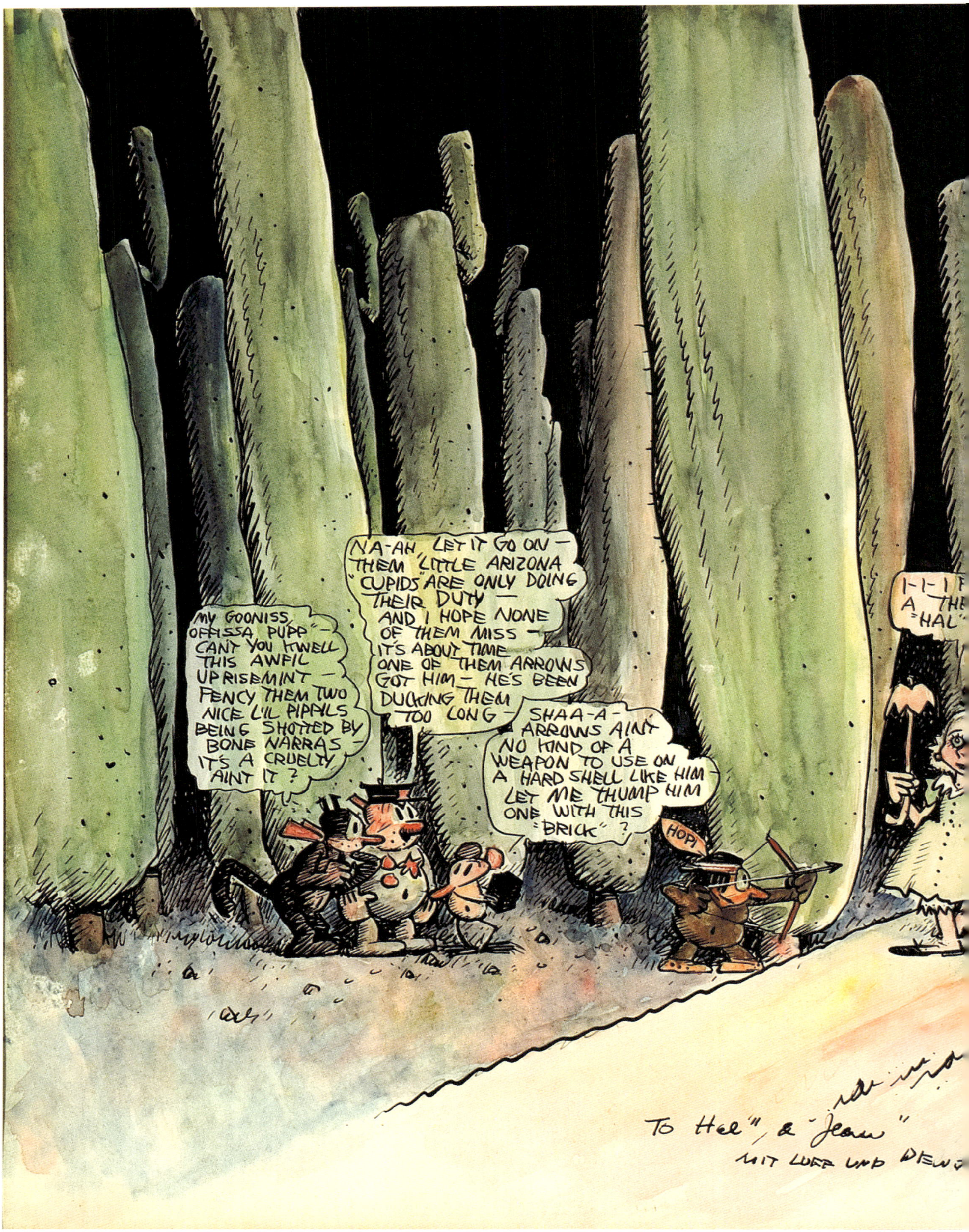
MY GOONISS, OFFISSA PUPP - CAN'T YOU KWELL THIS AWFIL UPRISEMINT - FENCY THEM TWO NICE L'IL PIPPILS BEING SHOTTED BY BONE NARRAS IT'S A CRUELTY AINT IT?
NA-AH LET IT GO ON - THEM "LITTLE ARIZONA CUPIDS" ARE ONLY DOING THEIR DUTY - AND I HOPE NONE OF THEM MISS - IT'S ABOUT TIME ONE OF THEM ARROWS GOT HIM - HE'S BEEN DUCKING THEM TOO LONG -
SHAA-A - ARROWS AIN'T NO KIND OF A WEAPON TO USE ON A HARD SHELL LIKE HIM - LET ME THUMP HIM ONE WITH THIS "BRICK"?
HOP!
To Hal", & "Jean"
MIT LUFF UND

ABOVE The inscription reads, "To Hal & Jean mit luff und dewotion—from ole man Herriman—Xmas 1933."

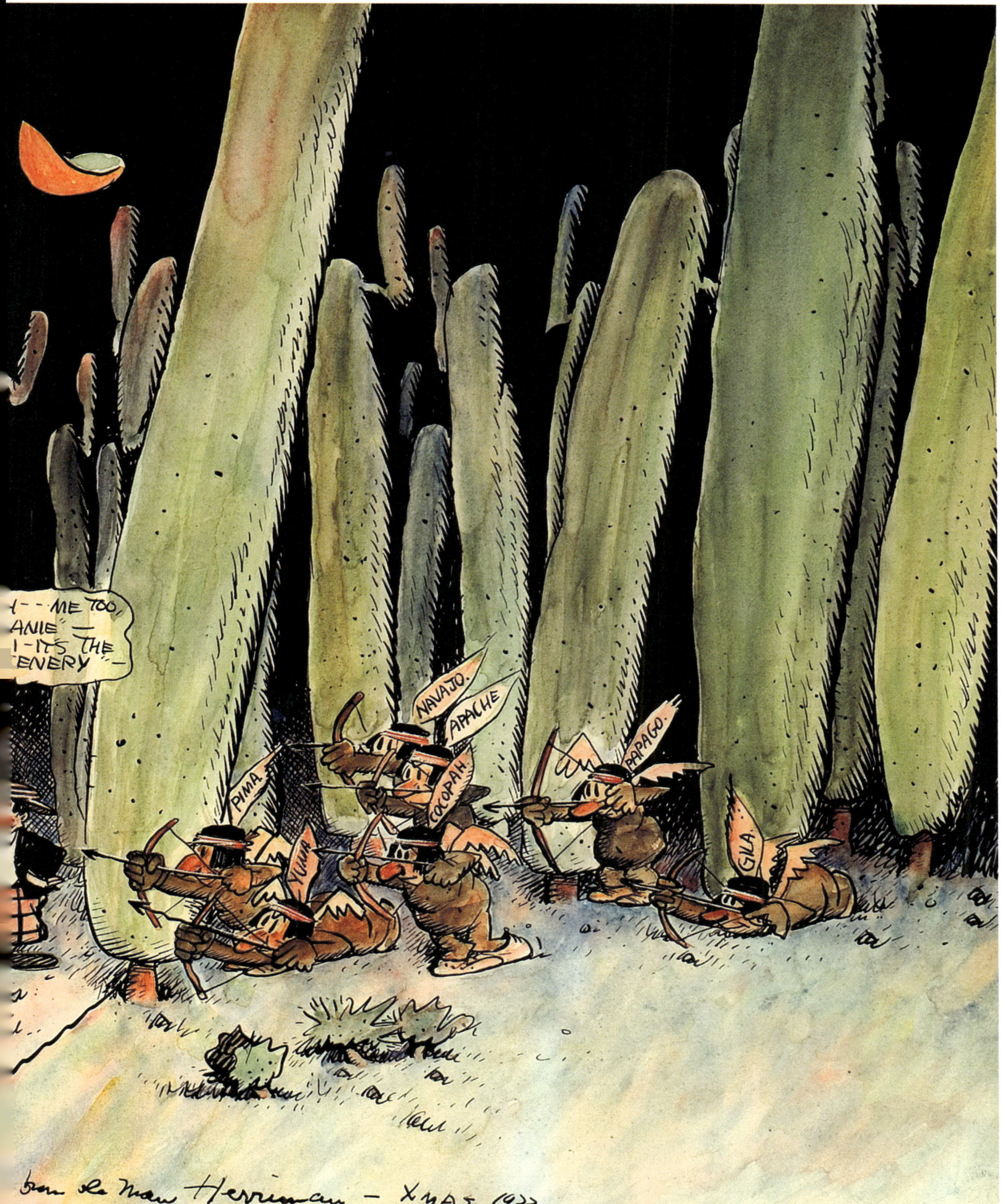
-- ME TOO,
ANIE —
-IT'S THE
ENERY
NAVAJO.
APACHE
PIMA
COCOPAH
YUMA
PAPAGO.
GILA
from da man Herriman — XMAS 1933.

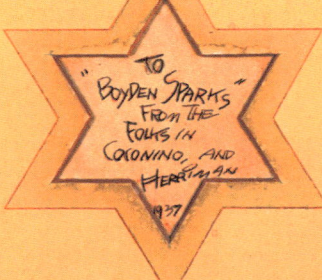

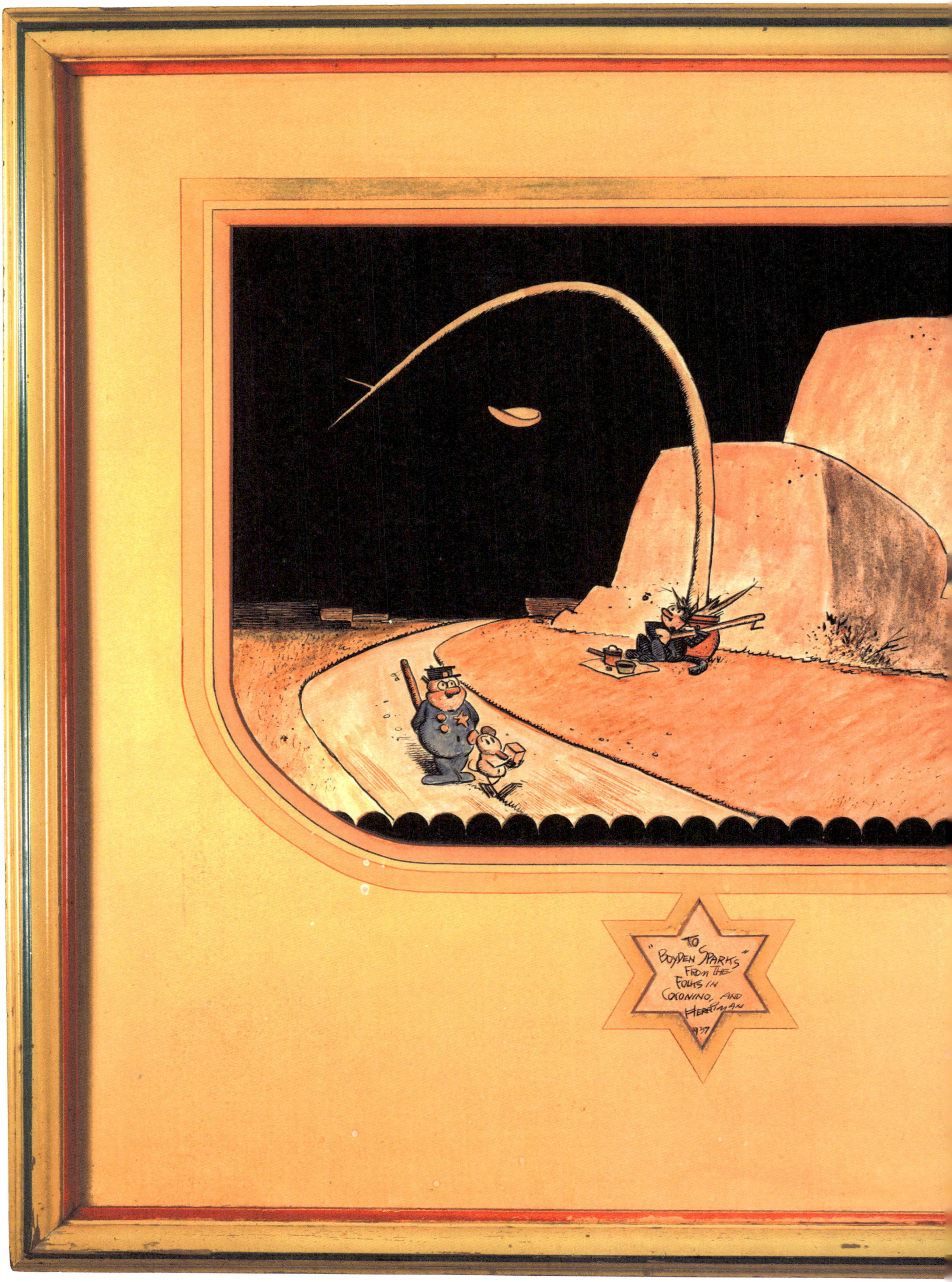

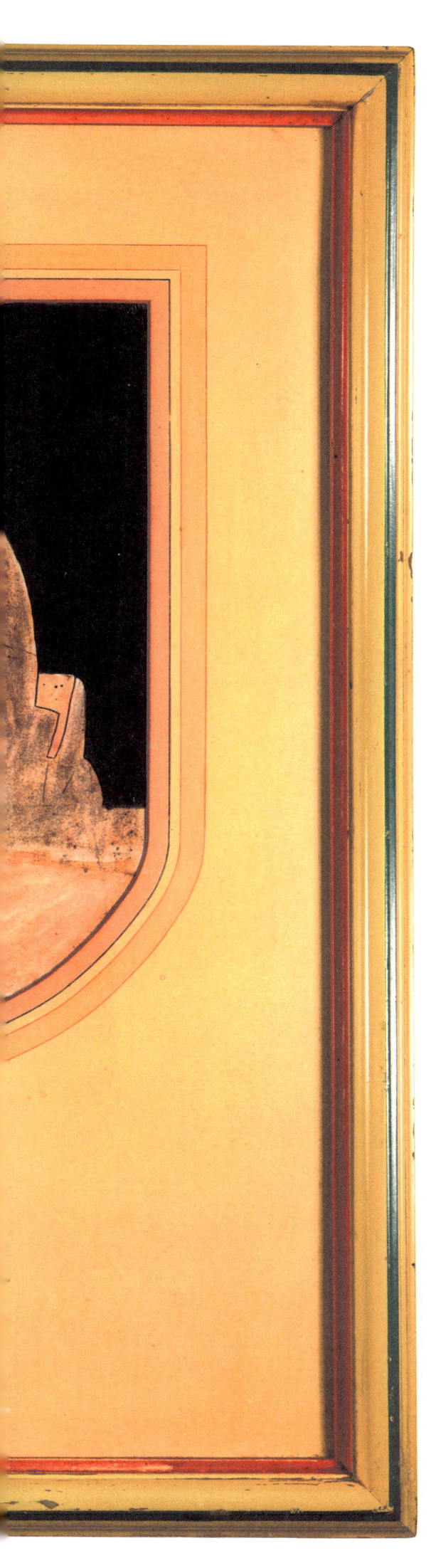

LEFT This painting is owned by the International Museum of Cartoon Art Collection, The Ohio State University Billy Ireland Cartoon Library & Museum. It's inscribed, "To 'Boyden Sparks' from the folks in Coconino, and Herriman, 1937."

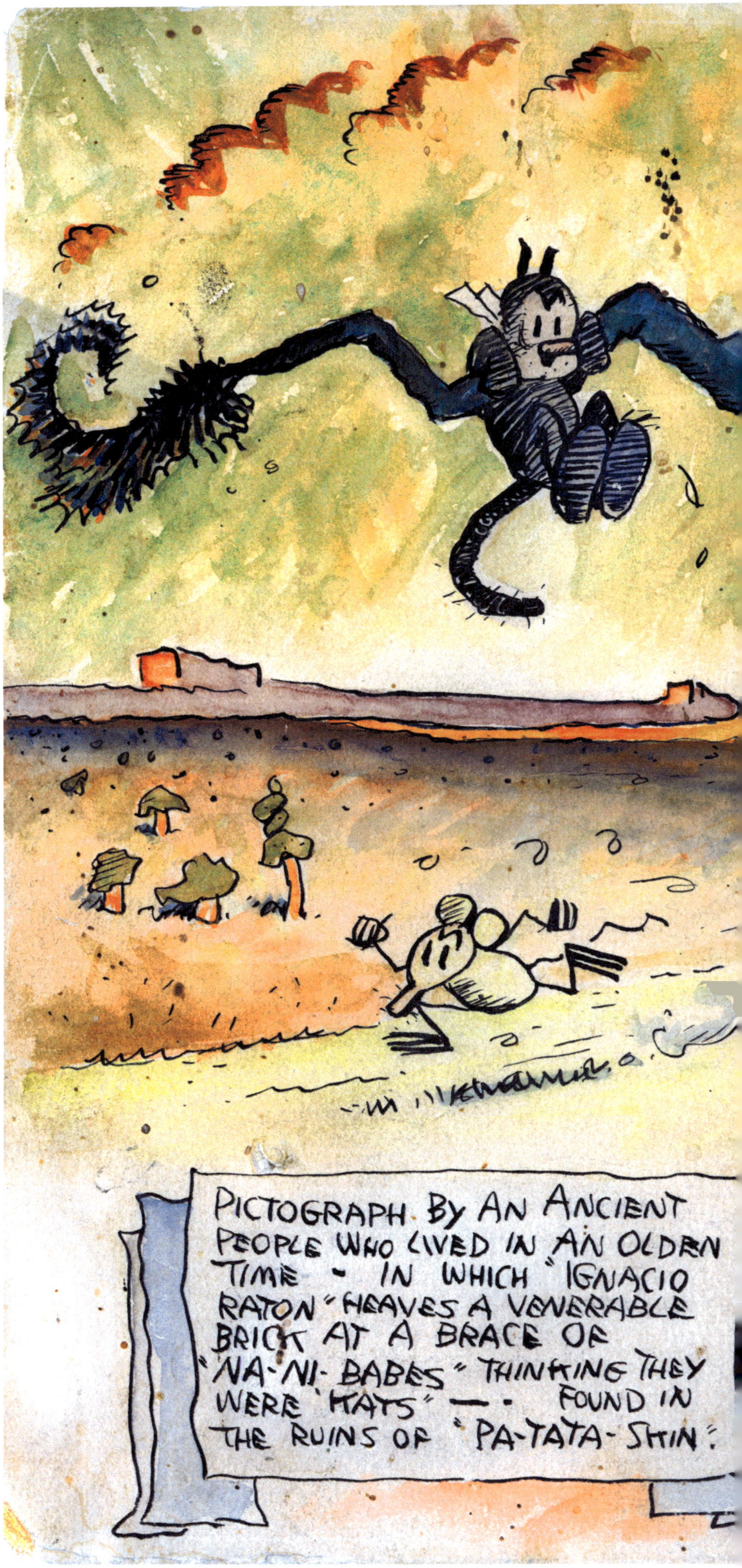
PICTOGRAPH BY AN ANCIENT PEOPLE WHO LIVED IN AN OLDEN TIME - IN WHICH "IGNACIO RATON" HEAVES A VENERABLE BRICK AT A BRACE OF "NA-NI-BABES" THINKING THEY WERE "KATS" — . FOUND IN THE RUINS OF "PA-TATA-SHIN".

RIGHT The inscription on this painting reads, "To Mr. & Mrs. John Wetherill—which is no way to repay them for their kindness & hospitality—BUT—what can you expect from a 'KRAZY KARTOONIST'?—Geo. Herriman, Aug. 1922."

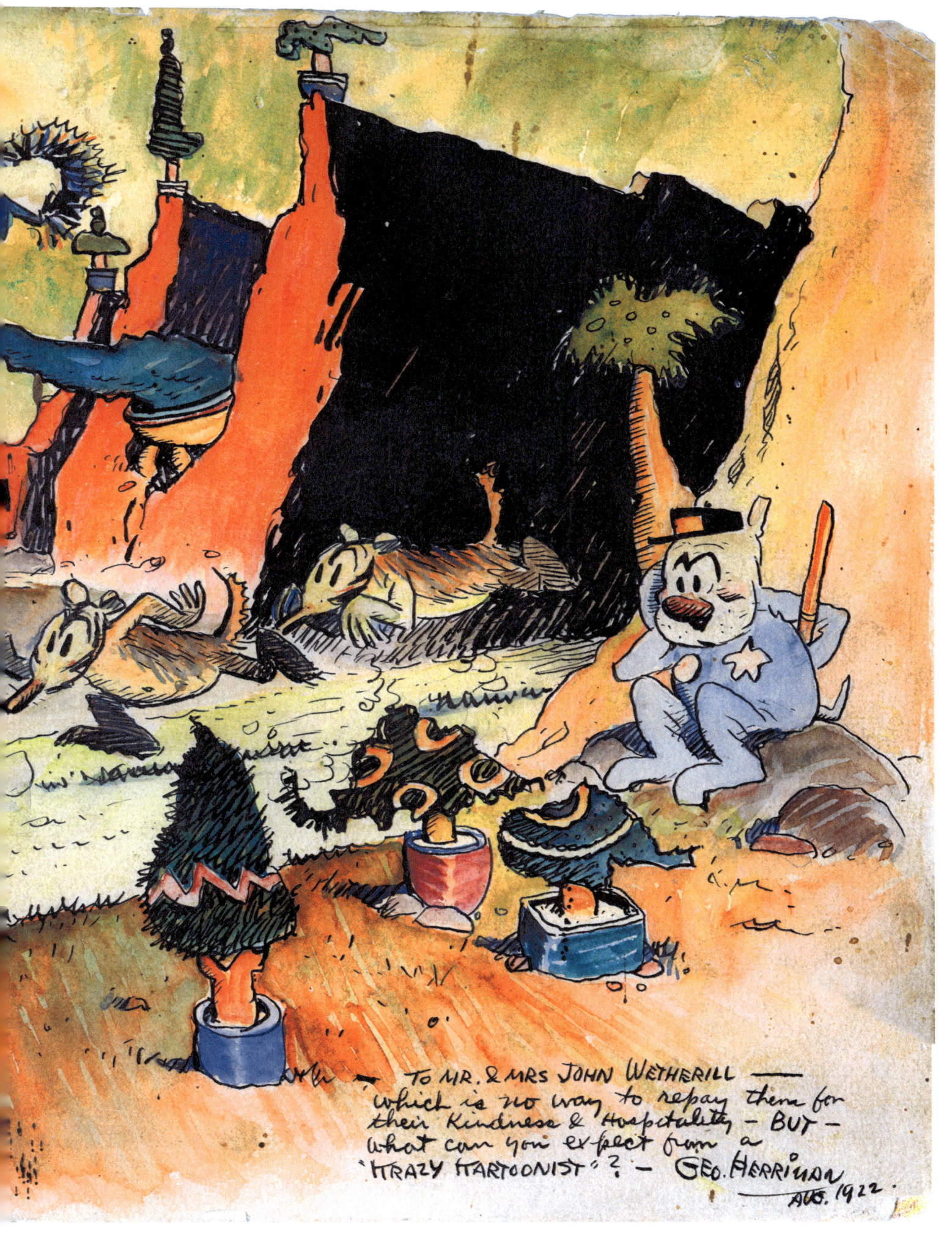

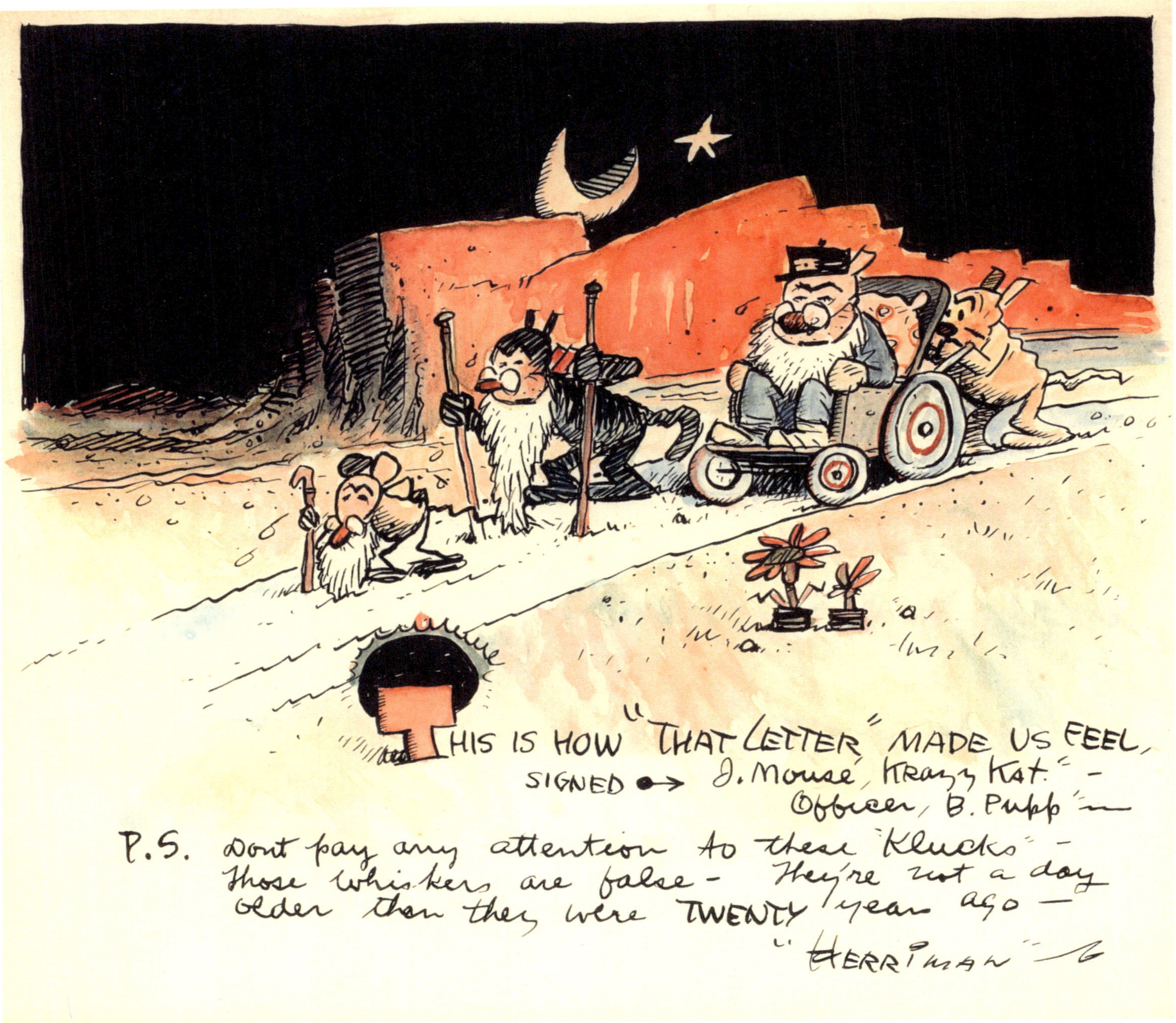
THIS IS HOW "THAT LETTER" MADE US FEEL,
SIGNED → I. Mouse, Krazy Kat, – Officer B. Pupp –
P.S. Dont pay any attention to these Klucks – Those whiskers are false – They're not a day older than they were TWENTY years ago –
"HERRIMAN"

ABOVE The inscription reads, "This is how 'that letter' made us feel, signed I. Mouse, Krazy Kat, Officer B. Pupp—P.S. Don't pay any attention to these 'klucks'—those whiskers are false—They're not a day older than they were TWENTY years ago—Herriman."

A Genius of the Comic Page

by Summerfield Baldwin

This essay first appeared in *Cartoons Magazine,* which normally featured political cartoons but made this unusual visit to Coconino County in June 1917.

There is a man named Herriman. All that I know of him is that he signs his name in curious letters to the most charming column of comic pictures that it has ever been my privilege to see. Do not recoil in horror before what you fear is going to be an apology for American vulgarism. The personalities that populate the world of *Krazy Kat* as they appear from day to day in the Hearst journals are not vulgar. They are rather the products of one of the most original and delicate of all contemporary American creative geniuses.

It is my purpose to point out in the following pages wherein that genius is original and delicate, and in some measure to show that its indigenous nature is something of which Americans might well be proud. A person with a fancy for the comic section is ordinarily prone to be ashamed of it, to excuse it as a means of relaxation, as an escape from reality, as a thousand and one other foibles. The shame and the excuses are right and natural, save in this single instance. For to follow the adventures of Mr. Herriman's fantastic animals is a delight which no one should underestimate or fail to enjoy.

I am not sure exactly when the series started. It must have been at least six years ago. For a number of years the sole actors on Mr. Herriman's stage were Krazy Kat and Ignatz Mouse. The motif of the drama they enacted was the perpetual chastisement of the Kat by the Mouse, a chastisement usually performed by the hurling of a brick at the former's head, and usually incited by some particularly atrocious manifestation of idiocy on the former's part. The origin of this conception is obvious enough, and is based solely on a reversal of the normal relations of the feline to the rodent.

Now it is a distinguishing characteristic of the technique of the comic artist that with the exhaustion of the situations suggested by the original protagonists and their primary raison d'étre, the material may be enlarged in two ways: first, and to the greatest possible extent, by the development of new phases in the old characters; second, as a last resort, by the introduction of new personages. In this respect, Mr. Herriman's craftsmanship does not differ from that of his fellow workers. While the original brick motif is still predominant, there has been introduced a minor motif which revolves around the indeterminate sex of the cat. The origin of this idea is again sufficiently obvious to need no explanation. That it contains the germ of a vast number of humorous situations must be equally clear. A third motif, of still more recent origin, is that of Krazy Kat's patient submission to, nay, actual delight in forever recurring maltreatment at the hands of his smaller fellow denizen of the animal world.

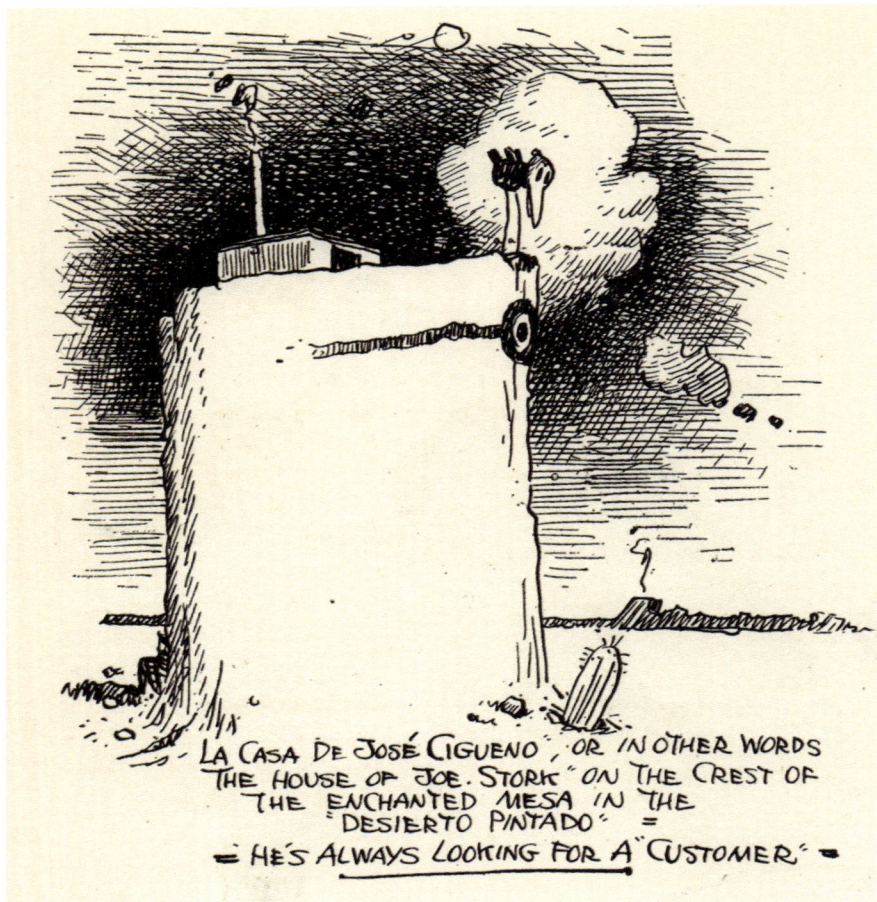

LA CASA DE JOSÉ CIGUENO", OR IN OTHER WORDS
THE HOUSE OF JOE. STORK" ON THE CREST OF
THE ENCHANTED MESA IN THE
"DESIERTO PINTADO" =
= HE'S ALWAYS LOOKING FOR A "CUSTOMER" =

Within the last two years Mr. Herriman has found it necessary to have recourse to the introduction of new characters. His enlarged dramatis personae includes a dog, known as Offissa Pupp, who protects the Kat (uncharacteristically enough) from the assaults of the Mouse. There are also a large number of other animals, who pass rapidly across the stage and serve largely as excuses for new vagaries on the part of the chief actors.

Mr. Herriman's medium is the pen and ink sketch. In the daily issues there are five of these. In the Sunday issues the form is less strictly limited. As a rule, each sketch contains an horizon line decorated with quaintly fantastic trees and houses. In the foreground the characters speak their lines and go through their business. Where speaking of lines predominates and the characters move little, the audience is entertained by a miraculous shift in the landscape from picture to picture. Such a shift is often made, indeed, where the movements of the protagonists are violent, but in these cases its value is not so great. I should like to speak at length of these charming landscapes, but they defy description. They consist almost exclusively of trees with extraordinarily large and bulging trunks crowned by the merest tuft of foliage (giving somewhat the effect of misshapen asparagus stalks) and of small, squat, one-storied houses with thatched roofs, evidently intended to suggest the hovels of Mexican peons.

The appearance of the actors themselves is also well-nigh incapable of reproduction in words. To be appreciated they must be seen. (I dare say few of my readers, however high their noses are, by this time, lifted, have failed to see them.) Krazy Kat is black, with a large body and short legs. His face is white, with two black dots for eyes, and a thick black line for a nose. His tail (also black) is a most remarkable creation, ending very squarely indeed, and almost always betraying one or two quite heart-rending kinks. Ignatz Mouse is done in line. His head and trunk are of approximately the same size. His legs and tail are single lines. His feet are made by a mere wiggle of the artist's pen. The other characters are also done in line, and are, if possible, of an appearance even more fantastic than that of Krazy and Ignatz. Offissa Pupp, for example, is exceedingly stout in the waist, wears a policeman's hat, and a belt from which is suspended a billy. He suggests, to be sure, a humanized bulldog, but his attitudes are far from canine. All the actors, of course, walk on their hind legs, and in general assume human postures.

From the point of view of drawing, Mr. Herriman's work is distinguished by the simplicity of the means whereby he secures the utmost subtlety of effect, by the fantastic nature of his conceptions, and (what appeals to me most of all) by his ability to create kinaesthetic illusion. No better example of the simplicity of his means could be found than in the face of Krazy Kat. It consists, as I have said, of a white patch in which are two black dots for eyes, a thick black line for a rather protruding nose, and a thinner line for a mouth. By almost infinitesimal variations in the position of the eyes and of the corners of the mouth, Mr. Herriman contrives to run the whole gamut of the emotions on Krazy's excessively stupid countenance. Fear, affection, devotion, wonder, surprise, amusement, content, all find a place. Before me, at this moment, he is depicted (in the somewhat more elaborate Sunday edition) as sitting rapt at the feet of Mr. Stork, and hearing from him the circumstances of his birth and the birth of many of his intimates. He has drawn his knees up and holds them clasped in his forelegs. His eye dots are raised a trifle nearer than usual to his arching eyebrows, and are somewhat extended vertically. His mouth line, of which little is visible, suggests the close-pressed lips of a child fascinated by a fairy story. Again, on the same page, he is depicted asleep in his natal washtub. His eye dots are now horizontal—clearly shut. His mouth, again barely visible over the edge of the tub, has become relaxed into a small triangle. His face is essentially asleep.

Mr. Herriman's conception, unlike his execution, is rather complex. It is, as I have said, fantastic, and yet fantastic in a way more quaint than out and out grotesque. Having turned the relations of the animal world upside down, he must perforce distort the animals themselves. Krazy and Ignatz are marvelous enough representations of the cat and mouse, but they are not comparable in this respect to some of their fellow performers. These last, I shall not attempt to describe. The bookworm with the pair of legs, the ostrich with the mittenlike feet, the turtle with the cigar, the duck with the shoes and the silk hat, the dog (not, in this case, Officer Pupp, with the spectacles and the barroom posture), are all utterly inimitable and, as a rule, so nonsensical as to transcend the vulgarity usually found in comic animals. Of his landscapes and trees, I have spoken. To those who would delve deeper, I can only say (as Philip to Nathaniel): "Come and see!"

ABOVE, OPPOSITE; OVERLEAF Drawings Herriman created especially for this article.

The third phase of Mr. Herriman's craftsmanship is his ability to create kinaesthetic illusion. Here again his means are fairly simple. The "arms" and legs of Ignatz Mouse consist, as I have said, of single lines. With these crooked at various angles, the artist contrives to depict almost perfectly the posture assumed in throwing. Thus, in those pictures wherein chastisement is inflicted on the unfortunate Krazy, one can feel, as it were metaphysically, just the sensations of the mouse as he hurls the brick, or the stone, or (once most charmingly) the watermelon. The preposterous disproportion between the thrower and the missile lends added fascination. Somehow or other the tremendous physical exertion required is brought out in every line of Ignatz' body. More ingenious and elusive still is the method by which the sense of Krazy's precipitation through space is conveyed. Sometimes, after being struck from behind, he comes hurtling directly at you. Again he moves along directly parallel with the horizon—moves, mark you, not merely hangs suspended in mid-air, as would inevitably be the effect were the artist's hand less skillful. I cannot speak in detail of other illusions of motion which Mr. Herriman conjures up. He understands perfectly how to depict slinking, hasty retreat, the walk of perfect indifference, the walk of those accustomed to ride, the walk of those with something on their minds, and heaven only knows what else. Follow his column for a week and you will realize his boundless versatility.

But Mr. Herriman's genius is almost as much manifested by his literary style as by his drawings. Krazy Kat, for example, indulges in a vast variety of most engaging idiosyncracies of diction. The flat "a" of "Ignatz" becomes the "e" of "Ignetz." Singular and plural are not very clearly differentiated, either. "Ignetz Mice" is usually Krazy's way of addressing his companion. On the page before me, I see such delightful specimens of Kat dialect as: "Wundafil, Mr. Stork, just simpfully wundafil," or, as Krazy renders a variation on a well-known ballad:

"How dear to my heart is the scene of my infinthood,
Where fond reckillection pr-e-e-e-zents tha-m-m-m to view.
The ole haunted house and the cellar undaneet it,
And the dear old wash-boila e-e-e-n which I was born. . . .
And every loved spot whom my infinthood knew."

On the same page, we discover Mr. Herriman in an altogether different vein as he writes this almost beautiful explanation of the significance of the day's pictures:

"The clocks of the universe are striking the hour of now and Joe Stork, who dwells on the topside of the enchanted mesa in the desierto pintado, and who pilots princes and paupers, poets and peasants, puppies and pussycats across the river without any other side of the shore of here, is telling Krazy Kat a tale which must never be told, and yet which everyone knows."

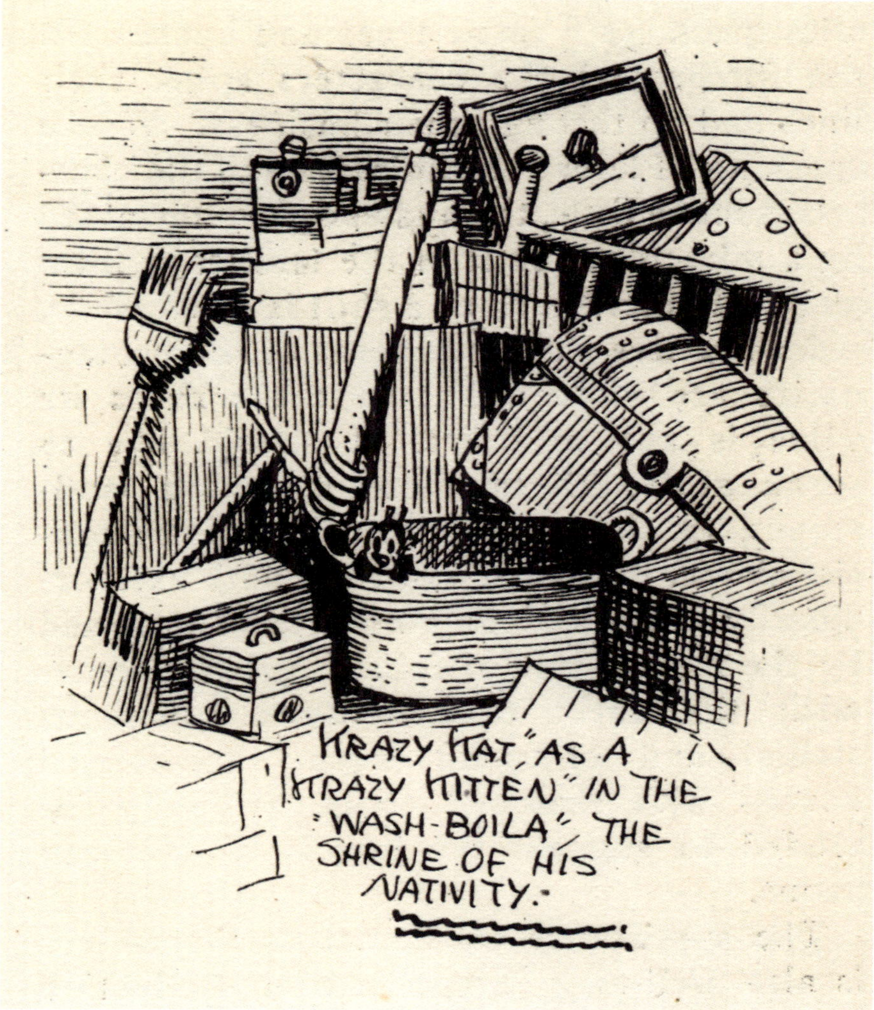
"KRAZY KAT" AS A "KRAZY KITTEN" IN THE "WASH-BOILA" THE SHRINE OF HIS NATIVITY.

One would like to see Mr. Herriman try his hand at writing fairy tales, for one has a feeling that he could do it in a most quaint and effective manner. "The river without any other side of the shore of here"—what a phrase! How miraculous in its suggestiveness! How steeped in that imagery which is always associated with childhood's notion of the origin of life.

Mesa and desierto pintado illustrate another feature of Mr. Herriman's verbiage. He is apparently well acquainted with Mexican dialect and employs it with startling frequency. I am myself ordinarily well-nigh unable to recall enough of my college Spanish to make out what he means. I am tempted to conclude that not a few of his phrases pass completely over the heads of a majority of his audience. I have a similar feeling with regard to his inexhaustible store of literary allusions. In one out of every five of his columns there occurs some indication that Mr. Herriman is by no means an unlettered man. Frequently, also, Krazy and Ignatz indulge in a sophisticated hair-splitting that might have delighted the heart of Socrates. Forgive me if, in all this, I seem to patronize. The experience of finding a genius in a comic section is novel enough to serve as excuse for any tactlessness.

Another charming feature of the conversations of his characters is their indiscriminate mingling of the choicest of diction with phrases scarcely in the best literary use. Thus on this single page to which I have referred so often, Mr. Ostrich speaks thus:

"There wasn't a grander castle in all the Kalahari than the one in which I was born. That was me starting

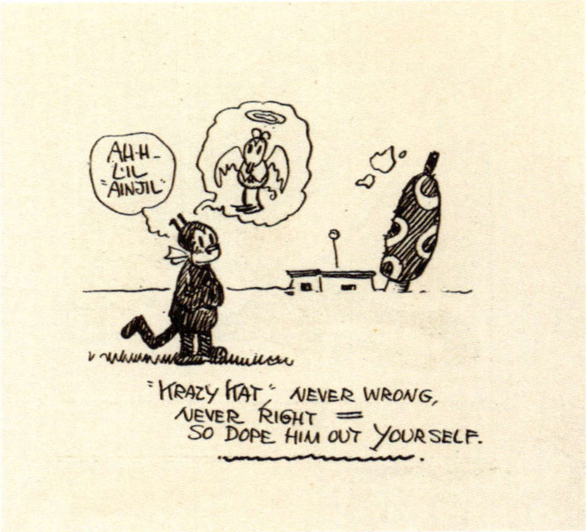
AH-H- LIL "AINJIL"
"KRAZY KAT" NEVER WRONG, NEVER RIGHT = SO DOPE HIM OUT YOURSELF.

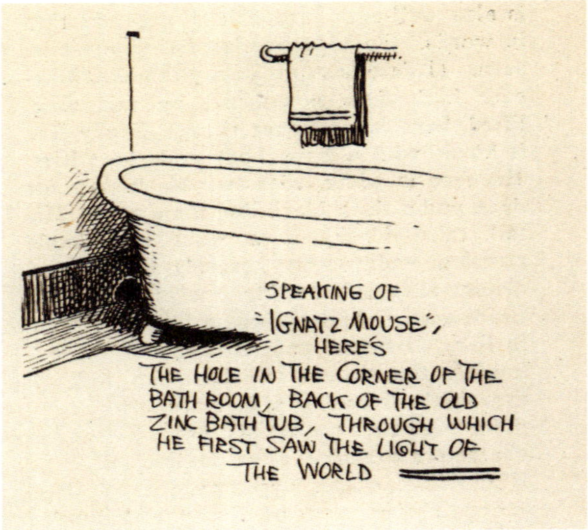
SPEAKING OF "IGNATZ MOUSE", HERE'S THE HOLE IN THE CORNER OF THE BATH ROOM, BACK OF THE OLD ZINC BATH TUB, THROUGH WHICH HE FIRST SAW THE LIGHT OF THE WORLD

life as a infant swathed in the purple of royalty, and a golden spoon in my mouth. Yizza-boy!"

Mr. Turtle goes on in the same vein as follows:

> *"Ha, you prate of castles and golden spoons, and you boast of the purple, but know you, my friends, that I, Terrapin Turtle, had all that stuff at my birth, and more, my swaddling clothes were diamonds. Segura Miguel!"* which, being interpreted is, presumably, "Sure, Mike!"

I should like to add a few words in connection with the incidents to illustrate which Mr. Herriman draws his pictures. I am unfortunately altogether dependent on my memory in this matter, and consequently cannot perhaps make citations so apt as if I had a number before me to choose from. One of the slightest and yet one of the most amusing series I recall is this: In the first picture, the artist has mixed his conversation. Krazy is made to say "Hello, Krazy," while Ignatz says "Hello, Ignatz." In the second picture, each glances at the other's remarks. In the third each has grasped the line which binds the words spoken to the lips of the speaker. In the fourth, we find these lines crossed, and in the fifth the remarks are arranged properly, while a look of contentment is writ large upon the features of both. This typifies that class of incident in which the artist in a manner introduces himself to his audience by emphasizing the limitations and general nature of his medium. Again I recall a series of which the first scene represents Krazy carrying a large framed picture. In the next we discover him hanging it, the picture being a representation of himself. He is mounted on a box during the process. In the third the picture is hung, and Krazy is departing with the remark that Ignatz will be delighted to see it. In the fourth picture, Ignatz is on the box eyeing it quizzically. In the last, we find the picture utterly ruined, as if something had been hurled at it, while Krazy looks at it regretfully and shows by his remark that he knows that Ignatz has already seen it. This is essentially a series designed to throw light on Krazy's pitifully submissive character, and the brutal way in which Ignatz tramples on his feelings. Finally, one of the most delightful of the incidents I recall is an allegorical depiction of birth control. Krazy, the epicene, is now become a tabby cat, and is revealed outside her cottage. The second picture shows a stork winging its way in the far distance. In the third, Krazy is running to her house, while the stork draws nearer. In the fourth, Krazy is seen partly emerging from the chimney, over which she is spreading a sheet. In the final scene, the chimney is covered, the stork flies over the cottage, and Krazy from the window peeps out at it with an exceedingly mischievous twinkle in her eye.

Let me say one word more of Mr. Herriman's ingeniously onomatopoetic way of representing sound. The passage of a brick through the air is usually represented by the letters Z-I-Z-Z strewn in its wake. The concussion of the brick on Krazy's head is rep-

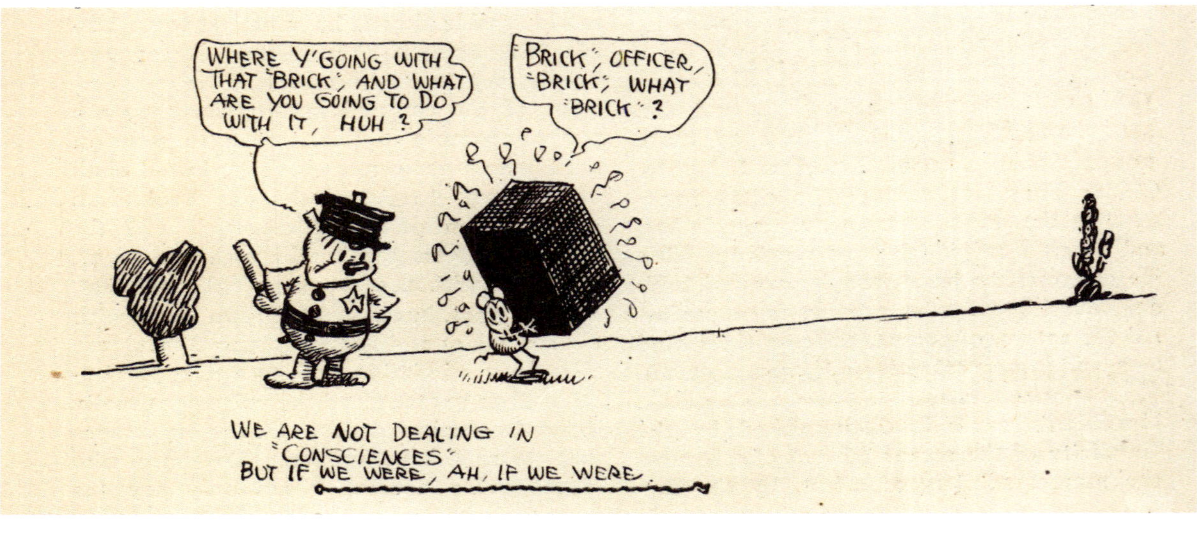
WHERE Y'GOING WITH THAT "BRICK", AND WHAT ARE YOU GOING TO DO WITH IT, HUH ?
"BRICK", OFFICER, "BRICK", WHAT "BRICK" ?
WE ARE NOT DEALING IN "CONSCIENCES" BUT IF WE WERE, AH, IF WE WERE.

resented by the greatest variety of symbols. I recall one in particular where the missile happened to be a watermelon, and where the sound it was supposed to make was represented most appropriately by some such combination of letters as *skobsh*. Here as always, Mr. Herriman's art is rather designed to suggest than to imitate.

Oscar Wilde has somewhere written that the only literary forms not devised by the Greeks are the sonnet, the ballad written in sham Scotch dialect, and American journalism. For the sake of Hellenic reputation, one cannot but rejoice that American journalism, indeed, finds no prototype in the age of Pericles. But at the same time, it is an obvious fact that without American journalism we should not have American funny pages, and without American funny pages we should not have Mr. Herriman's *Krazy Kat*. And I hope I am not making myself too ridiculous in suggesting that even the age of Pericles need not have been ashamed to stand sponsor for this last.

In the foregoing pages, I have surveyed Mr. Herriman's work in an exceedingly cursory and careless fashion. I have endeavored to point out the poignant originality and innate delicacy of his drawing in respect to both their conception and execution. I have tried to cite illustrations of his delicious literary style, and of his ingenuity in devising plots in which to set his artistic and literary creations. I have been compelled to leave many things unsaid that I should have liked to say. I have been incompetent to devise any consistent critical theory that would do justice to his genius and vindicate his work of the charge of vulgarity so justly levied against that of many of his contemporaries.

My sole purpose has been to bring him to the attention of thinking people as a phase of American art well worth thinking about; in other words, to perform what is really the sole function of criticism, the function of discovering genius wheresoever it may be concealed. If I have in any measure accomplished my purpose or performed my function, I shall rest content.

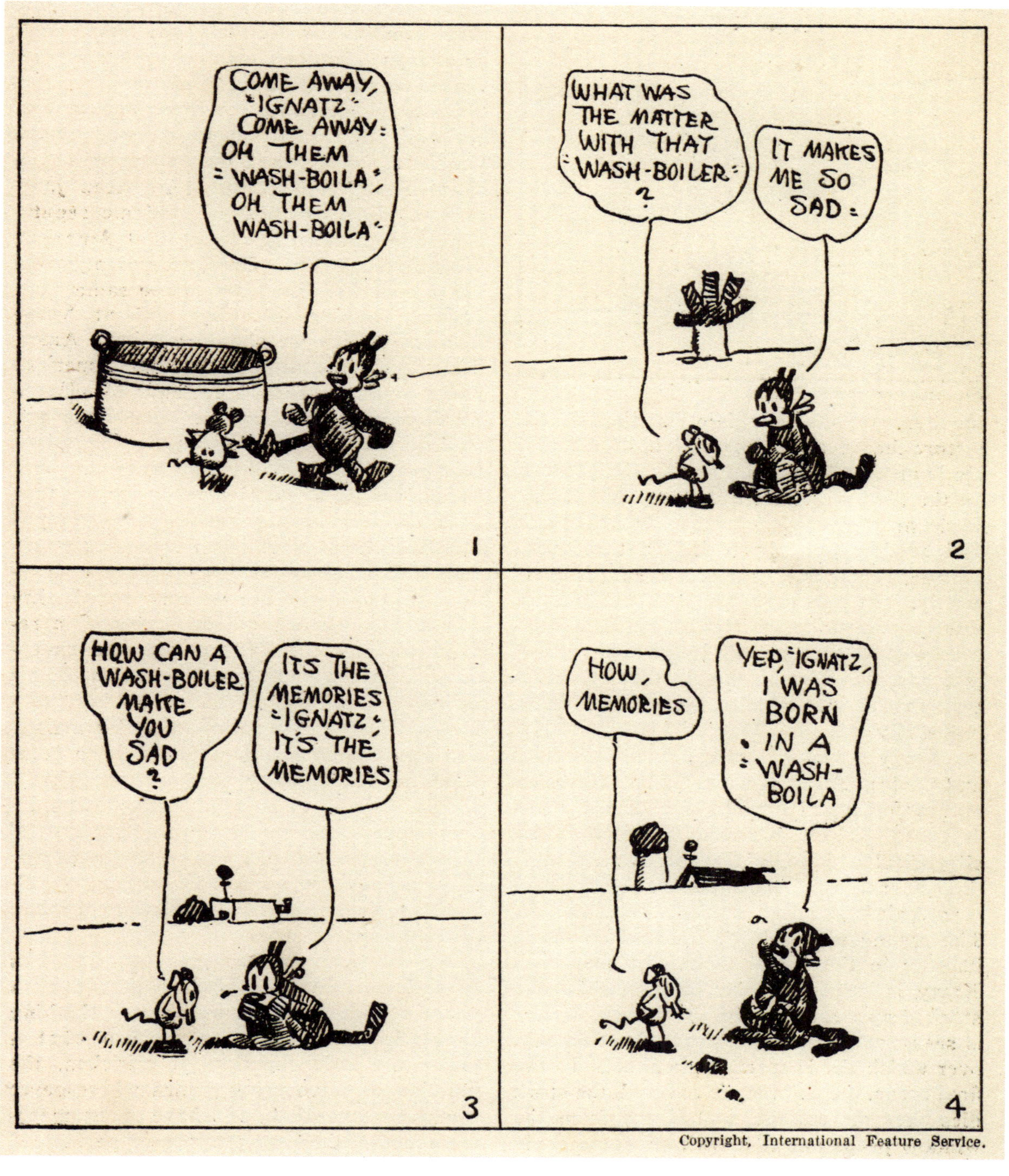

COME AWAY, IGNATZ COME AWAY: OH THEM WASH-BOILA; OH THEM WASH-BOILA
WHAT WAS THE MATTER WITH THAT WASH-BOILER ?
IT MAKES ME SO SAD
HOW CAN A WASH-BOILER MAKE YOU SAD ?
ITS THE MEMORIES IGNATZ IT'S THE MEMORIES
HOW, MEMORIES
YEP, IGNATZ, I WAS BORN IN A WASH-BOILA
Copyright, International Feature Service.

LEFT The original caption from the article reads, "How dear to my heart is that li'l ole wash boila."

Kat Books

Krazy, Ignatz Mouse, and Offissa Pupp have graced the pages of many books and special publications.

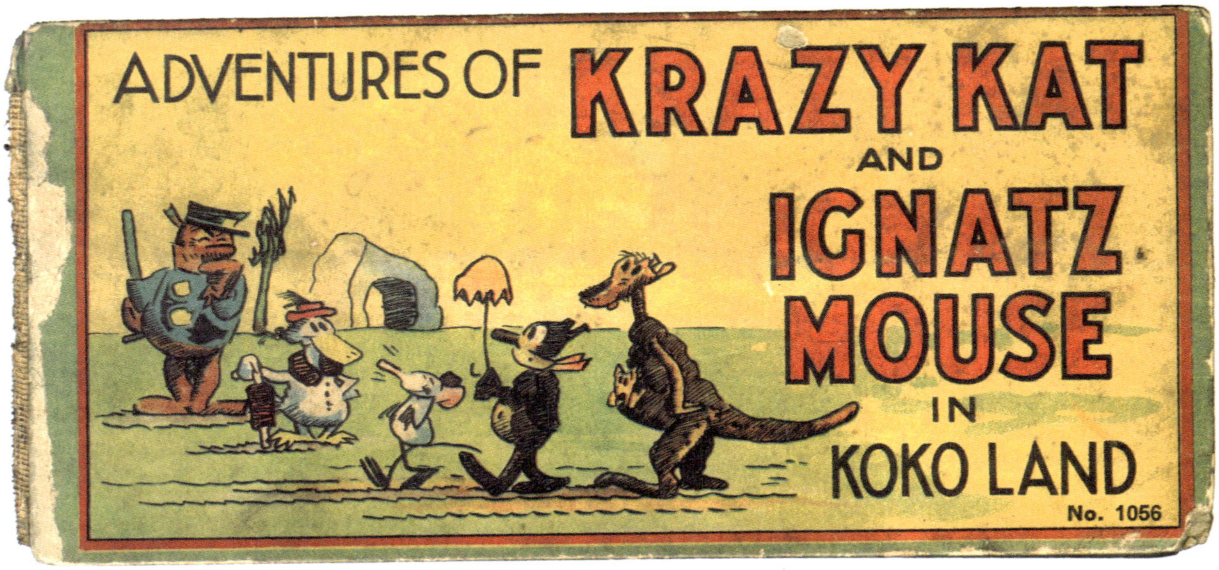
ADVENTURES OF KRAZY KAT
AND
IGNATZ MOUSE
IN
KOKO LAND
No. 1056

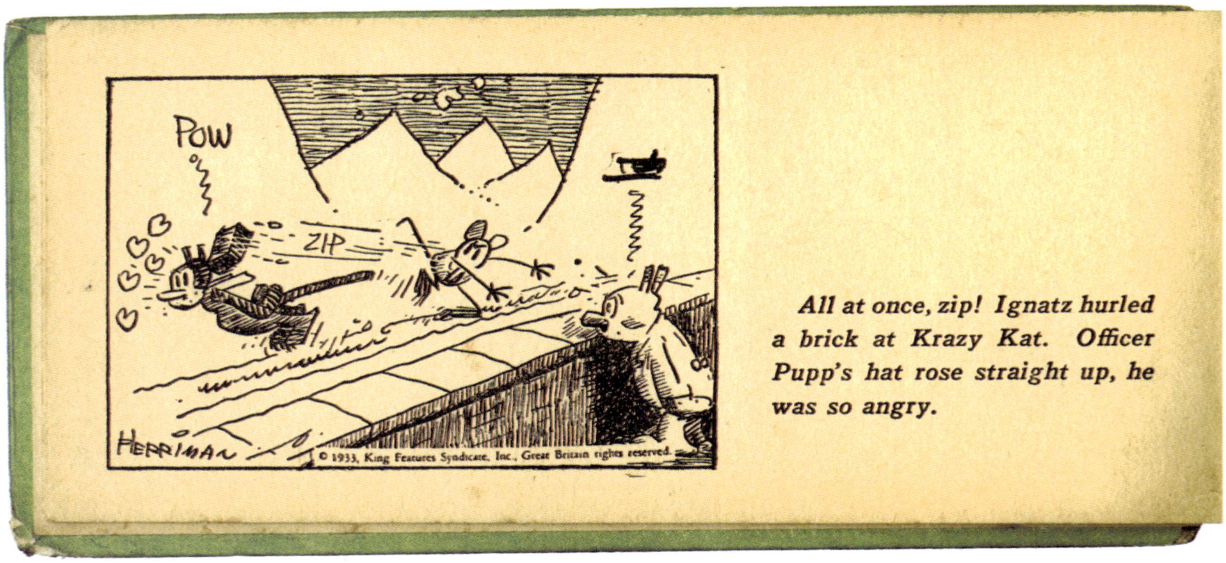
POW
ZIP
HERRIMAN
© 1933, King Features Syndicate, Inc., Great Britain rights reserved.
All at once, zip! Ignatz hurled a brick at Krazy Kat. Officer Pupp's hat rose straight up, he was so angry.

ABOVE Although the inside reprints images from the *Krazy Kat* strip, the illustration on the cover of this 1934 book, published by the Saalfield Publishing Company, is an interpretation of Herriman's characters by an anonymous artist.

OPPOSITE Cover of *Krazy Kat,* a collection of Sundays and dailies published by Henry Holt in 1946, two years after Herriman passed away. The book has an introduction by E. E. Cummings.

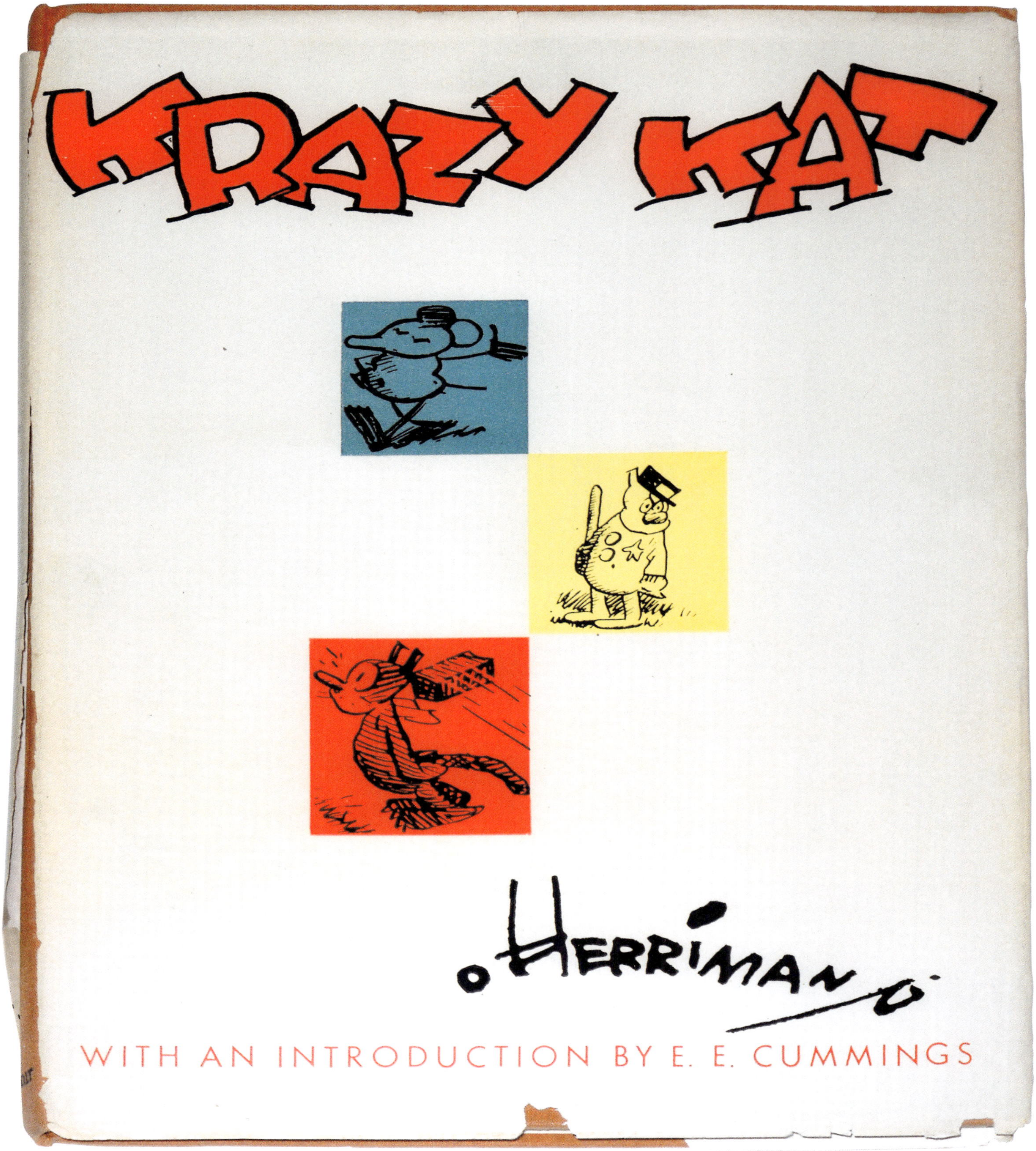
KRAZY KAT
HERRIMAN
WITH AN INTRODUCTION BY E. E. CUMMINGS

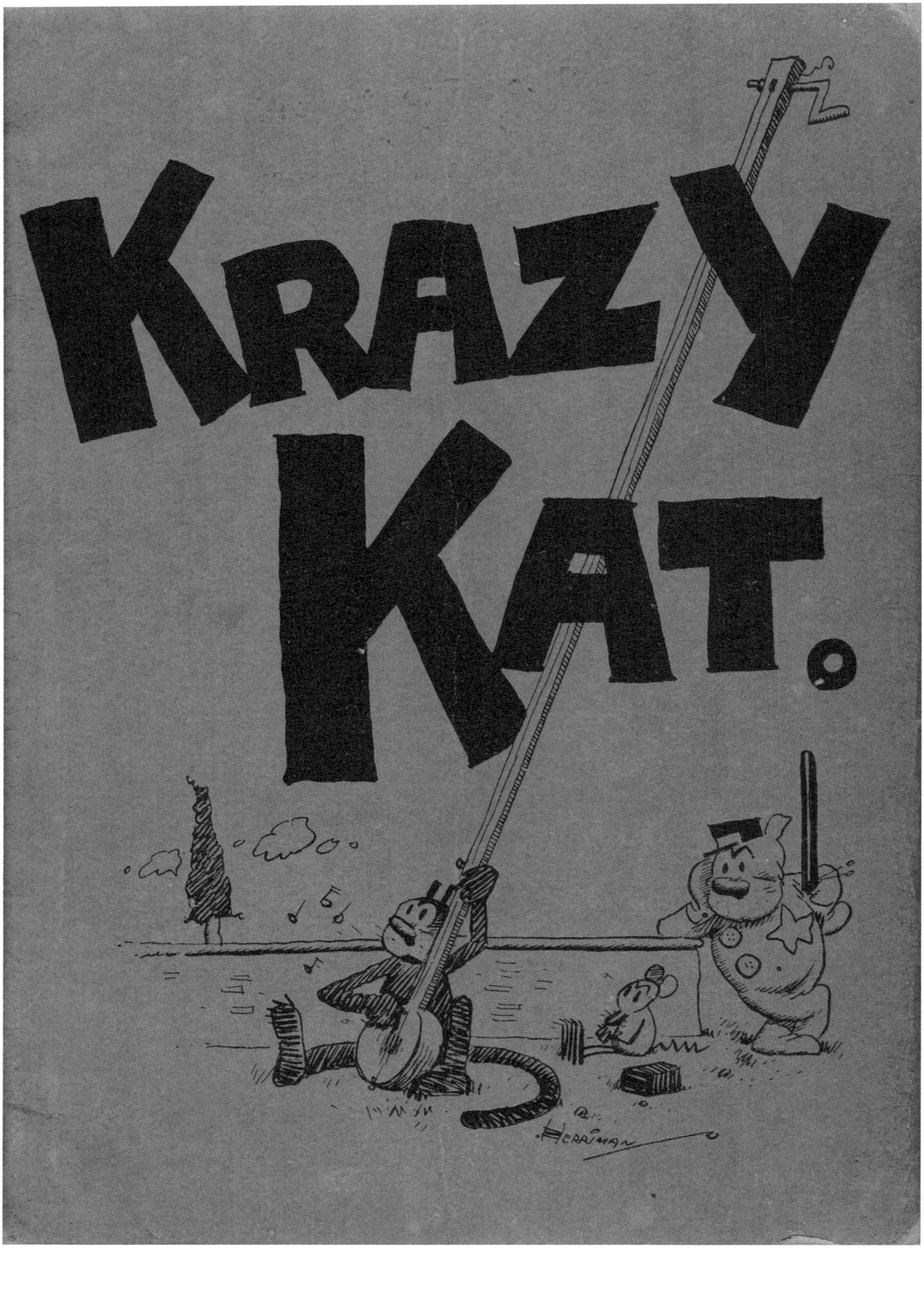
KRAZY
KAT.
HERRIMAN

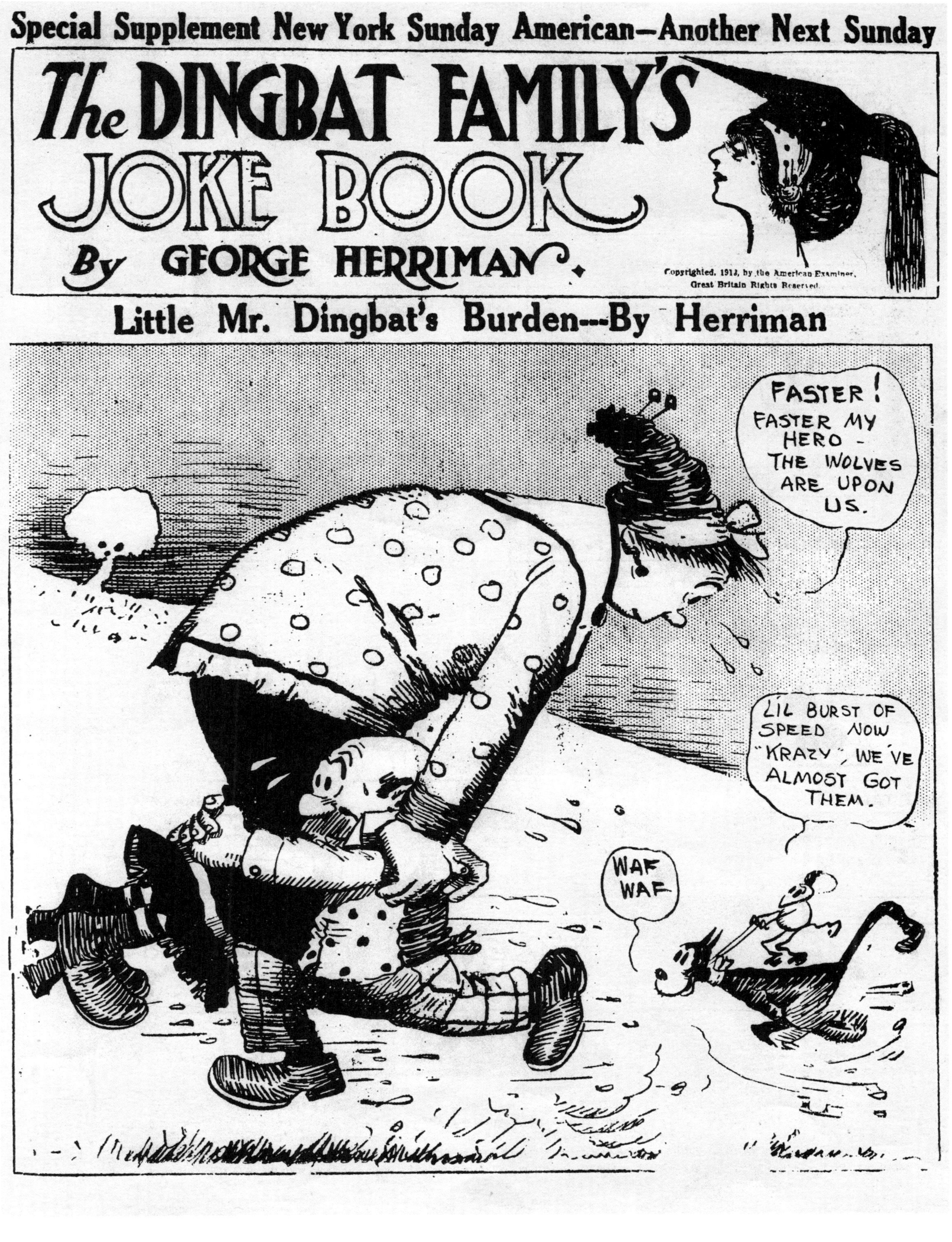
Special Supplement New York Sunday American—Another Next Sunday
The DINGBAT FAMILY'S JOKE BOOK
By GEORGE HERRIMAN
Little Mr. Dingbat's Burden---By Herriman
FASTER! FASTER MY HERO - THE WOLVES ARE UPON US.
LIL BURST OF SPEED NOW "KRAZY", WE'VE ALMOST GOT THEM.
WAF WAF

OPPOSITE The cover of a program book for a jazz pantomime ballet written by John Alden Carpenter in 1922.

ABOVE A supplemental book that appeared with the *New York Sunday American* in 1916.

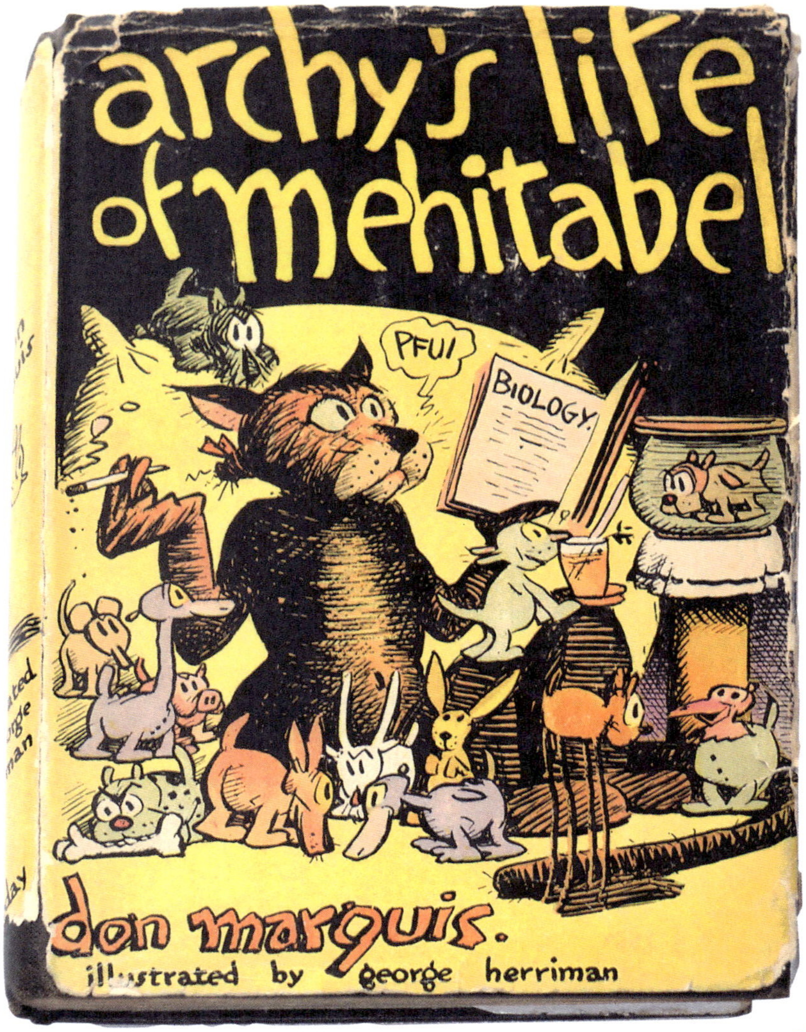
archy's life of mehitabel
PFUI
BIOLOGY
don marquis.
illustrated by george herriman

Doubleday, Doran & Company, Inc., 1933.

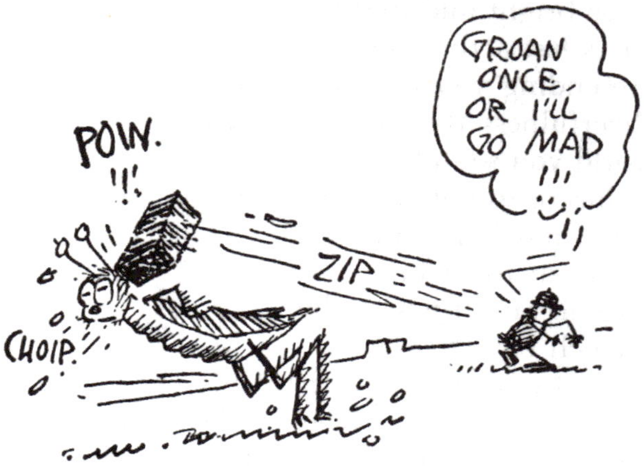
GROAN ONCE, OR I'LL GO MAD !!!
POW. !!
ZIP
CHOIP

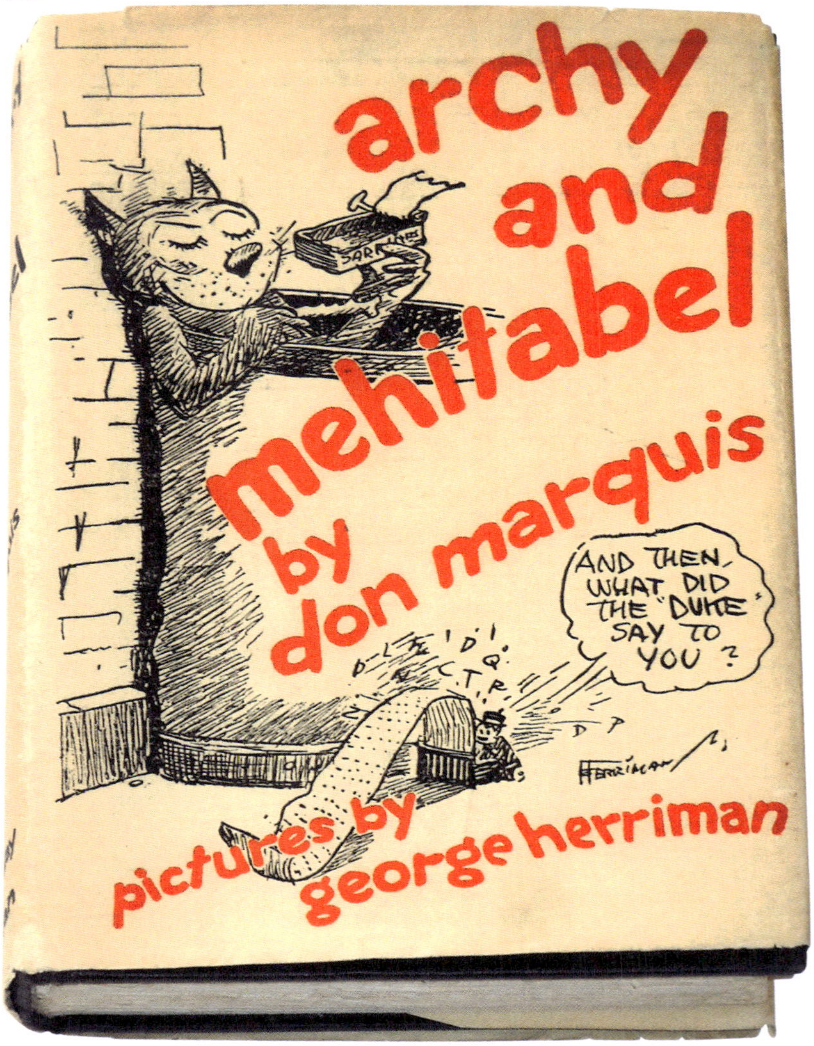
archy and mehitabel
by don marquis
AND THEN, WHAT DID THE "DUKE" SAY TO YOU ?
HERRIMAN
pictures by george herriman

Doubleday, Doran & Company, Inc., 1934.

ABOVE AND FOLLOWING PAGES Don Marquis created the characters Archy, a poet cockroach, and Mehitabel, an alley cat who claims she was Cleopatra in a previous life, in Marquis's 1916 newspaper column, later collected into books illustrated by Herriman.

ABOVE, RIGHT In Marquis's delightful books even bugs throw bricks!

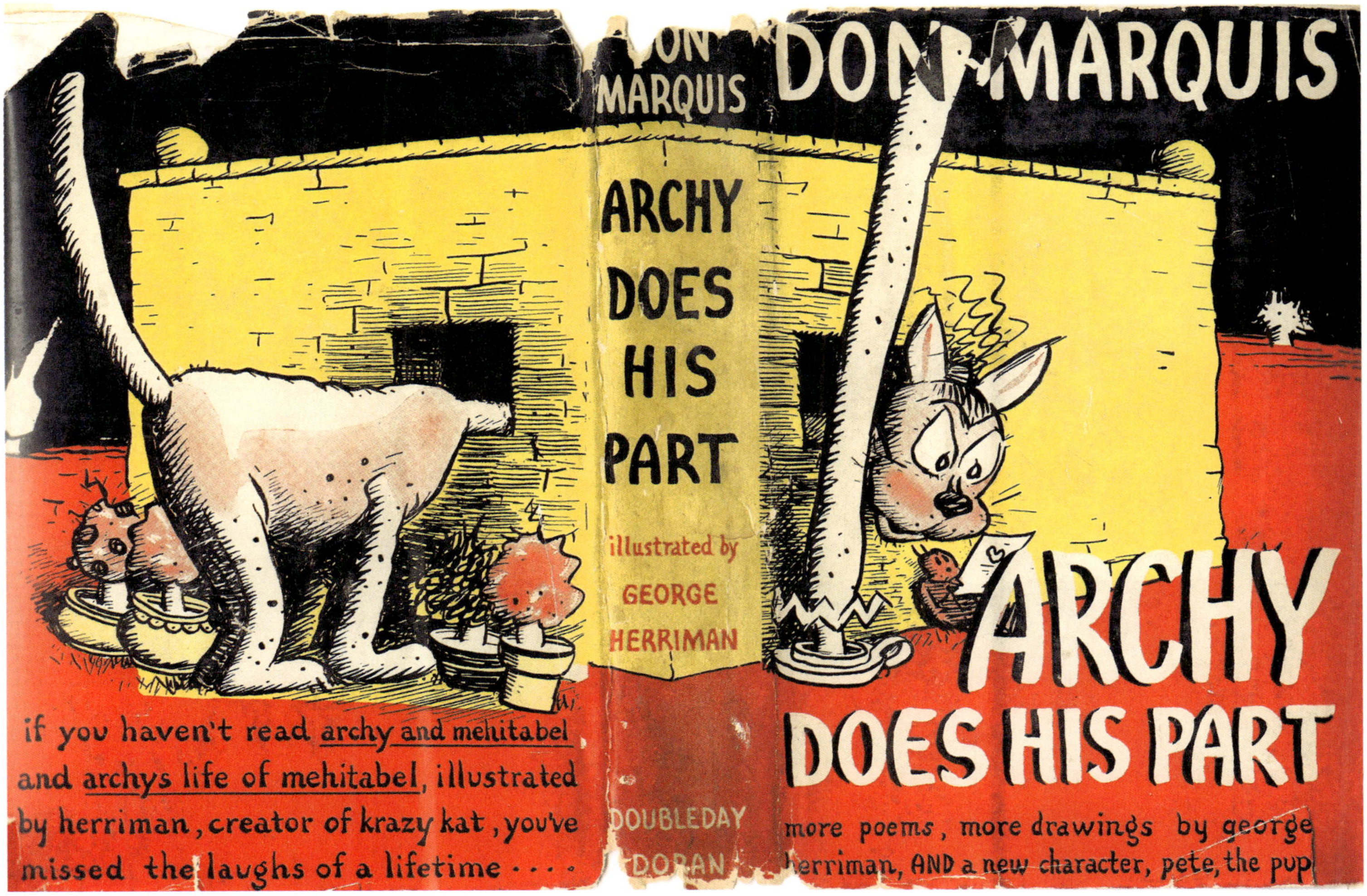
DON MARQUIS
ARCHY DOES HIS PART
illustrated by
GEORGE HERRIMAN
DOUBLEDAY DORAN
DON MARQUIS
ARCHY DOES HIS PART
if you haven't read archy and mehitabel and archys life of mehitabel, illustrated by herriman, creator of krazy kat, you've missed the laughs of a lifetime . . . .
more poems, more drawings by george herriman, AND a new character, pete, the pup

Doubleday, Doran & Company, Inc., 1935.

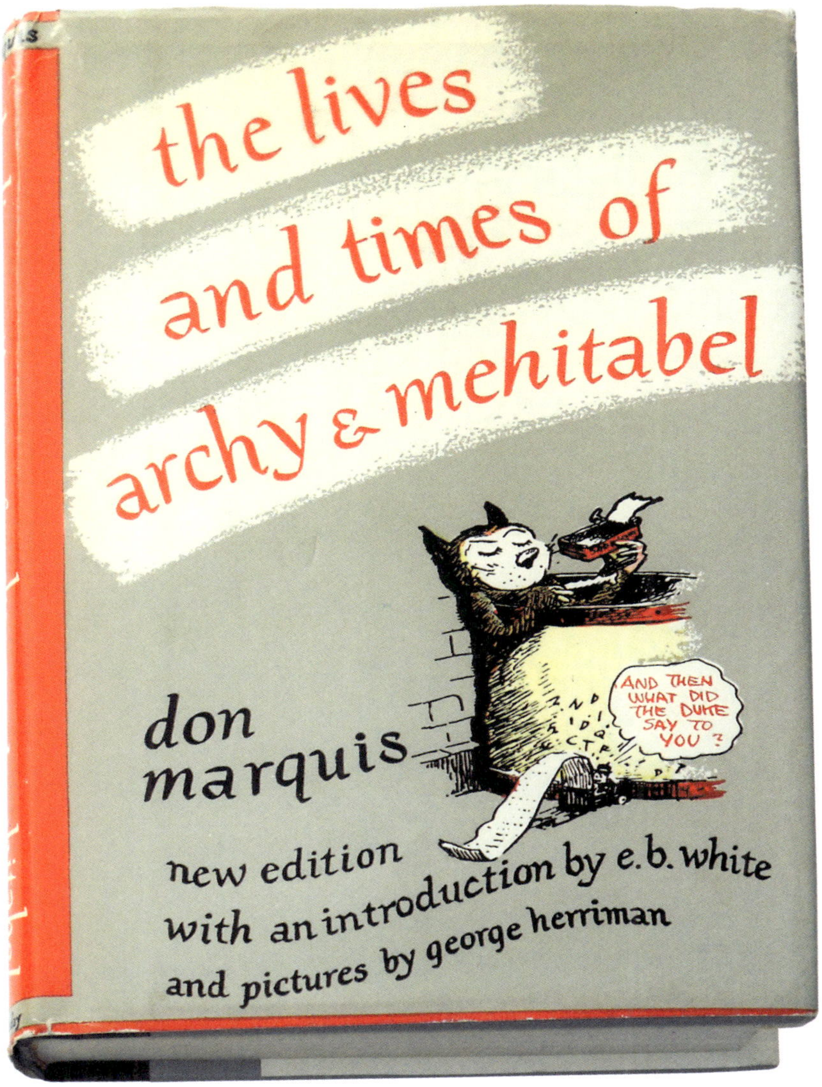
the lives and times of archy & mehitabel
AND THEN WHAT DID THE DUKE SAY TO YOU ?
don marquis
new edition
with an introduction by e. b. white
and pictures by george herriman

RIGHT E. B. White called George Herriman's art for this book "double-barreled illustration." White went on to say, "It seems to me Herriman deserves much credit for giving the right form and mien to these willful animals. They possess (as he drew them) the great soul. It would be hard to take Mehitabel if she were either more catlike, or less. She is cat, yet not cat; and Archy's lineaments are unmistakably those of poet and pest." Doubleday & Company, Inc., 1950.

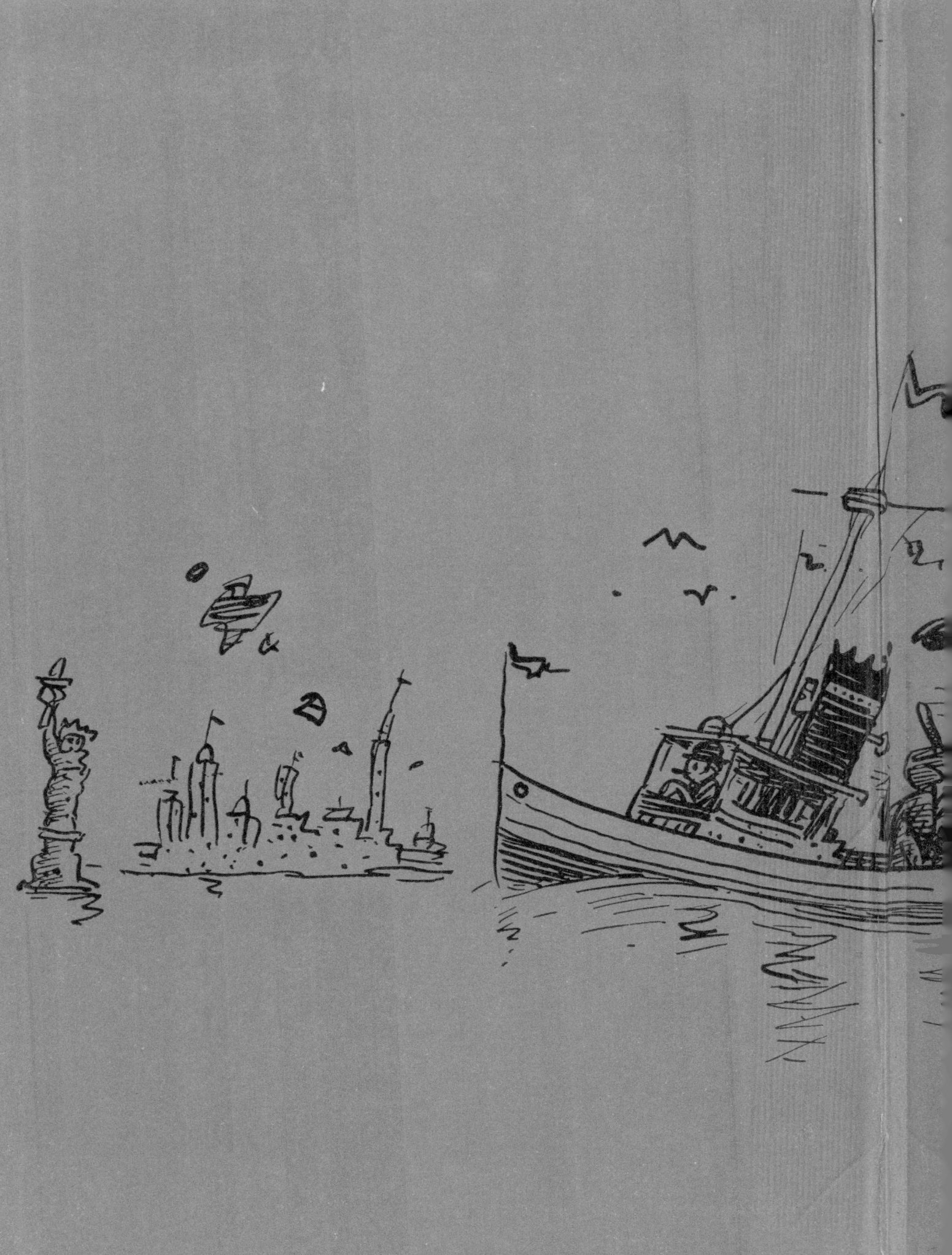

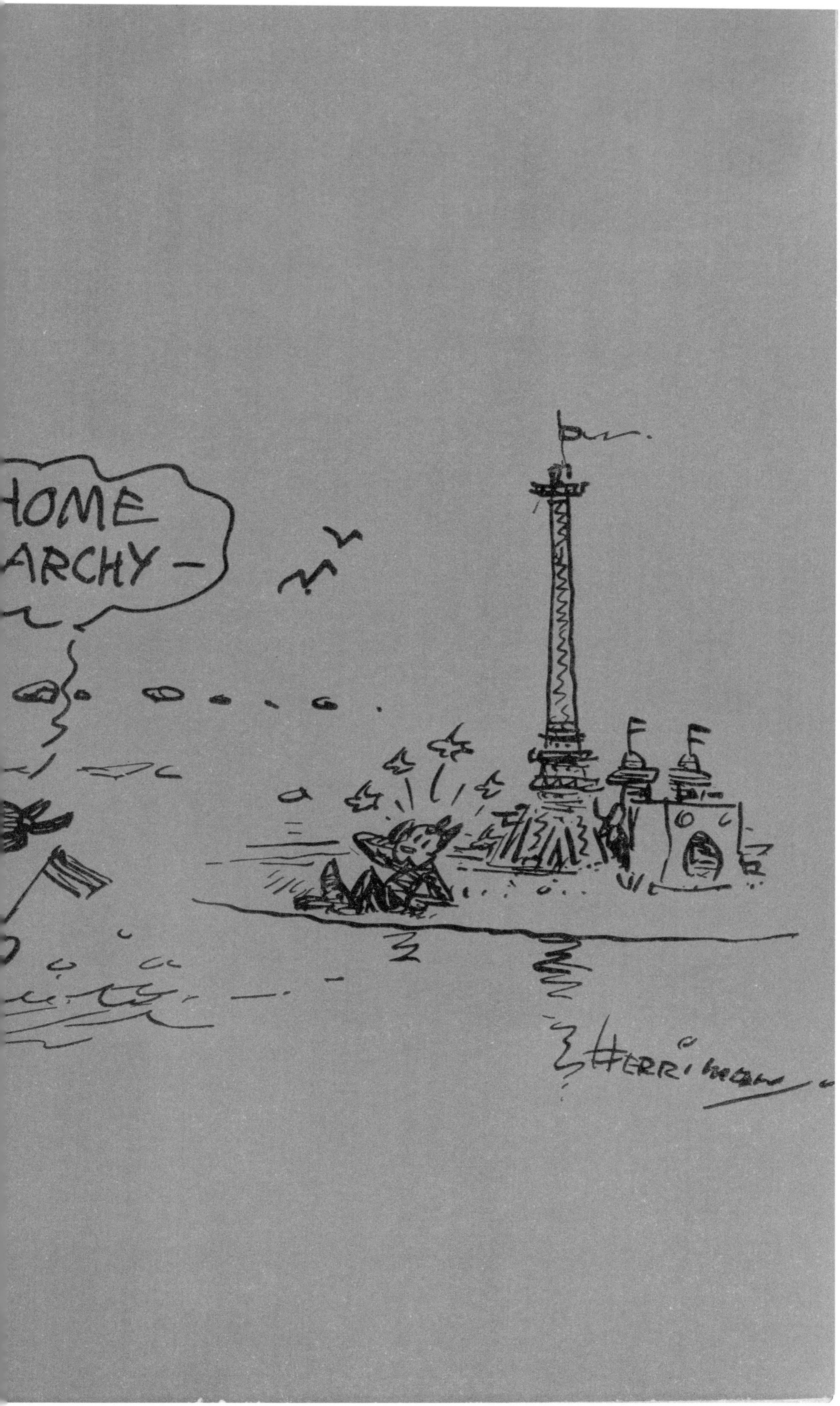
HOME
ARCHY –
HERRIMAN

LEFT The endpapers for *Archy and Mehitabel*.

OVERLEAF Frontispiece for the book *Archy's Life of Mehitabel*.

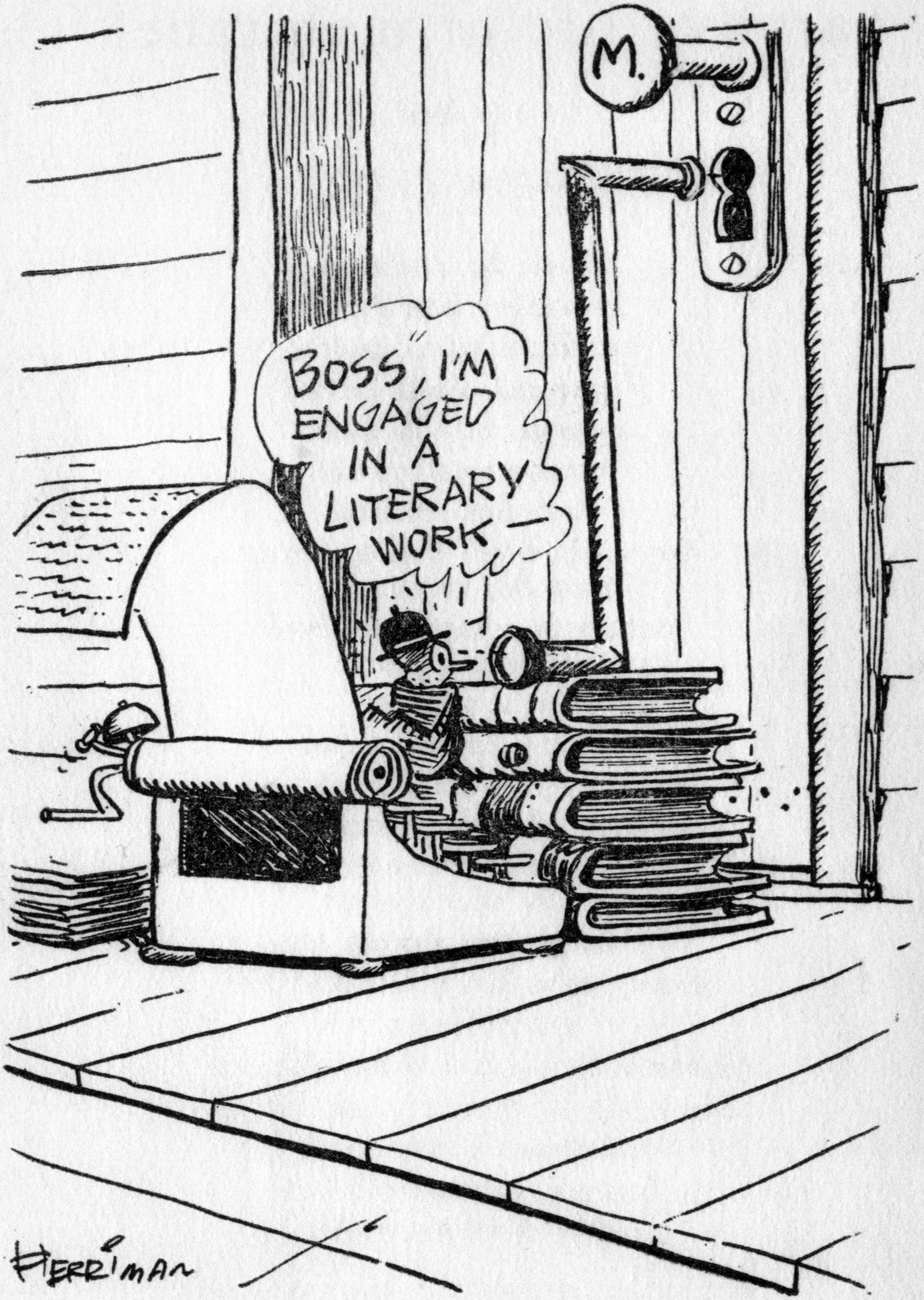
M.
BOSS, I'M ENGAGED IN A LITERARY WORK—
HERRIMAN

Reply to an Inquiry by Ignatz Mouse

by Jay Cantor

Me? No. Definitely not. I never resented her the name above the title. She was and always should be the headliner. Pupp and I knew that from the first moment we saw her. Oh, sure I was cleverer, he was "wiser" (if by wiser, you mean less cutting edge, more conventional, which is to say on the side of the law, instead of the avant-garde adventurer). Look at the way she moves, for God's sake—the girl has star quality. You can see immediately that she's the one who created our show's style—off-kilter, slightly syncopated, that *I don't know what it is* that makes you feel replete, filled with energy, wanting to dance; and at the same time that you're feeling full, you still want more—more of the ever-changing same.

Krazy reinvents herself every day, just enough so that she could remain Krazy yet hold our interest, not that she cared. Other stars, like Madonna, they freshen up the franchise to keep the suckers sucking, but Krazy didn't want to sell you anything, not even herself. She just tootled to the stars above and capered. And you heard. And you danced like her, best you could anyway. Our recording angel, Mr. George Herriman, he got it right in his jazzy, freshly minted, improvisatory style (and don't tell me it's an accident—mice are like Marxists or Freudians or Calvinists, we don't believe in accidents—that J. R. Morton, Louis Armstrong, and Mr. H, as we always called him, came from New Orleans, or that we've recently let that place drown—one humongous brick to the Big Easy's noggin).

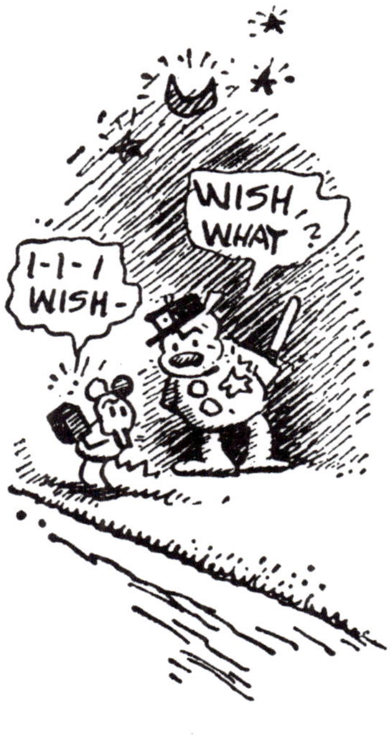
I-I-I WISH-
WISH, WHAT?

Krazy shaped our style, shaped us, from that first moment we saw her; *bang-oh,* see Krazy, be Krazy, or

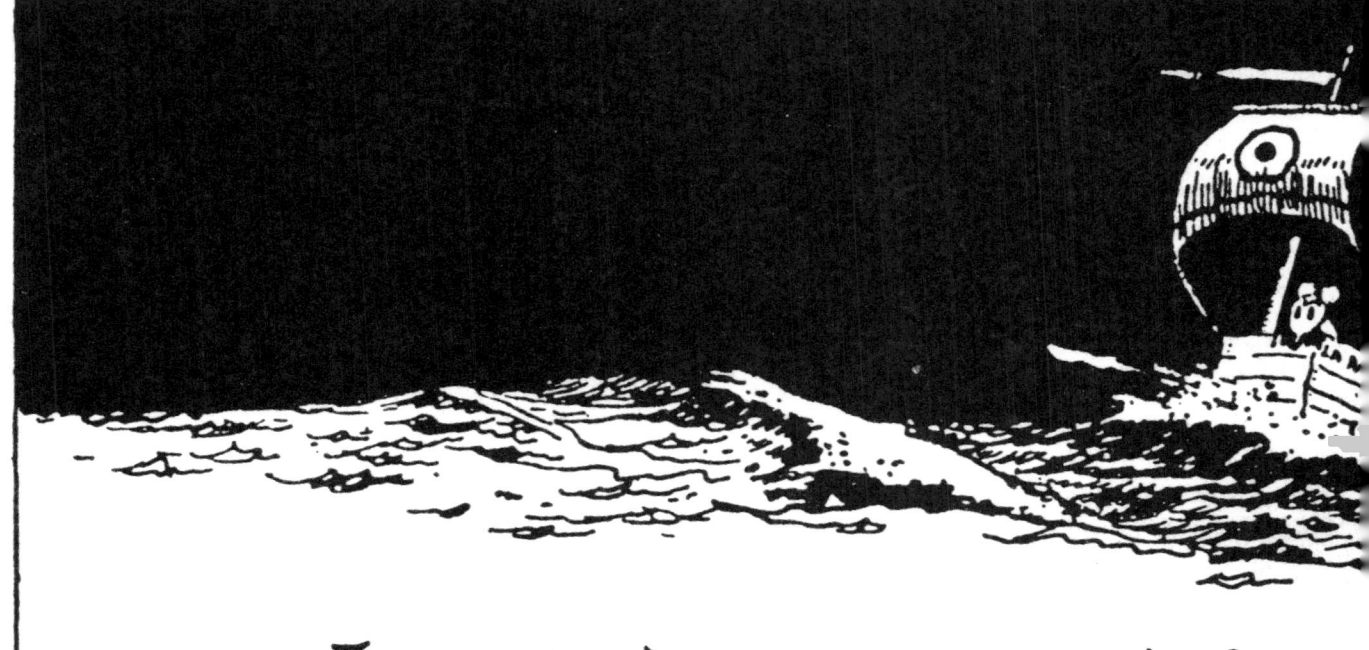

There is a storm tossed mariner mouse on the bluster

wanna-be Krazy. And I mean how annoying is that? "Baby, you make me lose control of myself," is something R&B sings about endlessly, but really, is *that* what people want—to lose control? If that's it, you could just go work at McDonald's or make a picture for Disney. But that's the effect Krazy had on all of us. I lost control (so did Pupp, but he didn't know it, he thought he was just fulfilling his calling, doing the Law and Lord's will). And unlike all the world's other wannabes, from St. Francis (in relation to the Madonna) or Gwen Ga Ga (in relation to Madonna), I knew I couldn't be her, because that girl, all the big and not-so-easy questions that knot up men and mice are ones she bears like she's bearing nothing, not even a feather. Take "Am I a man or a woman?" or "a man or a mouse?" the question that drives hysterics so mad from junior high on, so that they pump themselves up with muscles, or dress like Madonna, or slag the fag—all that was all no question at all to Ms.-sometimes-Mr. Kat.

So what could I do to this frustrating beauty to show her who was boss? You know what, of course, I bricked her. This brick she not only bore but delighted in. She would probably also have delighted in my *not* bricking her, but that I never found out, because, once again—*I couldn't control myself*. I bricked her because she made me lose control, and I bricked her to regain control, and either way, *she was in control*. So I may not be the headliner here, nor was meant to be, but I was the perverse motor of the thing. There is nothing perverse about KK, by the way; if you feel the brick is love then it ain't perverse to say so, it's just love, and who doesn't want that. But to throw the brick, day after day, knowing that you intend disdain but that it will be received as a valentine, that takes . . . not willpower, or endurance, but something that is the stupidity that lies beyond stupidity, the motor at the heart of existence. The one who knows *that* has actually to bear it; he's the repetitive, unsatisfied, inevitable perverse one, the mouse in a million, the one whose existence is its own trap.

Every great work of *modern* art requires a knotted up little perverse heart like that, the very essence of our existence without essence, our climbing to fall, our falling so we can climb again. It's as new and old and inevitable as the flatted fifth in the blues. Krazy's the headliner; she called me the "lil' angil," but to my tiny ears that only sounded like more of existence's mockery, because me it wasn't; Krazy's what made us sublime. But if you ask me, *I'm* the one who made us modern. I'm the unhappy, perverted hero of the show, the necessary Judas without whom no resurrection. I'm the Sisyphus, not that you did ask, not that anyone ever will. I know that, too, and still I persevere. *Ecce Mus*.

Jay Cantor has written the novels The Death of Che Guevara *and* Great Neck, *but nothing has made him prouder than the cooperation of Krazy and Ignatz in his research for* Krazy Kat: A Novel in Five Panels, *published by Knopf in 1987. He teaches at Tufts University.*

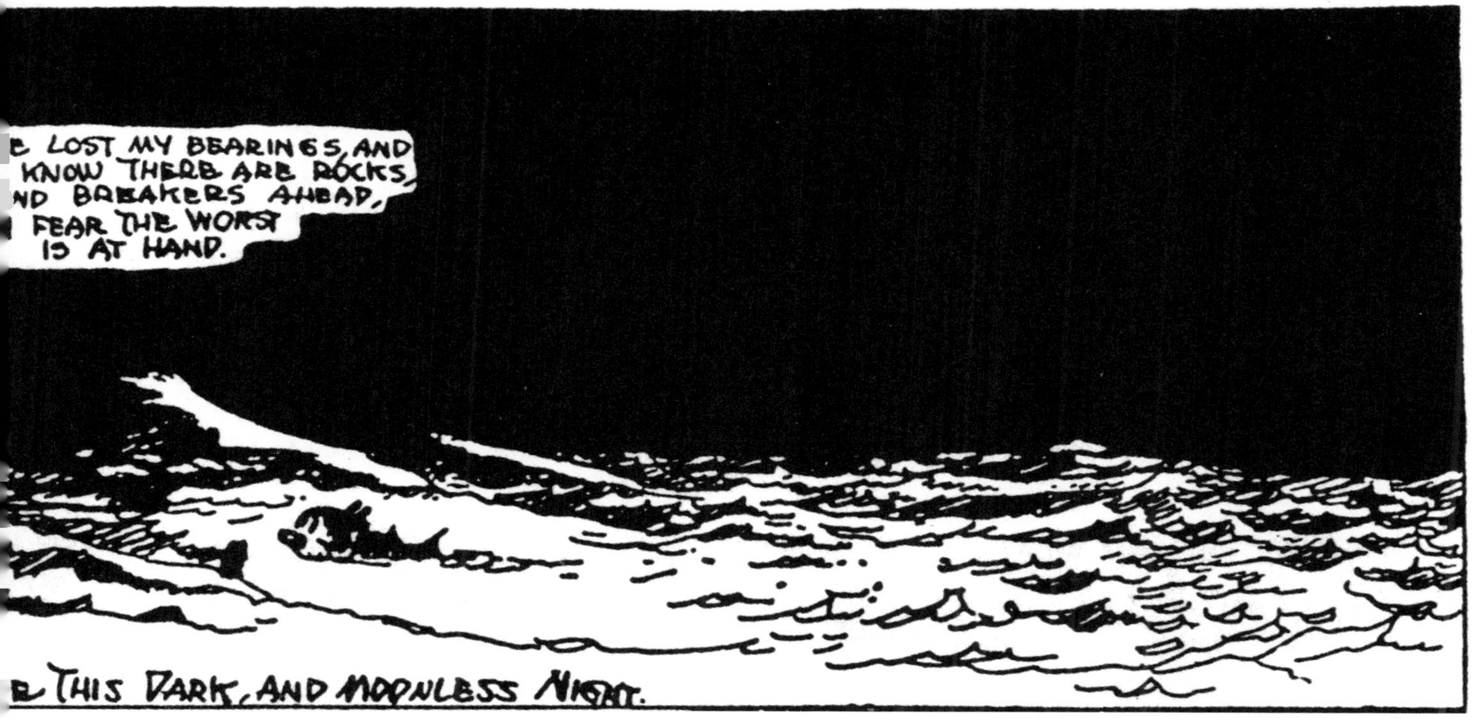
E LOST MY BEARINGS, AND
KNOW THERE ARE ROCKS,
ND BREAKERS AHEAD,
FEAR THE WORST
IS AT HAND.
E THIS DARK, AND MOONLESS NIGHT.

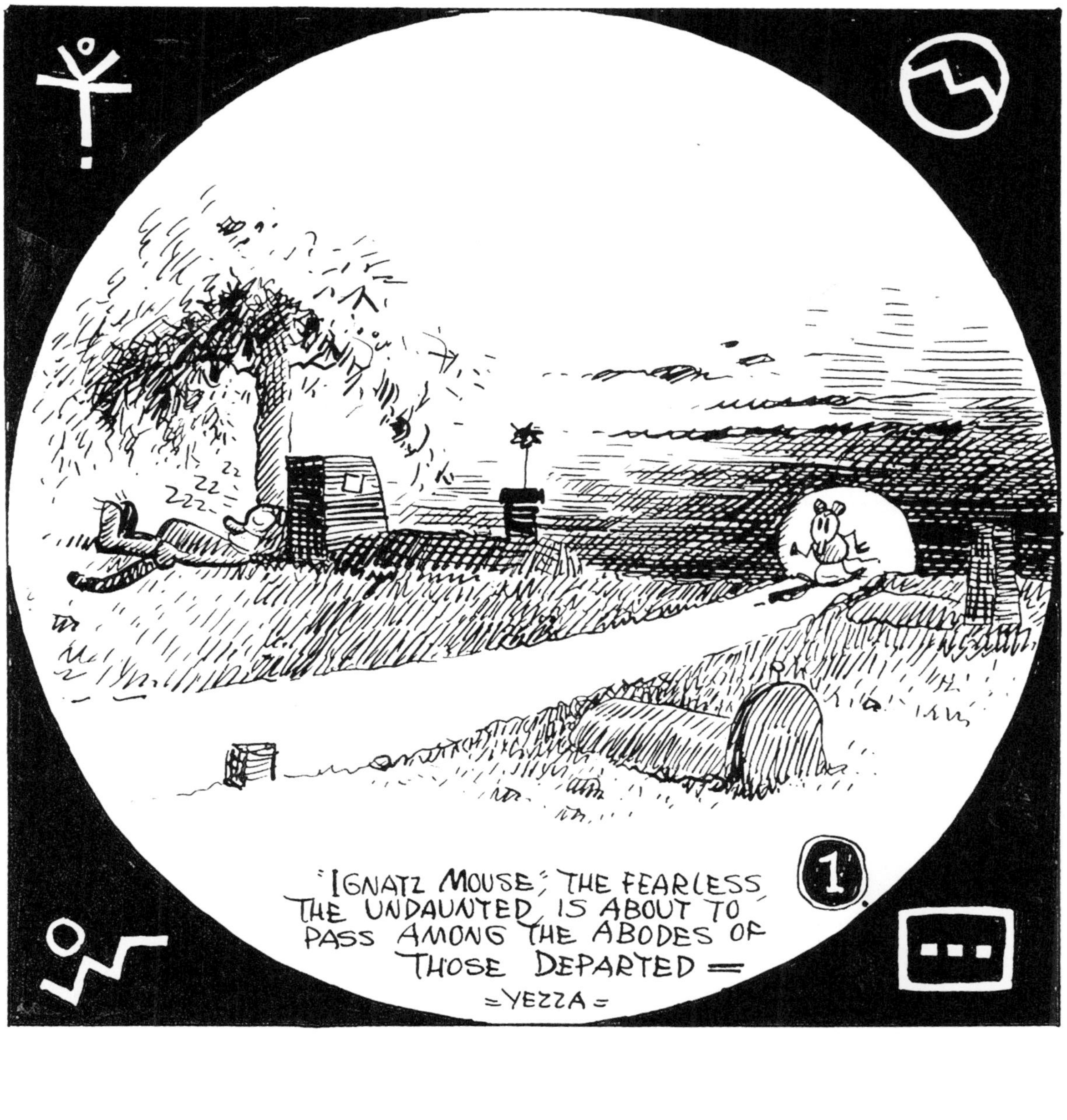
ZZ
ZZ
ZZZ
1
"IGNATZ MOUSE," THE FEARLESS
THE UNDAUNTED, IS ABOUT TO
PASS AMONG THE ABODES OF
THOSE DEPARTED =
=YEZZA=

Greetings from Coconino County

Herriman created many personal greetings, including cards for his family, Christmas promotional illustrations for his syndicate, and even a holiday card for Gilbert Seldes. Here are a few, including some courtesy of his granddaughter, Dee Cox (Dinah Pascal), published for the first time.

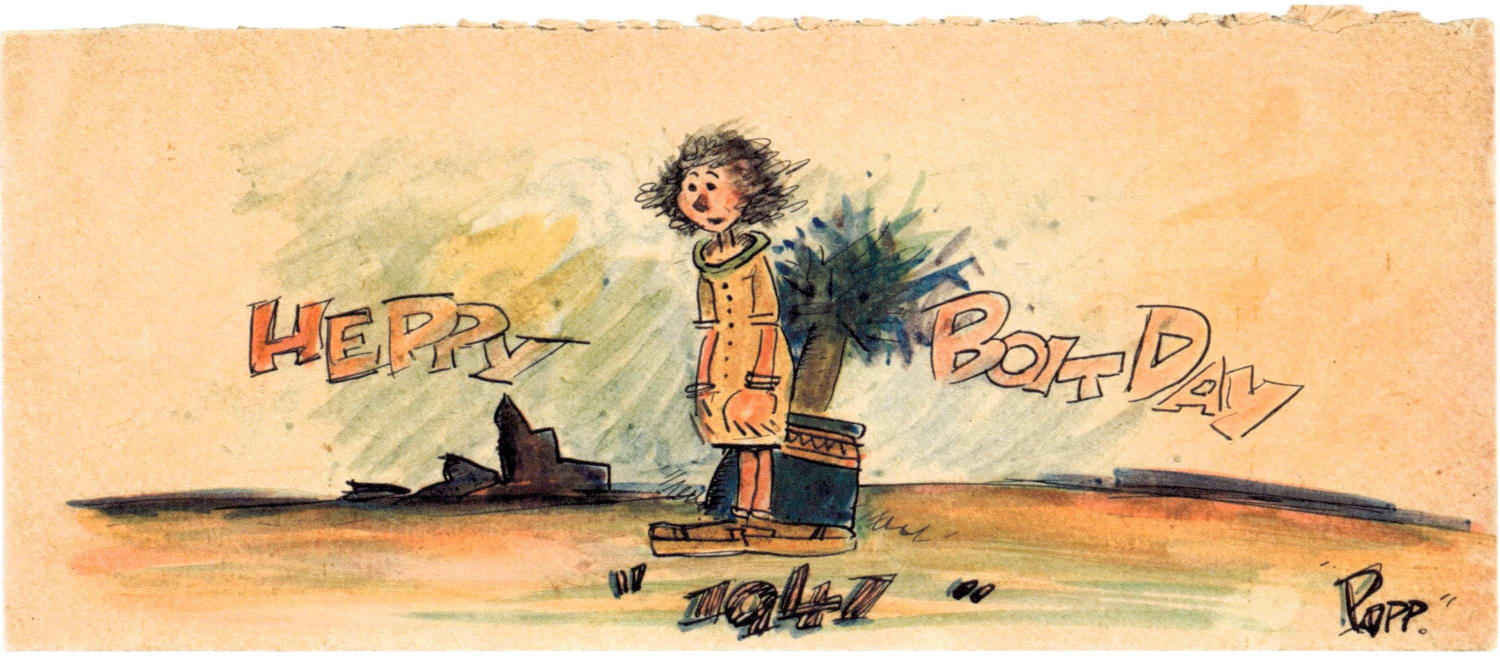
HEPPY BOIT DAY
"1941"
"POPP"

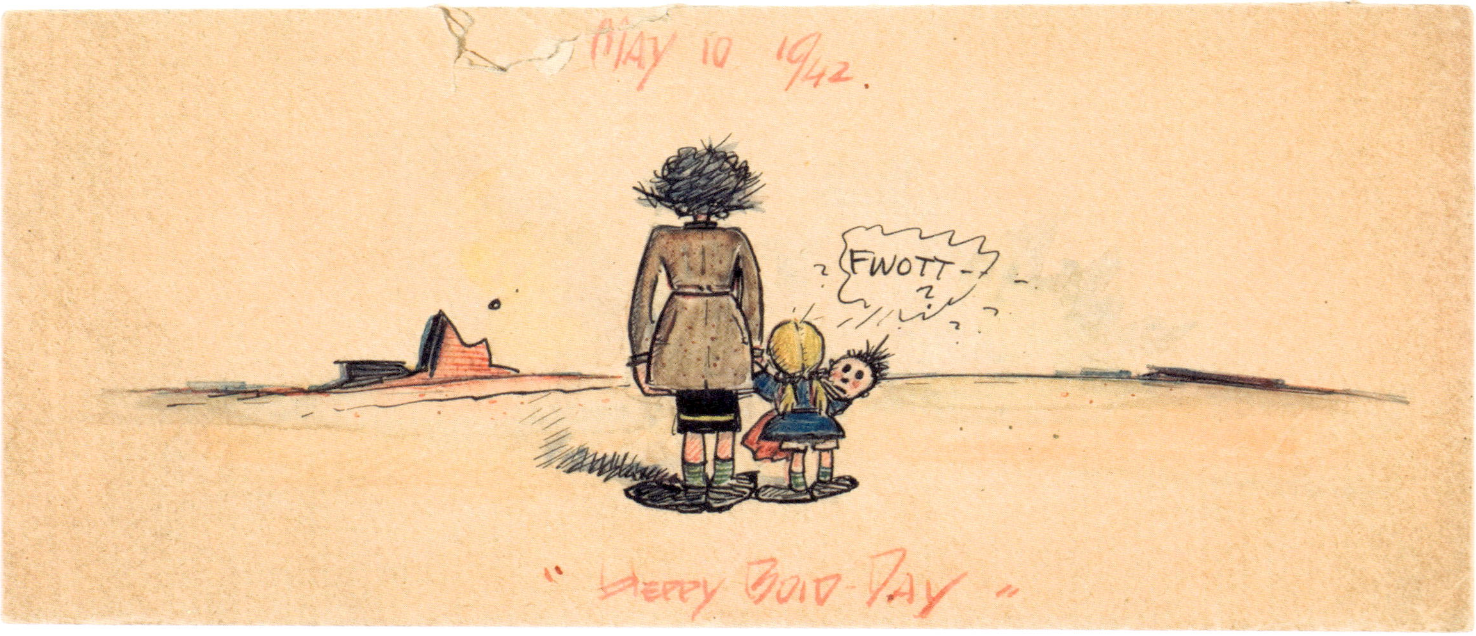
MAY 10 1942.
FWOTT-
"HEPPY BOID-DAY"

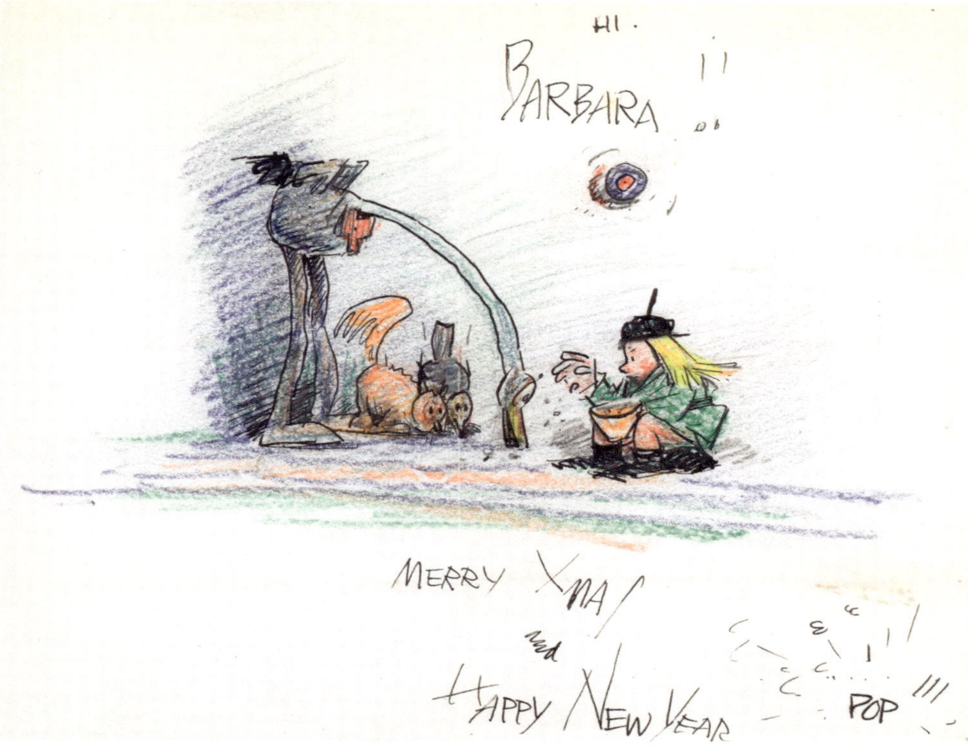
HI.
BARBARA !!
MERRY XMAS!
and
HAPPY NEW YEAR
POP !!!

OPPOSITE Birthday cards for Herriman's daughter Toots from 1941 and 1942. Bobbie's (Barbara's) daughter, Dee, is pictured in the second card. After Bobbie passed away, Toots raised Dee.

ABOVE Herriman's granddaughter Dee says this card is "from Pop's imagination—we had no pet ostrich!"

RIGHT Dee relates, "Aunt Toots was known to take a drink or two, and used to party with the Hollywood actor family the Carradines."

BELOW A valentine to his granddaughter Dee (Dinah), "walen Dinah" being a play on "valentine."

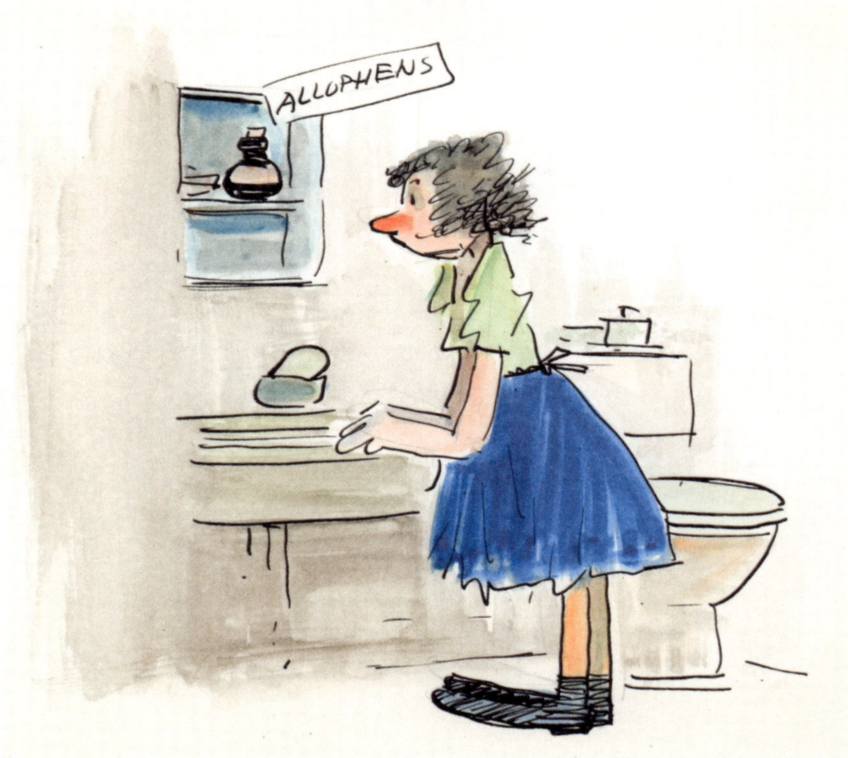
ALLOPHENS

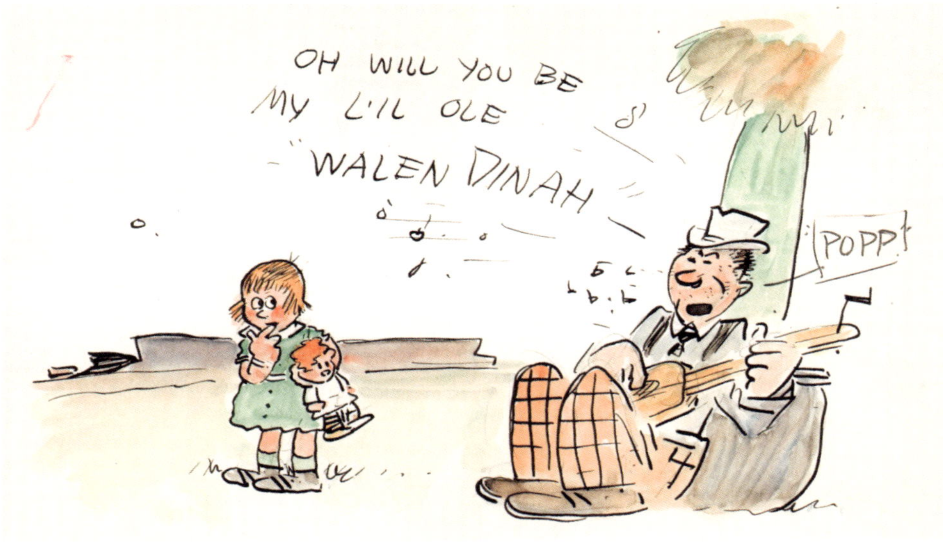
OH WILL YOU BE
MY L'IL OLE
"WALEN DINAH"
POPP!

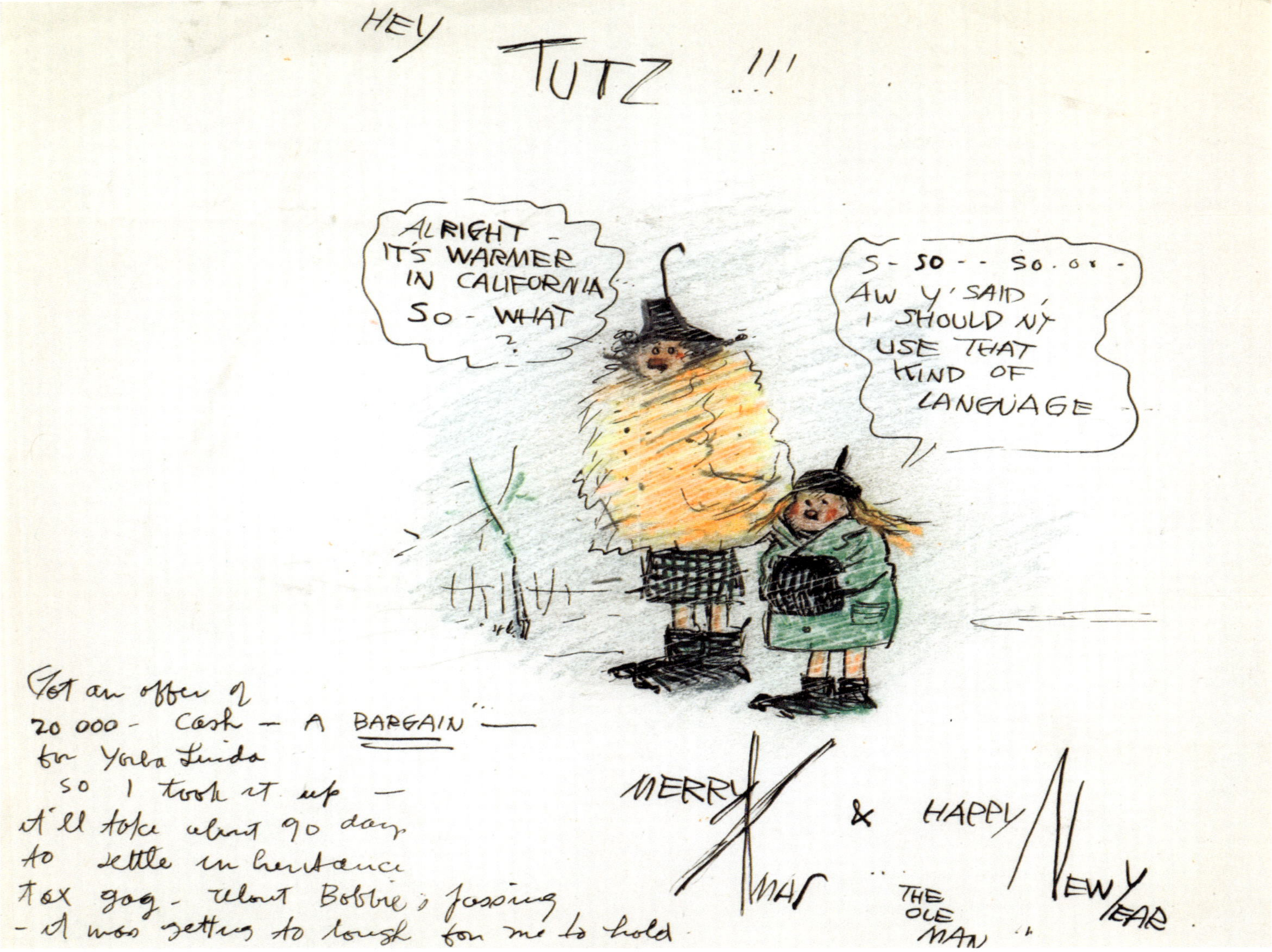
HEY
TUTZ !!!
ALRIGHT - IT'S WARMER IN CALIFORNIA SO - WHAT ?
S- SO - - SO . . . AW Y'SAID, I SHOULD N'T USE THAT KIND OF LANGUAGE
MERRY XMAS & HAPPY NEW YEAR
THE OLE MAN

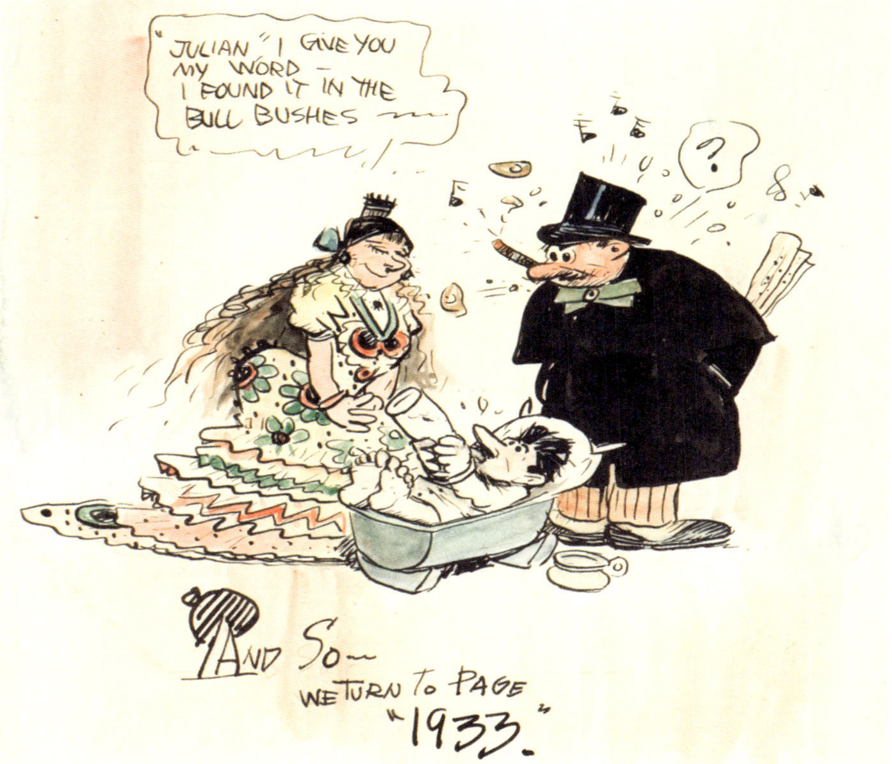
"JULIAN" I GIVE YOU MY WORD - I FOUND IT IN THE BULL BUSHES
?
AND SO - WE TURN TO PAGE "1933."

ABOVE Hey Tutz!!! This card to Toots from 1943 has a revealing note in the bottom left corner. Dee tells us, "Pop was good with money. He planned well and was skilled with investments." This note refers to him selling land in the Yorba Linda area of Southern California. The area probably painfully reminded Herriman of the death of his daughter Bobbie, who passed away in 1939 at the age of thirty.

RIGHT A birthday card from 1933 for Herriman's son-in-law, Ernest Pascal, pictured here as Moses, with his father, Julian, and his Jewish mother, Annette.

OPPOSITE A thank-you card to John and Louisa Wetherill. Their trading post became a regular vacation spot after he discovered Mesa Verde. Louisa is the geisha, while Herriman is in bed. Circa 1930.

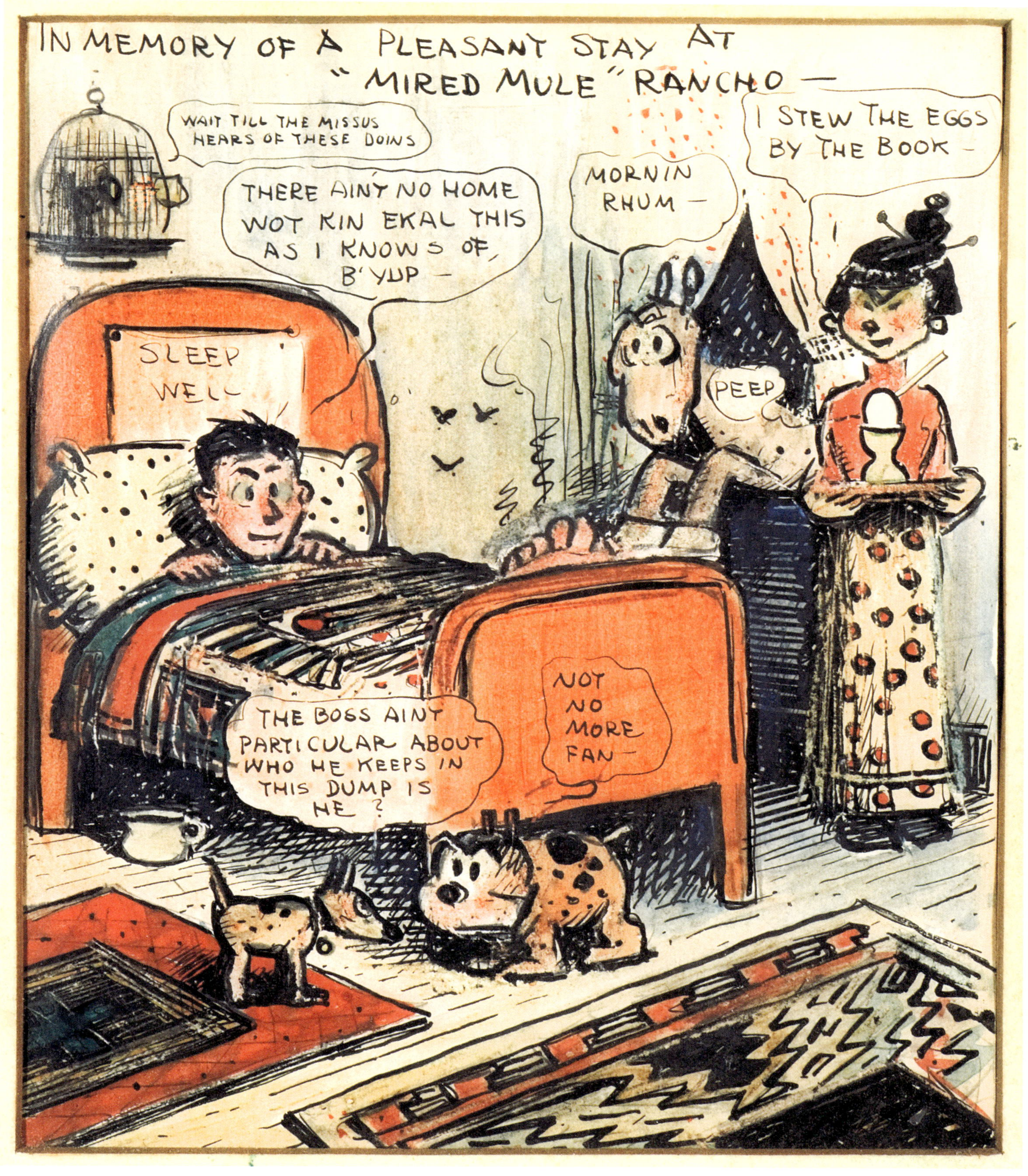
IN MEMORY OF A PLEASANT STAY AT "MIRED MULE" RANCHO —
WAIT TILL THE MISSUS HEARS OF THESE DOINS
THERE AINT NO HOME WOT KIN EKAL THIS AS I KNOWS OF, B'YUP —
MORNIN RHUM —
I STEW THE EGGS BY THE BOOK —
SLEEP WELL
PEEP
NOT NO MORE FAN —
THE BOSS AINT PARTICULAR ABOUT WHO HE KEEPS IN THIS DUMP IS HE ?

THIS PAGE A Christmas and New Year's greeting designed for Gilbert Seldes, who had celebrated Herriman in his book *The Seven Lively Arts*. The top illustration is the front of the card. The bottom drawings are the inside, with room for Seldes to add his inscription. 1922.

OPPOSITE In 1943 the top artists of King Features Syndicate devised a special, one-of-a-kind, handmade, red leather book to give to their boss, William Randolph Hearst, for Christmas. The cartoonists included George McManus (*Bringing Up Father*), Harold Knerr (*The Katzenjammer Kids*), Percy Crosby (*Skippy*), Otto Messmer (*Felix the Cat*), and many others, including George Herriman. Herriman's dedication reads, "It is Xmas time in Coconino County, so to our NAH-TA NIH AH-LAH-HA-NIH SIKIS—Geo. Herriman." Previously unpublished.

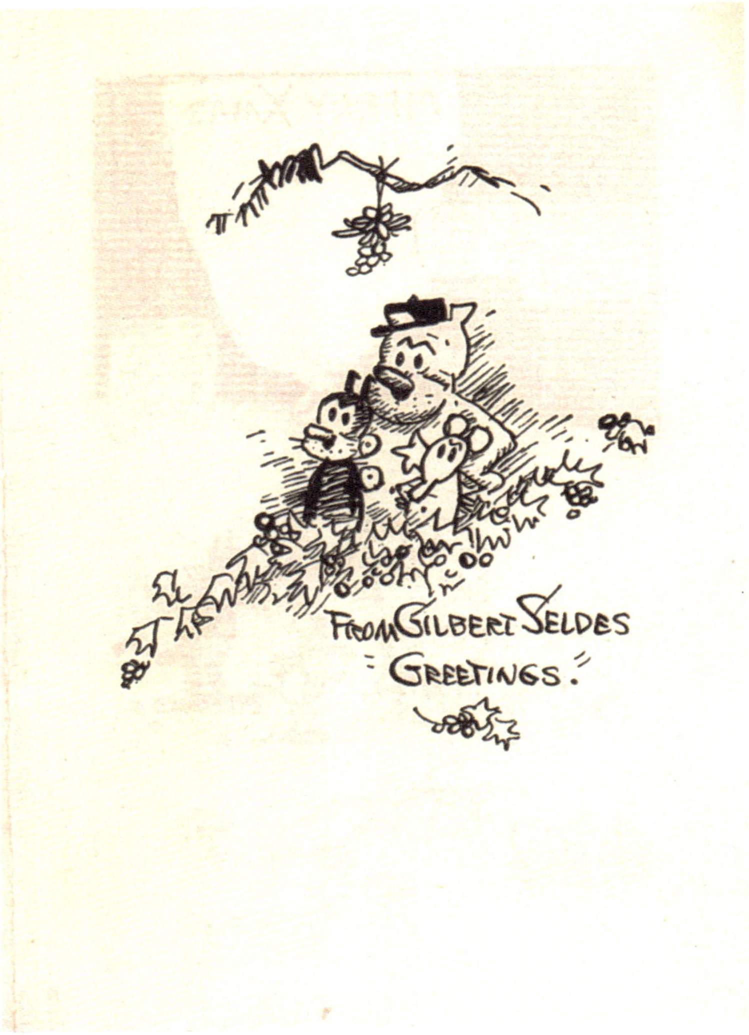
FROM GILBERT SELDES
GREETINGS.

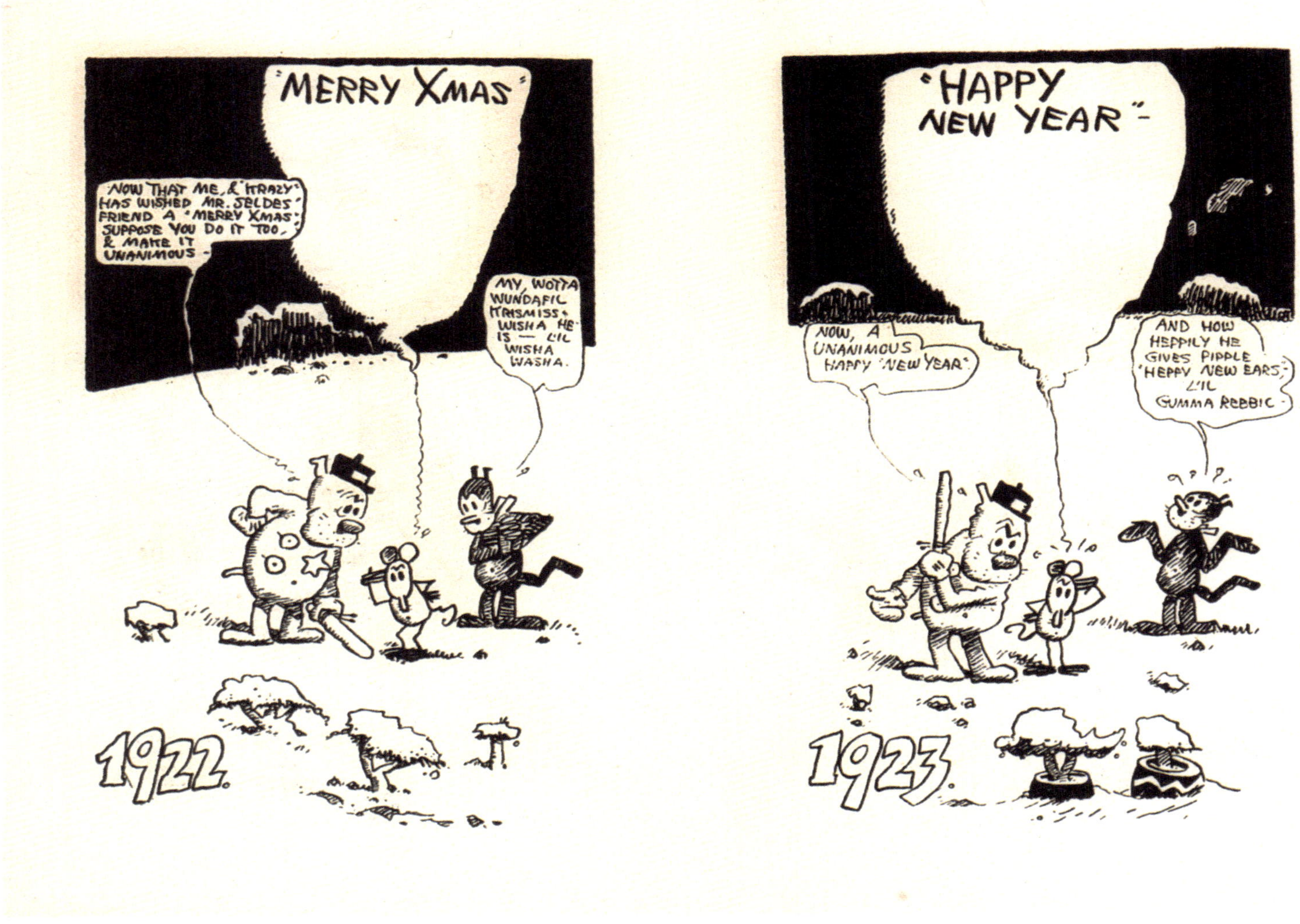
"MERRY XMAS"
NOW THAT ME, & 'KRAZY' HAS WISHED MR. SELDES' FRIEND A 'MERRY XMAS' SUPPOSE YOU DO IT TOO, & MAKE IT UNANIMOUS -
MY, WOTTA WUNDAFIL KRISMISS. WISHA HE IS — L'IL WISHA WASHA.
1922.
"HAPPY NEW YEAR"
NOW, A UNANIMOUS HAPPY 'NEW YEAR'
AND HOW HEPPILY HE GIVES PIPPLE 'HEPPY NEW EARS,' L'IL GUMMA REBBIC -
1923.

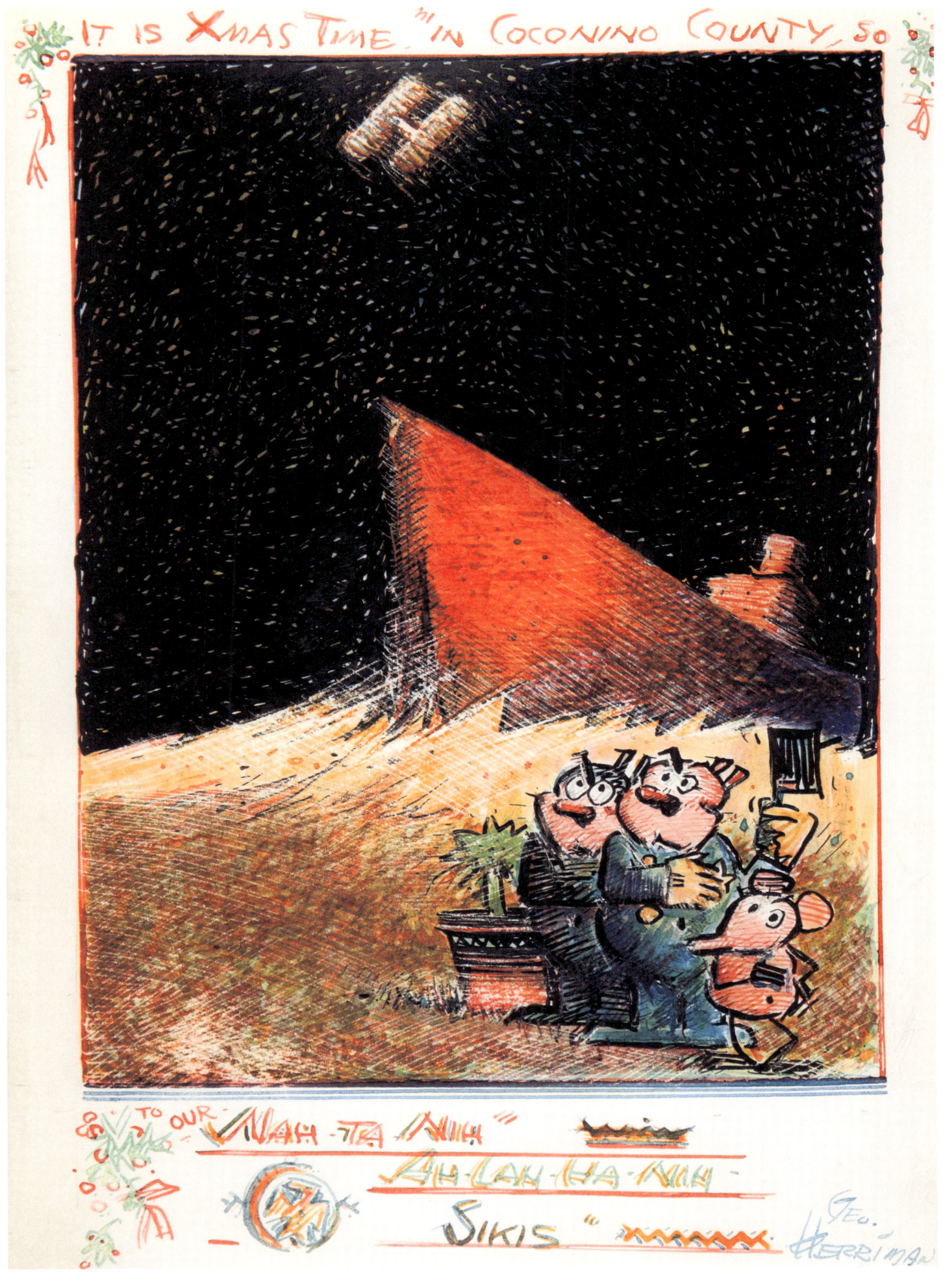

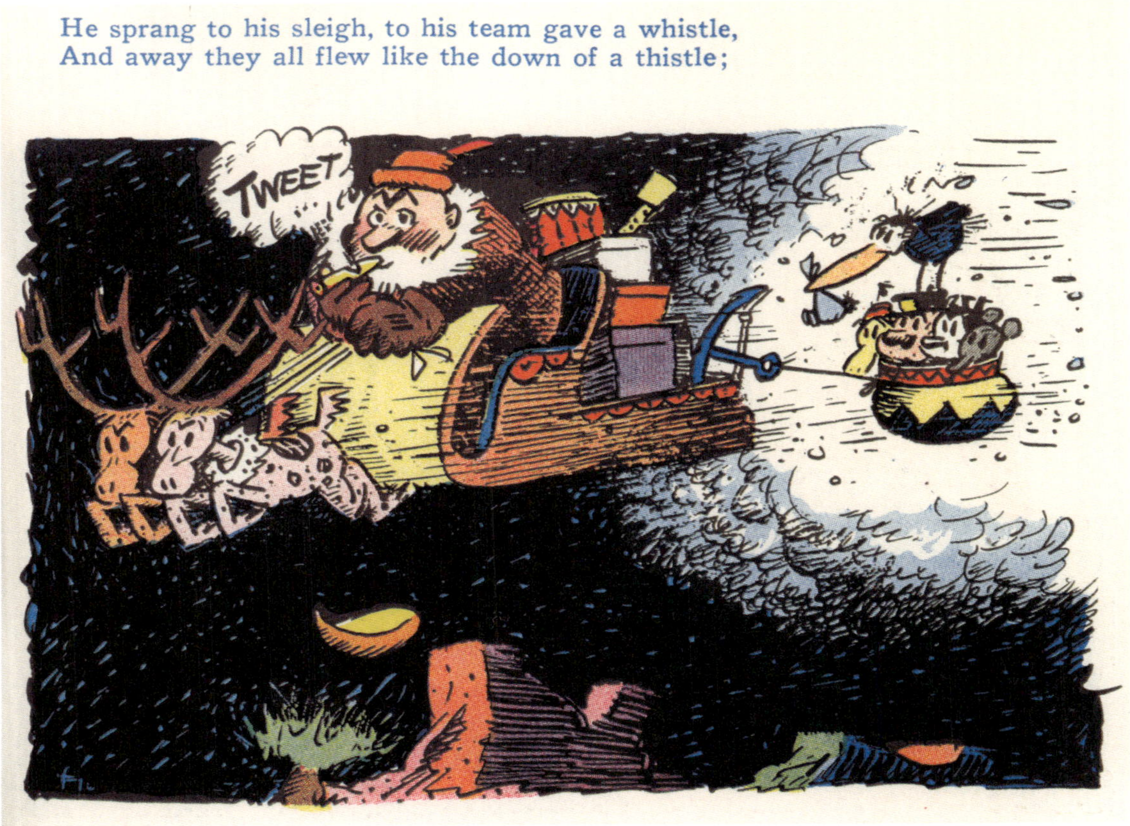
He sprang to his sleigh, to his team gave a whistle,
And away they all flew like the down of a thistle;
TWEET

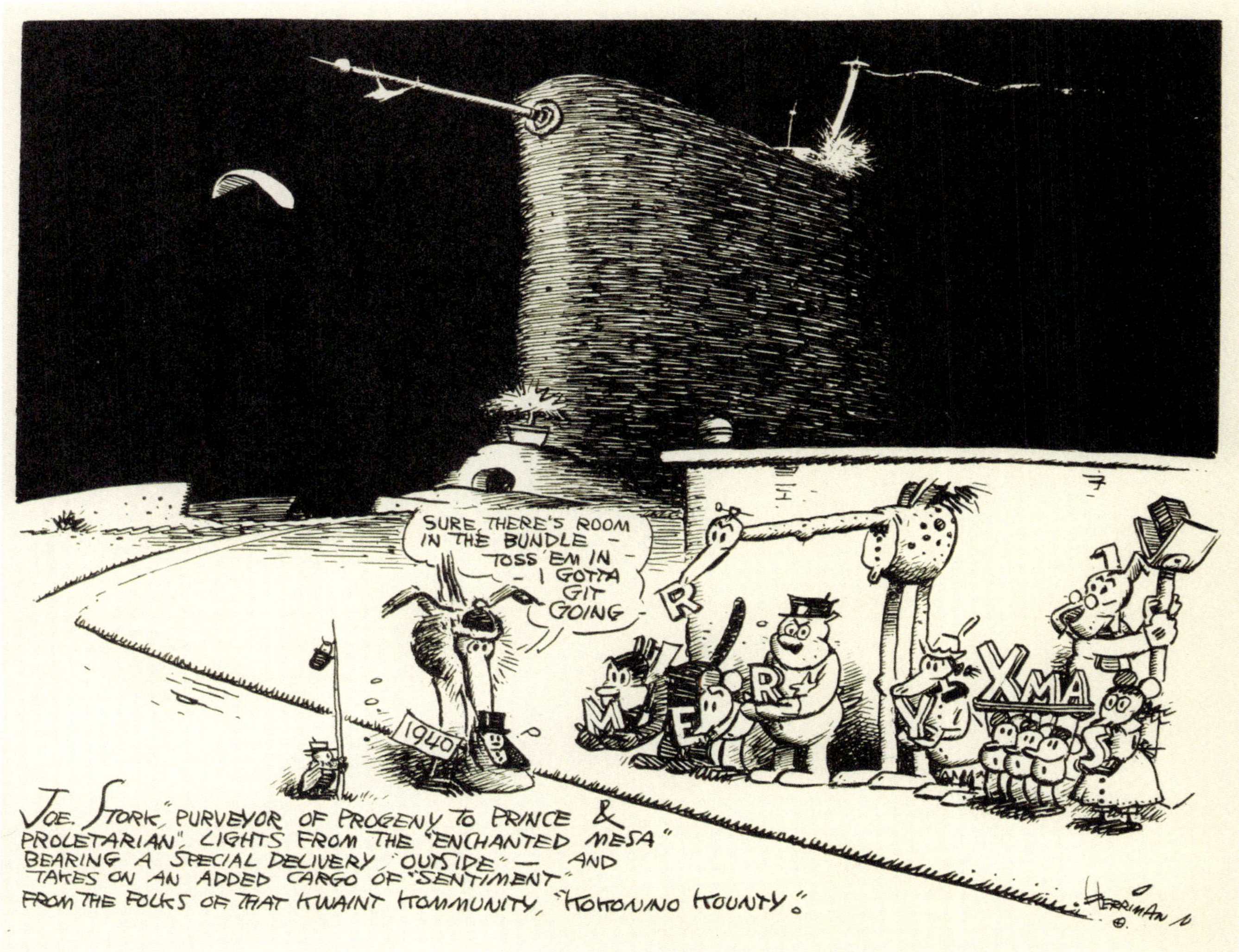
SURE, THERE'S ROOM IN THE BUNDLE - TOSS 'EM IN - I GOTTA GIT GOING -
1940
JOE. STORK "PURVEYOR OF PROGENY TO PRINCE & PROLETARIAN", LIGHTS FROM THE "ENCHANTED MESA" BEARING A SPECIAL DELIVERY "OUTSIDE" — AND TAKES ON AN ADDED CARGO OF "SENTIMENT" FROM THE FOLKS OF THAT KWAINT KOMMUNITY, "KOKONINO KOUNTY."
HERRIMAN

TOP Promotional Christmas greeting for King Features Syndicate. 1922.

BOTTOM Promotional Christmas greeting for King Features Syndicate. 1935.

The Gift

By Douglas Wolk

Krazy Kat is always funny—funny peculiar, as well as funny ha-ha. The most peculiar thing about its humor is that it often comes off as mild whimsy rather than outright hilarity. But every strip George Herriman drew is funnier than it looks, and it's part of his funny-peculiar gift that his comedy sneaks up on you. What he offers is the kind of funny-peculiar gift that comes wrapped in inky newspaper, one that can sit on the mantel of your mind for a while instead of offering its candied delights all at once. Contemplate it, and it yields something darker and sweeter.

The real comedy of *Krazy Kat* is almost always slower than its surface humor, which is appropriate for a strip whose central joke is miscommunication on a grand scale. The one way you can't read it for pleasure is *quickly*. Everything from Herriman's crabbed hand-lettering and batty phonetic spellings to his habit of showing Ignatz's brick flying from right to left (against the flow of reading) to the way he constructs his panels and pages—with vistas so wide the eye can't take them in all at once—means you need to slow down and be mindful of each element of his work to know how funny it really is.

So, reading *Krazy Kat* can be a kind of meditation practice, a slow process of opening yourself to its funny-peculiar pleasure. Analyzing most humor kills it by slow torture, but the perverse joy of Herriman's work is that the more you contemplate it, the funnier it becomes. Take a single Sunday page—basically any page—as the object of your reflection. (It's convenient to have all the strips together in beautiful volumes, but they were made to be read one at a time; in the early years, Hearst newspapers even ran *Krazy Kat* in the arts section, out of the company of other comic strips.) Empty your mind and concentrate on what's in front of you. Try to think of it as a present that George Herriman made for you, to amuse and baffle you, and ultimately to make you happier for a few minutes, if you're willing to read it slowly and receptively enough.

Krazy Kat meditation begins by contemplating the form of the day's page, even before you read a word. Try not to read its words, or follow the narrative. (It can be difficult, but hold off as long as you can.) Admire the strip as a pure aesthetic object of light and shade, of shapes and colors and proportions. Turn it upside down for a while, if that helps. See how playful its design is, and how its broadest strokes are balanced with one another.

Then read the strip's words—and with Herriman, more than almost any other cartoonist, it's crucial to read it out loud, or at least under your breath. "Fancy those foolish fingers fashioning a fabric, ah, the futile foof, and fuff of it—a waste of warp, a wanton wear of weft, and woof—foowy—" If you can read that aloud without cracking up a little, either you are made of stone or you are Gerard Manley Hopkins. Even the unnecessary-for-meaning commas are there to indicate the pacing that makes the line kick and whinny when it's read aloud. Everything about the language of *Krazy Kat* is at least a little bit funny: the bombastically high-flown diction of the strip's narration, Krazy's accent and the spelling with which Herriman renders it instantly burlesque, the proliferating quotation marks that throw the veil of indeterminacy over the commonest nouns.

Next look at Herriman's figures: more awkward and bulbous than any human being could be, more indefinite in form than virtually any other comic strip's denizens. (It's almost impossible to imagine model sheets for the *Krazy Kat* characters; Krazy, of course, refuses even to be pinned down on the question of gender.) But they're perfectly graceful, balanced in space, with the angles and bends of their tails serving as commentary on whatever they're doing. They are natural comedians, funny from the moment they stroll onto the strip's stage, before the first pratfall is fallen or the first brick is flung. Cats are natural comedians, too, and some of the most hilarious moments of Krazy's body language in particular have to have come from Herriman's observations of real cats—especially when Krazy sings, head thrown back and mouth wide open, clearly yowling off key.

Consider the minds of Herriman's characters—so different from one another that their difference is not just the fuel of the strip but its entire point. The much-quoted 1918 strip in which Krazy opines that "lenguage is, that we may mis-unda-stend each

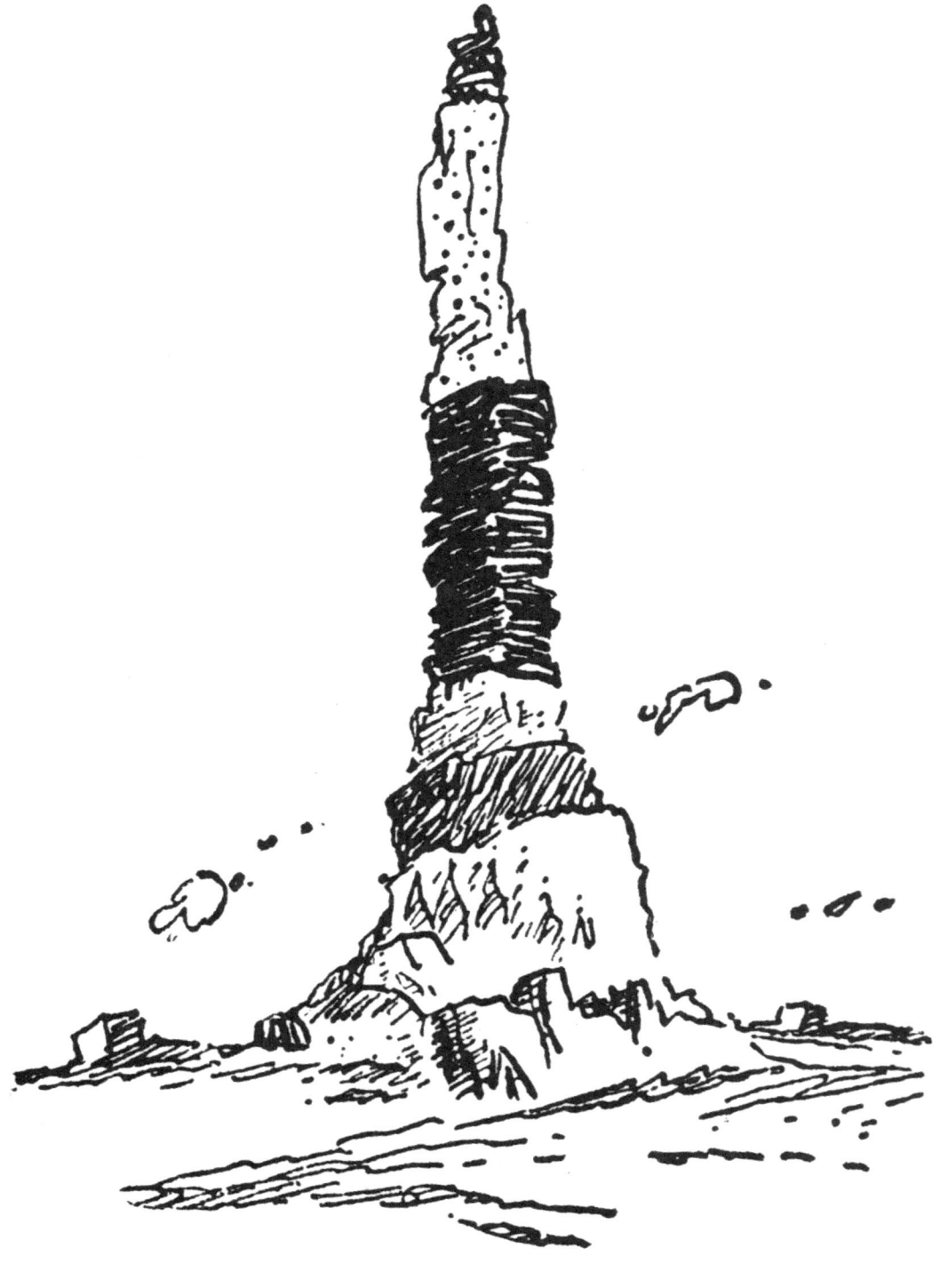

udda" is only part of the story: every form of communication in Krazy Kat is miscommunication, because all of the strip's principals believe they comprehend the others' desires and motivations, and none of them do. That makes for a breed of comedy that's exceptionally dark, but no less funny for it.

The biggest joke in Krazy Kat is, of course, that it had variations on a single theme nearly every day for decades on end: the brick, the mis-unda-stending, the jailhouse. So notice the space and movement in the strip in front of you that *doesn't* directly relate to its most obvious gag, and direct your mind slowly outward to Herriman's entire cosmic thirty-year comedy. In the early Krazy Kat strips, especially the dailies, Herriman often goes for a simple *ba-dump bump* gag: Krazy sets up some kind of misunderstanding, Ignatz plays straight man, Krazy delivers the punch line, and Ignatz delivers the brick. Even then, though, Herriman often makes the end of the strip not the delivery of the brick but its promise or its aftermath. The deepest and funniest moments of Krazy Kat meditation can come from the time before and after he addresses an individual strip's conceit, especially the tiny panoramic "kicker" panels that appeared at the bottom of the Sunday page beginning in 1938; they were probably instituted to allow newspapers some flexibility in the strip's printed dimensions, but they're a delicious little postgag lagniappe, a squat but very wide space in which the day's joke, and its laughter, echoes.

Those echoes can go beyond the page, too: the final stage of meditating on a Krazy Kat strip is to open yourself to what it says about the humans who are never seen in Herriman's Coconino County. You can be Ignatz, intent on dramatic but ultimately meaningless actions whose consequences land you in the same place every time, sending out a message that's always misunderstood. You can be Offissa Pupp, the protector of the law and preserver of order, never to know the joys of transgression. Or you can be Krazy, curious and accepting and "heppy," unbound by anybody's language or definitions, believing that the world was made for your pleasure and that every brick-blow to the head is a lil' ainjil's kiss.

That, of course, would mean that you're crazy.

Douglas Wolk writes about comics for the New York Times, *the* Savage Critics, *the* Washington Post, *and other publications. He's the author of* Reading Comics: How Graphic Novels Work and What They Mean, *published by Da Capo Press in 2007.*

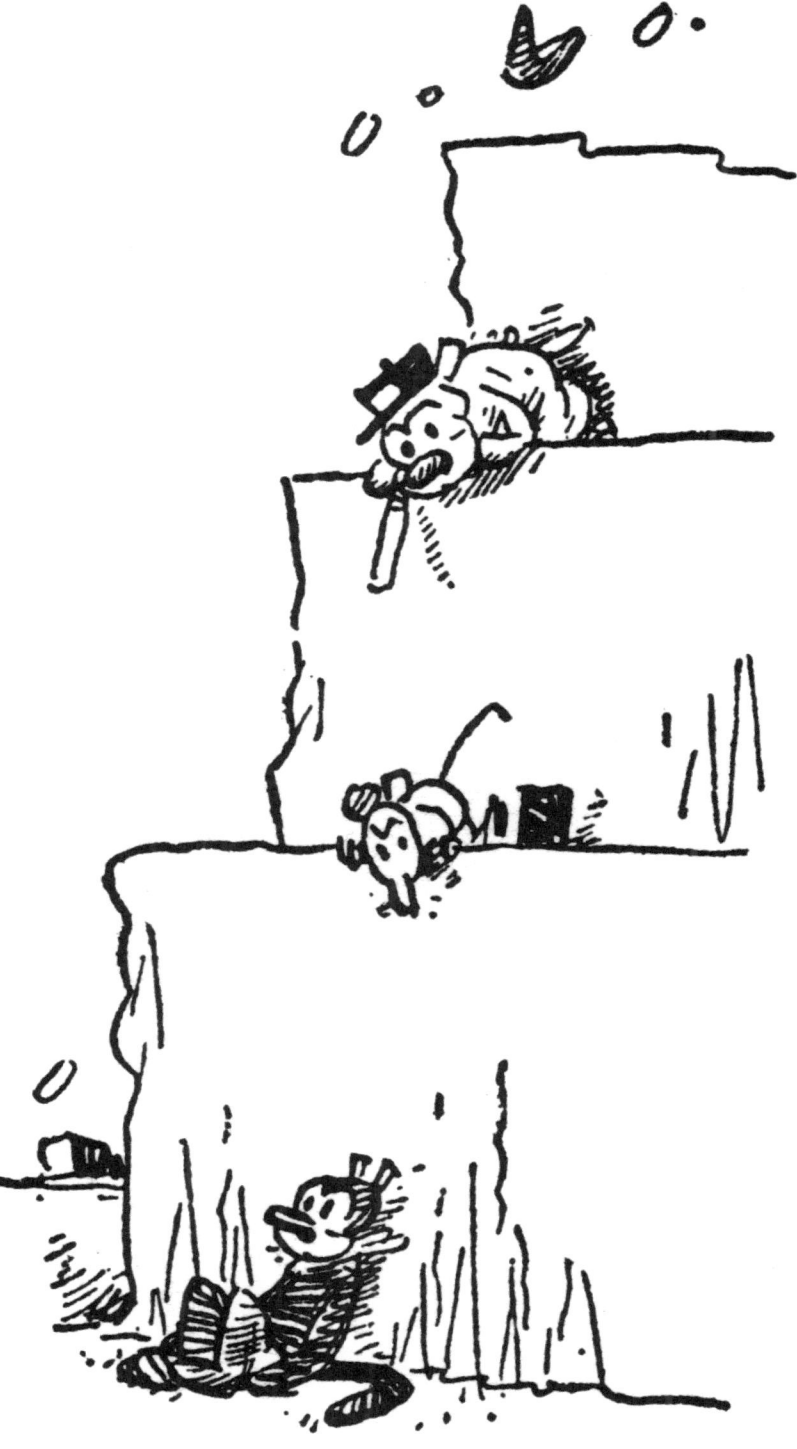

Special Specialty Drawings

Specialty drawing is a term used by comic-art collectors to denote drawings done for fans and friends. They were often private commissions or gifts from the artist. Specialty drawings don't get any more special than George Herriman's.

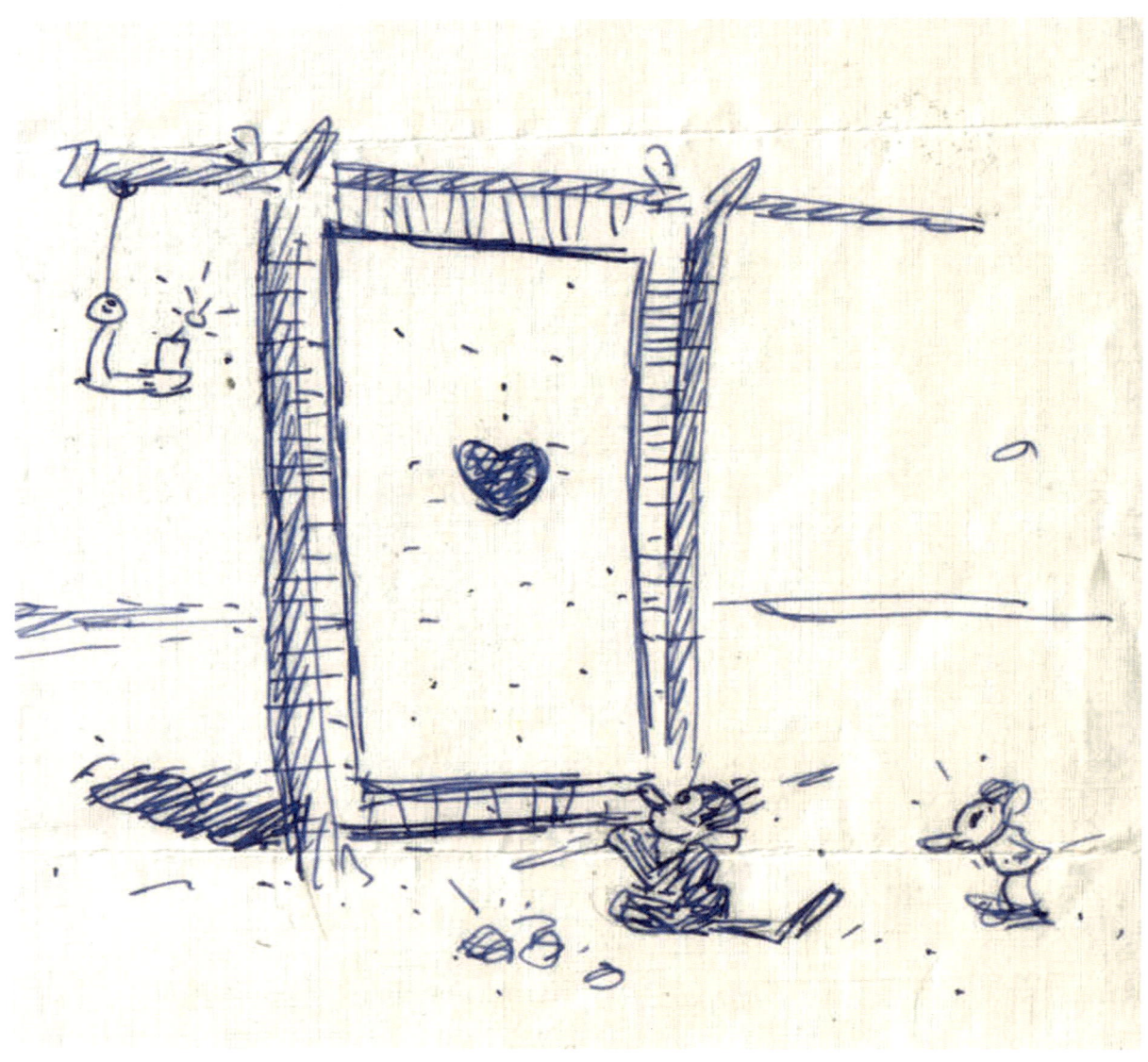

ABOVE A Herriman doodle becomes a work of art.

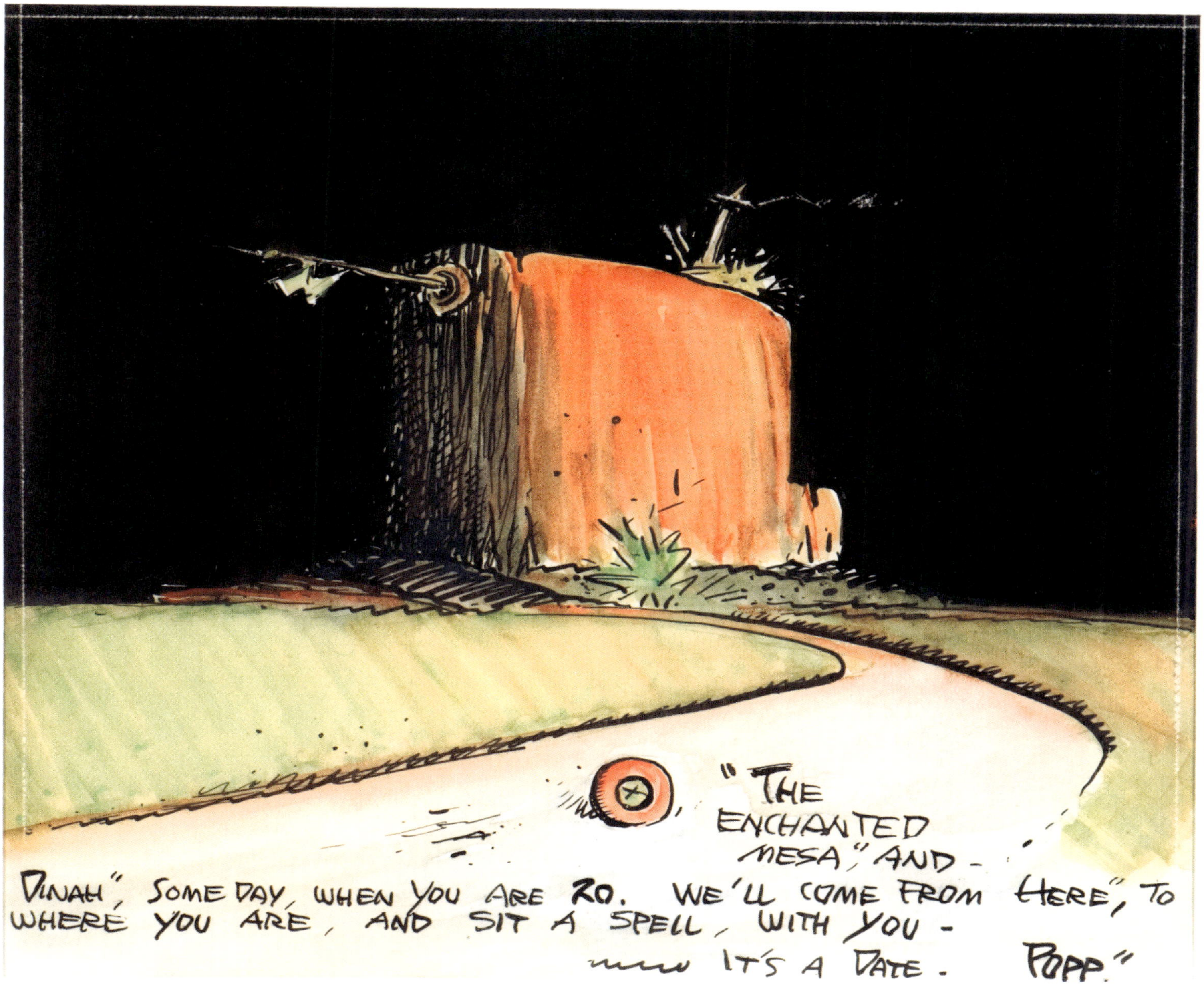
"THE ENCHANTED MESA", AND -
DINAH", SOME DAY, WHEN YOU ARE 20. WE'LL COME FROM HERE", TO
WHERE YOU ARE, AND SIT A SPELL, WITH YOU -
IT'S A DATE. POPP."

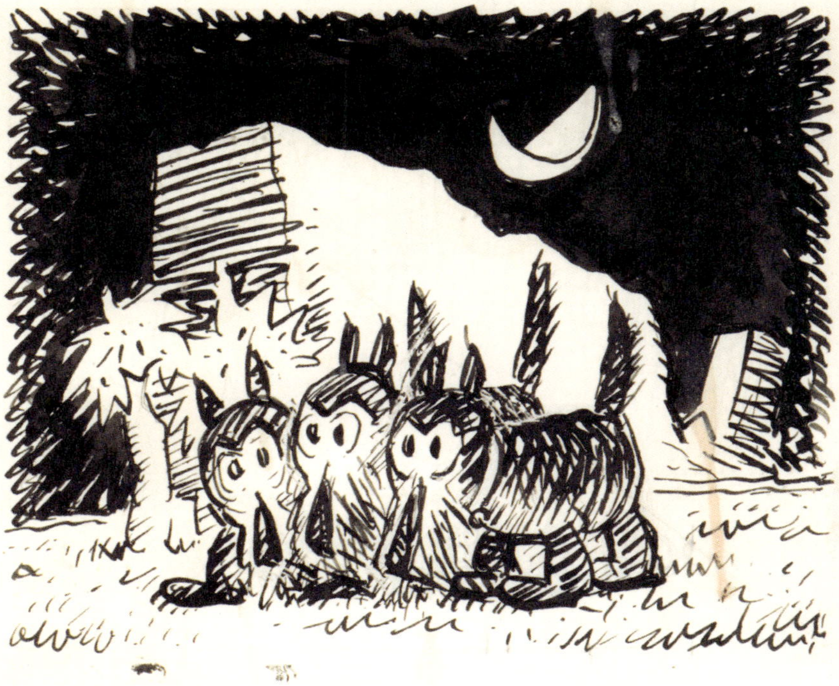

THIS PAGE Two of Herriman's great loves, the Southwest desert and Scottish terriers. The inscription at the top reads, "'The Enchanted Mesa,' and 'Dinah.' Some day, when you are 20, we'll come from 'here,' to where you are, and sit a spell with you—It's a date. Popp." Previously unpublished.

OVERLEAF, TOP Herriman's sketches for a jazz pantomime ballet written by John Alden Carpenter in 1922 (see page 120). Top left, "Ignatz Mouse appears." In the bottom left of the top right, "Kat dances on—oblivious of what's going on over here." In the bottom right of the top right, "Just as Ignatz is about to toss the brick—'Officer Pupp' appears and tells him to beat it." Bottom left, "Ignatz leaves—angry—Officer Pupp also leaves—with satisfaction." Bottom right, "Kat has stage all to himself—Dances wildly." Previously unpublished.

OVERLEAF, BOTTOM A specialty drawing done for cartoonist Jud Hurd, editor and publisher of *Cartoonist PROfiles*. The inscription reads, "To Jus Hurd [probably as in "just heard"]—mitt luff—Herriman." 1930s.

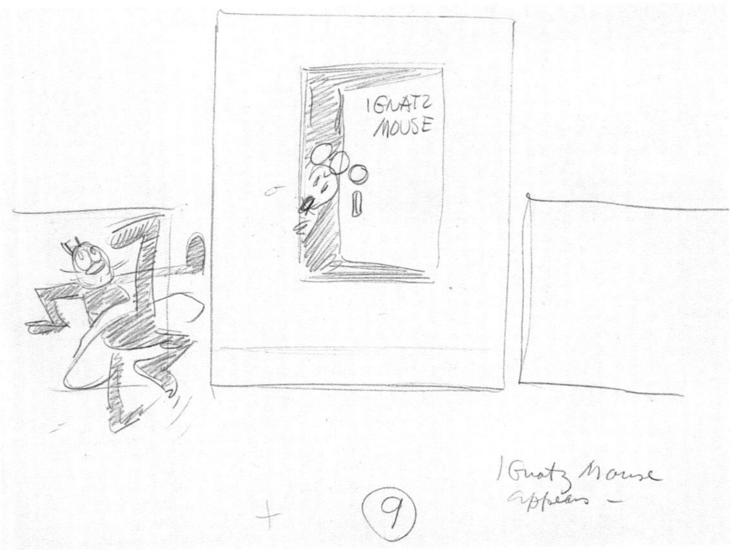
IGNATZ MOUSE
Ignatz Mouse appears -
9

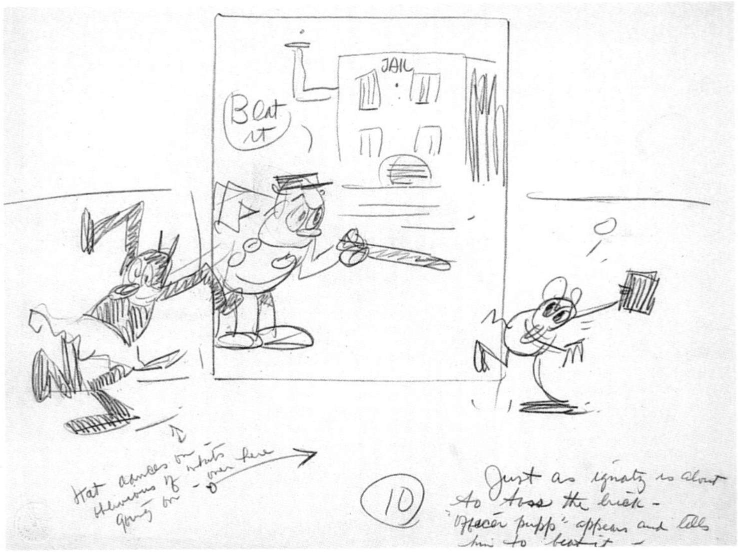
JAIL
Beat it
Kat dances on oblivious of what's going on - over here
10
Just as Ignatz is about to toss the brick - "Officer Pupp" appears and tells him to beat it -

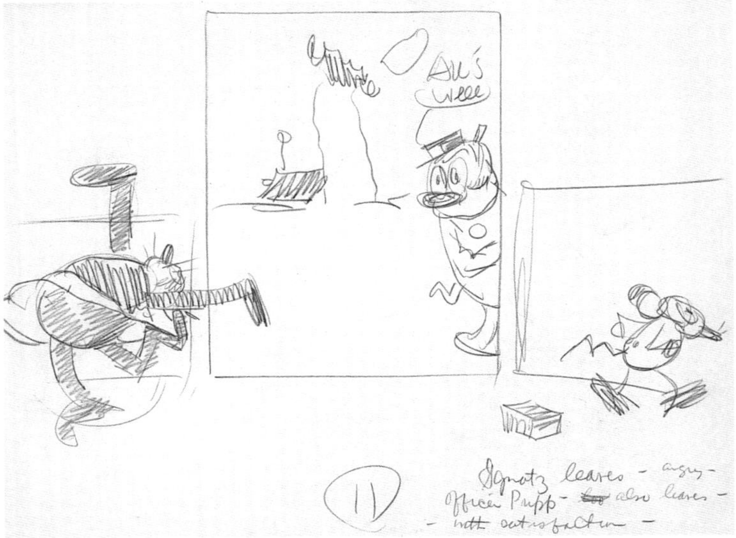
All's well
11
Ignatz leaves - angry - Officer Pupp - also leaves - with satisfaction -

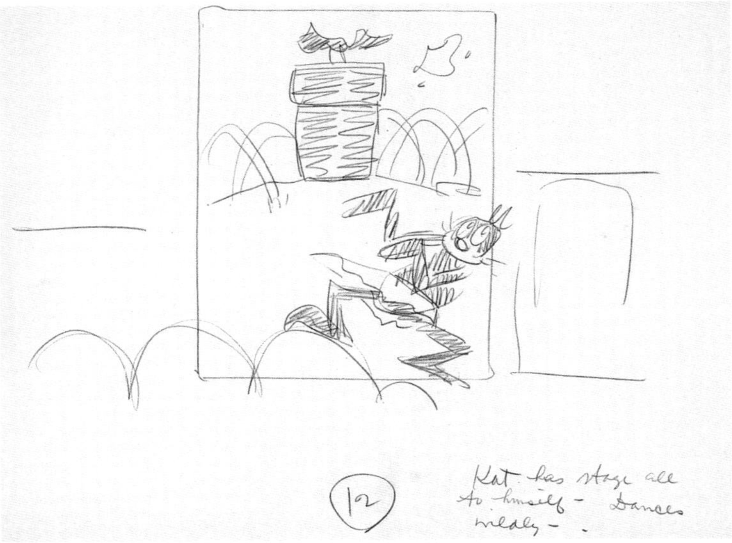
12
Kat has stage all to himself - Dances madly -

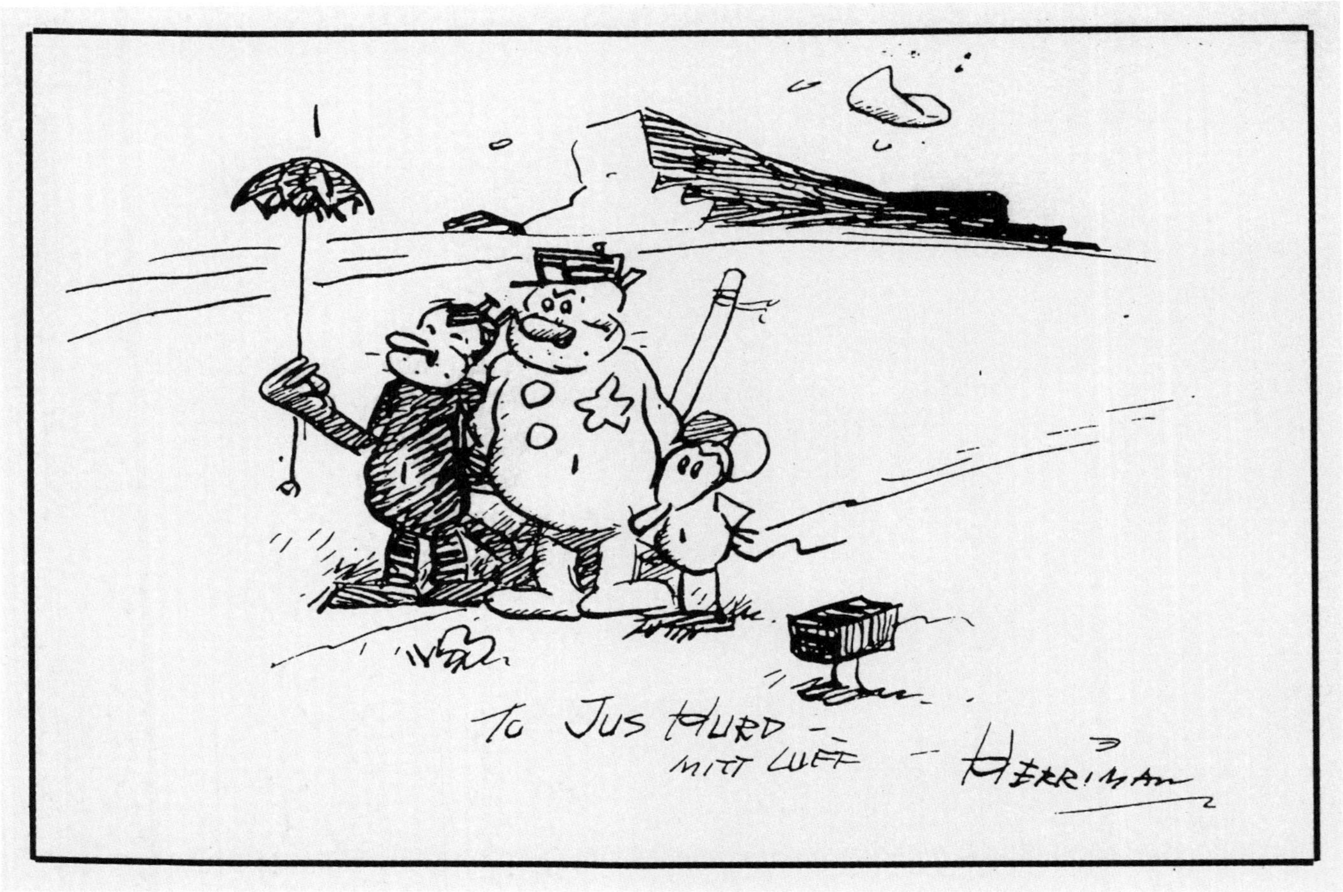
To Jus Hurd -
Mitt Luff
Herriman

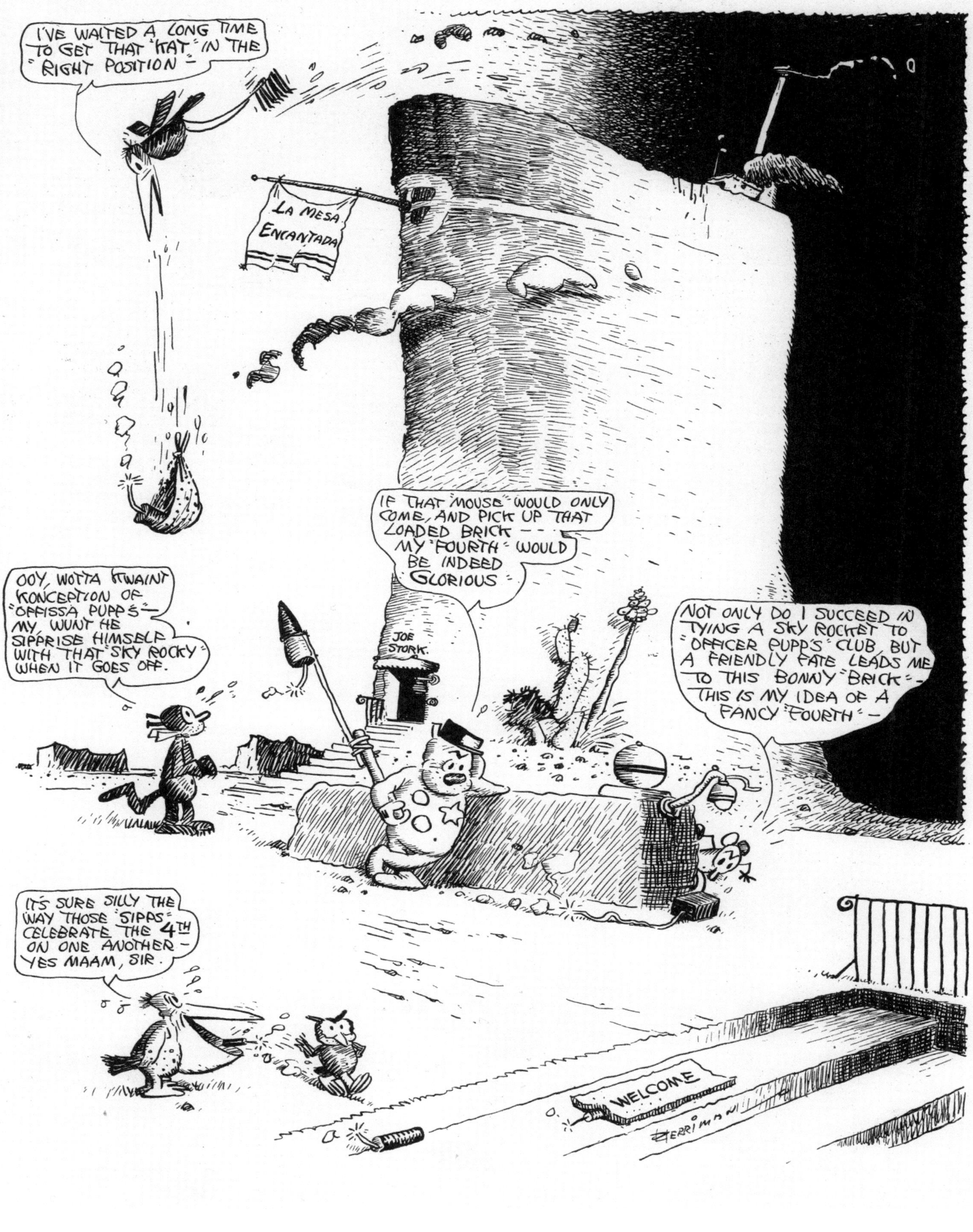
I'VE WAITED A LONG TIME TO GET THAT "KAT" IN THE RIGHT POSITION –
LA MESA ENCANTADA
IF THAT MOUSE WOULD ONLY COME, AND PICK UP THAT LOADED BRICK – – MY "FOURTH" WOULD BE INDEED GLORIOUS
OOY, WOTTA KWAINT KONCEPTION OF "OFFISSA PUPP'S" – MY, WUNT HE SIPPRISE HIMSELF WITH THAT "SKY ROCKY" WHEN IT GOES OFF.
JOE STORK.
NOT ONLY DO I SUCCEED IN TYING A SKY ROCKET TO "OFFICER PUPP'S" CLUB, BUT A FRIENDLY FATE LEADS ME TO THIS BONNY BRICK – – THIS IS MY IDEA OF A "FANCY FOURTH" –
IT'S SURE SILLY THE WAY THOSE "SIPPS" CELEBRATE THE 4TH ON ONE ANOTHER – YES MAAM, SIR.
WELCOME
HERRIMAN

ABOVE From the Hearst trade publication *Circulation*. July 1923.

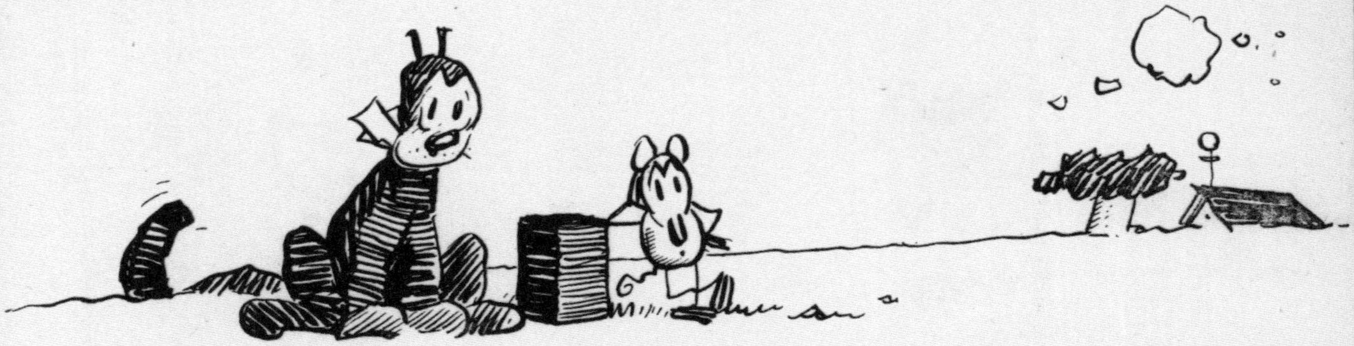

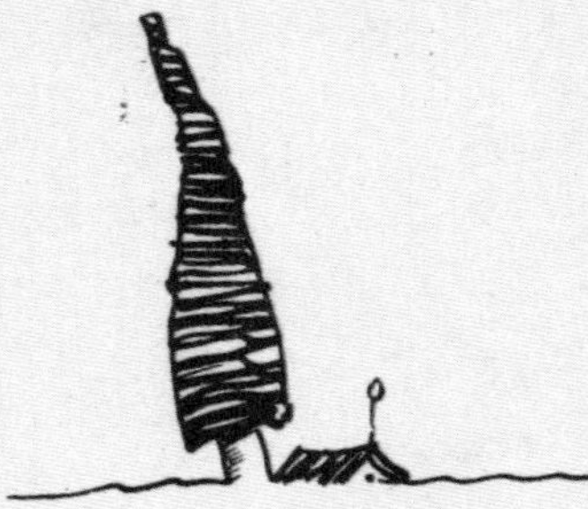

GEORGE HERRIMAN

THIS introduces Herriman, the clever, ever merry man who gives us "Krazy Kat" and "Baron Bean." He takes us to the house of the worthy Ignatz Mouse, whom you've very often seen on page and screen.

In sunny California, three dozen years ago, George Herriman, the merry man, began to see and grow.

This artist's boyhood was ideal and one most boys would prize. His father had a bake shop full of cookies, cakes and pies. But George had never leaned toward cake. He saw it by the tons. He worshipped Art for Art's sweet sake and did not yearn for buns.

One Summer morning, on the sly, while father was away, George drew a picture of a pie and put it on a tray. A customer came in the store in search of something sweet, and when he looked the picture o'er he thought 'twas good to eat. He bought it then and took it home and nearly had a fit—the only thing George ever drew that didn't make a hit.

For sixteen years in New York town he's been a comic star, and many a pawn since then he's drawn—you know how good they are. The little Kat, the little Mouse, each drawn with simple Art, have scurried into many a house and gladdened many a heart. And this, beyond all question, is a greater Art to prize than spreading indigestion drawing wagons full of pies.

Yes, George, you've brightened countless houses with "Krazy Kats" and "Ignatz Mouses."

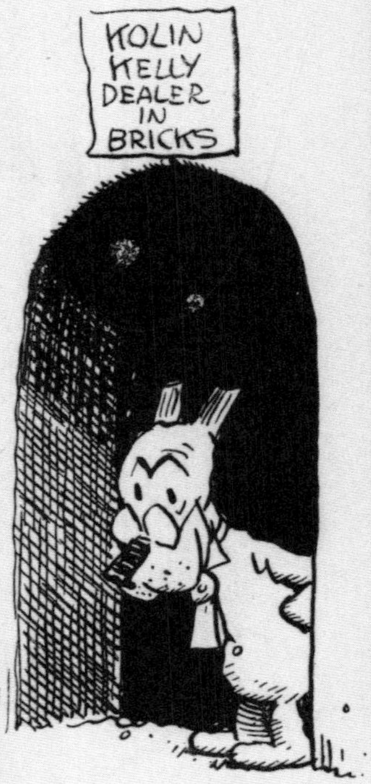
KOLIN KELLY DEALER IN BRICKS

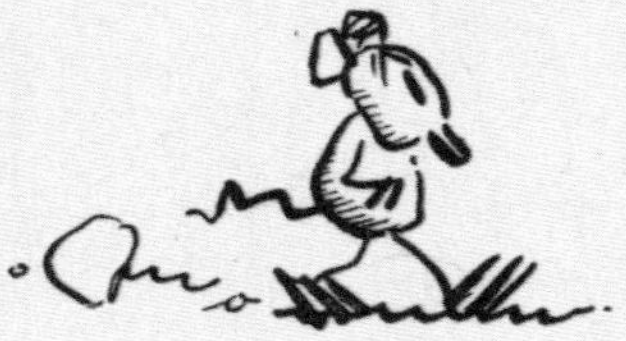

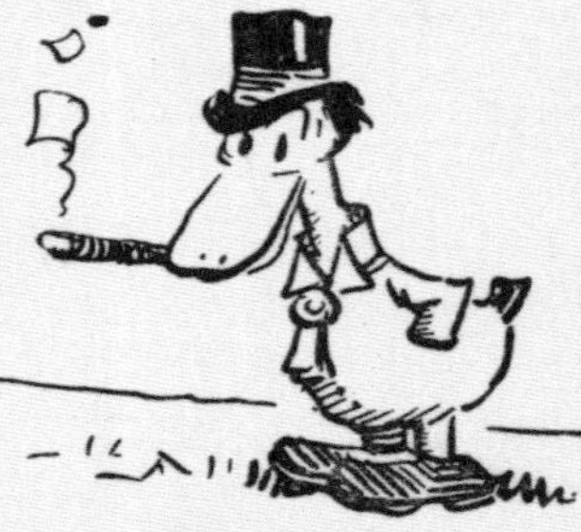

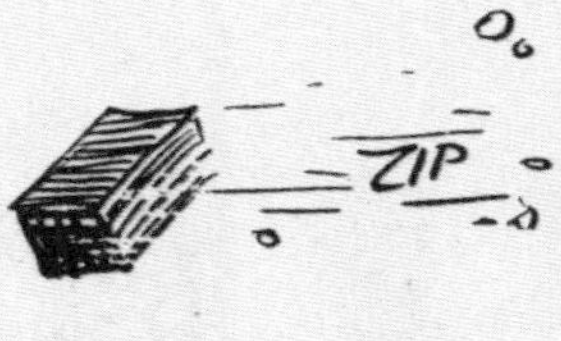
ZIP

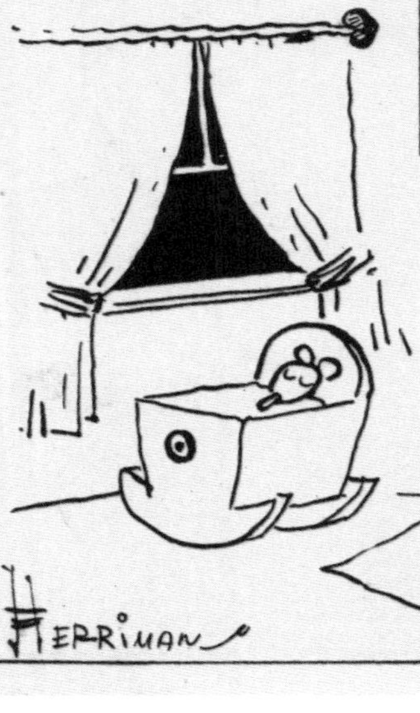
HERRIMAN

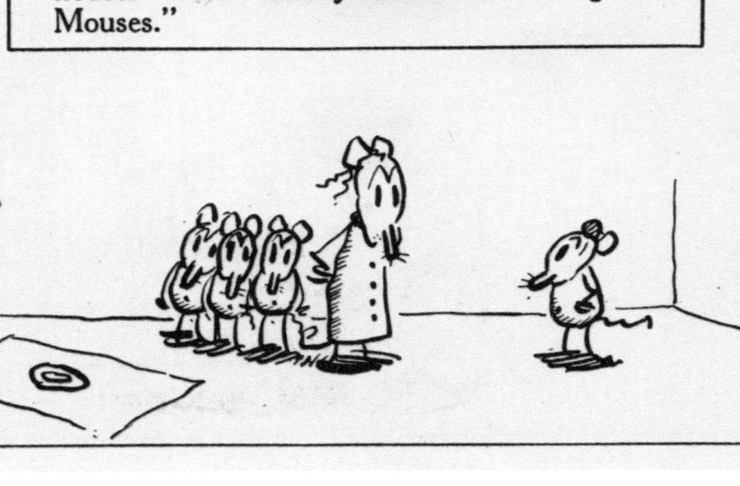

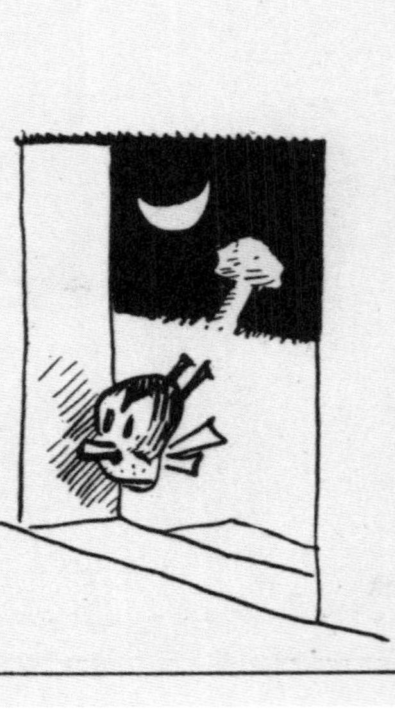

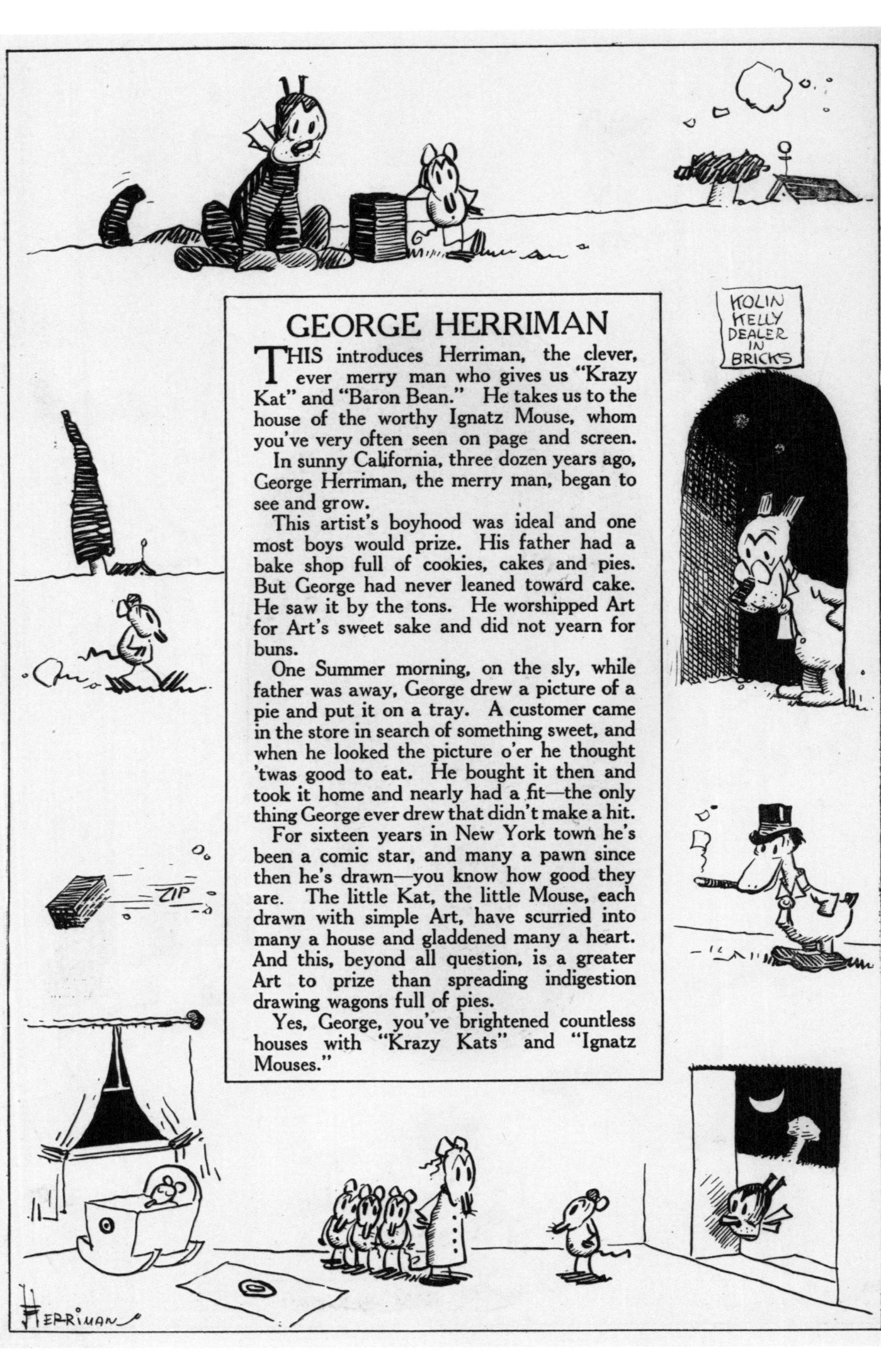

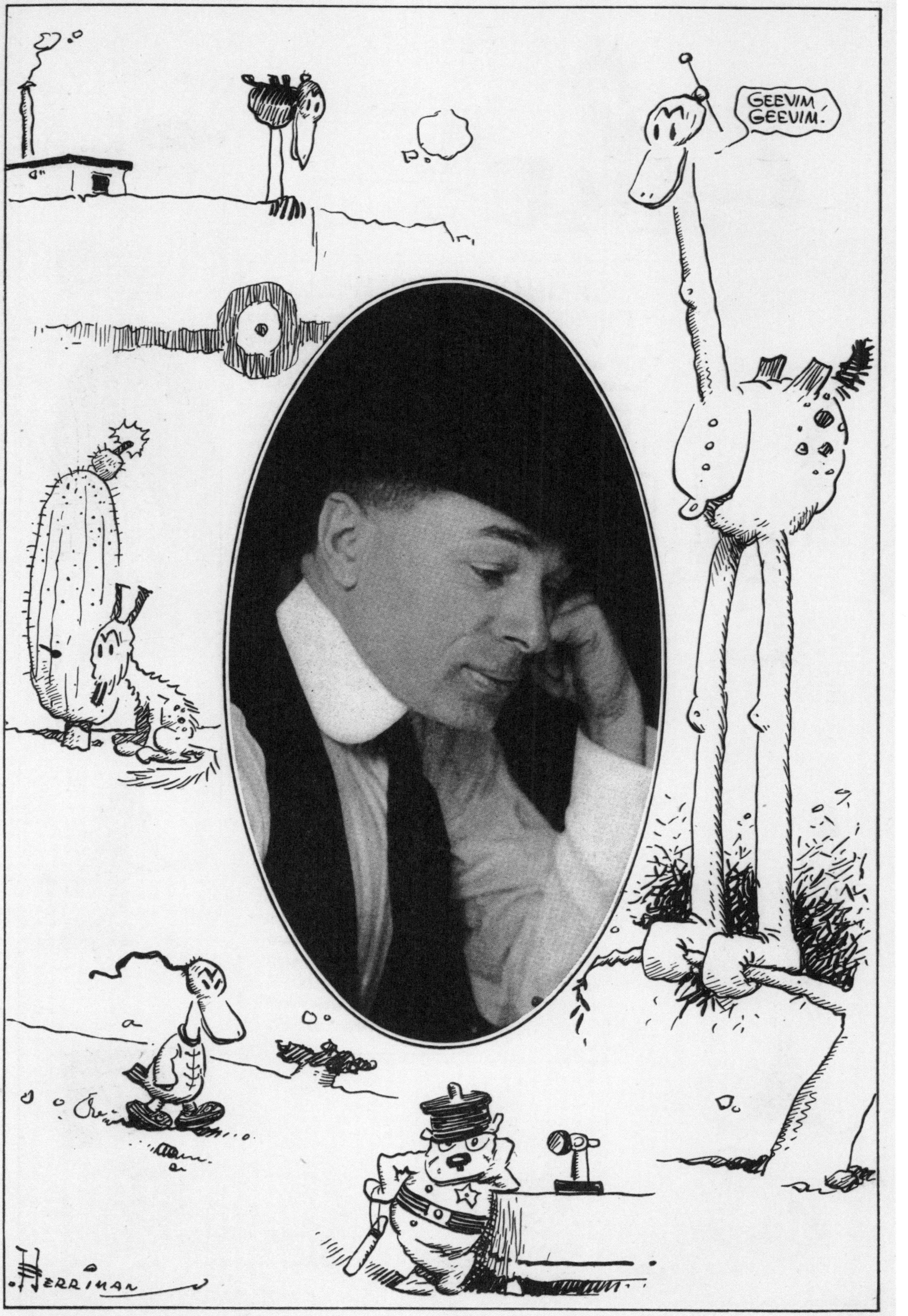
GEEVIM GEEVIM!
HERRIMAN

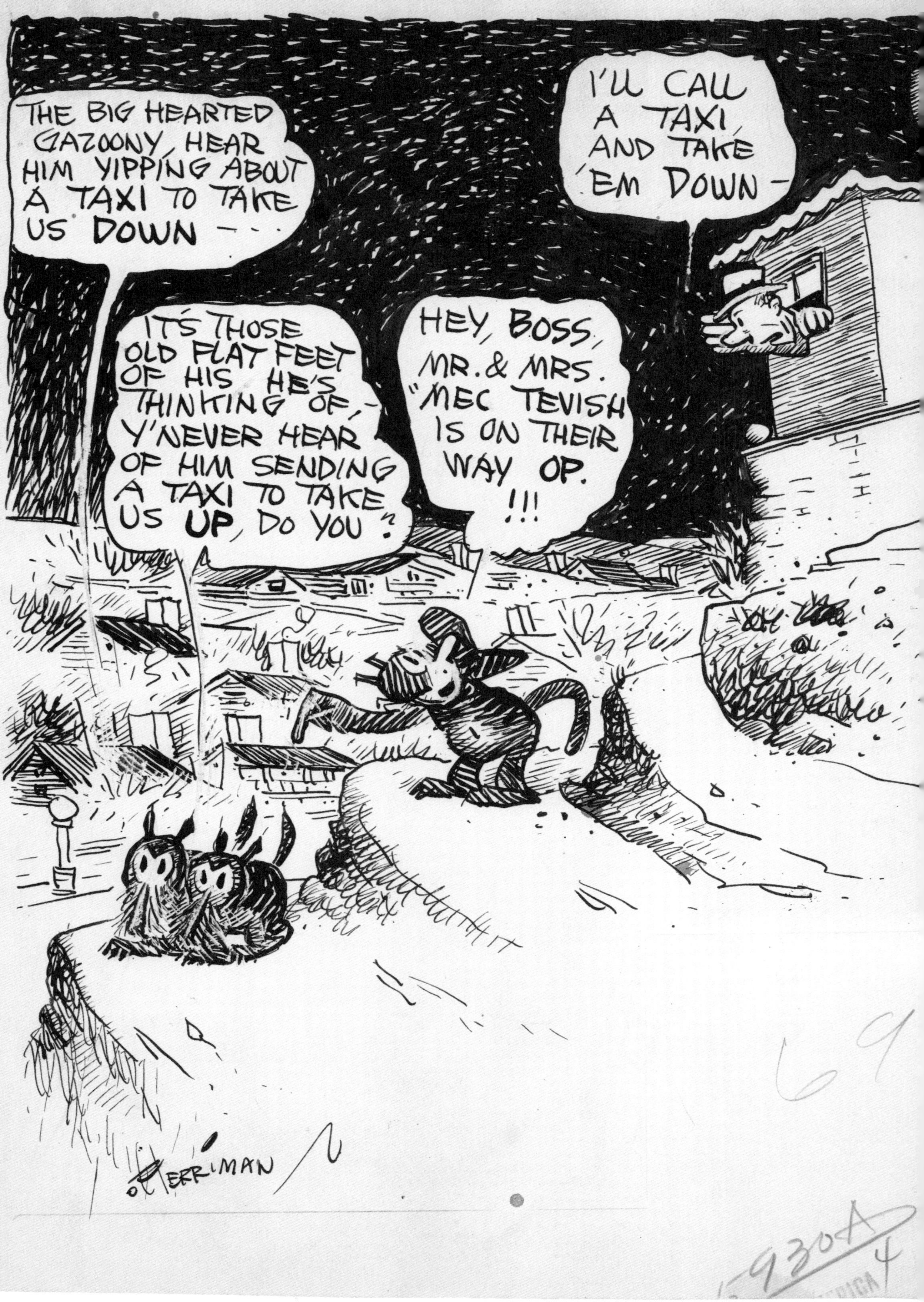
HEY, BOSS, MR. & MRS. "MEC TEVISH IS ON THEIR WAY UP. !!!
I'LL CALL A TAXI AND TAKE 'EM DOWN -
THE BIG HEARTED GAZOONY, HEAR HIM YIPPING ABOUT A TAXI TO TAKE US DOWN - - -
IT'S THOSE OLD FLAT FEET OF HIS HE'S THINKING OF, - Y'NEVER HEAR OF HIM SENDING A TAXI TO TAKE US UP, DO YOU ?
HERRIMAN

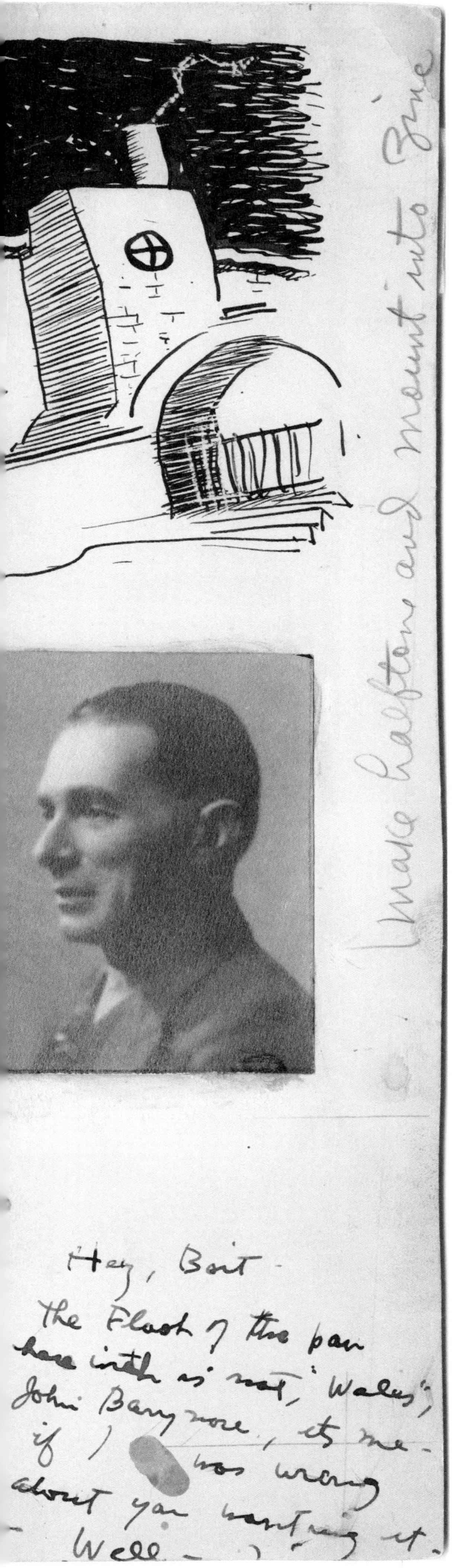

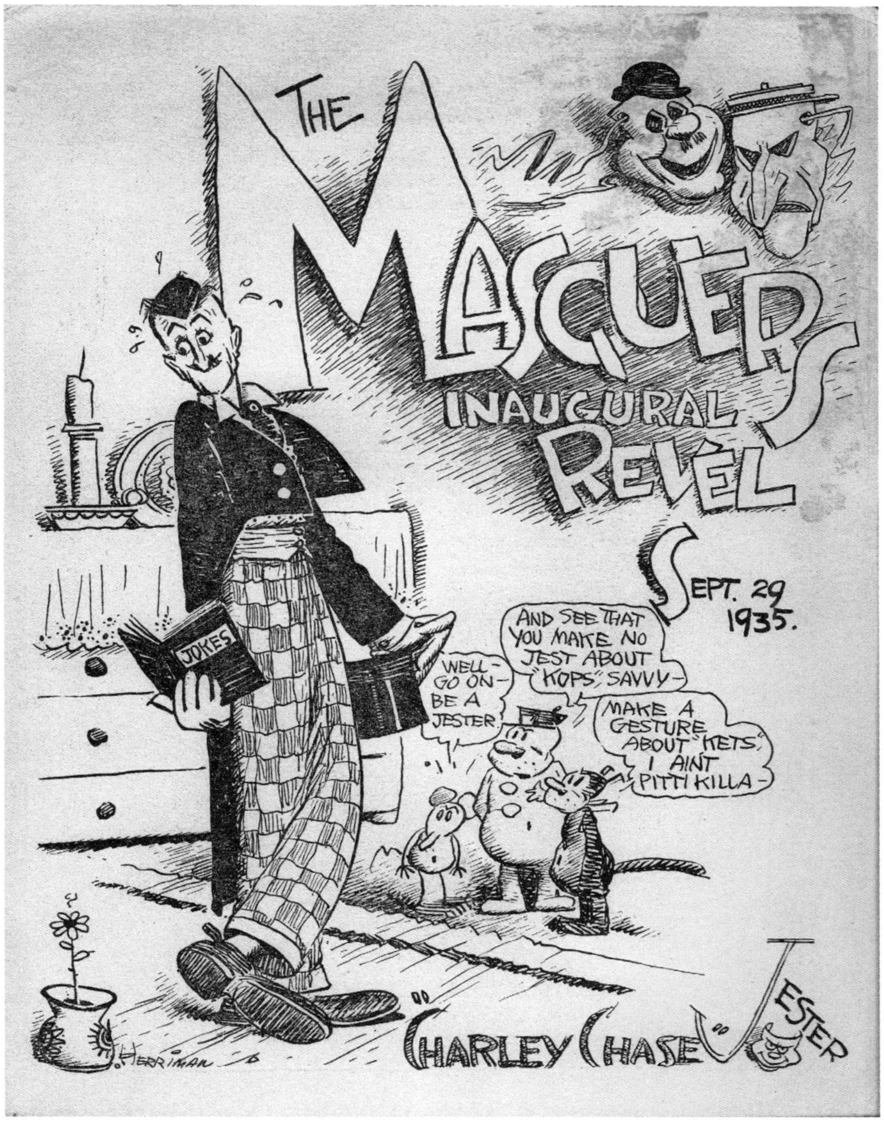
THE MASQUERS INAUGURAL REVEL
SEPT. 29 1935.
AND SEE THAT YOU MAKE NO JEST ABOUT KOPS, SAVVY-
WELL- GO ON- BE A JESTER
MAKE A GESTURE ABOUT KETS, I AINT PITTI KILLA-
JOKES
HERRIMAN
"CHARLEY CHASE" JESTER

PREVIOUS SPREAD Rudolph Block was the editor of the comics supplement for Hearst newspapers. In 1917 Block wrote a book of verses about the cartoonists in Hearst's stable. The poetic biographies were collected in a booklet titled *A Half Million Dollar Feature Service,* with the artists adding specialty borders. This artwork and biography are reproduced from the personal copy of one of the cartoonists in the booklet, Winsor McCay.

LEFT The inscription for this illustration reads, "Hey, Boit [?]—the flash of the pan here [. . .] is not 'Wales,' or John Barrymore, it's me—if I was wrong about you wanting it—well . . ."

ABOVE Program cover for the September 29, 1935, "Masquers Inaugural Revel," which included performances by Lionel Barrymore, Dorothy and Lillian Gish, and Harry Carey. The Masquers were an Hollywood actors' club whose motto was "We laugh to win!" Pictured on the cover is Charley Chase, who was a comedian and actor. In 1921, Chase became director-general of Hal Roach Studios. George Herriman had an office there, where he worked on his comic strips.

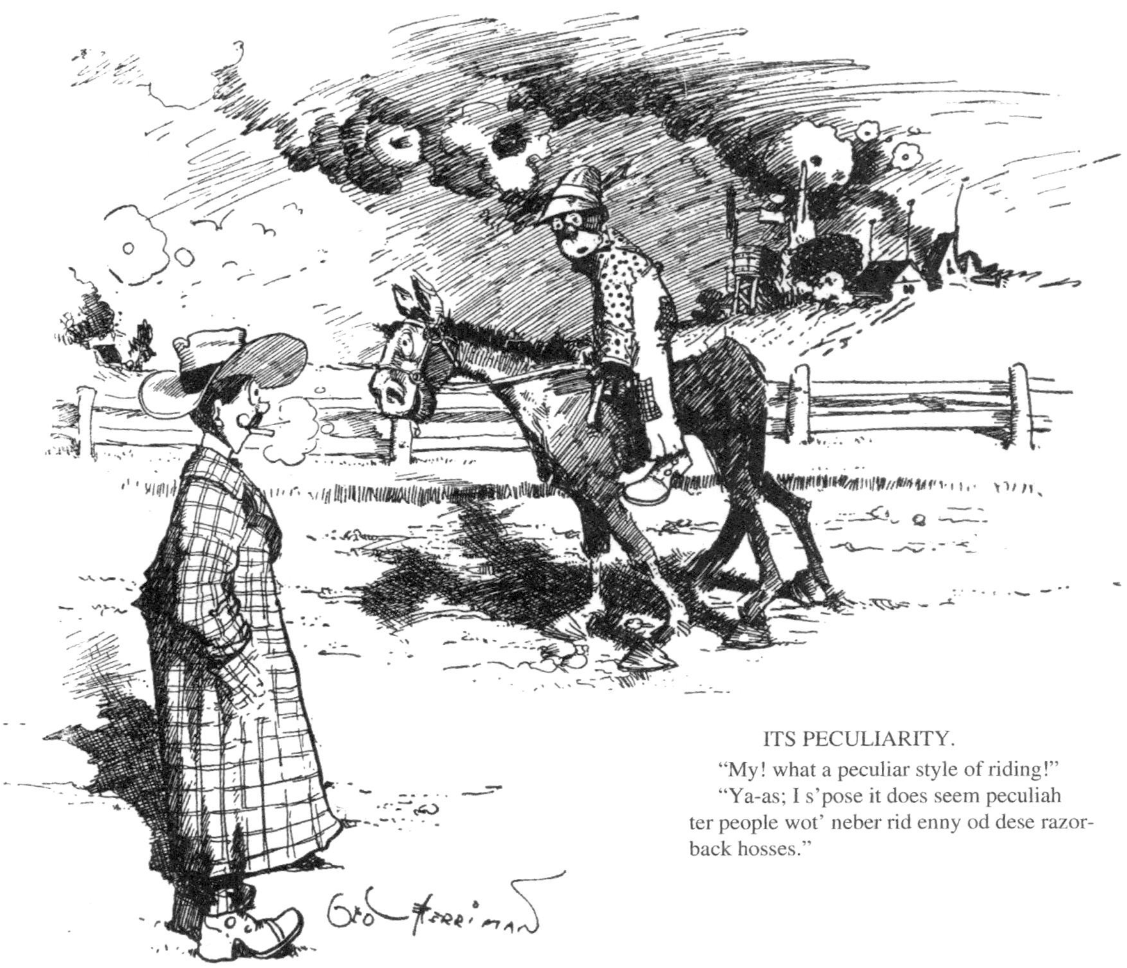
Geo Herriman

ITS PECULIARITY.

"My! what a peculiar style of riding!"

"Ya-as; I s'pose it does seem peculiah ter people wot' neber rid enny od dese razor-back hosses."

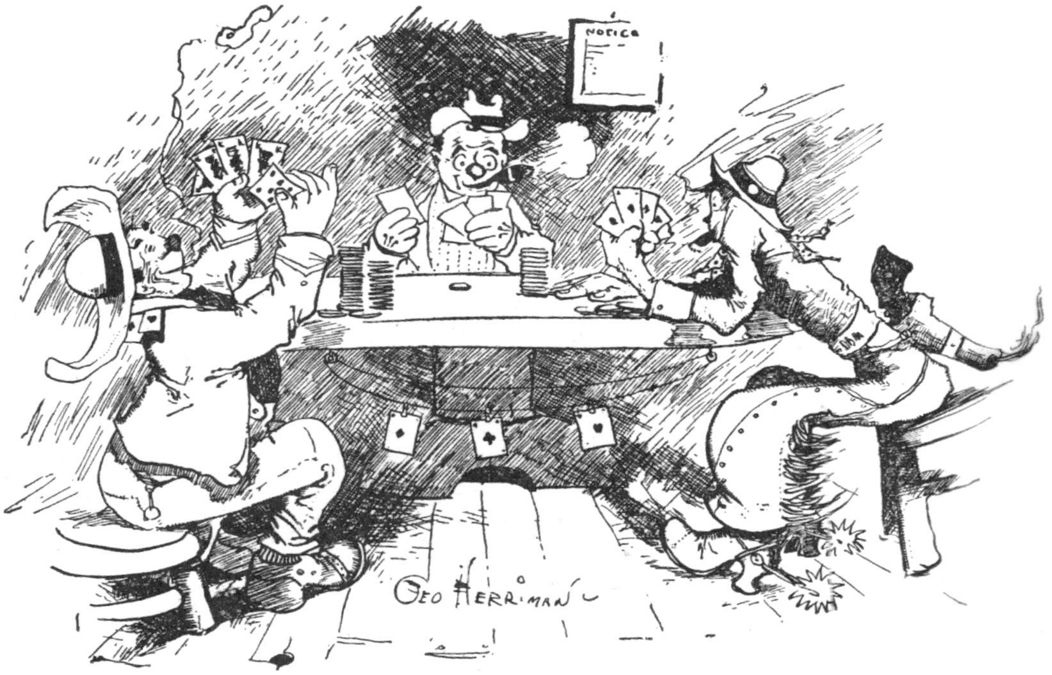
NOTICE
Geo Herriman

HOW THEY WORKED IT.

BILL BITTERS—"As I said before, stranger, Hank an' I, here, has carried on some purty nifty deals."

Stranger—"Working hand-in-hand, I suppose?"

Bill Bitters—"Thet's it—handin' hands."

THIS PAGE Herriman amazingly found time to draw cartoons for the humor magazine *Judge*. These are circa 1910.

OPPOSITE Drawing by TAD. From left, Harry Hershfield (*Abie the Agent*); Walter Hoban (*Jerry on the Job*); TAD (*Indoor Sports*); George Herriman; T. E. Powers (*Our Moving Pictures*); Cliff Sterrett (*Polly and Her Pals*); in the poster on the wall, Tom McNamara (*Us Boys*). *Circulation,* March 1923.

This Is About Garge Herriman

by Tad Dorgan

This article first appeared in *Circulation*, March 1923.

HERRIMAN. That's the monicker you see signed to the *Krazy Kat* drawings. His first name is George, but the boys calls him Garge, because that's the way he pronounces it himself.

Now I'm not going to sit here and chuck the swell about the guy. I'm going to tell the truth.

Garge came from somewhere out west, we think it's Los Angeles. He came here on a side door Pullman. Of course, he wouldn't want me to say so if he was here, but it's a fact just the same. He hangs around with a lot of painters, poets, and authors these days, but when I first saw him he still had grease from the box cars on his pants.

He looked like a cross between Omar the tent maker and Nervy Nat when he eased into the art room of the *New York Journal* twenty years ago. We didn't

CIRCULATION
YES MEYER— BUT LISTEN— THAT'S A LOTTA MONEY
HERSHFIELD
GO ON GREEK KNOCK HIM STIFF.
ARE YOU READY GARGE?
TAKE THAT CIGAWR OUTA YA MOUTH
NOW—AHEM! BREAK CLEAN BOYS—PST—
HEAVENLY DAYS!! YOU DONT THINK THEY'RE ANGRY DO YOU TOM?
RUBBER NOSE MCNAMARA
MY STARS STERRETT.
TO CASHIER
HOBAN.
METHUSELAH POWERS
ME
GARGE
BOXING IN THE ART ROOM WITH GARGE HERRIMAN THE GREEK
TAD

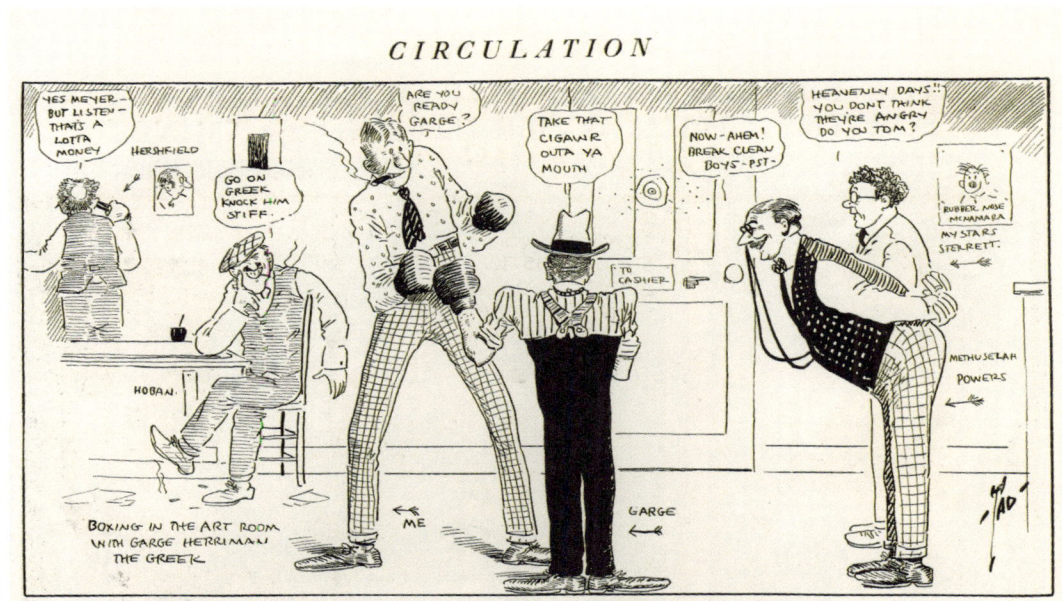

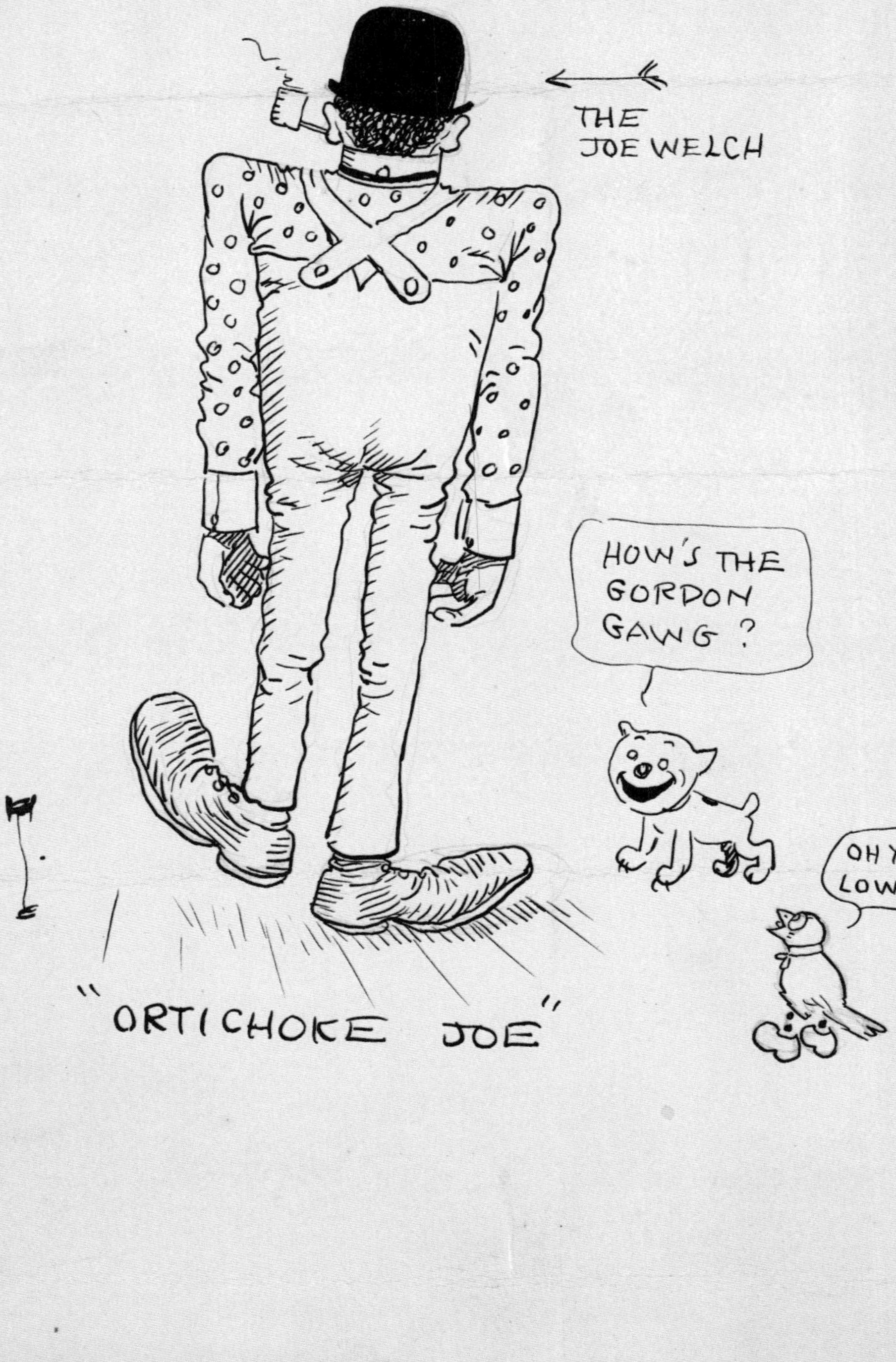
THE JOE WELCH
HOW'S THE GORDON GAWG ?
OH YOU LOWSE
"ORTICHOKE JOE"

"TAD'S PALE BLUE EYES
POPPED LIKE CHINEE
NEW YEAR AS THEY
LAID THEMSELVES ON
"BOB'S" PASSION FLOWER

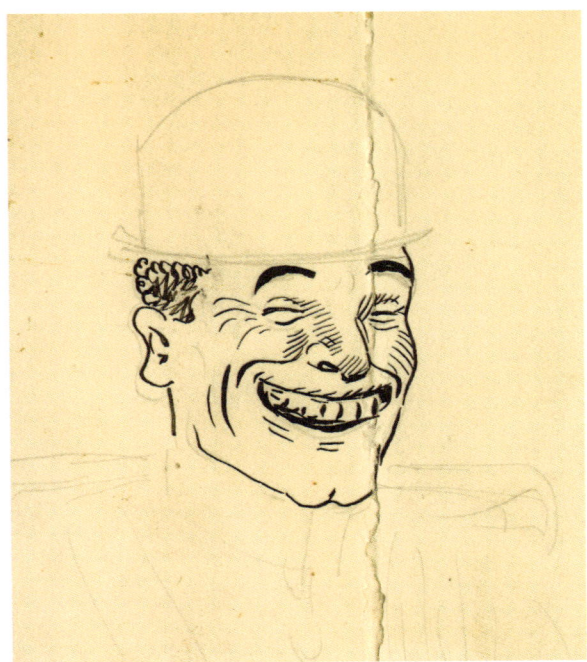

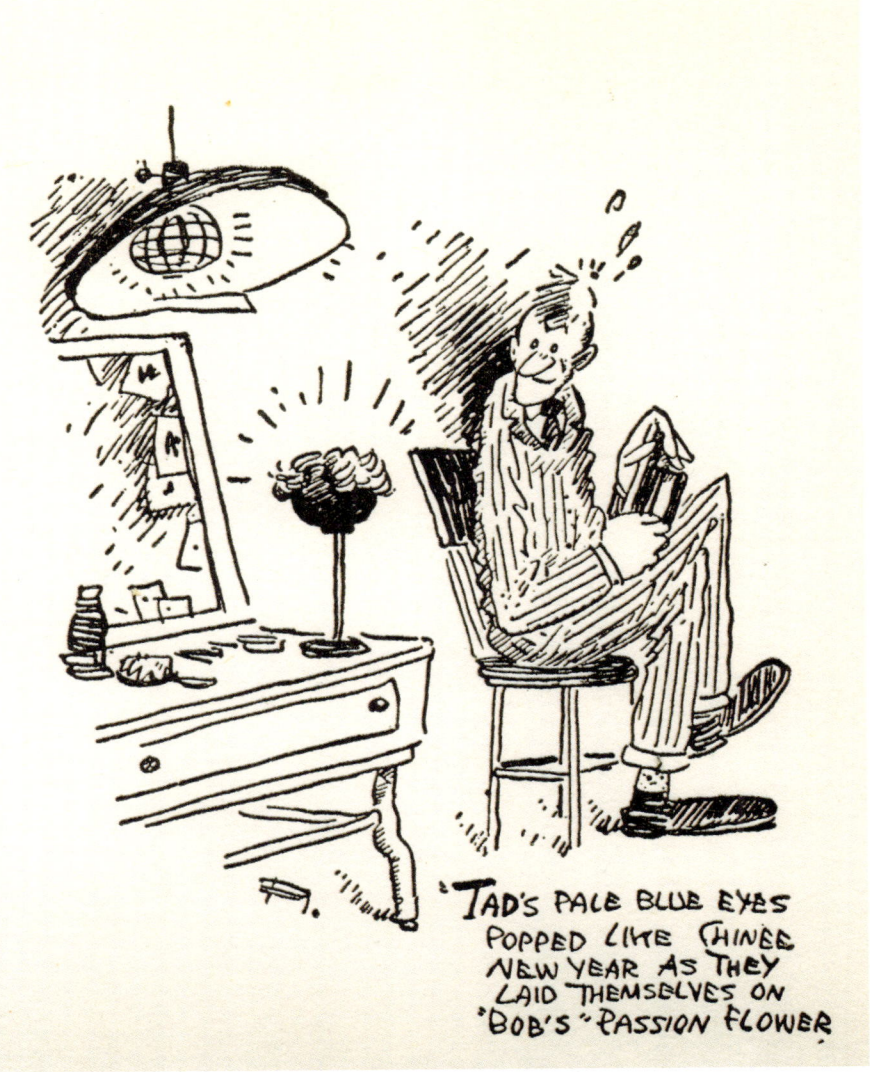

know what he was, so I named him The Greek, and he still goes by that name.

Garge is short and wide, like the door of a safe, and as Johnny Dunn, the announcer, used to say of his wrestler, "He is strong. He can bend IRUN BARS WITH HIS NAKED HANDS."

Garge also has a peculiar way of drawling. He is never in a rush as he drawls his words. He calls garden GORDON, he calls harness HORNESS, he calls cigars CIGORS, and so on.

He ALWAYS wears a hat. Like Chaplin and his cane, Garge is never without his skimmer. Hershfield says that he sleeps in it.

Garge has three hobbies. They are Arizona Indians, chili con carne, and boxing gloves. He once knocked a guy cold on the elevated station at Forty-second street, New York City, and has been living on that rep ever since.

No one has ever found out what this knocked out gent did to Garge, but it must have been something AWFUL, because he has never once lost his temper with us and he has been through some tough afternoons and evenings. No matter what happens Garge is always the same. You can steal his pens, but he only smiles. You can knock California, but he merely smiles. You can cut up rubber in his tobacco pouch and he'll smoke it just to let you laugh. He is like the old rye the guy told of. Not a harsh word in a whole barrel of it. There never was a smoother tempered gent. I'll bet right now that if you asked Garge what the brick that hits Krazy Kat was made of he'd say VELVET. Then he'd add, "You don't think I'd want that poor lil cat to be hurt, do you?" Garge is a great reader and a great movie fan. His favorite author is CHORLES DICKENS and his favorite movie guy is CHORLIE CHAPLIN.

He will sit by the hour and talk of them. That is, he used to before the soda stores took the places once held by the Pilsner peddlers.

He brags about his favorites, Garge does, but never about himself.

The violet imitated Garge when it assumed that attitude of shyness.

He thinks he's the rottenest artist that ever got behind a pen, and no matter how many boosting letters he gets about his stuff he's of the same opinion still. Of course WE KNOW BETTER.

Half the guys that never get a boosting letter admit that they're good. Garge doesn't and never will. He is always last. He laughs, though. Yes, he gets his giggles. When he laughs you'd think he had just taken a sniff of snuff. It isn't a laugh, it's a sort of internal explosion.

Thomas Aloysius Dorgan (April 29, 1877–May 2, 1929), who signed his name TAD, worked alongside Herriman at the New York Journal *in the early 1900s. As both a sportswriter and cartoonist, TAD was busy as a "one-armed paperhanger," one of the many phrases he popularized in his comics.*

OPPOSITE An original drawing by TAD of George Herriman as seen from the rear. Early 1920s.

ABOVE, LEFT The back of the drawing on the facing page shows a preliminary sketch drawn by TAD of George Herriman. Previously unpublished.

ABOVE, RIGHT A drawing by Herriman titled "TAD's stealing Bob Fitzsimmons' wig." This appeared in the book *Give Us a Little Smile, Baby,* by Harry J. Coleman, published by E. P. Dutton in 1943.

Toyland, Toyland. Krazy Kat and Ignatz-land

The limited amount of merchandising around *Krazy Kat* produced timeless treasures.

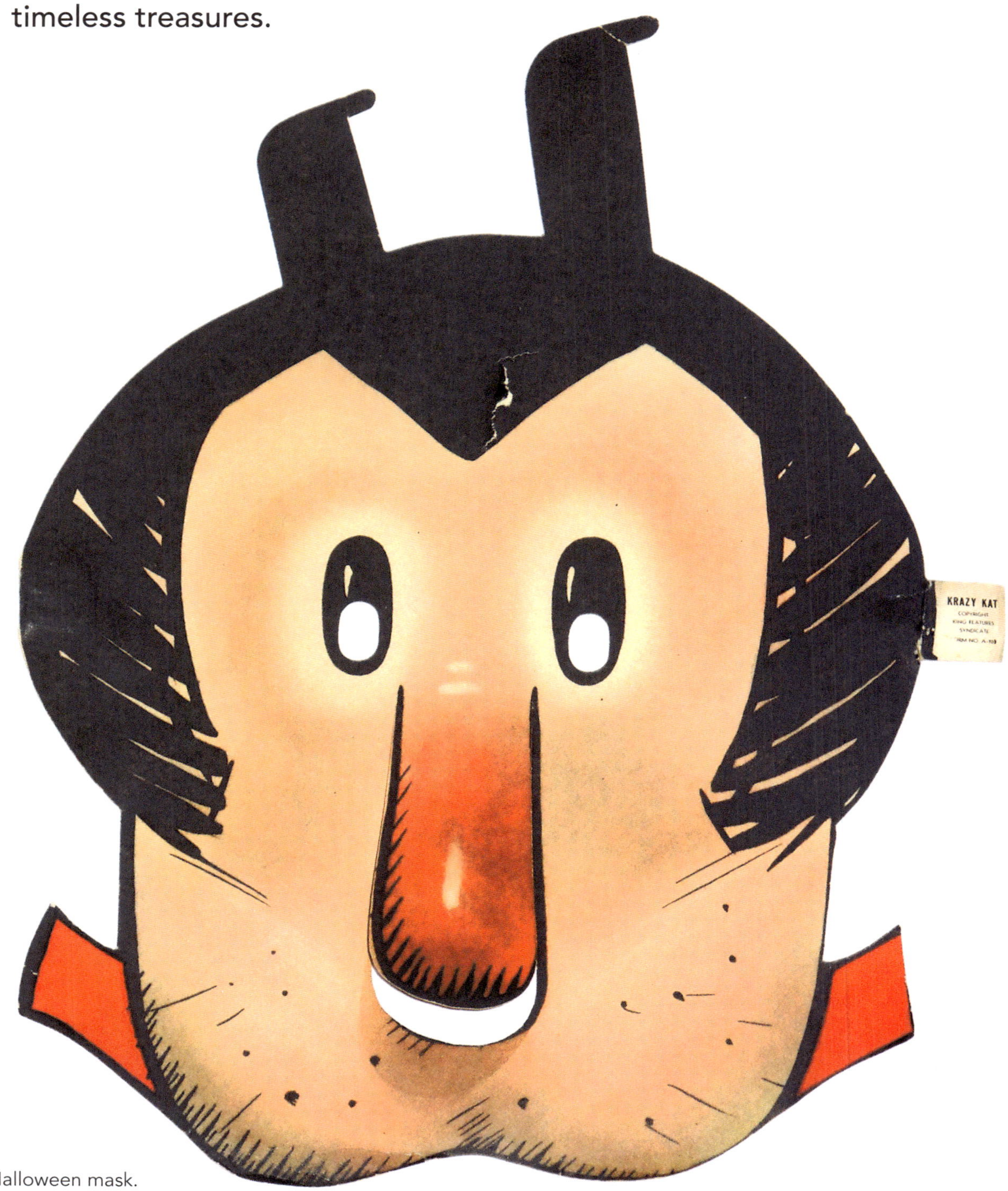
KRAZY KAT

ABOVE A fragile Krazy Kat Halloween mask.

OPPOSITE Krazy Kat dolls came in a variety of colors (see pages 164–65 and 170).

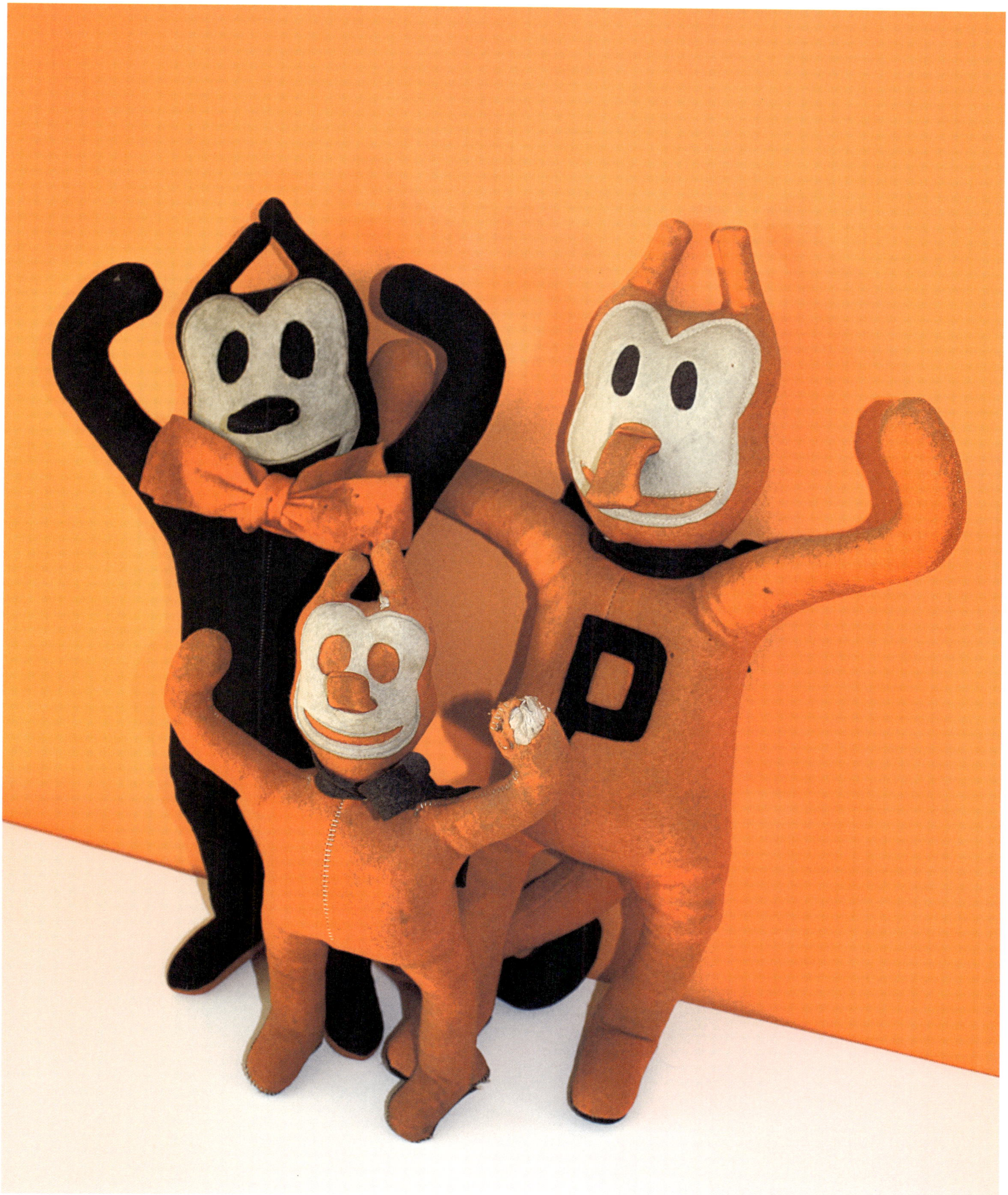

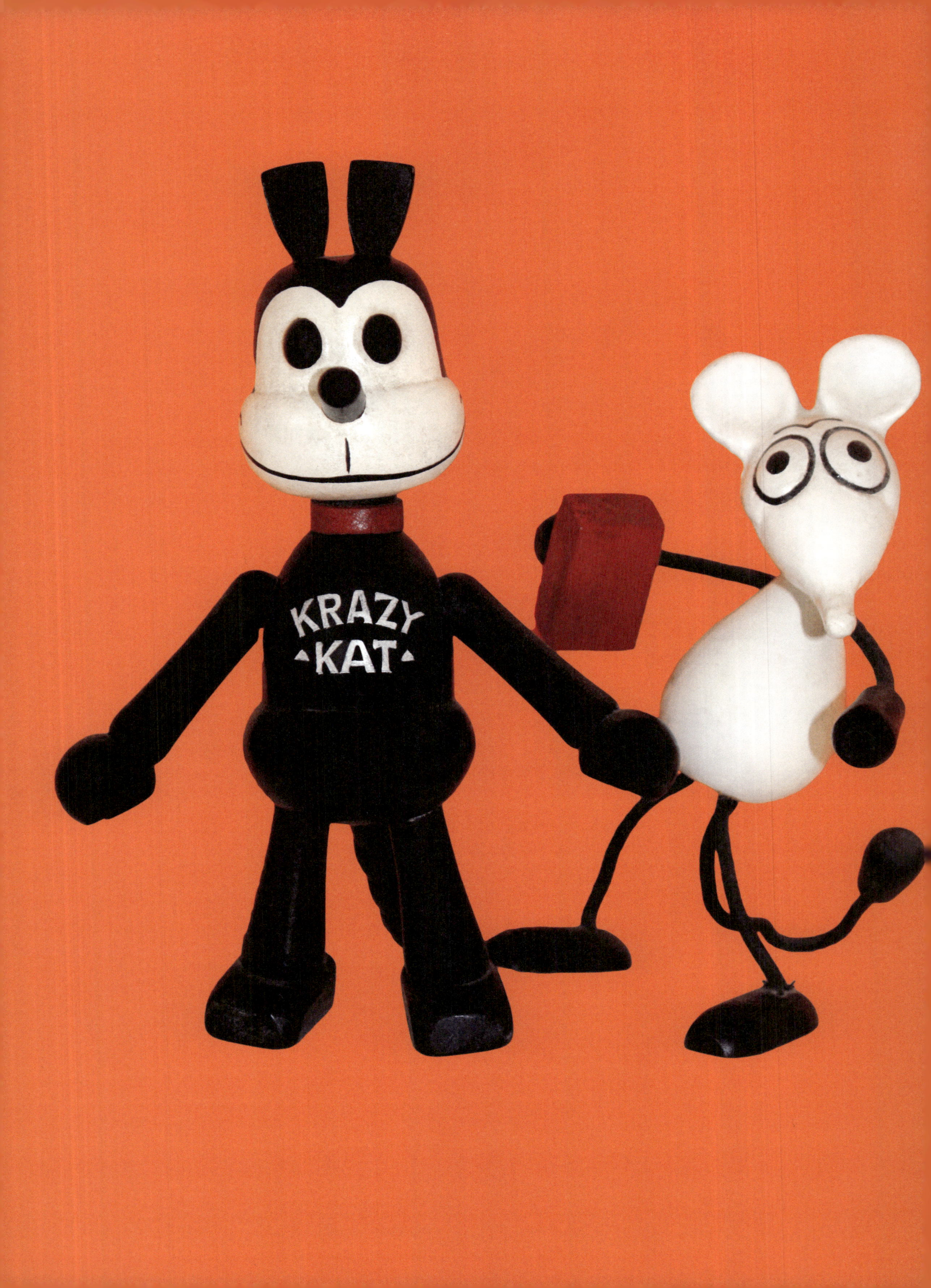
KRAZY
KAT

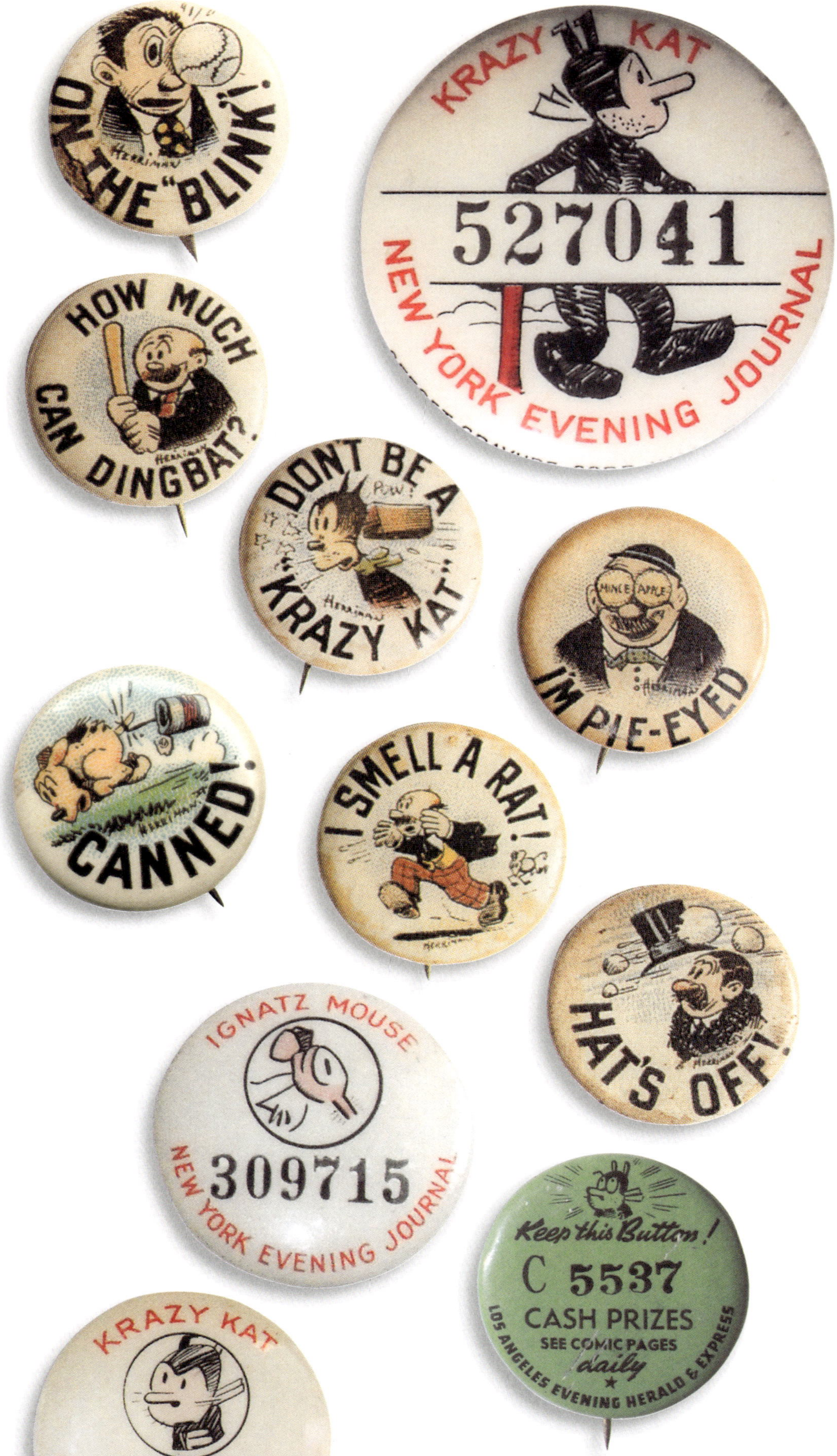
ON THE "BLINK"!
KRAZY KAT
527041
NEW YORK EVENING JOURNAL
HOW MUCH CAN DINGBAT?
DON'T BE A KRAZY KAT!
POW!
MINCE APPLE
I'M PIE-EYED
CANNED!
I SMELL A RAT!
HAT'S OFF!
IGNATZ MOUSE
309715
NEW YORK EVENING JOURNAL
Keep this Button!
C 5537
CASH PRIZES
SEE COMIC PAGES
daily
LOS ANGELES EVENING HERALD & EXPRESS

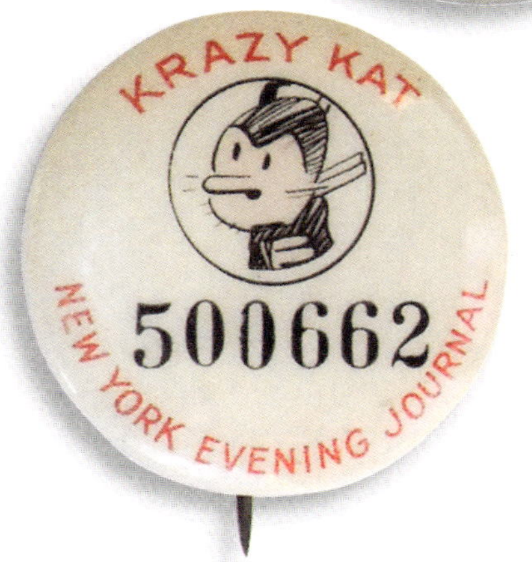
KRAZY KAT
500662
NEW YORK EVENING JOURNAL

OPPOSITE Krazy and Ignatz joined Felix and Mickey in being made into posable, wooden toys.

ABOVE George Herriman, along with Rube Goldberg and TAD, drew buttons for the Hassan cigarette company. The premiums were distributed inside the cigarette packs in the 1920s. The top right button and the two on the lower left were promotional items for the *New York Evening Journal*. 1930s. The green button on the bottom right was for the *Los Angeles Evening Herald Examiner*. 1930s.

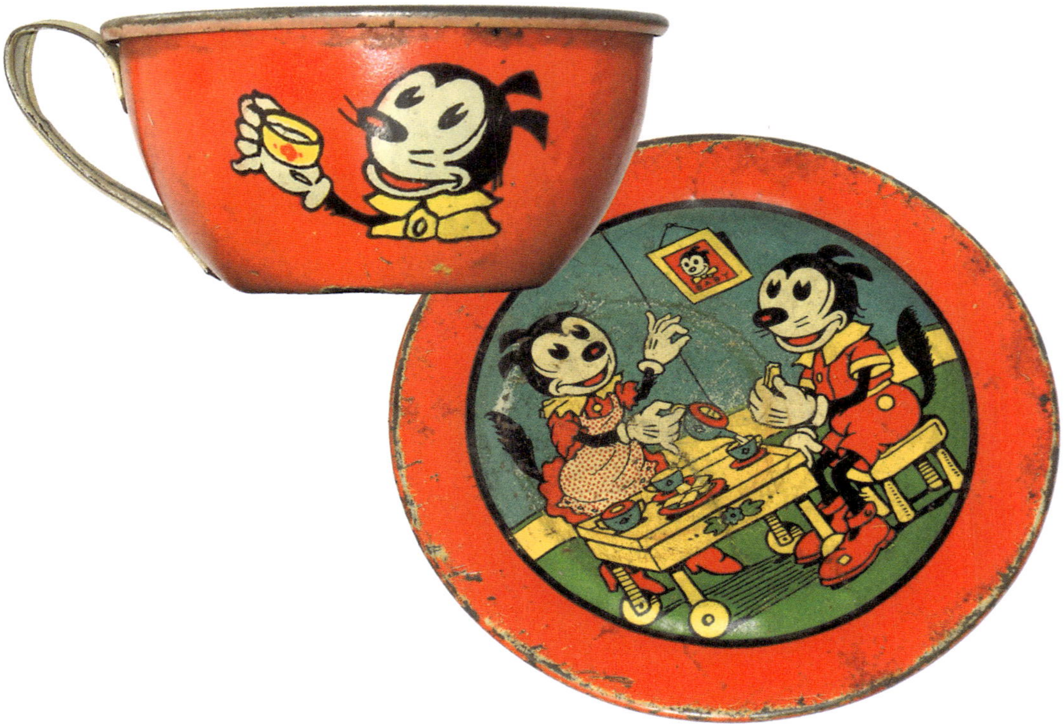

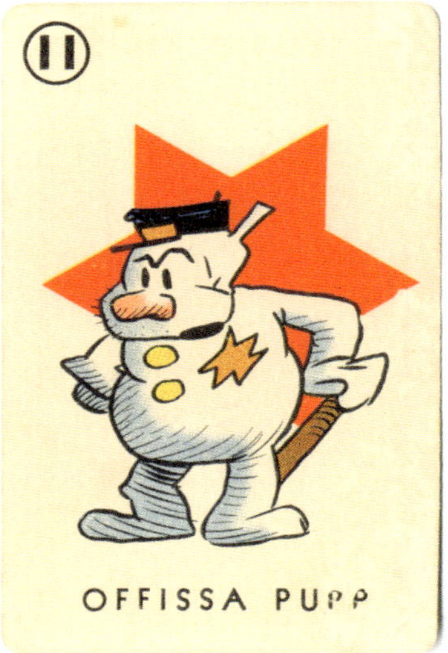
11
OFFISSA PUPP

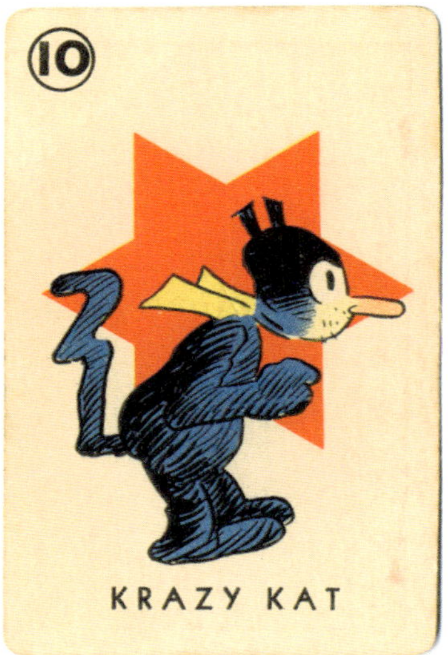
10
KRAZY KAT

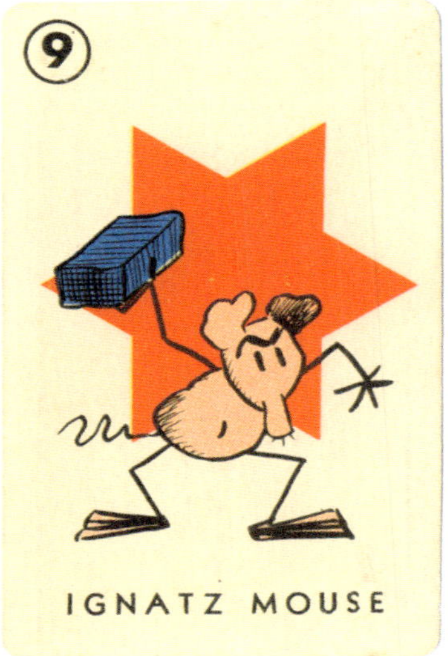
9
IGNATZ MOUSE

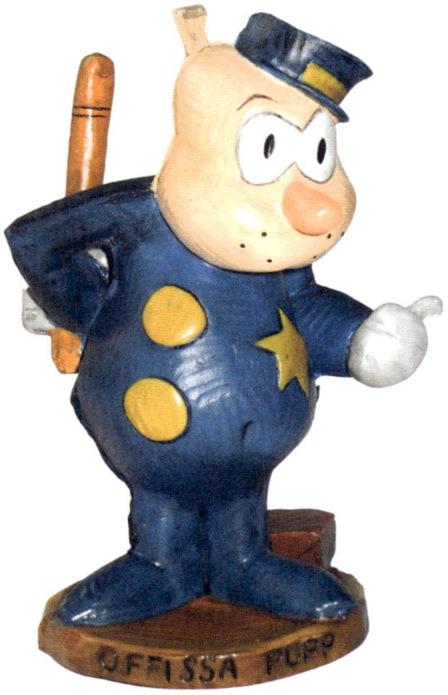
OFFISSA PUPP

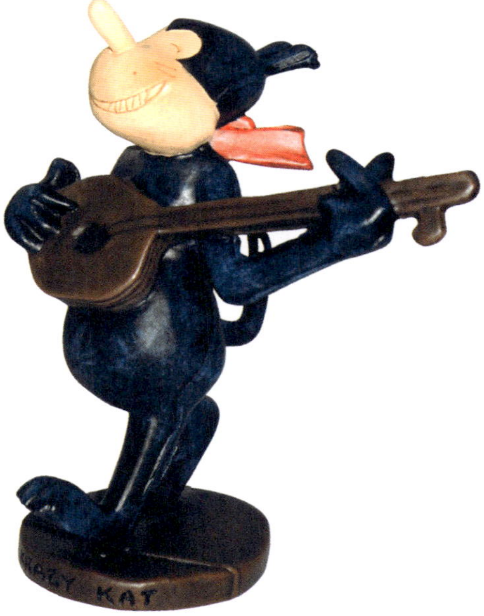

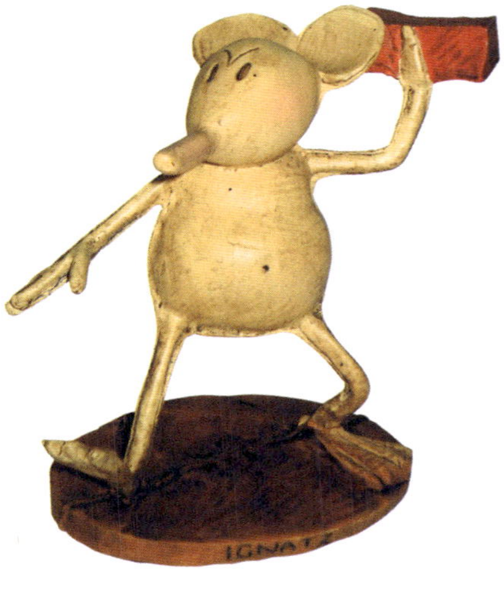

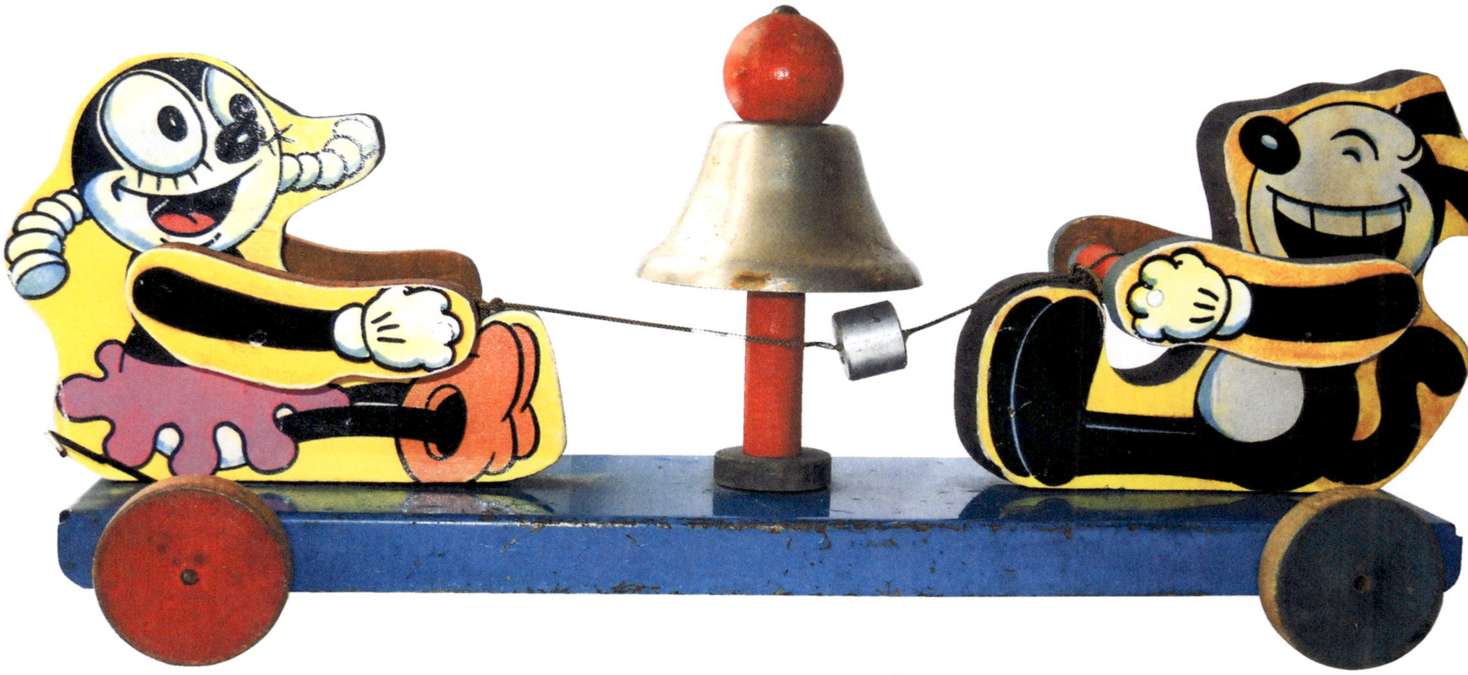

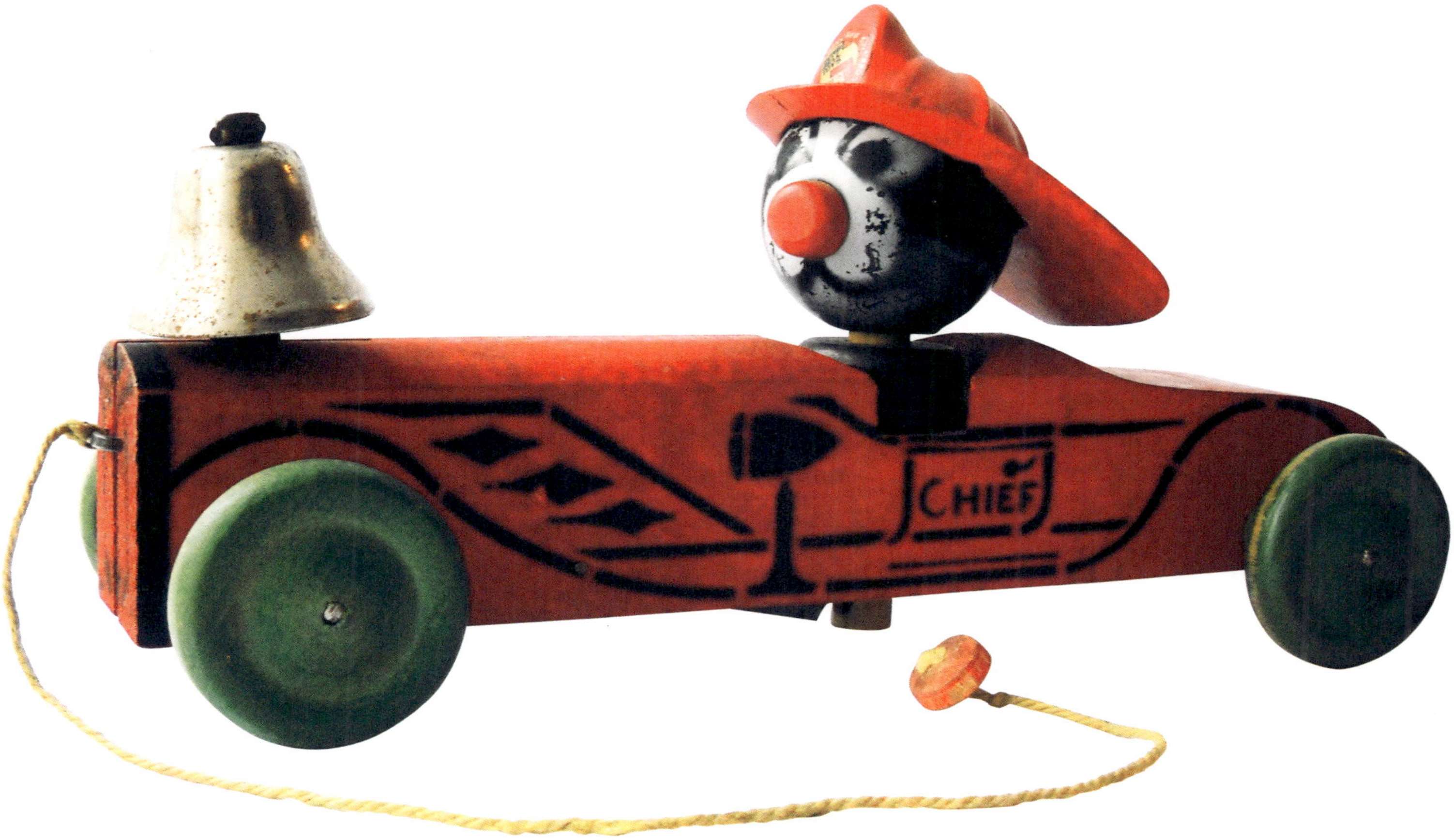
CHIEF

OPPOSITE, TOP Tea for toons! This tin tea set from the 1930s was manufactured by J. Chein & Co.

OPPOSITE, MIDDLE These playing cards depicted characters from King Features Syndicate. Here are the characters from Coconino County.

OPPOSITE, BOTTOM Statues created for Dark Horse Comics. Sculpted by YOE! Studio, 1999.

TOP Krazy Kat and friend are working on the railroad in this Columbia Pictures toy from the 1930s.

BOTTOM Krazy Kat is a firefighter in this toy made by Gong Bell Manufacturing Company. 1930s.

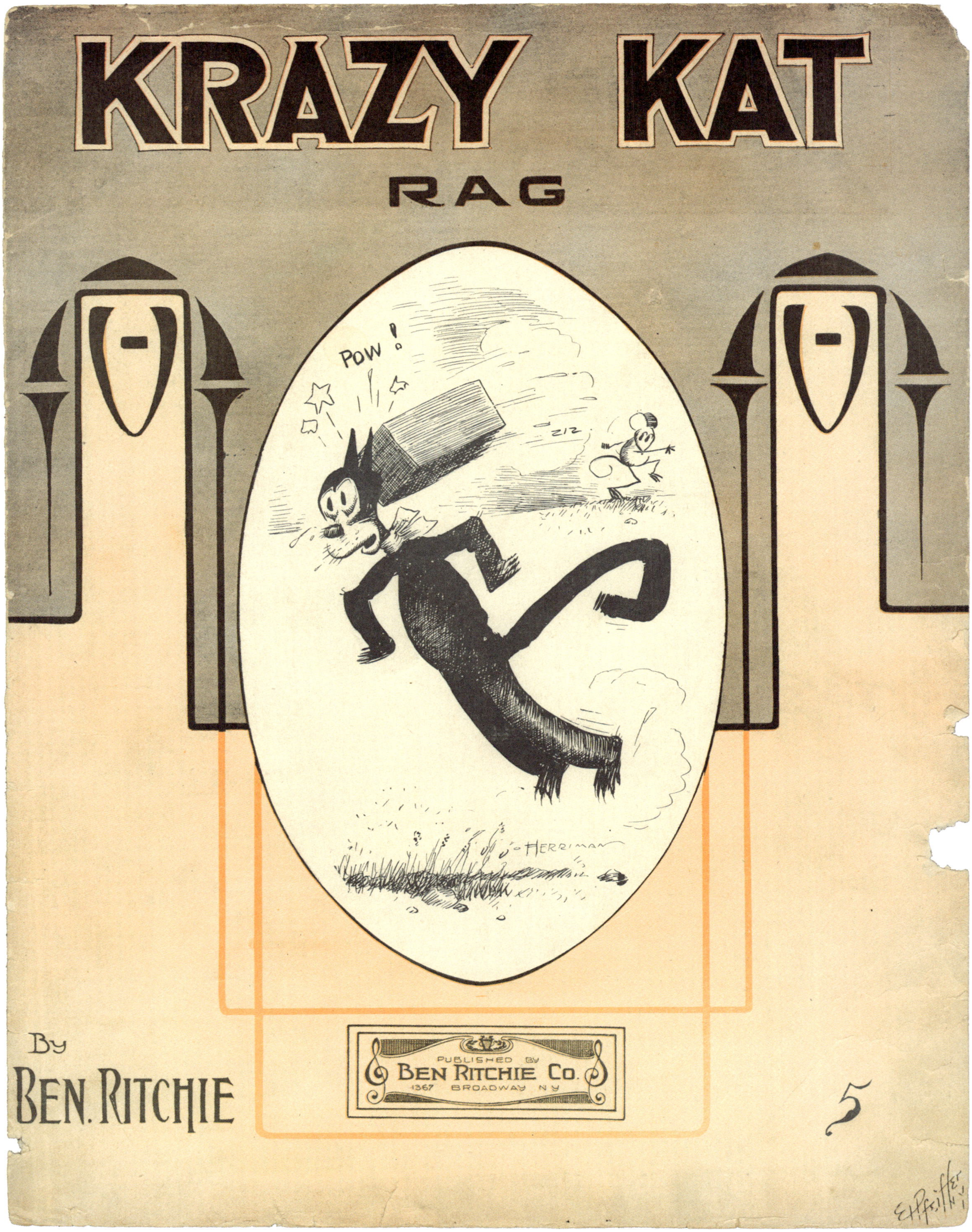
KRAZY KAT
RAG
POW!
ZIZ
HERRIMAN
By
BEN. RITCHIE
PUBLISHED BY
BEN RITCHIE CO.
1367 BROADWAY N.Y.
5

ABOVE "Krazy Kat Rag" sheet music by Ben Ritchie from 1911. Although the depiction of Krazy Kat is a bit unusual, it is by Herriman.

Toots Herriman Tells the World About Krazy Kat

by William Paul Langreich
This rare article first appeared in the trade journal *The Cartoonist*, volume 1, number 2, January 1922.

First, let us tell you who "Toots" Herriman is. Being the oldest daughter of Mr. and Mrs. George Herriman, she quite naturally becomes managing head of the Herriman family, even if the law recognizes Mr. Herriman as the legal head. So, when we learned that George Herriman shuns matters of publicity just as he does matters pertaining to business, we appealed to the fixer of all fixers, Tom McNamara (Skinny Shaners' Boss). McNamara is acquainted with the Herrimans well enough to know who is boss, so an interview with "Toots" was arranged.

"Toots," we learned later, was the name of a comic strip character appearing in a contemporary paper about the time of the young lady's appearance on this little green earth of ours, and it has clung to Miss Herriman much closer than the name her teachers use—Mabel.

Toots has a favorite comic strip and a favorite comic strip artist. They are, quite naturally, *Krazy Kat* and Krazy's boss—George Herriman. Little Ignatz Mouse, Krazy's comrade in foolishness, doesn't get one bit of encouragement from Toots. In fact, we are informed, the whole family accepts Ignatz with contempt. Officer Pupp is tolerated because he protects Krazy from Ignatz's flying brick now and then but Krazy—our leading character—is just loved as much as a kat can be loved.

Miss Herriman is surprised by her mother and her younger sister, Barbara (Bobbie), in her opinion of these characters. Only Mr. Herriman disagrees, but Toots just blames it on his modesty and assures us that even if he had little or no respect for his entire cast of strip actors, the reader wouldn't allow him to harm a single hair on even Ignatz. Herriman is dissatisfied with the strip, however, and is in a rather peculiar situation. While he regards his work as an inferior attempt at humor, his efforts to improve it have raised the standard of his strip to a plane far above the usual run of strips; his drawings are inimitable and his humor both subtle and original. But early in its existence, he made a mistake by allowing Ignatz to abuse Krazy. Little did he know that the public would acclaim this action as real humor and demand its repetition. As a result, he tries to omit his signature as often as the editors will let it get by, which does not happen very frequently.

Proofs of Herriman's work pulled on a good coated paper instead of the usual newsprint brings out re-

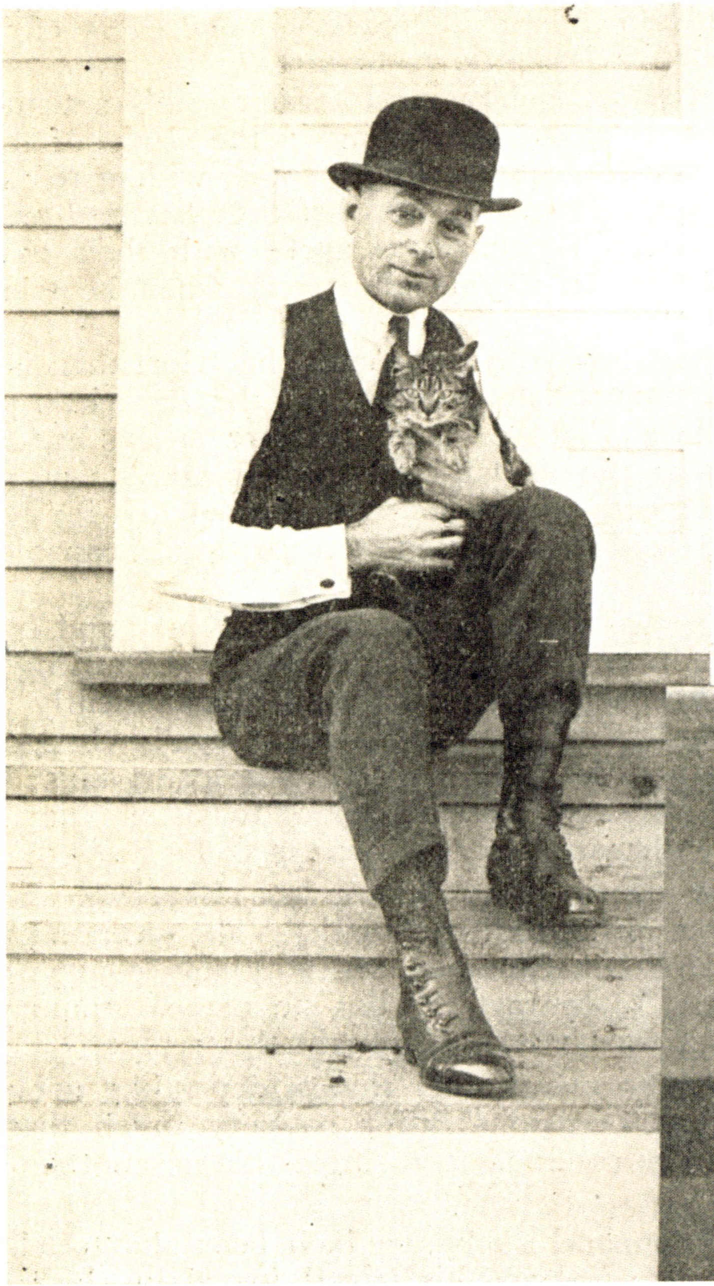

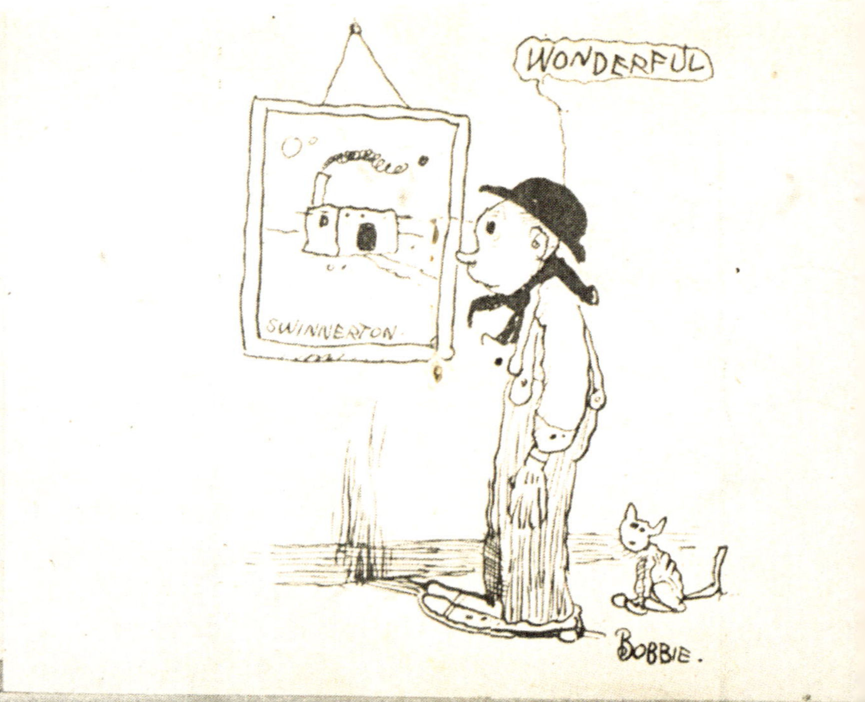
WONDERFUL
SWINNERTON
BOBBIE.

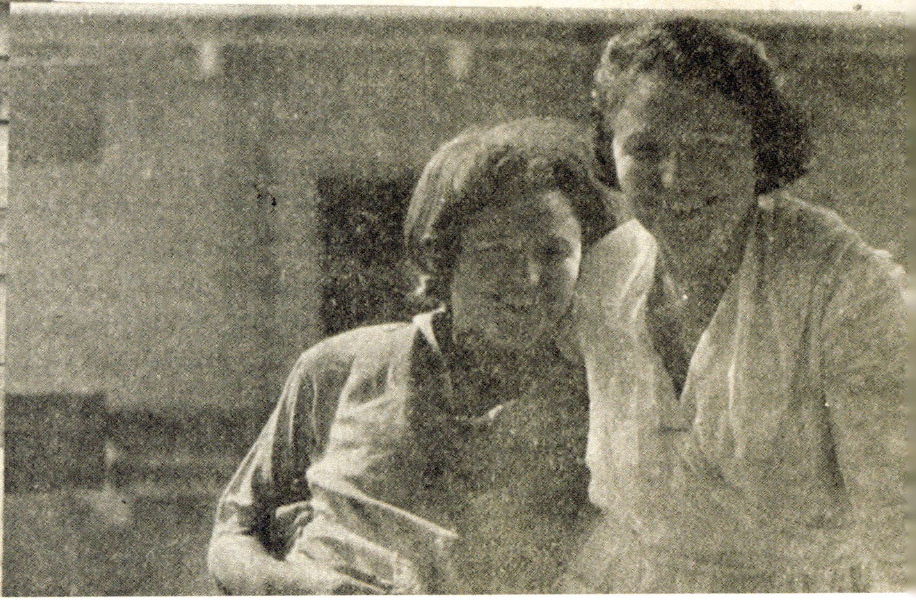

markable qualities unusual in ordinary work of this kind. Not only his drawings, but his ideas on which he bases strips are "different," and while he tries to discount favorable comment on his drawings, men prominent in the field of journalism acclaim this man as the "genius of the comic strip."

The story of *Krazy Kat* is interesting. A good many years ago, while Toots' dad was drawing sport cartoons for a Los Angeles paper, a daily feature was a little picture of a cat sketched in the corner of his sporting page picture. While it resembled a cat in many ways, the little creature assumed so many properties of a human being that the artist was called upon quite often for verification of the little animal's identity, whereupon Herriman decided that it was something different from a cat—possibly a Kat. Not only a Kat, however, for even as a Kat it looked ridiculous, so he dubbed it "Krazy Kat."

Krazy fared well by himself—or herself—or itself (Herriman tells his readers the creature is sexless), and came to New York when Herriman moved East to draw *The Dingbat Family* for the *New York Evening Journal* and other papers of the Hearst group. Here Krazy was adopted as the family pet of the Dingbats.

In any well-regulated family, a cat is supposed to earn its milk and liver by acting as a guard against the ravages of mice. However Krazy was not a regular cat in the first place and the Dingbats were not at all well regulated as a comic-strip family might be, so what should be more logical, then, than that the appearance of Ignatz should spell woe for Krazy. Ignatz' first appearance was marked by his picking up a marble and hitting Krazy squarely between the eyes. The whole affair was subordinated to the doings of the Dingbats, but Willie, one of the *Journal*'s office boys, insisted that the Krazy-Ignatz affair was the funniest thing he had ever seen.

Toots' dad, as explained, doesn't care for this type of humor at all, but, let it also be said, he was experienced enough to have learned to respect the opinions of an office boy, and so, Krazy and Ignatz appeared oftener and oftener until the editors decided that they were popular enough to own a strip of their own. This was printed directly beneath the Dingbat strip.

The newcomers were treated indifferently by Herriman, but despite the neglect of its originator, the

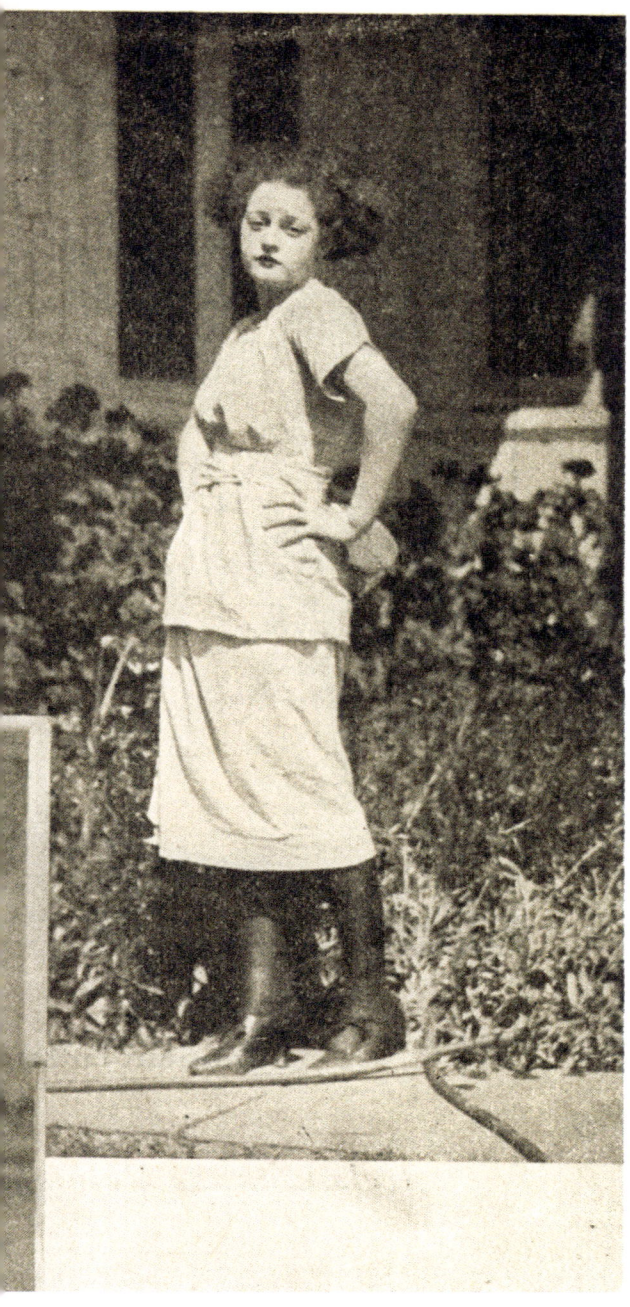

strip outlived the *Dingbats* and the *Dingbats*' successor, *Baron Bean*. It not only outlived, but also outgrew these two bigger brothers, for, in addition to a daily strip, *Krazy* also monopolizes the greater portion of a page in the *Sunday American*.

The backgrounds in the *Krazy Kat* pictures are more than incidental parts of these little drawings, for they allow the reader to peek behind the scenes to get a fleeting glimpse of the artist's hobby—the study of Mexico, Mexicans, and their history. Every now and then his followers are not at all surprised to see a sombrero on Krazy or a bit of Mexican chatter on the part of Officer Pupp. And it's real Mexican, too, for Herriman picked up quite a smattering of the language of our southern neighbors while he spent his early days in California. Mexican furniture, cliff dwellings, and hot tamales are dragged in without rhyme or reason.

Then too, he is interested in the Navajo Indians and spent several summers among them, so what would be more natural than to have Toots' dad introduce backgrounds with trees decorated Indian blanket fashion or to introduce a dog whose spotting is decidedly like an Indian design.

Languages don't faze Herriman one bit, and it is common to find a strip whose individual pictures are numbered by spelling out the names of the numbers in Spanish, French, German, or Honky Tonk. Can it be surprising, then, that his stuff shoots over the heads of his readers unless every effort is exerted on his part to "keep down to earth"?

Toots and her sister Bobbie inherit their dad's artistic inclinations. The former is specializing in the study of textile and costume design while the younger tot is willing to tackle anything as may be indicated by the sketch of her dad printed on another page. Both youngsters agree with their mother that the originator of Krazy is all wrong when he tries to underestimate his strip.

Authorities, too, agree with the writer that Herriman is one of the cleverest comic artists drawing for the American press and that his is the work of a genius. However, his endeavor to gear it down to the demand of the everyday newspaper reader causes a loss in the value which results in work far below the standard he sets for himself and is quite capable of reaching.

Like other strip characters, Toots tells us, Krazy and Ignatz step out of the strip now and then and play havoc among real folks. For instance, a man named Ignatz Maus recently went to a local court and asked to have his name legally changed to one commanding a little more respect. The court must have been a follower of Krazy and his tribe, for permission was granted to the gentleman to choose any name he desired.

"Yes," inquiry informed us, "there is a Herriman family cat," and he was produced forthwith. The creature was picked up in Maine last summer, but strangely enough, was not named "Krazy." In fact, he has no name. Inquiry of Toots as to why it wasn't Krazy brought this reply:

"Oh, he is called so many other things, depending upon the occasion, and these occasions differ so very much that his name could never be confined to a single title as another cat's might be."

So, thanks to Toots and Bobbie, we have been able to tell you not only about Krazy Kat and his crowd, but about the Herriman family as well.

OPPOSITE AND ABOVE The Herriman family, including Kat Herriman. Clockwise from left: Mr. George Herriman; Mr. Herriman as Barbara sees him "admiring his favorite artist," James Swinnerton, a pioneer of early comics who, later, took up painting in the Southwest; "Toots" vampishly inclined; Barbara and Mrs. Herriman.

Picture Perfect

A handful of casual photographs, a studio portrait of Herriman, and previously unpublished family photos taken at his home in Hollywood Hills, Los Angeles.

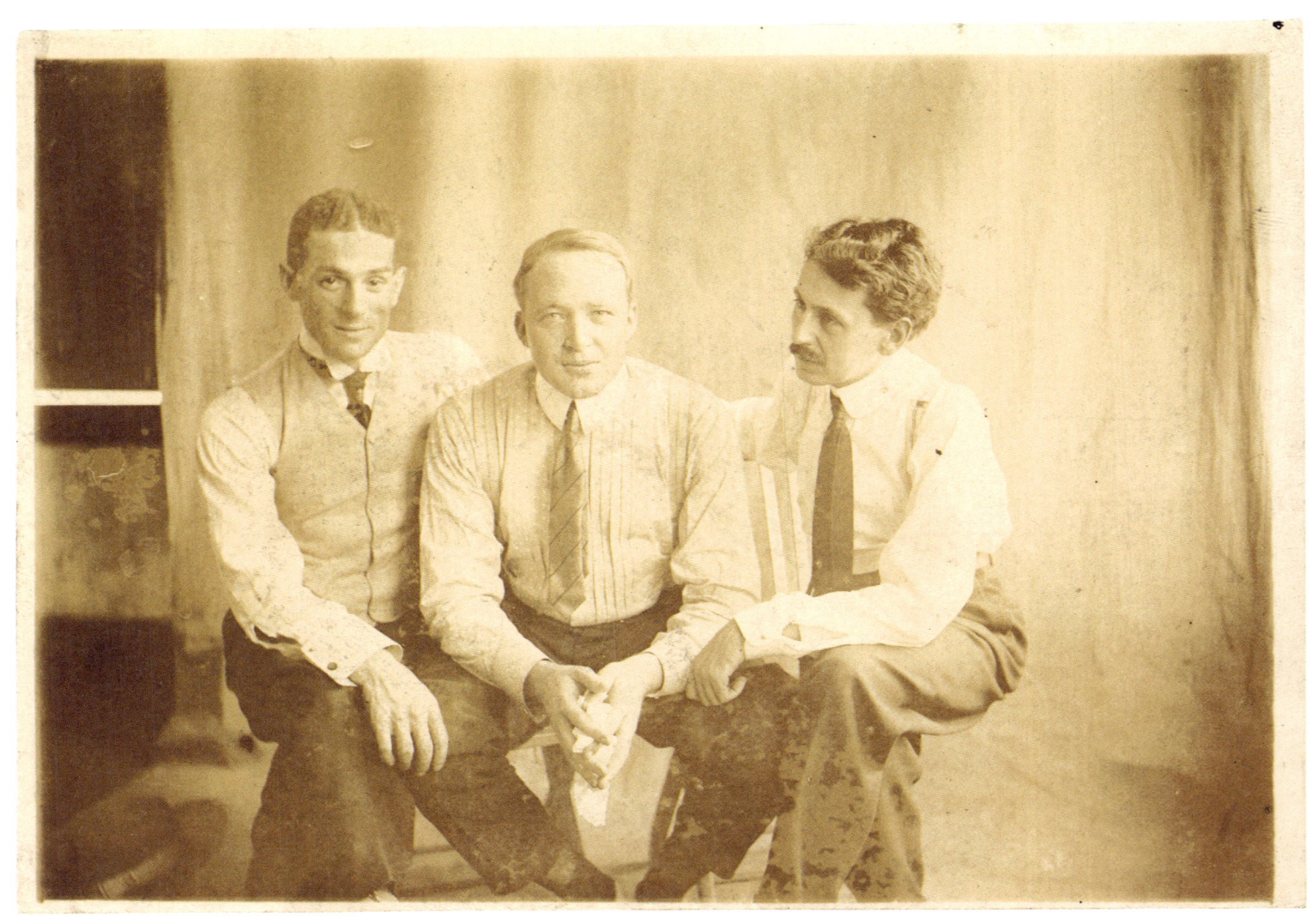

ABOVE A young George Herriman, left, with two unknown associates. Early 1910s. Previously unpublished.

OPPOSITE A rare studio photograph from a 1937 publicity photo shoot.

162

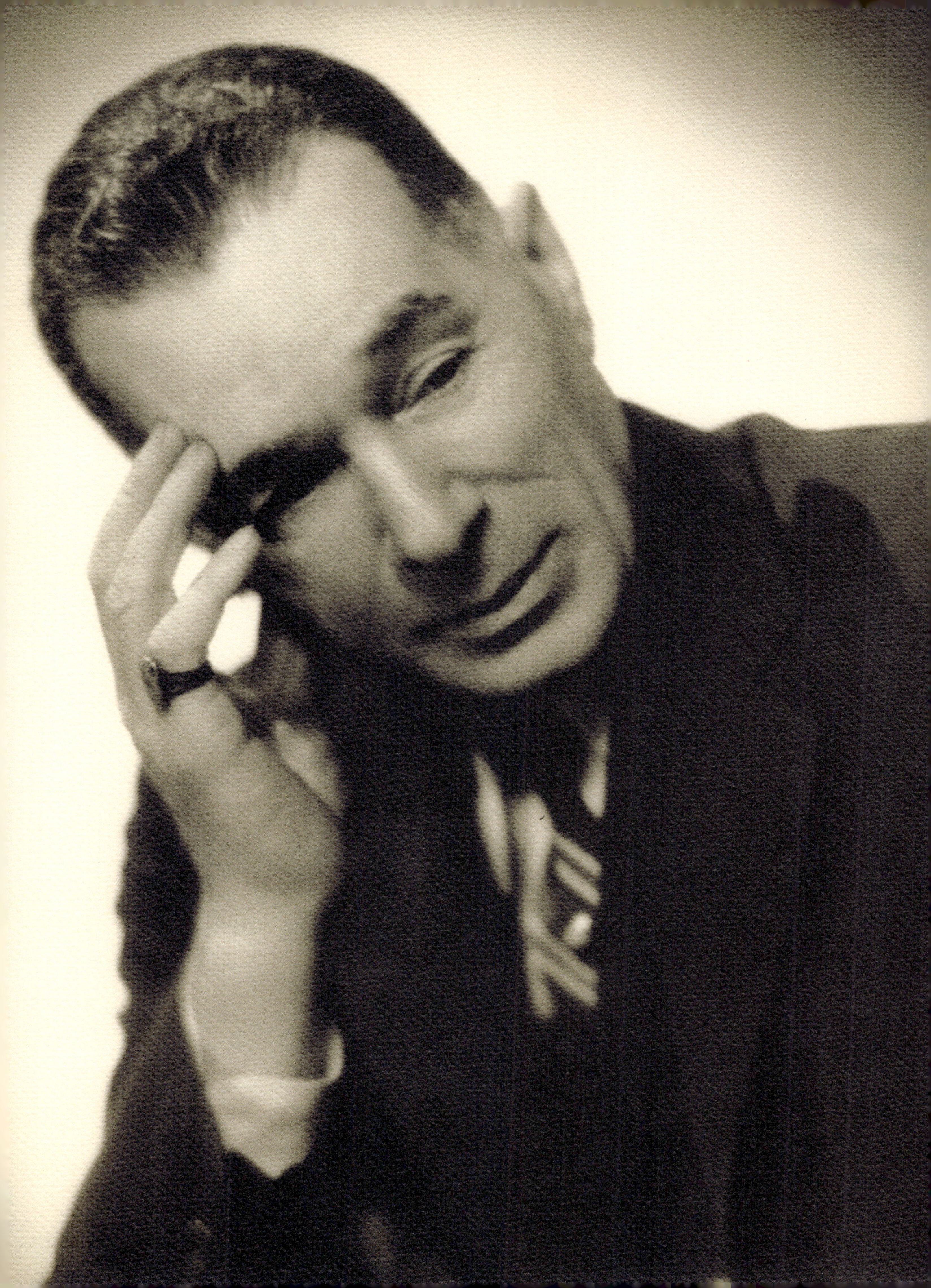

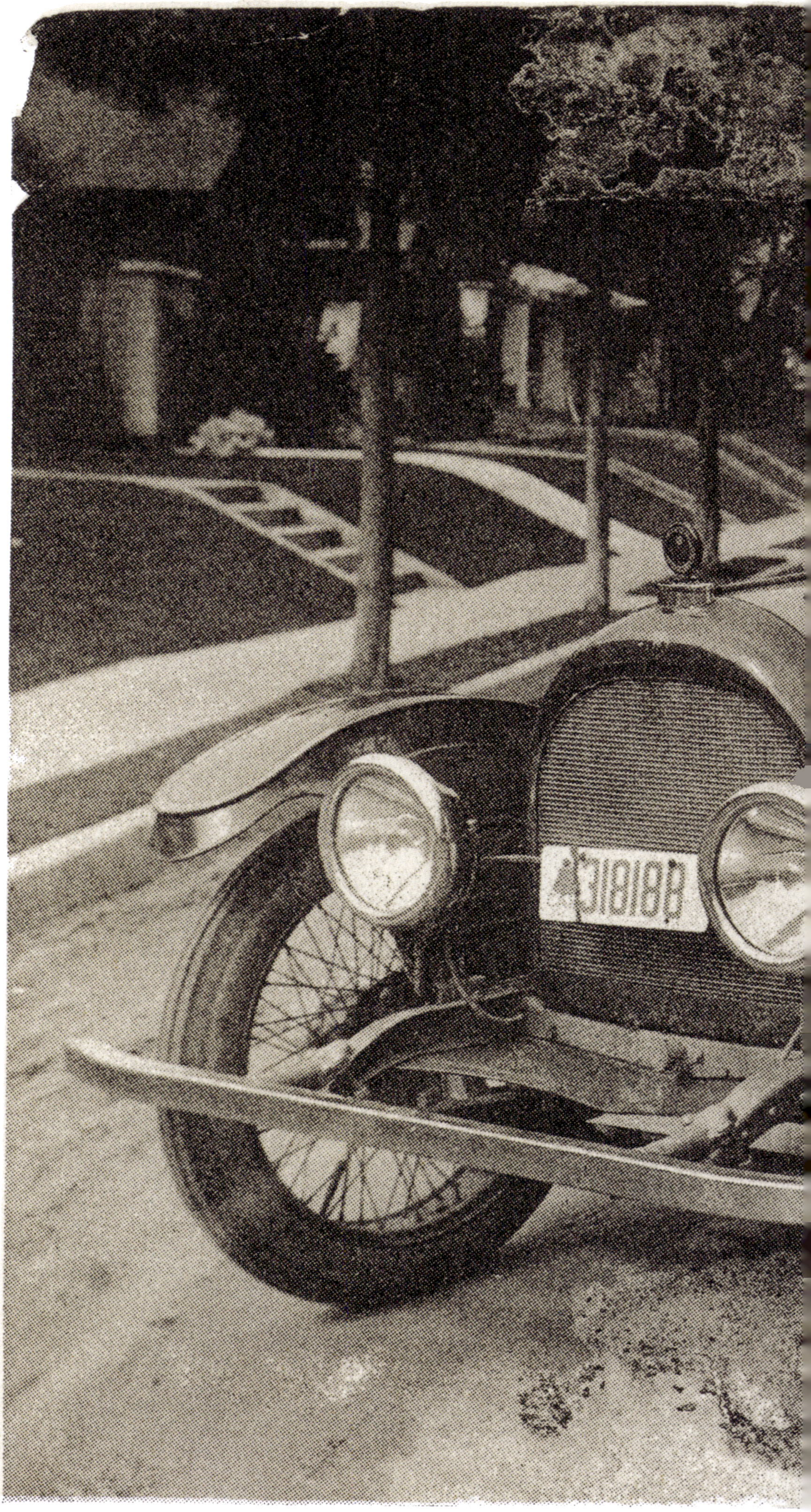

318188

RIGHT George Herriman pens a sketch for a group of youthful admirers. 1918.

OVERLEAF, TOP The home Herriman designed for his family at 2217 Maravilla Drive. Popeye cartoonist Bud Sagendorf, who had been tutored by the creator of Popeye, E. C. Segar, wrote: "Shortly before Herriman's death in the Forties, Mrs. Sagendorf and I had the opportunity to spend an afternoon with this great man. Driving up a narrow road to the top of one of the Hollywood Hills, we came to a rambling home perched on the edge of a cliff. It had to be Herriman's home. It looked as though he had drawn it there— the brick wall, the brilliant house trim and the potted plants were right out of *Krazy Kat*." Previously unpublished.

OVERLEAF, BOTTOM Herriman designed this weather vane, with an angel and his beloved Scottie dog, for his home.

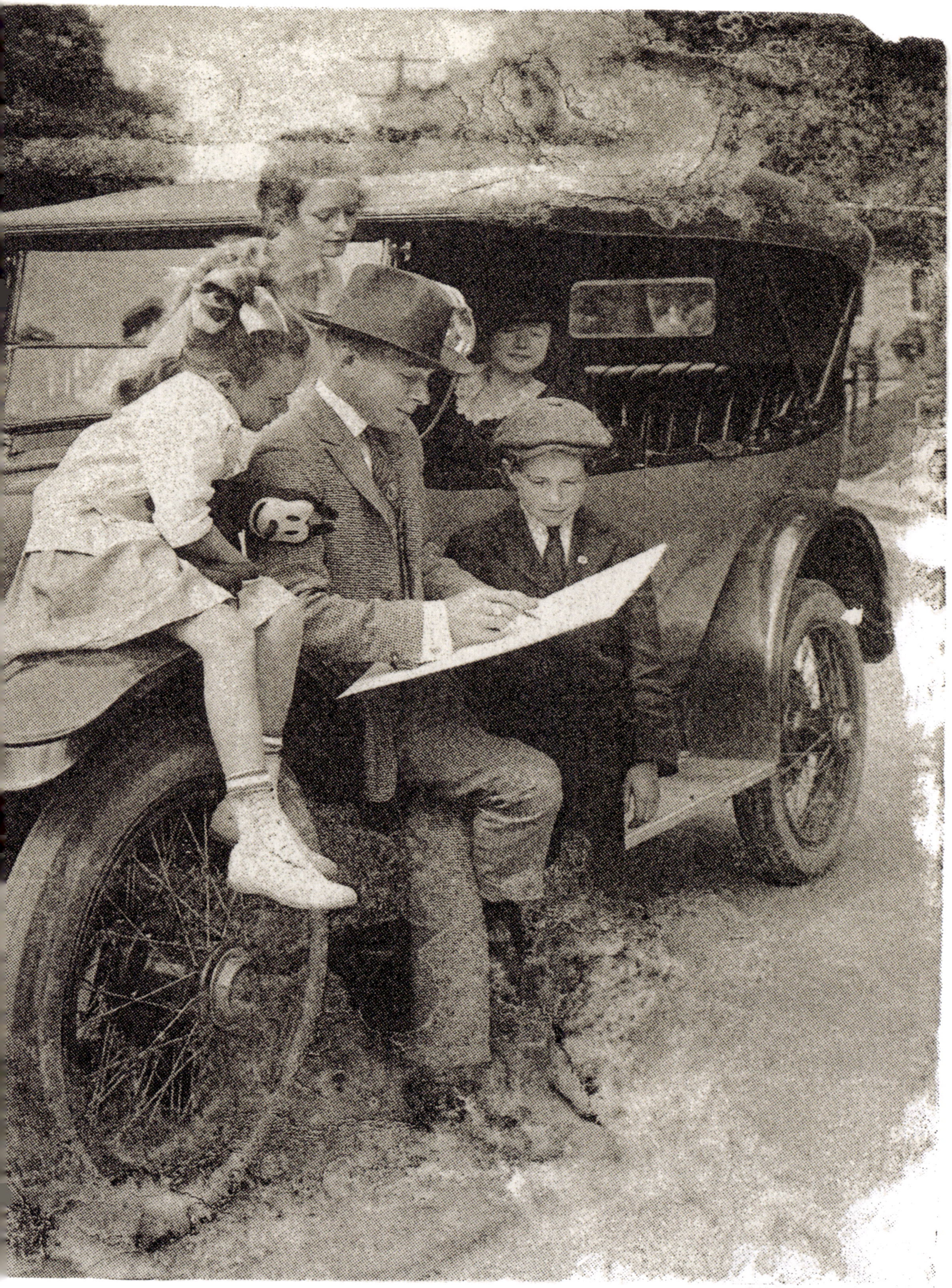

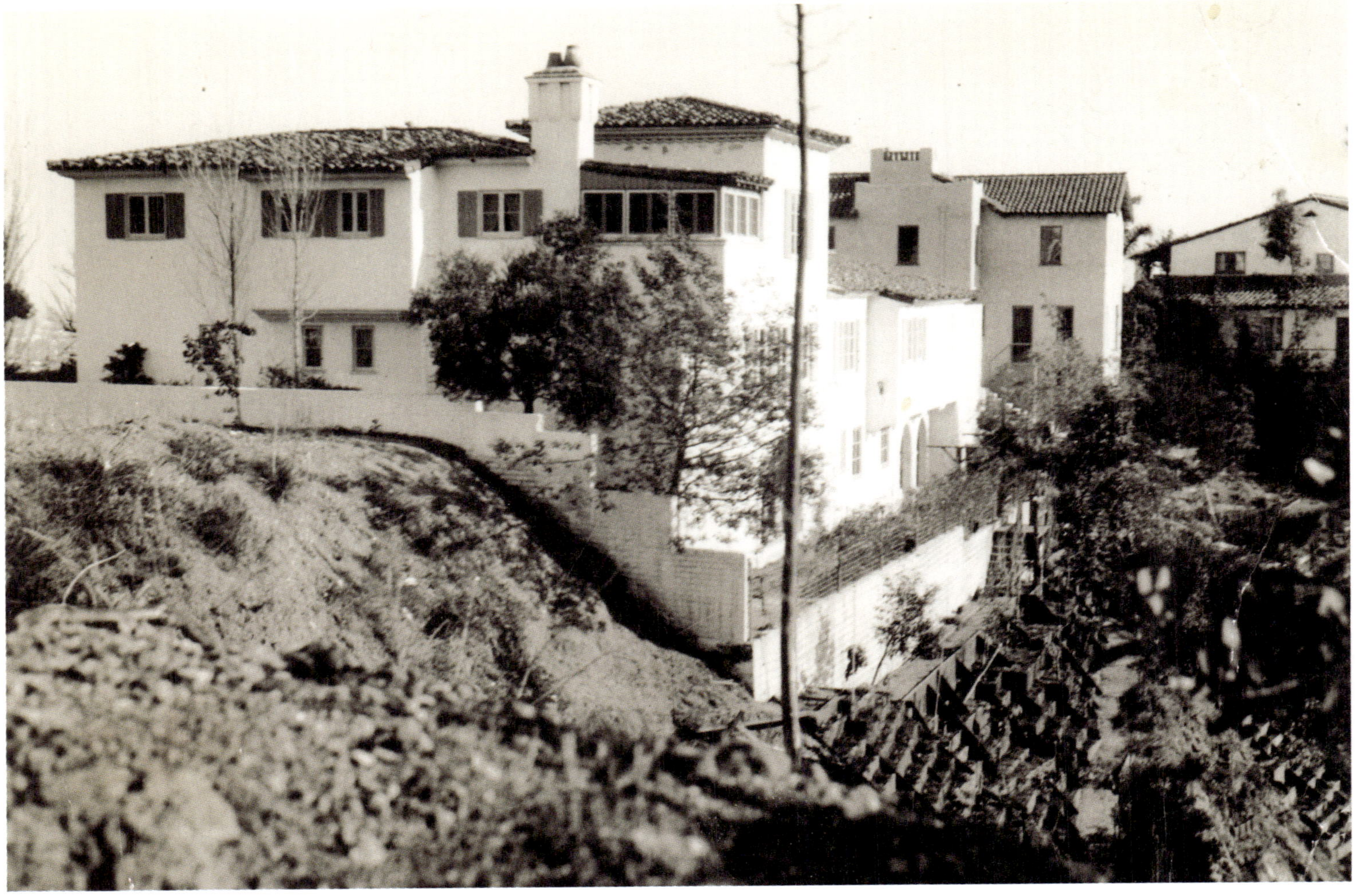

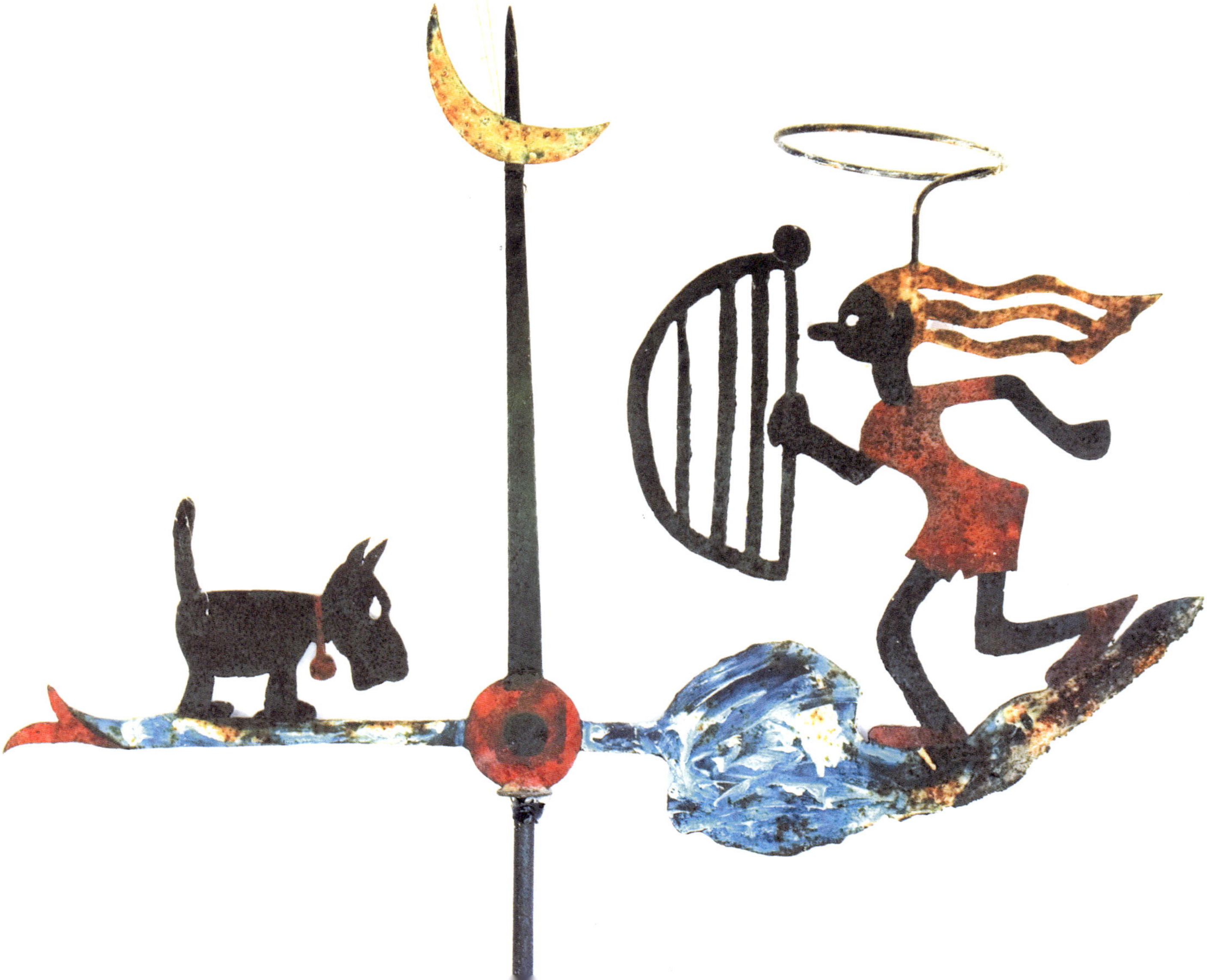

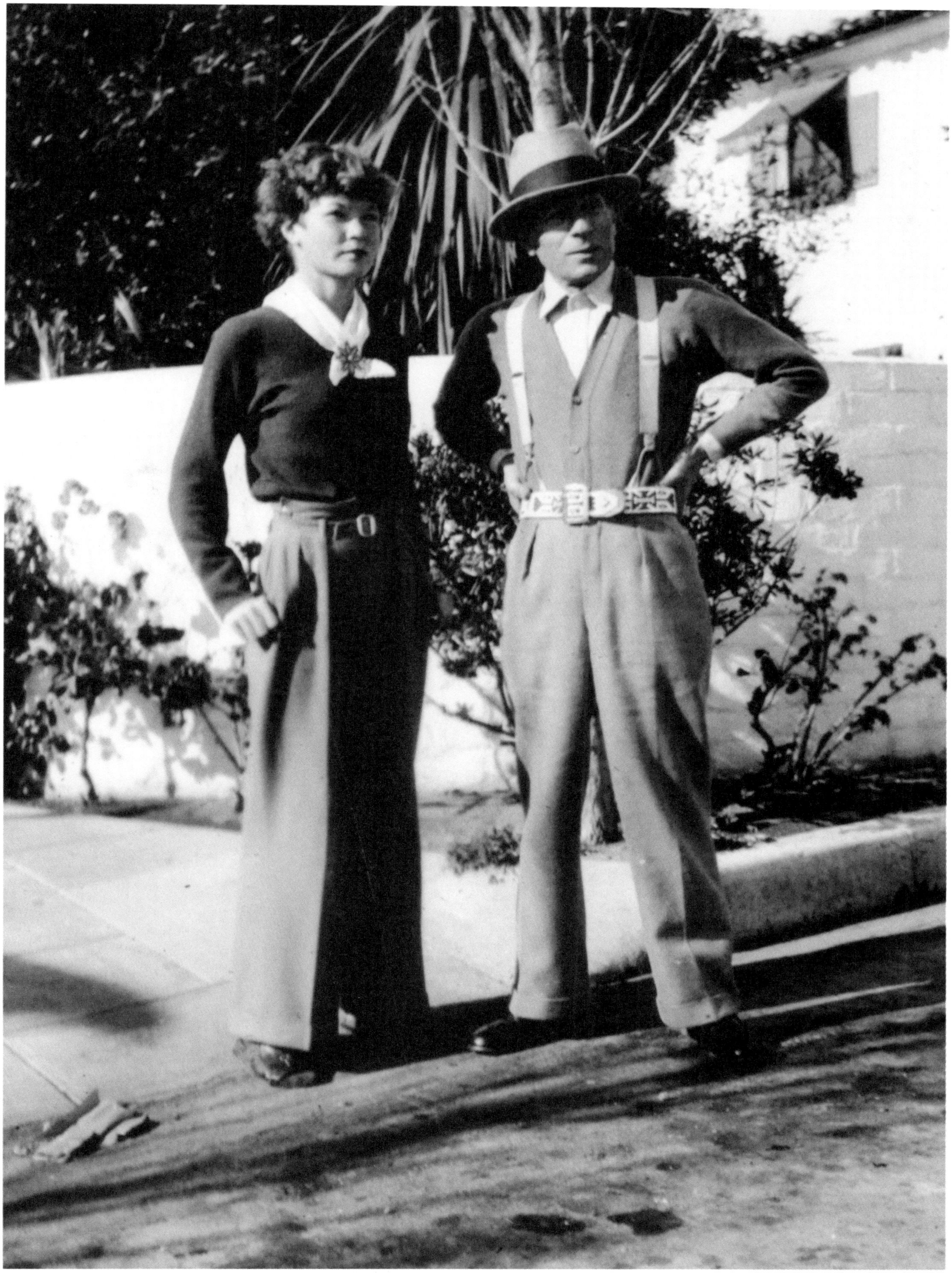

ABOVE George and his daughter Bobbie. 1933. Previously unpublished.

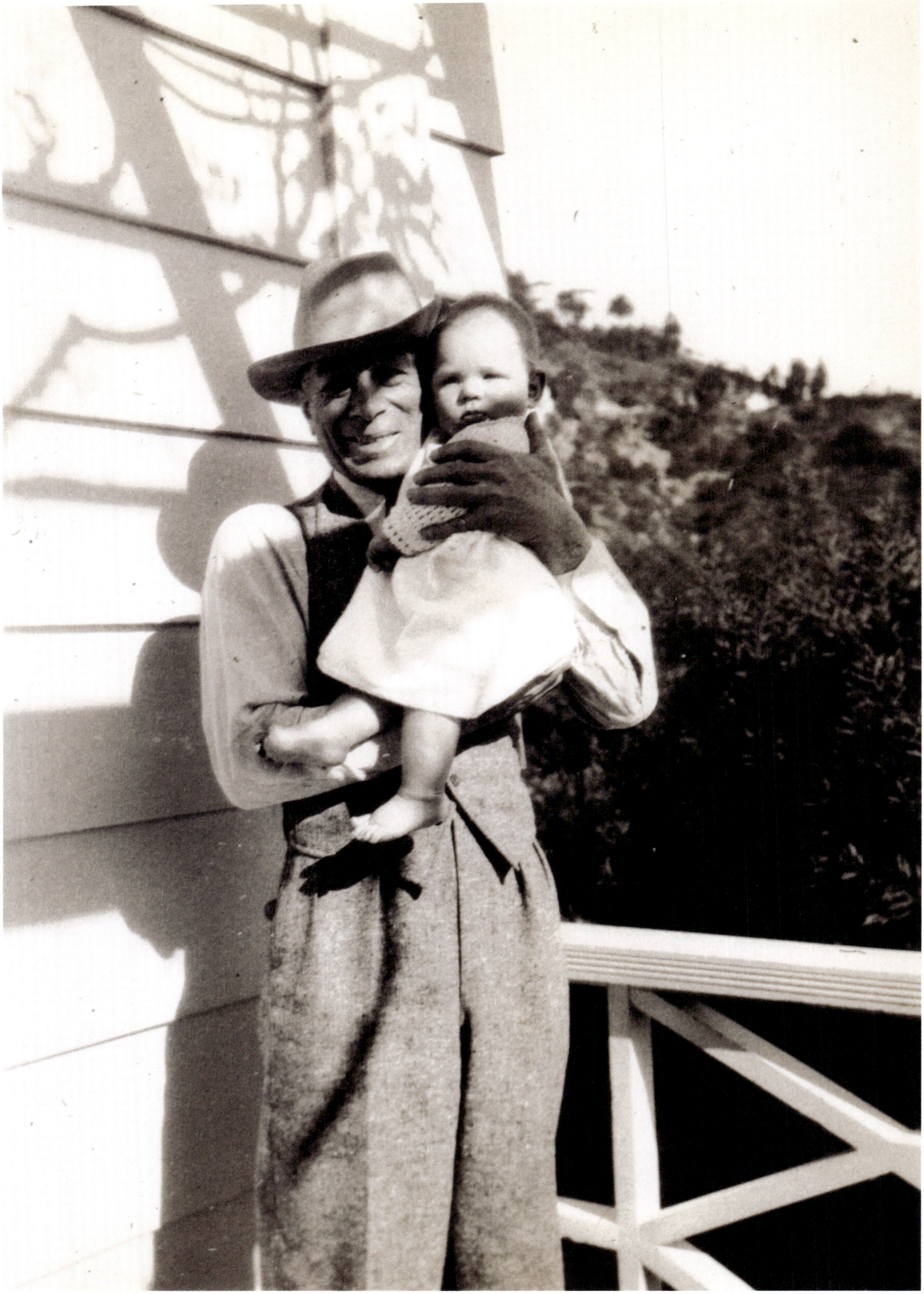

Remembering My Grandfather, George Herriman

by Dee Cox

I did know George Herriman as I was about eight when he died and I was at his house a lot. As my mother (his youngest daughter) died when I was four, Toots, his older daughter, took care of me, but lived with him and took care of him as well. William, his Japanese houseboy, was sent to the internment camps after Pearl Harbor.

Around me he was always gentle and soft-spoken and he laughed easily. Toots liked to say that he loved to argue, but I never saw this. He loved his dogs. He had five Scotties, and I remember him saying once that he had to go to the butcher shop to buy a leg of lamb for the dogs. My father used to note that the dogs were not awfully well house-broken.

I have no idea of his connections to the community, nor am I aware of any of his cartoonist friends on the West Coast. When I knew him, his daughter and wife had already died and his health was not so good—and the house seemed very quiet. I never saw another visitor in the house.

His home was on Maravilla Drive in the Outpost (Hollywood Hills). It was California Spanish—very pretty. I mostly saw him working. He sat at a drawing table in the living room. While he worked, he smoked "roll your own" Bull Durham cigarettes—the tobacco pouch always in his shirt breast pocket with the tab hanging out. There were Indian zigzag designs and *Krazy Kat* characters painted on the living room wall and other places.

My grandfather had a very beautiful garden and, when he wasn't drawing, he was gardening. The garden was a brick patio in the front of the house—walled in with a covered porch over part of it. There were lots of large planters full of gardenias and camellias.

George Herriman's love of, and connection to, the Navajo people and the land of the reservation was always stressed. I suspect that when he drew the strip he was "there" (on the res) in his head and heart. Perhaps this was because it was a happier time for him. I just had the feeling of his being totally immersed in his drawing.

It is of course a delight to be related to George Herriman—a treasure.

Dee Cox has fond memories of visiting her grandfather's studio. She lives in the Southwest, where George Herriman obtained so much inspiration.

OPPOSITE George Herriman holding his six-month-old granddaughter Dee. 1936. Previously unpublished.

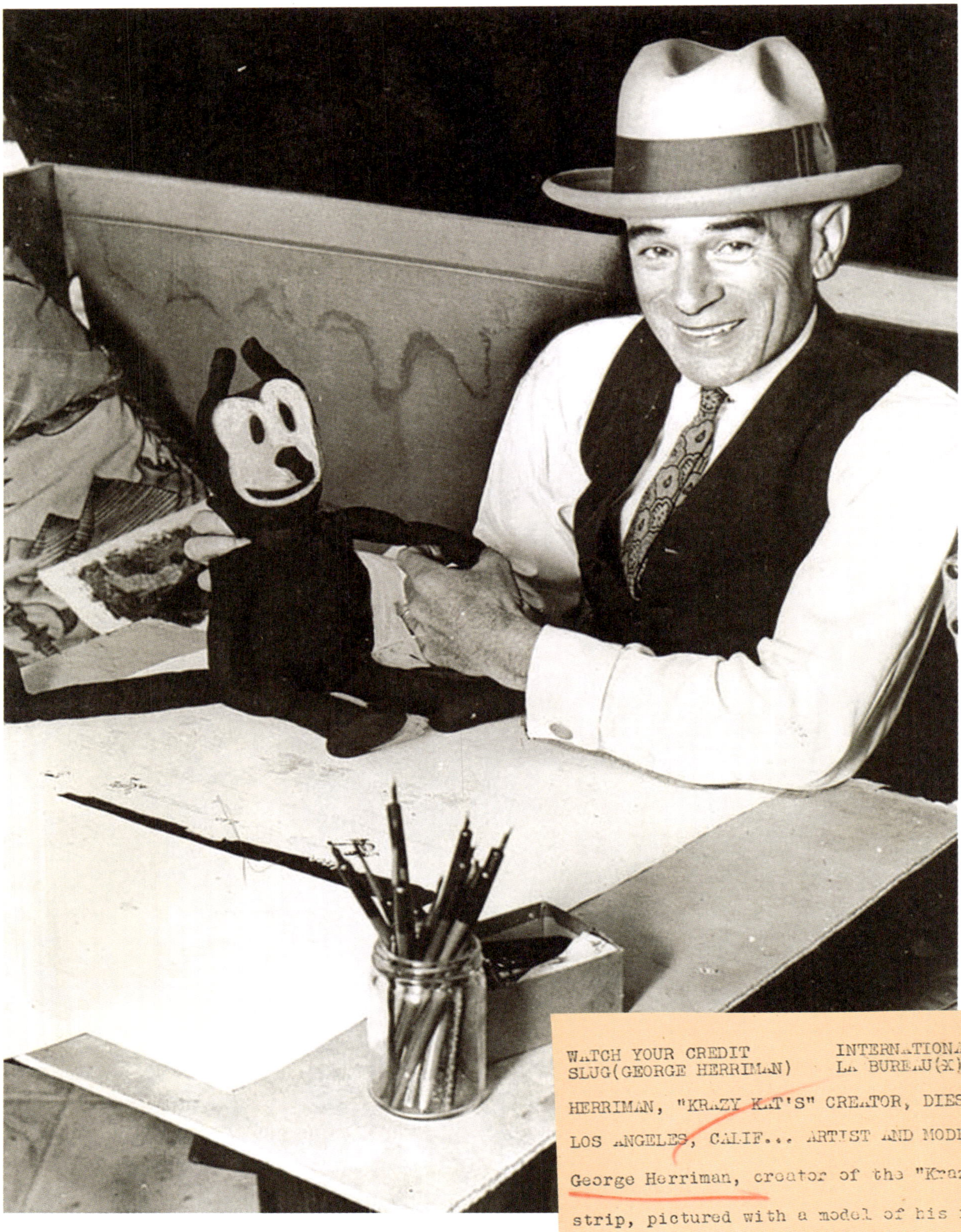

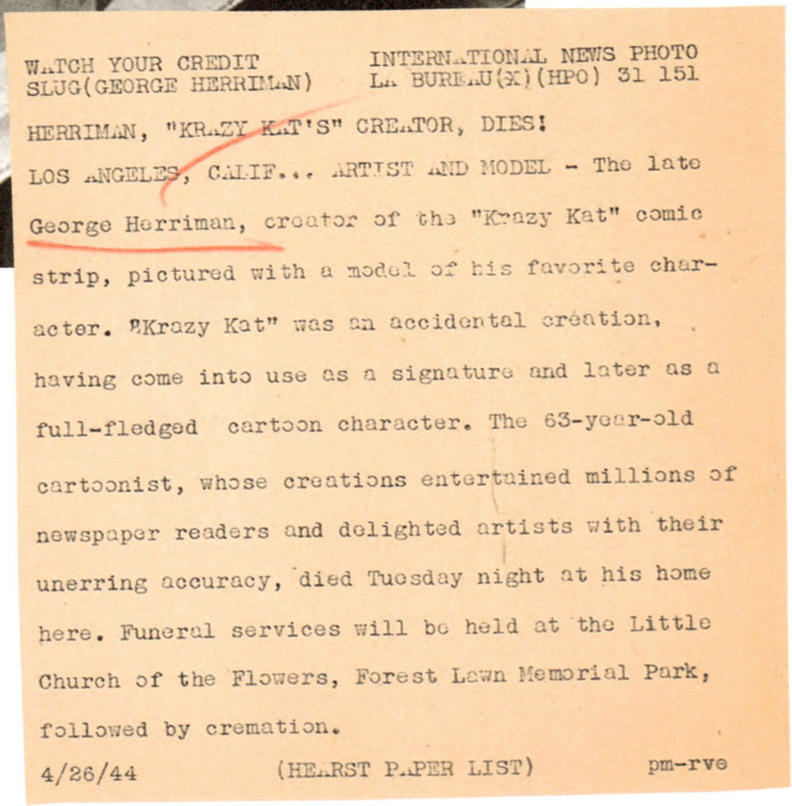

WATCH YOUR CREDIT INTERNATIONAL NEWS PHOTO
SLUG(GEORGE HERRIMAN) LA BUREAU(X)(HPO) 31 151

HERRIMAN, "KRAZY KAT'S" CREATOR, DIES!

LOS ANGELES, CALIF... ARTIST AND MODEL - The late George Herriman, creator of the "Krazy Kat" comic strip, pictured with a model of his favorite character. "Krazy Kat" was an accidental creation, having come into use as a signature and later as a full-fledged cartoon character. The 63-year-old cartoonist, whose creations entertained millions of newspaper readers and delighted artists with their unerring accuracy, died Tuesday night at his home here. Funeral services will be held at the Little Church of the Flowers, Forest Lawn Memorial Park, followed by cremation.

4/26/44 (HEARST PAPER LIST) pm-rve

THIS PAGE This photo and the caption adhered to the back were sent to newspapers upon George Herriman's death on April 25, 1944.

WALT DISNEY

May 6, 1944

Dear Miss Herriman:

I am taking this opportunity to express to you my sorrow at the untimely loss of your father.

As one of the pioneers in the cartoon business, his contributions to it were so numerous that they may well be never estimated.

His unique style of drawing and his amazing gallery of characters not only brought a new type of humor to the American public but made him a source of inspiration to thousands of artists.

My staff joins me in paying tribute to his memory.

Sincerely,

Walt Disney

Miss Mabel Herriman
2217 Maravilla Drive
Hollywood, California

WED:KC

ABOVE A letter of condolence to the Herrimans' only surviving daughter, Mabel, from Walt Disney and his staff. May 6, 1944.

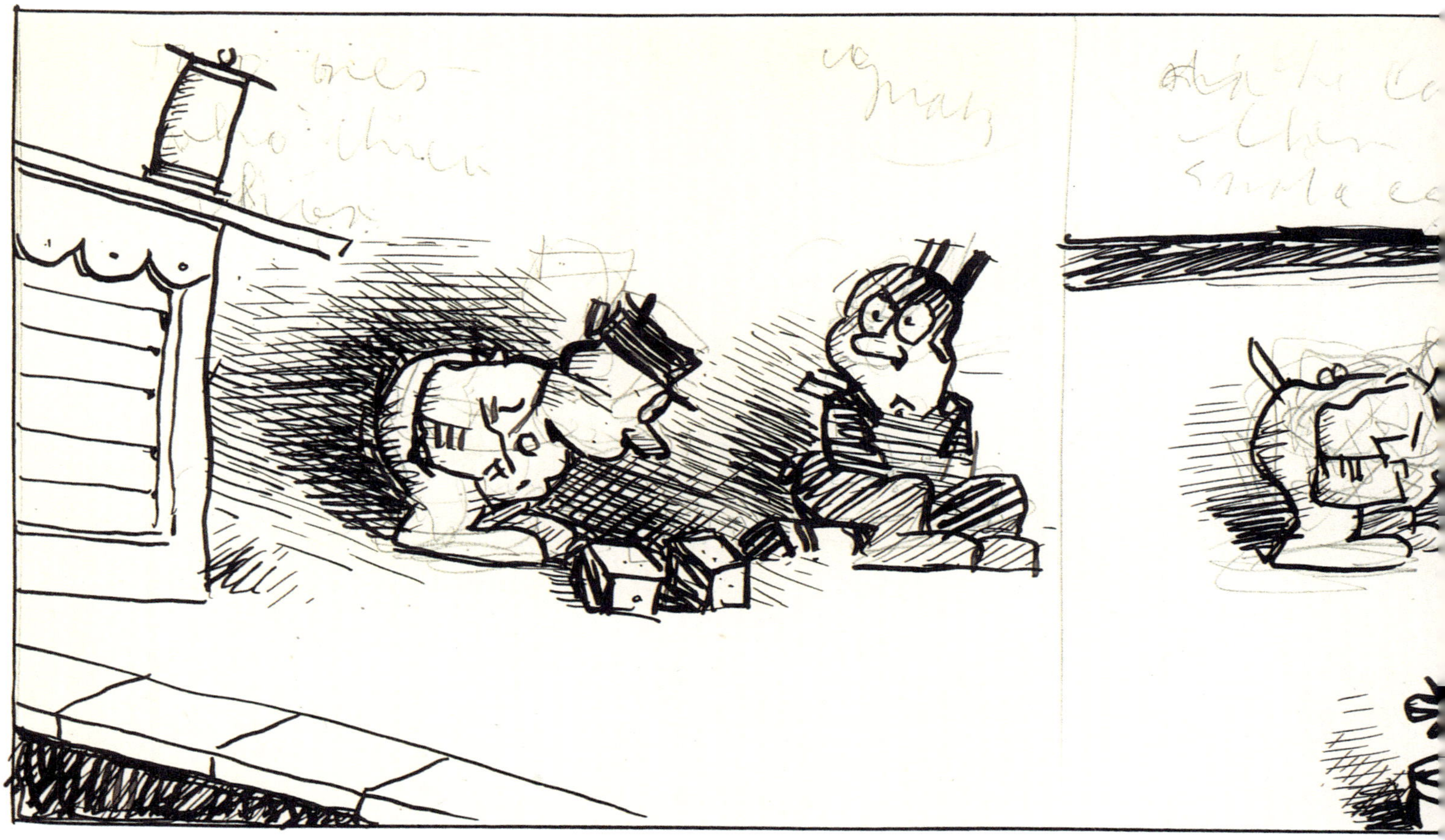

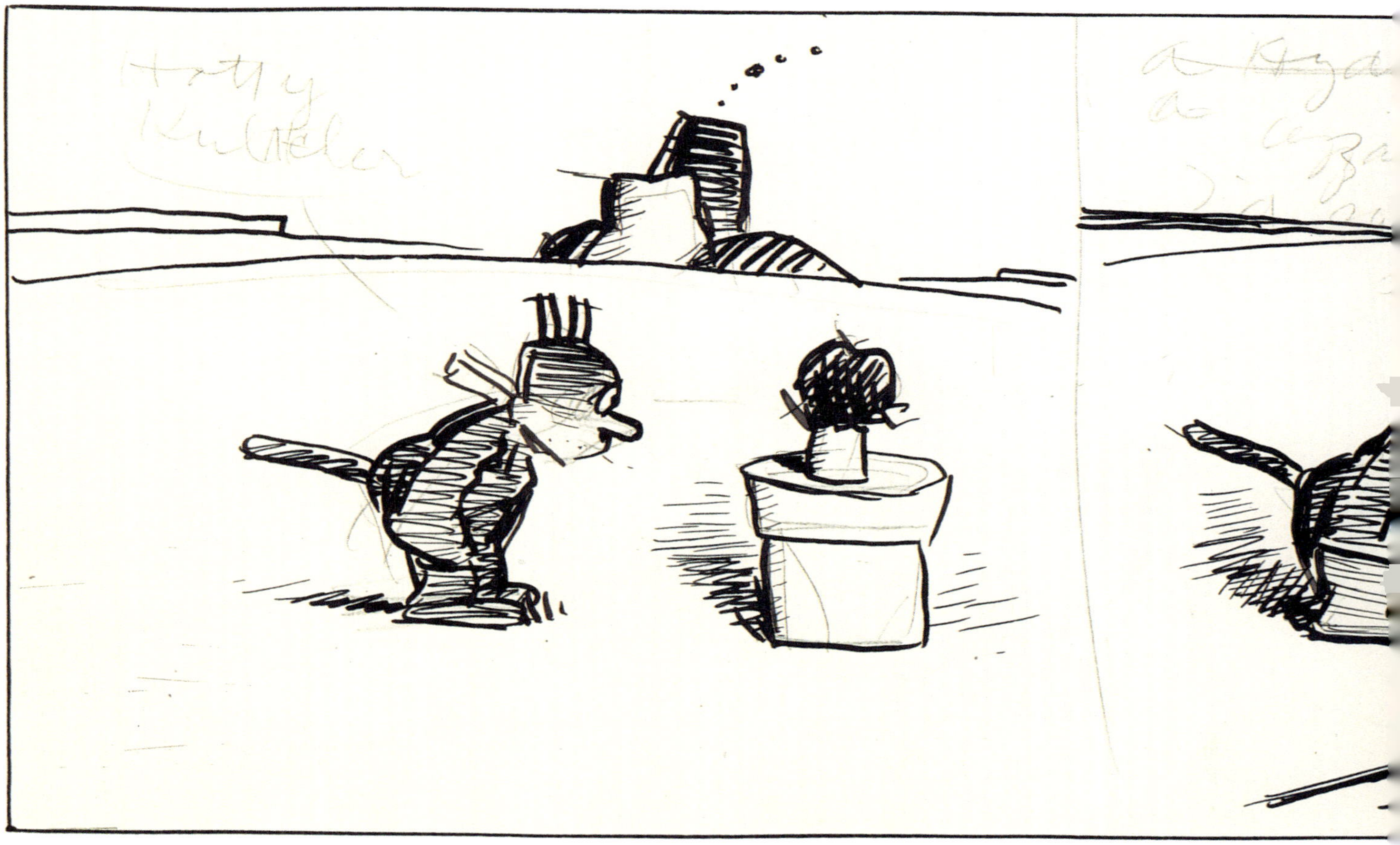

ABOVE

Unfinished *Krazy Kat* strips found on George Herriman's drawing board at the time of his death. Herriman's ashes were scattered over Monument Valley in Arizona. Previously unpublished.

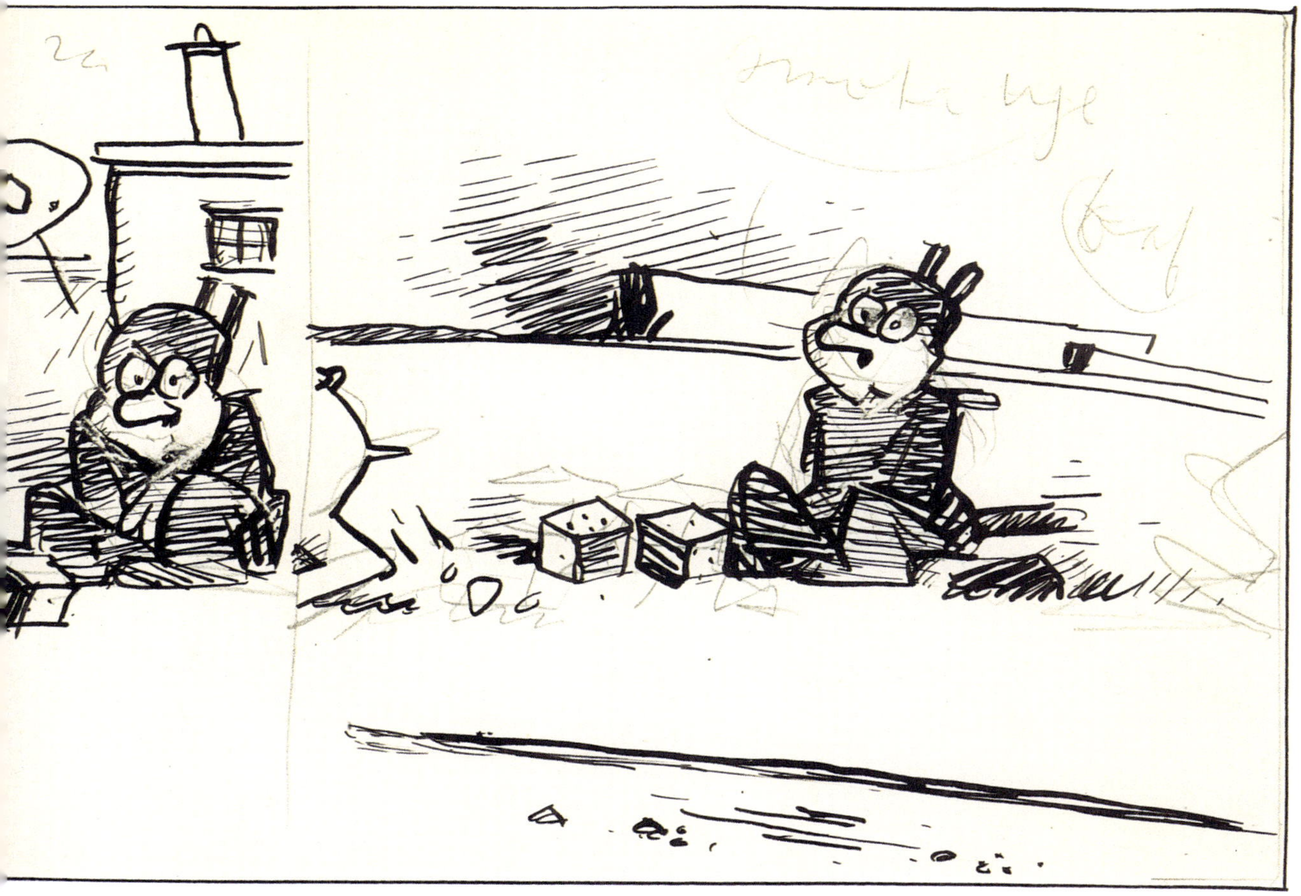

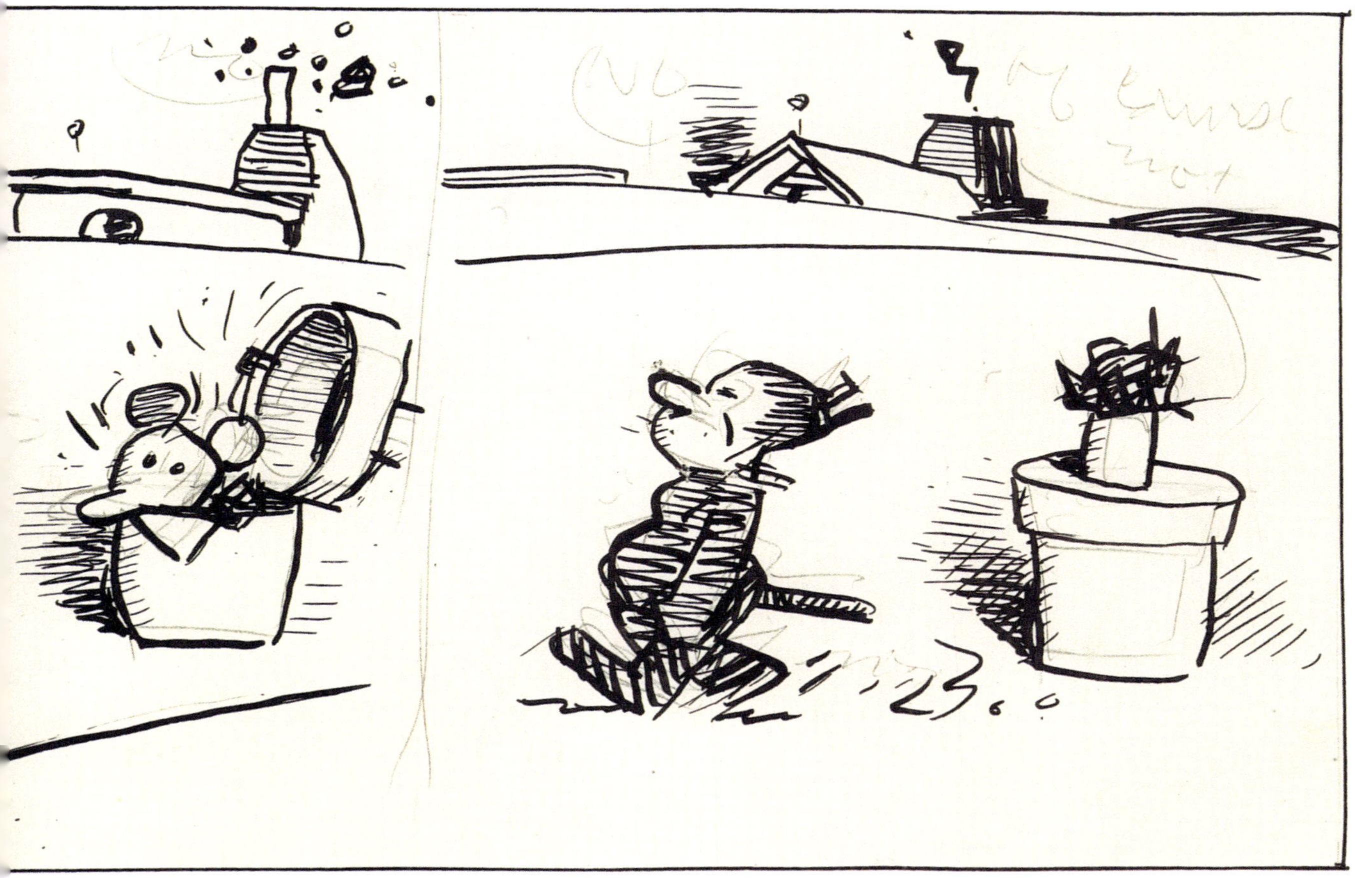

Bibliography

Blackbeard, Bill. *The Komplete Kat Komics.* Edited by Bob Callahan. 9 vols. Forestville, CA: Turtle Island/Eclipse Books, 1988–1992.

Blackbeard, Bill, ed. *The Family Upstairs: Introducing Krazy Kat.* New York: Hyperion Press, 1977.

Blackbeard, Bill, ed. *Krazy and Ignatz: The Complete Full Page Comic Strips.* 11 vols. Seattle: Fantagraphics Books, 2002–10.

Block, Rudolph. Illustrated by various artists. *A Half Million Dollar Feature Service.* New York: International Feature Service, ca. 1917.

Carlin, John, Paul Karasik, and Brian Walker, eds. *Masters of American Comics.* New Haven and London: Yale University Press, 2005.

Coleman, Harry J. *Give Us a Little Smile, Baby.* New York: E. P. Dutton & Company, 1943.

Herriman, George. With an introduction by E. E. Cummings. *Krazy Kat.* New York: Henry Holt and Company, 1946.

Marquis, Don. Illustrated by George Herriman. *Archy and Mehitabel.* New York: Doubleday, Doran & Company, Inc., 1934.

Marquis, Don. Illustrated by George Herriman. *Archy Does His Part.* New York: Doubleday, Doran & Company, Inc., 1935.

Marquis, Don. Illustrated by George Herriman. *Archy's Life of Mehitabel.* New York: Doubleday, Doran & Company, Inc., 1933.

Marquis, Don. Illustrated by George Herriman. *The Lives and Times of Archy & Mehitabel.* New York: Doubleday & Company, Inc., 1950.

Marschall, Richard, ed. *The Komplete Kolor Krazy Kat Vol. 1. 1935–1936.* Remco Worldservice Books, 1990.

McDonnell, Patrick, Peter Maresca, eds. *Krazy Kat: A Celebration of Sundays.* Palo Alto, CA: Sunday Press Books, 2010.

McDonnell, Patrick, Karen O'Connell, and Georgia Riley de Havenon. *Krazy Kat: The Comic Art of George Herriman.* New York: Harry N. Abrams, Inc., 1986.

Yoe, Craig, ed. Introduction by Paul Krassner. *George Herriman's Krazy + Ignatz in "Tiger Tea."* San Diego, CA: IDW/Yoe Books, 2010.

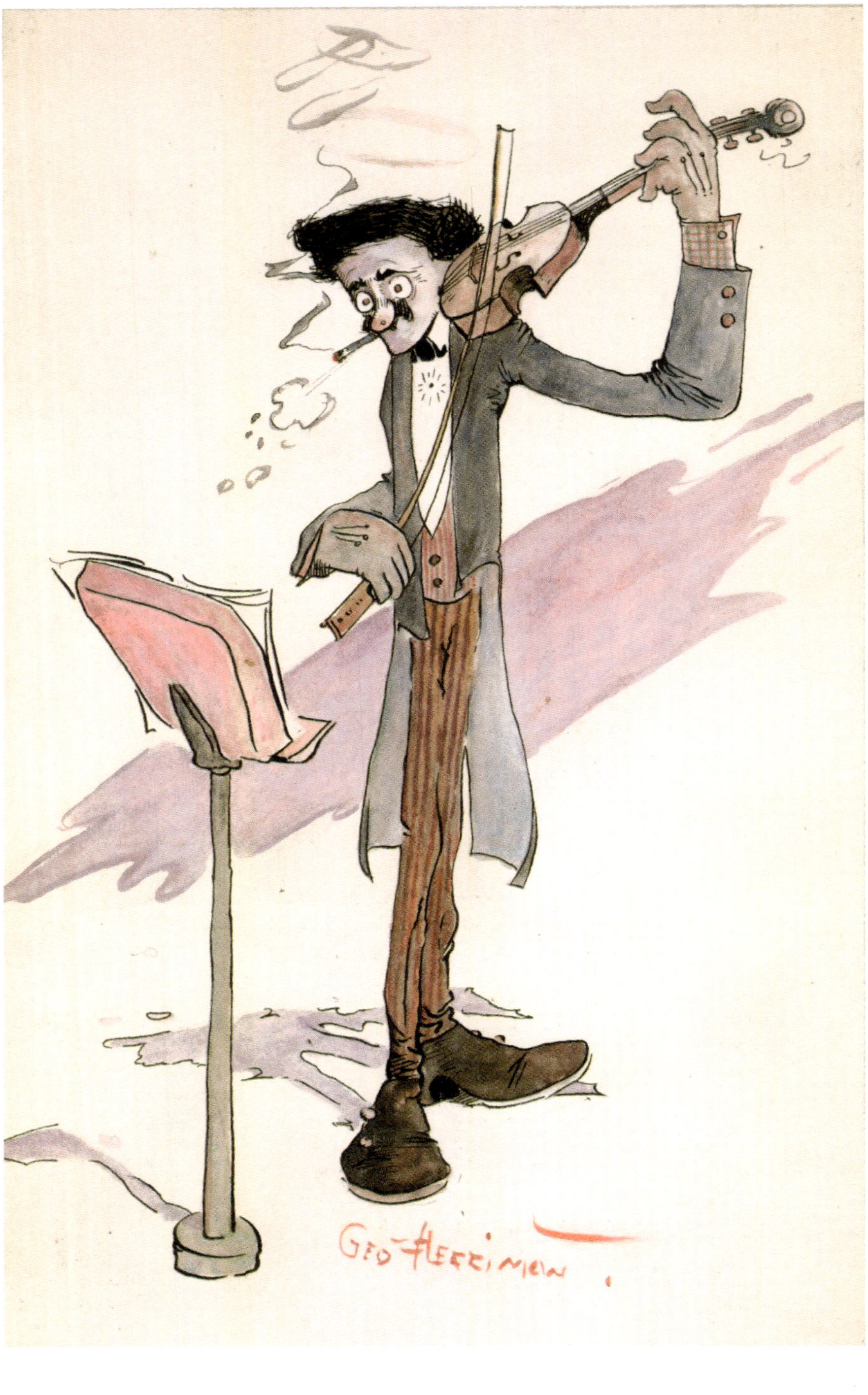

Geo Herriman

LEFT An early watercolor of a Groucho-esque musician. Previously unpublished.

Index

Page numbers in italic refer to illustrations.

A
Acrobatic Archie, 13
animation, 78–84
Archy and Mehitabel, 125
Archy's Life of Mehitabel, 125

B
backdrops, 38, 87, 114, 161
Baldwin, Summerfield, 113–17
Baron Bean, 38, 43, 161
Beats, 29
Bernie Burns panel, 50
Bierstadt, Albert, 28
Block, Rudolph, 147
books, 118–25
Boos, John, 30
Bray, John, 78
brick motif, 38, 87, 113, 116–17, 128, 139
Brisbane, Arthur, 38
Bronis, Jimmy, *83*
buttons, 155

C
Cantor, Jay, 127–29
Carpenter, John Alden, 121, 141
Carr, Jack, *83*
cartoon genre, 28
Chase, Charley, 147
Coconino County, 10, 11, 17, 29, 38, 87
color comics, 18–26
comic strips
    business of, 75, 85–86
    daily, 42–50
    genre, 28
    medium of, 9–10
    Sunday, 18–26, 54–74
Cox, Dee (Dinah Pascal), 6, 130, 131, 132, *168*, 169
Crosby, Percy, 134
Cummings, E. E., 17, 51–53, 118
Currier, Richard, 34

D
daily comic strips, 42–50
Davis, Art, *83*
DeNat, Joe, *83*
The Dingbat Family, 13, 16, *16–17*, 27, 38, 43, *44–45*, 86, 160
Dirks, Rudolph, 29
Disney, Walt, 171
Dixon, Maynard, 96
dolls, 152, *153–54*
Don Koyote and Sancho Pansy, 38

Dorgan, Tad, 28, 29, 148, 149–51, 155
drawing style, 10, 87, 114–15

E
Embarrassing Moments panel, 36, *36*, 50

F
family home, 164, *166*
The Family Upstairs, 16, 27, 37–38, 43
Feininger, Lyonel, 28
Fisher, Bud, 27
Foster, Hal, 92

G
Goldberg, Rube, 155
Gooseberry Sprig, 13
Gould, Manny, *83*
greeting cards, 130–36

H
Halloween mask, *152*
Hal Roach Studios, 6, 17, 147
Harrison, Ben, *83*
Hearst, William Randolph, 17, 27, 29, 76, 92, 134
Herriman, Barbara (Bobbie), 17, 159, *161*, 161, *167*
Herriman, George
    artistry of, 27–29
    career of, 13, 27–28
    death of, 170–73
    Dorgan on, 149–51
    greetings by, 130–36
    ink-and-watercolor paintings by, *88–112*
    life of, 13–17, 27–29, 149–51, 169
    photos of, *5, 160, 162–65, 167, 168, 170*
    self-portraits, *30–36*
    specialty drawings of, 140–48
Herriman, Mabel (Toots), 159–61, *161*, 171
Herriman, Mabel (wife), 17, 35, *161*
Hershfield, Harry, 35, 148
Hoban, Walter, 148
humor, 137–39
Hurd, Jud, 141

I
Ignatz Mouse, 9, 11–12, 38, 51–53, 127–28
    appearance of, *85*, 114
    in *The Dingbat Family*, 16, *16–17*, 160
ink-and-watercolor paintings, *88–112*
International Film Service (IFS), 78
irony, 40

J
Judge, 148

K
Katz, Harry L., 27–29
Knerr, Harold, 134
Krazy Kat (character), 9, 38, 52–53, 127–28
    animations of, 78–84
    appearance of, 85, 114
    beginnings of, 160–61
    in *The Dingbat Family*, 16, *16–17*, 160
    gender of, 16–17, 138, 160
Krazy Kat
    art of, 37–41
    beginnings of, 86–87
    in books, 118–25
    characters in, 9, 11–12, 16–17, 51–53, 114
    in color, 18–26
    daily strips, 42–50
    fans of, 76
    format of, 114
    humor of, 9–10, 137–39
    merchandise, 152–58
    plot of, 9, 38, 113
    Sunday comics, 54–74
    theme of, 38–40
    unfinished, *172–73*
Krazy Kat dolls, 152, *153–54*
Krazy Kat Halloween mask, *152*
Krazy Kat in Wedding Bells, 83, *84*
"Krazy Kat Rag" sheet music, 158

L
Lange, Dorothea, 96
Langreich, William Paul, 159–61
language, 16, 17, 40–41, 115–16
Los Angeles Herald, 13
love, 52–53, 128
Love, Harry, *83*
love triangle, 16–17, 38, 86–87

M
Major Ozone's Fresh Air Crusade, 13
Marquis, Don, 122–23
Mary's Home from College, 13
Masquers, 147
McCay, Winsor, 28, 147
McCracken, Craig, 75–77
McDonnell, Patrick, 29
McManus, George, 35, 134
McNamara, Tom, 35, 148, 159
merchandise, 152–58
Messmer, Otto, 134

Index

Mintz, Charles B., 78, *83*, 83
miscommunication, 139
Moran, Thomas, 28
Musical Mose, 13
Mutt and Jeff, 27
Mutts, 29

N
Nolan, Bill, 78

O
Offissa Pupp, 9, 11, 38, 51–53, 85, 114
O'Keeffe, Georgia, 28

P
paintings, *88–112*
Pascal, Ernest, 132
Peanuts, 86
photographs, *162–68*
pity, 39–40
playing cards, *156*, 157
plot, 9, 38, 113
political cartoons, 15
Previously unpublished images, endpapers, *1, 2–3, 4, 5, 8, 18, 32, 33, 34, 46–47, 74, 90–91, 92–93, 97, 99, 135, 141, 142, 151, 162, 166, 167, 168, 172–73, 174, 176*
Professor Otto and His Auto, 13

R
Raguse, Elmer "Al" Sr., 6
Raymond, Alex, 92
Ritchie, Ben, 158
Rose, Al, 83

S
Sagendorf, Bud, 164
Seldes, Gilbert, 17, 27, 37–41, 51, 56, 134
self-portraits, *30–36*
setting, 10, 11, 17, 87, 114, 161
sheet music, 158
Sloan, John, 28
sound (representation of), 116–17
Southwest, 28–29
specialty drawings, *140–48*

sports cartoons, 15
statues, *156*, 157
Sterrett, Cliff, 29, 148
Stumble Inn, 38
Sunday comics, 18–26, 54–74
Swinnerton, Jimmy, 29, 33, 161
Swinnerton, Louise, 33, 34

T
TAD. *See* Dorgan, Tad
tea set, *156*, 157
theme, 38–40
Thompson, Richard, 85–87
Tiger Tea sequence, 48
toys, *154*, 155, *156*, 157

V
violence, 11, 16–17

W
Watterson, Bill, 9–10
Weiss, Morris, 100
Wetherill, John and Louisa, 132
White, E. B., 17, 123
Winkler, Margaret J., 78
Wolk, Douglas, 137–39
writing style, 10, 17, 115–16

Y
Young, Chic, 92
Young, Roland, 90

Z
Ziff Davis, 13

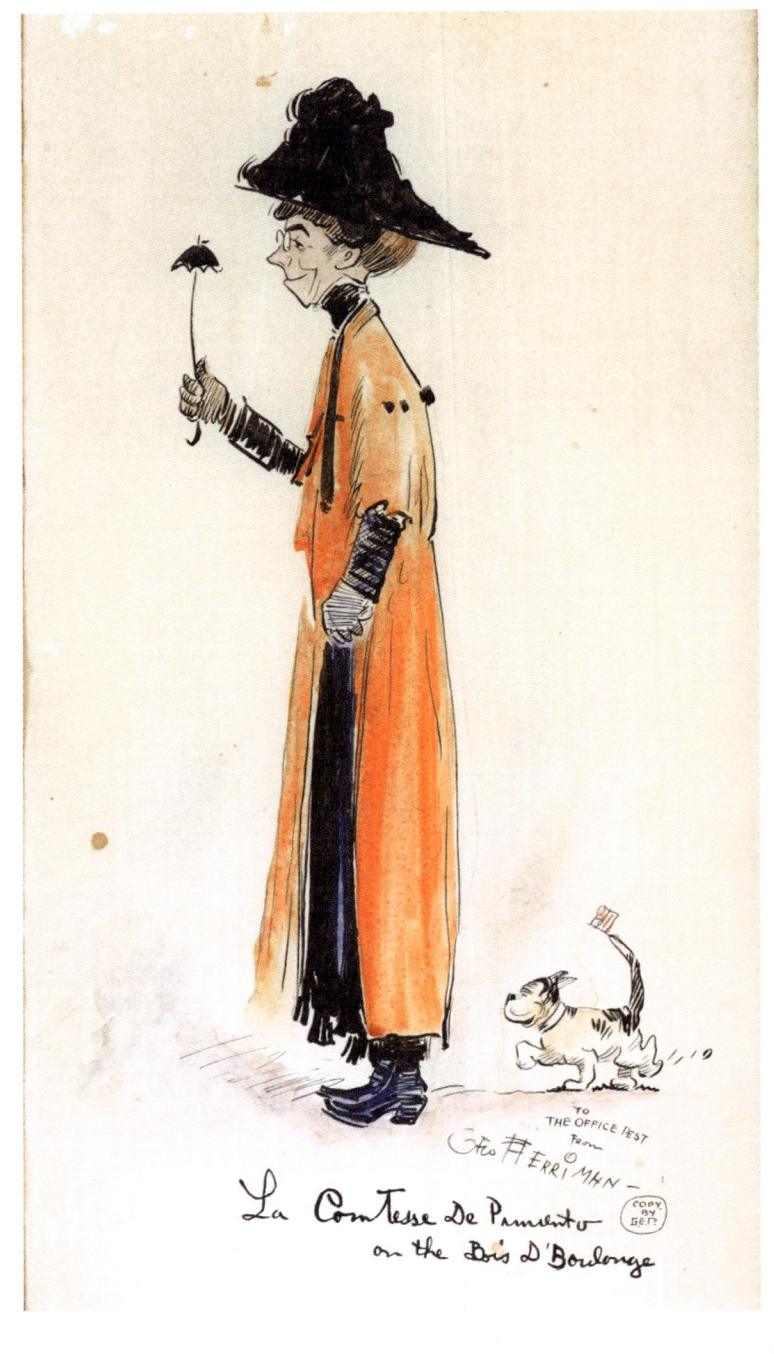

RIGHT The inscription on this early watercolor reads, "To the office pest from Geo. Herriman—La Comtesse De Pimiento on the Bois D'Boulonge." Previously unpublished.